Londinopolis

Politics, culture and society in early modern Britain

General editors

PROFESSOR ANN HUGHES
DR ANTHONY MILTON
PROFESSOR PETER LAKE

This important series publishes monographs that take a fresh and challenging look at the interactions between politics, culture and society in Britain between 1500 and the mid-eighteenth century. It counteracts the fragmentation of current historiography through encouraging a variety of approaches which attempt to redefine the political, social and cultural worlds, and to explore their interconnection in a flexible and creative fashion. All the volumes in the series question and transcend traditional inter-disciplinary boundaries, such as those between political history and literary studies, social history and divinity, urban history and anthropology. They contribute to a broader understanding of crucial developments in early modern Britain.

Londinopolis

Essays in the cultural and social
history of early modern London

edited by
Paul Griffiths and Mark S. R. Jenner

Manchester
University Press
Manchester and New York

distributed exclusively in the USA by St. Martin's Press

Published by Manchester University Press
Oxford Road, Manchester M13 9NR, UK
and Room 400, 175 Fifth Avenue, New York, NY 10010, USA
www.manchesteruniversitypress.co.uk

Distributed exclusively in the USA by
Palgrave, 175 Fifth Avenue, New York NY 10010, USA

Distributed exclusively in Canada by
UBC Press, University of British Columbia, 2029 West Mall,
Vancouver, BC, Canada V6T 1Z2

British Library Cataloguing-in-Publication Data
A catalogue record for this book is available from the British Library

Library of Congress Cataloging-in-Publication Data
A catalog record for this book is available from the Library of Congress

ISBN 0 7190 5152 5 *paperback*

First published 2000

First digital, on-demand edition produced by Lightning Source 2005

Contents

Contents

List of tables and figures

TABLES

FIGURES

Notes on the contributors

IAN W. ARCHER is Fellow, Tutor and University Lecturer in Modern History at Keble College, Oxford. He is the author of *The Pursuit of Stability: Social Relations in Elizabethan London* (1991) and *The History of the Haberdashers' Company* (1991). He is working on taxation and on guilds and civic government in early modern England.

MICHAEL BERLIN lectures in History at the Faculty of Extra-mural Studies, Birkbeck College, University of London. He is also a research associate of the Centre for Metropolitan History, Institute of Historical Research, and the author of several articles on the cultural and social history of early modern London.

JEREMY BOULTON is Senior Lecturer in Social History at the University of Newcastle. He is the author of *Neighbourhood and Society: A London Suburb in the Seventeenth Century* (1987) and has written about other aspects of London's social and economic history. He is completing a study of the poor in the West End, 1550–1725, to appear as *The Making of the London Poor* (Manchester University Press).

FARAMERZ DABHOIWALA is a Fellow and Tutor in Modern History at Exeter College, Oxford. He works on the social and intellectual history of early modern England, and is writing a book about sex and society in seventeenth- and eighteenth-century London.

LAURA GOWING is Senior Lecturer in History at the University of Hertfordshire. She is the author (with Patricia Crawford) of *Women's Worlds in Seventeenth Century England: A Sourcebook* (1999) and *Domestic Dangers: Women, Words, and Sex in Early Modern London* (1996).

PAUL GRIFFITHS lectures in early modern British history at Iowa State University. He is the author of *Youth and Authority: Formative Experiences in England 1560–1640* (1996) and co-editor of *The Experience of Authority in Early Modern England* (1996). He is completing *The First Bridewell: Petty Crime, Policing, and Prison in London 1545–1645* for publication.

MARGARET R. HUNT is Professor of History and Women's and Gender Studies at Amherst College. She is author of *The Middling Sort: Commerce, Gender and the Family in England 1680–1780* (1996) and is working on the Court of Exchequer in late seventeenth- and early eighteenth-century London, focusing particularly on women as litigants.

MARK S. R. JENNER is lecturer in History at the University of York. The author of articles on various aspects of the cultural and social history of early modern England, he is completing books on English conceptions of 'cleanliness' and 'dirt' as reflected in the environmental regulations of London *c.* 1530–*c.* 1700 and on water supply in London *c.* 1500–*c.* 1830.

MARGARET PELLING is Reader in the Social History of Medicine in the Modern History Faculty, University of Oxford, and is supported by the Wellcome Trust. Her publications include a volume of her essays, *The Common Lot: Sickness, Medical Occupations and the Urban Poor in Early Modern England* (1998). She is completing a monograph on the College of Physicians and 'irregular' practitioners in early modern London.

SARA PENNELL'S research interests range across early modern foodways, material culture and post-medieval archaeology. She is presently working as a researcher on the Robert Boyle Project at Birkbeck College, and writing a book on the uses of food in early modern England.

TIM WALES is a research editor on the *New Dictionary of National Biography*. He was a Leverhulme Research Fellow at the University of Essex, 1994–97, and is preparing a book on the decline of infant mortality in Essex, 1880–1940. His chapter in this volume is the first publication from a long-term project on thief-takers in seventeenth- and eighteenth-century London.

List of abbreviations

APC J. R. Dasent *et al.* eds, *Acts of the Privy Council* (46 vols, 1890–1964)

Archer, *Pursuit* Ian W. Archer, *The Pursuit of Stability: Social Relations in Elizabethan London* (Cambridge, 1991)

BCB Bridewell Hospital Court Books

Beier & Finlay, *London* A. L. Beier and R. Finlay eds, *London 1500–1700: The Making of the Metropolis* (1985)

BL British Library

BODL Bodleian Library, Oxford

Boulton, *Neighbourhood* Jeremy Boulton, *Neighbourhood and Society: A London Suburb in the Seventeenth Century* (Cambridge, 1987)

Chamberlain, *Letters* *The Letters of John Chamberlain*, ed. N. E. McClure (2 vols, Philadelphia, 1939)

CLRO Corporation of London Record Office

CSP City Sessions Papers

CSPD Calendar of State Papers, Domestic

CSPSpan. Calendar of State Papers, Spanish

CSPVen. Calendar of State Papers, Venetian

CTB Calendar of Treasury Books

DNB Dictionary of National Biography

EcHR Economic History Review

GCL Goldsmiths' Company Library

GL Guildhall Library, London

Gowing, *Domestic* Laura Gowing, *Domestic Dangers: Women, Words and Sex in Early Modern London* (Oxford, 1996)

HCC House of Correction Calendar

HJ Historical Journal

HMC Historical Manuscripts Commission

HOL House of Lords Record Office

Howes, *Annals* Edmund Howes, *Annales, or a Generall Chronicle of England Begun by John Stow: Continued and Augmented with Matters Foraigne and Domestique, Ancient and Moderne, unto the End of the Present Year 1631* (1631)

HWJ History Workshop Journal

JJ John Johnson collection, Bodleian Library, Oxford

Jour. Journal of Common Council

KB King's Bench

LJ London Journal

LMA London Metropolitan Archives

Londinopolis James Howell, *Londinopolis: An Historical Discourse or Perlustration of the City of London, the Imperial Chamber and the Chief Emporium of Great Britain* (1657)

LRS London Record Society

Machyn, *Diary* *The Diary of Henry Machyn, Citizen and Merchant Taylor of London 1550–1563*, ed. J. G. Nichols (Camden Society, old series, XLII, 1848)

MP   Main Papers, House of Lords

Pearl, *London*   Valerie Pearl, *London and the Outbreak of the Puritan Revolution: City Government and National Politics 1625–1643* (Oxford, 1961)

OBSP   Old Bailey Session Papers

P&P   Past and Present

PCR   Privy Council Register

Pepys, *Diary   The Diary of Samuel Pepys*, ed. Robert Latham and William Matthews (11 vols, 1970–83)

PRO   Public Record Office, London

Rappaport, *Worlds*   Steve Rappaport, *Worlds within Worlds: Structures of Life in Sixteenth Century London* (Cambridge, 1989)

RCP   Royal College of Physicians, London

Remb.   Remembrancia Books

Rep.   Repertory of the Court of Aldermen

SP   State Papers

STAC   Star Chamber

Stow, *Survey*   John Stow, *A Survey of London*, ed. C. L. Kingsford (2 vols, Oxford, 1971)

Stow, *Survey 1633*   John Stow, *The Survey of London ... Now Completely Finished by the Study of A.M., H.D. and Others this Present Yeere 1633* (1633)

Stow, Wheatley   John Stow, *The Survey of London*, introduced by Valerie Pearl, ed. H. B. Wheatley (1987)

Strype, *Stow*   John Strype, *A Survey of the Cities of London and Westminster ... by John Stow ... Corrected, Improved, and very much Enlarged* (1720)

WCA   Westminster City Archives

WPL   Westminster Public Library

In the notes the place of publication is London unless otherwise stated. 'The City' refers to the area of London under the jurisdiction of the Court of Aldermen.

Chapter 1

Introduction

Mark S. R. Jenner and Paul Griffiths

'[I]t is ... above thirty foure years ... since any thing was written of London, and Westminster her collateral Sister', declared James Howell in the preface to his *Londinopolis* (1657).[1] No contemporary historian could make such a claim. In the first place, numerate reviewers would delight in pointing out that only twenty-four years had elapsed between the 1633 recension of Stow's *Survey of London* and the publication of Howell's study. More importantly, there has been a renaissance in the history of early modern London.

This revival is of comparatively recent origin, for the capital was somewhat sidelined by the dominant themes in early modern British history during the 1970s and early 1980s. During this period influential revisionist political historians like John Morrill and Conrad Russell focused mainly on the aristocracy and gentry, while social historians concentrated on village and county studies. In the introduction to their seminal 1986 collection *London 1500–1700: The Making of a Metropolis*, Beier and Finlay thus noted a 'relative dearth' of historical writing about the early modern capital and expressed surprise that 'despite London's national and international importance ... it has not inspired the new generation of urban historians'.[2]

This dearth has been followed by a rich harvest. Three substantial histories of the city appeared during the 1990s.[3] They were complemented by studies of many fundamental aspects of metropolitan existence between the sixteenth and eighteenth centuries.[4] New and more reliable data about wages and prices have been assembled;[5] the work of John Landers in particular has taken the capital's demographic history to new levels of methodological sophistication;[6] early modern London's policing and criminal justice systems have been outlined with rigour and clarity.[7] London's reformations have been explored by Susan Brigden and David Hickman;[8] the complex religious and political cultures of seventeenth- and eighteenth-century London have prompted much research, with scholars investigating the links between patterns of mercantile investment and allegiance during the Civil War and party-political preference after 1688.[9]

This renewed interest in early modern London is hardly surprising. Despite losses occasioned by the Fire, war and local government reorganization, the capital possesses exceptional sources.[10] Aspects of early modern London, such as the Plague, the Fire, and the Globe, remain prominent in popular notions of the past and in versions of 'national heritage'. Furthermore, early modern London experienced truly dramatic change. Its population soared from about 50,000 in 1500 to some 200,000 in 1600, passing its previous (pre-Black Death) peak of between 80,000 and 100,000 in the mid-sixteenth century, and continued to grow thereafter. In 1650 Londoners numbered approximately 375,000; in 1700 they totalled at least 490,000, and probably considerably more, and by 1750 roughly 675,000.[11]

This demographic explosion transformed the nature of the city. In the early sixteenth century London was a relatively bounded community, largely defined by its walls and the jurisdiction of the mayor and aldermen. By the 1630s, however, Westminster and the suburbs had grown dramatically and only a minority of Londoners fell under City rule. By the 1690s extramural London parishes like St Dunstan Stepney and St Martin's in the Fields were as large as any other city in the British Isles.[12] This growth was relative as well as absolute. Whereas London contained perhaps 4 per cent of the English population in 1500, its population was over 11 per cent of the nation's by the mid-eighteenth century. It had become one of the world's great metropolises. Indeed, many Augustan and Georgian Englishmen and women reckoned that London was, in the words of a 1694 proposal to publish a revision of Stow's survey, 'no less than the great Mart and *Metropolis* of the Kingdom ... the largest as well as noblest City of the World'.[13]

The authors of this broadsheet were myopically Eurocentric – Istanbul and Edo were almost certainly at least as populous.[14] Nevertheless, the capital was quite unlike any other place in the British Isles. When the Scottish cleric, Robert Kirk, visited London in the 1680s, he wrote that the city was 'a great vast wilderness'.[15] Ned, a Somerset lad, was even more horrified when he came to the capital at about the same time:

> Thorn going on London city z' did view
> And when z' did zeet schor a ready to spew
> What with the neeze and what with the smoake
> Twas Death in my ears, and schor a ready to choake.
> But oh how the coaches did vlee up and down
> Iz thought the whole world had a bee in ye town.[16]

Not surprisingly he turned tail and fled home. Many commentators have stressed the confusing rootlessness which these visitors found in the city and the way this changed people's behaviour. Kirk suggested that because Londoners numbered a million and a half and so did not know the people around them, they relied instead upon 'public printed papers' to discover what was happening.[17] London was certainly a far more literate society than anywhere else in the country. David Cressy noted how its servants and apprentices were 'extraordinarily literate' in the seventeenth century – only one-fifth of apprentices deposing in the ecclesiastical courts signed with a mark. By the 1690s, moreover, roughly half the women witnesses in these courts could also sign their names. Although the labouring poor of the capital had fewer literacy skills,[18] London was an obvious location for the effloresence of print culture in the seventeenth century and for the birth of the newspaper.[19]

In a classic article, E. A. Wrigley estimated that one-sixth of England's population lived in London at some point in their lives and argued that this was a powerful solvent of traditional mores throughout the land.[20] He and other commentators now present a less cataclysmic account of how far London may have changed early modern mentalities.[21] Nevertheless, many historians have argued that the size of London and the diversity of its markets and material culture helped create new social and sexual identities and dissolve older, more hierarchical, forms of social organization.[22]

This book seeks to convey something of the dynamic and changing nature of early modern London and to bring together some of the exciting new research currently being done on the city. The contributors also offer fresh approaches to the history of the early modern metropolis. For while the last two decades' research has added immensely to our knowledge, it has not altered the metanarratives of London history as fundamentally as one might expect. Indeed, the structure, periodization and literary techniques of Roy Porter's well received *London: a Social History* are not particularly different from earlier syntheses of London history.[23]

By drawing together research on London from the sixteenth century to the eighteenth, *Londinopolis* challenges some of the chronological enclosure of early modern English history.[24] There has recently been much excellent work which crosses the boundary between late medieval and early modern, which shows the intellectual benefit of examining the sixteenth century alongside the fifteenth, and many historians now work on medieval and Tudor London.[25] Despite this example of the permeability of periodization, one would have thought from much of its historiography that the Civil War, Restoration, and the Fire together formed a total hiatus in the history of the capital. Yet only a fifth of London's housing stock was destroyed in 1666.[26] Furthermore, influential general accounts of late seventeenth-century politics portray it as a continuation of the conflicts of the mid-century.[27] Arguably, the foundation of the Bank of England in 1694, and the expansion of servant-keeping in the late seventeenth century, have at least as great a claim to be viewed as a turning point in Londoners' lives as the high politics of the 1640s or 1660s.[28] Recent work, moreover, has revealed that joint stock companies and nascent political parties did not simply supplant other older cultural forms. Guilds, apprenticeship, wardmotes and other aspects of specifically civic culture remained important in London life long into the eighteenth century.[29] They coexisted with and adapted to newer patterns of metropolitan living in ways which paralleled the vitality of civic forms in other chartered boroughs.[30]

An awareness of work on both sides of this chronological divide brings great intellectual benefits. In particular, it inoculates historians against seeing the birth of the 'modern' or of consumer culture in the particular period which they are studying.[31] This desire to challenge the conventional distinction between pre- and post-Restoration London is one of the reasons we have appropriated the title of James Howell's *Londinopolis*. Published in 1657, Howell's account of the city obviously lies at the chronological midpoint of this collection; its form and content also face both forward and backwards. It has received less attention from London historians than the surveys of John Stow in the late sixteenth and John Strype in the early eighteenth centuries. In many ways this is not particularly surprising. In the engraved portrait incongruously inserted as the frontispiece to some copies of *Londinopolis*, Howell chose to be portrayed according to Arcadian conventions. For all his prefatory protestations of affection towards the capital, he regularly depicted London as a seedbed of sedition.[32] *Londinopolis*, furthermore, was written fairly hastily, when Howell was largely devoid of patronage and was apparently making a living as an author.[33] It is not as detailed as Stow or Strype, and is, in fact, singularly uninformative about the reconstruction of mayoral culture and the efforts at godly reformation in the capital during the 1650s.[34] Nor is it an antiquarian gold mine to compare with William Dugdale's account of St Paul's published in the following year, even though Howell, like Dugdale, was horrified by iconoclasm and by the desecration of the cathedral.[35]

Nevertheless, Howell's text and its hybrid title reveal some of the processes by which London became a metropolis and yet also retained its older civic identities. Within the pages of *Londinopolis* the literary form of Stow is combined with the quantification that characterized the political arithmetic of William Petty and John Graunt,[36] and with the emphasis upon London's role as an international trading centre that is so clear in Daniel Defoe and William Maitland.[37] Adopting Howell's title marks a desire to discuss sixteenth- and eighteenth-century London within the same covers.

The contributors also share Ian Archer's concern that historians of early modern London have been 'too accepting of an "urban" historical agenda' and his desire to move beyond it. This agenda has largely resulted in two modes of writing about early modern English towns and cities. The first has traced the *impact* of economic and demographic change of urban society, and the *response* to such economic and demographic problems; the second has produced forms of economic history which often reify towns. As we show below, most of the authors in this book implicitly or explicitly problematize the distinction between 'the social' and 'the economic', and focus rather upon the relationships and experiences of Londoners.

The existing urban historiography has often been organized around the antithesis between crisis and stability, or that between order and disorder. The work of Peter Clark and Paul Slack in the 1970s made these terms central to early modern English urban history.[38] They have been explored particularly explicitly with reference to sixteenth- and early seventeenth-century London. Several scholars have suggested that in this period London teetered on the brink of economic catastrophe and violent social conflict because of inflation, falling real wages and widespread unemployment.[39]

In the late 1970s and early 1980s, however, Valerie Pearl and Steve Rappaport fundamentally challenged this image. Pearl stressed the integrative culture of City office holding, while Rappaport demonstrated that real wages did not fall and prices did not rise as violently as earlier historians had suggested, and argued more controversially that there was little social conflict. In the eyes of many commentators, Ian Archer's *The Pursuit of Stability* resolved many of these debates, demonstrating that, while there was undoubted tension and hardship during the 1590s, conflict was largely (though not entirely) averted. This was substantially due to human agency: the governing elite worked closely with parish elites and balanced the repression of crime and disorder with displays of charity and neighbourliness which helped sustain their hegemony within the City.[40]

As Michael Berlin notes, these exchanges mirrored wider political debates of the 1970s and 1980s. Their somewhat Manichaean terms seem rather dated when compared with recent, finer grained, analyses of social relations. Rather than analysing early modern society within a functionalist framework, asking how far a particular institution or series of events contributed to the maintenance of social stability, these studies explore the *process* of social change, tracing the contestations of power, the reproduction of inequality, and the shifting balance of economic and social relations.[41]

With the exception of the 1790s,[42] discussions of late seventeenth- and eighteenth-century London are rarely preoccupied with how stability was maintained, even though during this period the capital witnessed industrial disputes, rioting, and political and religious conflict far more violent than the disorders of the late Elizabethan capital.[43] Admittedly, many historians argue that by this period the economic situation of the lower orders was less desperate and poor law provision more generous than in *c*. 1600.[44] Other historians of the Restoration and Augustan capital have highlighted its growing prosperity and the abundance of luxury goods within it. Peter Earle, for instance, has argued that a distinctive middle class appeared in the artisanal, mercantile and business sector of late seventeenth-century London.[45] Roy Porter, John Brewer, Peter Borsay and others have highlighted London's place at the heart of eighteenth-century polite and leisured culture, and the example which it gave to the urban renaissance.[46] London's cultural centrality was complemented by the increasing importance of its financial sector and joint stock companies.[47] Its trading interests reached out across the globe, and, as Karen O'Brien has demonstrated, from the late seventeenth century London was increasingly imagined as a centre of empire, not just as a political capital or the chamber of the realm.[48]

These triumphalist narratives of growth and economic expansion ignore the turbulence of the Exclusion crisis, the rage of party and the Jacobite rebellions.[49] Nevertheless, they do not write of a London that was stable. One does not have to follow modern management consultants' mantras of the need for perpetual change in business to suggest that the pursuit of prosperity in early modern London against a background of regular European wars, cycles of unemployment and trade depression, the South Sea Bubble, and appalling levels of mortality did not lead to a stable existence.[50]

The language of crisis is a similarly unhelpful analytical category with which to explore any period of early modern metropolitan history. Firstly, there is no consensus on what constitutes a social crisis. Consequently the terminology provokes sterile semantic debates, which are compounded by the unhelpful tendency to view the outbreak of the Civil War either as the normal response to social tensions or as an ideal type of early modern social crisis. More importantly, the term 'crisis', deriving as it does from the word used to describe the moment a fever breaks, easily leads to forms of functionalist analysis which do not address change. Historians thus write of towns, cities or societies 'weathering the storm', of the social fabric holding.[51] In so doing, they often fail to explore how those societies changed over the period in question, to ask who gained and who lost. Moreover, some versions of this crisis historiography imply that social and political tensions were clearly resolved in the mid-seventeenth century.[52] Not only does a greater awareness of the uncertainties of the later seventeenth and early eighteenth centuries call this model of social change into question, but some would doubt whether antagonistic human relations can be resolved so easily. Laura Gowing, for instance, has suggested that gender is most usefully analysed as being always in crisis, and argues below that one should see 'urban identity and gender identities ... [as] in the making', rather than ever being ultimately resolved or 'erased'.[53]

Admittedly, an important strand of eighteenth-century historiography explores rather than erases the misery which accompanied London's economic expansion. Dorothy George's *London Life in the Eighteenth Century* remains the crucial point of reference for such work, and it has been supplemented by important studies of prostitution, illegitimacy, poverty and of the policies developed towards them.[54] Recent work has paid more attention to the ideologies behind social regulation and charitable relief,[55] but there is still a tendency to follow George in describing them as a *response* to economic problems.[56] For, as Adrian Wilson has observed, George wrote her history by juxtaposing appalling poverty, poor housing and drunkenness with the achievements of *improvement*.[57] In her account social problems were objective categories, and *economic* circumstances, the misery of the indigent, led to governmental and philanthropic response.

Recent historiographical developments have raised important intellectual objections to this approach. Many would now stress that economistic categories such as the extent of poverty or the level of crime do not of themselves explain administrative and political initiatives. Social problems, they would argue, are constituted ideologically, rhetorically and politically.[58] This is not to deny the reality of hunger or suffering in the past, as some embattled critics of the linguistic turn have suggested.[59] Rather it is to acknowledge that people's hunger can be attributed to their alleged indolence or to the failure of their richer neighbours' charity. *Political* contests or debates over the *meanings* of indigence or disorder determine social responses. One cannot read them off from economic circumstances. Thus Paul Griffiths shows how the campaigns to make goldsmiths return to Cheapside were driven as much by Charles I's identification of architectural uniformity with social order as by economic imperatives. Similarly, Tim Wales suggests that the mind set of late seventeenth-century politics structured contemporary models of criminal association at least as much as any objective spread of organized crime.

The narrative of changing economic circumstances, however, remains the most common way to emplot the history of early modern London. As Margaret Pelling notes below, 'growth' is a dominant trope within early modern urban history. It has been a remarkably enduring one. F. J. Fisher's fifty-year-old studies of the metropolitan market for food and luxury goods remain important items on the reading list of London history, not only because of their clarity and fine scholarship, but also because the historiography of London has retained basically the same problematic.[60] At the heart of Beier and Finlay's collection are articles which trace London's demographic and economic transformation. In outlining the capital's male occupational structure, social topography, the geographical origins of its apprentices and the city's involvement in foreign and domestic trade, these articles render London history as a series of graphs and tables, or as a succession of maps.

Such statistical techniques and histories thus construct a 'London' as the object of analysis and then examine 'its' growth, problems and triumphs. In recent years there have been criticisms of this kind of approach. Firstly, women's historians have drawn attention to the gendered biases in the definition of categories like employment in historical sources and in modern economic history.[61] Peter Earle and Tim Meldrum have drawn attention to the myriad irregular forms of work by which London women supported themselves and contributed to household economies. By demonstrating the overwhelming continuities in women's work between the seventeenth and nineteenth centuries they, like Judith Bennett and Amanda Vickery, suggest that underneath the masculine economic history of mechanization, labour discipline and growth lies another history of women's economic experience revolving around poorly paid and unpaid casual and domestic labour.[62]

Secondly, this mode of history writing reifies towns and cities. It treats areas of human activity like work or buying things as economic abstractions. As a result it does not investigate either human agency or the culture of which such activities are a part. Recent works have suggested that this approach does not capture the complexities of early modern life. Craig Muldrew, for instance, has shown that in a poorly monetarized economy like pre-industrial England's credit in the sense of credibility was vital to the maintenance of economic activity.[63] Other historians, meanwhile, would stress that positivistic economic history largely ignores questions about how the city was *experienced* and about the social relations of its inhabitants.

Such questions are the central themes of this book. Its chapters do not isolate something called London and trace its fortunes. Rather they treat the history of London (and, one might add by extension, the history of any town) as the history of the social relations and social practices of its inhabitants. One might say that they are histories *about* but not necessarily *of* London. The contributors thus present a turbulent multiplicity of simultaneous and overlapping narratives reminiscent of the scene in Borough Market place depicted on our cover, not a single view of the capital from afar like the panoramas of Visscher and Hollar, which are often favoured on the dustjackets of other works of London history.[64]

Laid end to end these essays do not constitute a comprehensive account of the early modern capital. In fact, the detailed (often micro-historical) research of recent years has made it harder and harder to write *the* social or cultural history of London. As Jenner stresses in his discussion of water supply, the experience of the eastern suburbs was quite different from that of the City. Similarly, Boulton emphasizes the particular social dynamics of West End parishes. More fundamentally, attention to the diversity of London's inhabitants and to the ways in which historical narratives often work by excluding as well as incorporating historical actors calls into question the very notion of a single history of London. The London of an indigent maidservant or street walker was, after all, quite different from that of James Boswell.[65]

Nevertheless, one methodological position runs through the collection. None invokes 'the economic' as something which is analytically separable from society or culture. Indeed, several chapters explicitly reject the notion that cultural change is a reflection or simple expression of economic or demographic forces. Michael Berlin, for instance, argues that the reordering of Elizabethan parish society was effected as much by the changes in ritual which he describes as by growing inequalities of wealth.

Such an approach is anything but idealist. Indeed, Sara Pennell, Margaret Pelling and Laura Gowing stress the significance of *material* culture in the construction of particular forms of urban living; Faramerz Dabhoiwala highlights how often in Restoration and early eighteenth-century London sexual encounters were entwined with various forms of material exchange, and Margaret Hunt's examination of Exchequer cases stresses the centrality of the material, of *maintenance*, in London marital disputes.

Such an integration of the economic and the socio-cultural has methodo-logical implications which do not apply solely to the history of London. There are strong parallels between the approaches adopted in these essays and recent work by James Farr on artisanal culture in early modern France and David Sabean on early modern Germany.[66] It is no surprise, therefore, that most of the following essays use Londoners' experiences to address wider historiographical issues and to engage in important general debates in early modern English historical studies.

A striking recent development in early modern historiography has been the rethinking of political history. On the one hand claims that politics was the preserve of a narrow social elite have been subjected to increasing criticism. On the other a growing interest in how power was exercised and authority contested at the local level has made many scholars uneasy with the conventional separation of political and social history.

Few would now doubt that mid- and late seventeenth-century London was highly politicized. Tim Harris's work revealed a city in which large Whig and Tory crowds competed for control of the streets. Some 18,000 Londoners petitioned against the Popish Plot. But, as Keith Lindley has detailed, the English Revolution had already stirred the passions of many humble London women and men – some 15,000 Londoners signed petitions for root-and-branch reform of the Church in 1641.[67] Many historians link these developments with the explosion of cheap print in London, and argue that they marked the emergence of a new form of politics in which it was important to appeal to something that might be called public opinion.[68] Indeed, the late seventeenth-century London coffee house has been identified as a key locus for the emergence of the bourgeois public sphere, pushing back the original dating proposed by the German social theorist Jurgen Habermas by between fifty and a hundred years.[69]

Yet, as Ian Archer shows, popular politics in London did not erupt *de novo* in 1640. Large and often partisan crowds attended the execution of Protestant and Catholic martyrs; bills and libels commenting on national affairs were stuck up in prominent places in 1601, in the 1550s and, indeed, in the 1450s.[70] With a high number of licensed and graduate preachers, London pulpits provided a commentary upon the affairs of the realm, sometimes on occasion much to the displeasure of the Crown and Privy Council. The capital also contained networks of heretics and recusants. There were many points of contacts between the royal court and citizens; the City and the livery companies knew, for example, how to exploit royal favour and parliamentary legislation. Nor did Londoners simply respond to political initiatives from above. For Archer identifies strands of distinctively civic political prejudice and sentiment. These included a sense of civic pride which resented any assertion of superiority by gentlemen, and a deep-seated hostility to 'foreigners', who were claimed to endanger citizens' livelihood. At the time of the proposed marriage between Prince Charles and the Spanish Infanta such xenophobia combined with a popular Protestant culture to form a potent language of criticism of the court.

Archer's stress upon the central role of citizenship in London political culture connects with wider definitions of politics espoused by other scholars. Most influentially, Keith Wrightson has foregrounded what he termed 'the politics of the parish', the broader exercise and contestation of social power within parochial society.[71] Certainly in early modern London religious and high political changes were played out in conflicts between pastors and parishioners, and in purges of vestries.[72]

Concerns with the day-to-day exercise of authority come through forcefully in Michael Berlin's account of London parishes. Whereas other scholars have constructed a history of the London 'parish community' through the quantitative analysis of churchwardens' accounts,[73] he foregrounds how changing power relations were articulated through the spatial and symbolic reorganization of parochial culture. In the early sixteenth century parish feasts were occasions of inclusive parochial commensality; by the early seventeenth century they had often been turned into private gatherings of self-selected parish elders. In many parishes the poorer sort found themselves barred from attending vestry meetings and from sitting in the increasingly privatized pews springing up in London churches. Like the hedges of rural enclosures, such physical exclusion both marked *and* accomplished the reordering of parish life.

Ironically, recent assertions of the fundamentally political nature of social relations and social regulation use definitions of the political which ressemble those used by James Howell. It is striking how, shortly after the rule of the major-generals, he spent many pages praising the quality of the City's traditional forms of government, declaring that 'it will appear to the impartial ... Reader, that if consideration be had to the Prerogatives and power of her chiefest Magistrates, to their plenty, magnificence and hospitality, to the security of Passengers up and down her streets at midnight, as well as at noon daies, the City of *London* admits no Parallel.'[74]

This stress upon the Aristotelian notion of politics as the affairs of the *polis* would find favour with many social and cultural historians. However, few would concur with Howell's halcyon picture of London's streets. As Tim Wales's study of thief-takers shows, theft and other forms of crime were a considerable problem for London shopkeepers and artisans as well as for the social elite.[75] During the 1690s such concerns about metropolitan crime and disorder increased markedly and were coupled with anxieties about Jacobite plotters and the threat posed to the nation's money by coiners and clippers. Central government, not least the Office of the Mint under the direction of Isaac Newton, accordingly took an even keener interest in serious crime in the capital.

Historians have recently emphasized how the 1690s saw a rapid and lasting increase in the fiscal and military power of the English state and the establishment of a quasi-professional fraternity of excise officers to collect revenue.[76] Wales demonstrates that the same pressures also opened the door to a spectacular growth in private enterprise in the policing of the capital. Londoners, he shows, had long used a variety of brokers to recover stolen goods in return for a fee. Such individuals served a useful (if ambiguous) function – many householders preferred to get stolen property back rather than to spend time and money pursuing malefactors and having them tried and punished. Wales has uncovered a dozen such brokers, and finds the same individuals helping to apprehend more serious offenders for the state. He reveals how thief-takers carefully cultivated sources of information and built up reputations as sources of occult information of the criminal 'underworld'. Like the 'public printed papers' which the Scottish minister Kirk highlighted and the linkmen who lit citizens' way home at night, these shadowy intermediaries helped a wide range of Londoners to negotiate the often seamy streets.

Policing during the 1690s was not directed only at thieves, highwaymen and coiners. The Reformation of Manners campaigns were also concerned with the prosecution of vice in all forms. Thousands of people were prosecuted by the campaigns' representatives for 'lewd and disorderly conduct'. These were overwhelmingly women 'accused of "nightwalking" and picking up men' – in other words, prostitutes.[77] Such trade in heterosexual sex lies at the heart of Faramerz Dabhoiwala's discussion of patterns of sexual immorality. Yet, as he demonstrates, the range of behaviour for which women were liable to be condemned and prosecuted as 'whores' was extremely wide. Attempts to reconstruct the lives of a distinct group of women who worked as 'prostitutes' are therefore misconceived: firstly, because '[o]ccasional prostitution was merely a variation' in the 'economy of makeshifts' by which thousands of young women scraped a living in the capital; and, secondly, because there was no clear line between prostitution, adultery and fornication.[78] The richer sort were less likely to be prosecuted for extra-marital sex, but, he suggests, their sexual behaviour did not vary significantly from those of poorer Londoners.

Whereas Dabhoiwala stresses the difficulty of determining the exact marital status of many couples cohabiting in London, Margaret Hunt draws attention to how Londoners' unions were exposed to public scrutiny through the law courts, and the extent to which the judicial system offered opportunities for women to defend and assert their interests. London women, in particular, might find some redress for mistreatment or other grievances through the many law courts within walking distance. Tens of thousands of London women initiated suits in Chancery and Exchequer; similar numbers defended cases there. Such legal agency was not restricted to widows and single women – '[w]arring spouses and their families haunted the common law courts', and their testimonies offer an unparalleled source from which to explore women's as well as men's understandings of marriage.

Two particularly noteworthy conclusions emerge from Hunt's analysis. The first is the extent to which marriage was grounded in the material. In reaction to Lawrence Stone's denial of the existence of love in early modern unions, historians have often given a rather disembodied account of the emotional lives of early modern couples. The notion of a good marriage, Hunt shows, included the husband's obligation to provide maintenance for his family and spouse. Hunt (like Amy Erickson) demonstrates that women did not submerge their individuality in marriage. Although they were by no means equal partners in these relationships and were frequently subject to emotional blackmail, physical and verbal abuse, women often went to great lengths to protect the goods which they brought to the union, building upon a legal right to retain them in the event of their spouse's death. The household economy was thus riven with tensions as husbands sought to use their wives' capital and wives tried to protect it either for their own commercial activities or for the sustenance of their children. Moreover, London women's lives and work made them more litigious than their rural sisters throughout the seventeenth and early eighteenth centuries.[79]

Laura Gowing, like Hunt, is concerned with the interface between the symbolic and the material, and with the contradictory ways in which women experienced patriarchal power. As she notes, an influential literature presents the modern metropolis as undermining traditional gender norms and, to a certain extent, emancipating women. Yet almost all these claims, Gowing shows, can also be made for Elizabethan and early Stuart London. London women frequented alehouses and moved through the city as a matter of course. The traditional ideology which prescribed that women should remain enclosed within domestic space could not be sustained when women moved about for their work, when houses were often shared with lodgers, and when neighbours could hear and sometimes see much of what went on inside the kitchens, parlours or bedchambers of adjacent households.

But, Gowing shows, this was not a simple case of *Stadtluft macht Frauen frei*. Urban femininity was imagined and performed in a restricted range of locations – the pump, the yard, the doorstep, the parish. Even there women might find themselves harassed by spitting, jostling and verbally aggressive men. Furthermore, sexual incontinence was imagined through metaphors of wandering abroad. Women who walked through the streets selling clothes or fruit, or who strolled in the fields outside the city for their recreation, were liable to be condemned as disorderly, and this disorder was articulated through strongly gendered languages of sexual promiscuity. Gender, she shows, was thus quite literally *grounded* in social and spatial practice.

Her chapter introduces three further essays on notions of space and place. All focus on London's growing suburbs. Norman Brett-James described the growth of seventeenth-century London as the first phase in the 'absorption and destruction of the countryside', and similar images abound in urban history. But Nicholas Green's influential study of early nineteenth-century French culture has outlined a more complex model of the relationship between city and country. From the 1820s, he suggests, environmentalist medicine juxtaposed Parisian unhealthiness and dirt with the aesthetic, moral and medical benefits of rural life. In his words, 'the ... working together of environmentalist priorities with Parisian modernity produced a nature not antithetical but *integral* to the living-out of metropolitan culture'. One practical consequence of this was a move out 'to the picturesque delights of the suburbs and beyond', part of 'a long invasion ... of surrounding regions by ... the Parisian spectator'.[80] Margaret Pelling's examination of the ambivalences of urban living has many parallels with Green's work. But whereas he sees 'nature' as produced within discourses of urban modernity, she argues that 'the natural ... pleasures ... on the outskirts of towns' helped constitute the metropolitan. Londoners' lives were structured by 'a set of attitudes, and a way of life [in which they] ... went in and out of the capital' at regular intervals. This might involve walking in the fields beyond the City bounds or expeditions to nearby villages for recreation. By the 1670s significant numbers of London merchants lived in villages like Hoxton and Islington and did business in the City. Moreover, environmentalist concerns not dissimilar to those of the early nineteenth century structured responses to early modern London. To walk in the fields and take the air in the appropriate season was standard medical advice. Plague altered perceptions of London's public space, not least because it was associated with miasma produced by insanitary conditions.[81] Pelling also shows that concerns about endemic disease, notably smallpox, served as an 'engine of social alienation'. Crucially this was articulated spatially, through the insistence upon *distance* between the sick and the healthy and between the living quarters of servants or apprentices and those of the master and the mistress.

While Pelling describes the ways in which London living negotiated the antithesis between *rus* and *urbs*, nature and culture, Paul Griffiths explores how in the early seventeenth century Cheapside became a site upon which different visions of city life were imagined. He stresses the congruence between Charles I's pursuit of political order and his aesthetic taste for uniformity. One aspect of this was Charles's pursuit of a two-pronged policy compelling all goldsmiths to return to Goldsmiths' Row in Cheapside and expelling the other traders who had set up shop there. However, Griffiths shows that Charles was reviving sets of orders initiated by his father, which had originated in appeals to the Crown by the Goldsmiths' Company. In order to maximize guild control, senior members of the Company sought from 1619 onwards to force goldsmiths working in the suburbs to return to the Row. Stuart commands for uniformity were thus an appropriation of a guild ethos. Both policies were highly divisive. 'Remote goldsmiths', those taking advantage of the lower rents and expanding business opportunities in the West End, dug in their heels and resisted orders to close their shops and move to Cheapside. The vocabulary of the guild's commands, harping on the dangers presented by 'strangers', was unable to accommodate these divisions, not least because there were far more goldsmiths than there were shops in the Row. In the early 1640s these contestations became linked to far-reaching calls for the Goldsmiths' Company to become more responsive to the wishes of the 'generality' of the guild and, through the persons of Parliamentarian activists like Francis Allein, to a national political critique of arbitrary rule.

The growth of luxury trades like the goldsmiths' in the West End is confirmed by Jeremy Boulton's wide-ranging discussion of this district. He shows that the population of St Martin in the Fields and the parishes carved out of it passed 100,000 by 1720. The western suburbs were thus bigger than the East End. Although the cultural patronage of the royal court declined in the late seventeenth century,[82] the occupational structure of St Martin's remained roughly the same. The clothing trades, victualling and domestic service predominated, with the St Martin's textile workers being tailors, who catered to individual customers following fashion, rather than weavers or dyers, who produced large quantities of workaday cloth, as was the case in other areas of London.[83] All these trades served the gentry staying in the parish and government officials who worked in nearby Westminster.

Boulton also challenges conventional characterizations of the West End as an exclusive and aristocratic district. In fact, the percentage of titled households *declined* considerably after the Restoration, and a fifth of St Martin's households were exempted from the Hearth Tax. Mapping the 1716 listing of the poor, Boulton demonstrates that within a few hundred yards of the most fashionable residences were concentrations of parish pensioners. Parish pensioners (some 2 per cent of the population of St Martin's in the late seventeenth and early eighteenth centuries) were not, Boulton argues, a self-evident group. Although there has been a tendency to suggest that there was an inexorable increase in the generosity of poor relief over the seventeenth century, he shows how only micro-studies of particular parishes can uncover and explain the forms and levels of relief. Between the 1620s and the 1650s, for instance, the St Martin's vestry clamped down on the poor, badging pensioners and reducing both pensions and the percentage of the population relieved. One parish's pension might be two, three, or even four times another's.

Together these essays exemplify the new interest in notions of space and place among social and cultural historians. Cynthia Wall has recently discussed the growing importance of languages of surveying in descriptions of seventeenth-century London, attributing this in part to a new spatial self-awareness after the Fire. Miles Ogborn has explored the public spaces and architecture of eighteenth-century London in the light of theoretical writings on modernity.[84] While Boulton's chapter develops the tradition of mapping urban topography and social structure, other work presents senses of space and place as culturally specific and socially constituted.[85] The essays on popular politics, for instance, all highlight particular spaces – St Paul's, the vestry room, the coffee house – as sites for the assertion of cultural authority. Griffiths's discussion of Cheapside, meanwhile, has many parallels with cultural geographers' work on the iconography of landscape and cityscape, the ways in which particular sites and particular representations of places come to bear ideological significance.[86] Pelling and Gowing show that the social spaces of early modern London cannot be captured from a depopulated bird's eye view – they were produced through social practice. The character of a particular location was marked by its cultural meanings, whether it was healthy or unhealthy, moral or not. It was also determined by formal and informal structures of power and so varied according to who you were and the circumstances in which you entered it. The street was different for women and for men, rooms were different for masters and for servants or apprentices.[87]

Such attention to social space also informs Sara Pennell's and Mark Jenner's explorations of the preparing and the eating of food and the acquiring of water for domestic tasks – basic aspects of consumption which are remarkably absent from most accounts of London life. Economic historians have long noted the importance of victualling in the economy of early modern London and the impact which the capital had upon food production in surrounding counties. Pennell, however, begins to unpack the meanings of victualling in a city where ovens were rare, kitchens far from universal, and the boundary between the domestic and the commercial preparation of food permeable in the extreme. Such meanings could be complex and ambiguous. Did passing left-over food to servants express commensality or superiority? Did the preparation of food for a lodger indicate a domestic or a commercial relationship? Food and drink were tokens of relationships, and markers of special events in the calendar like Bartholomew Fair or vestry feasts. Metropolitan foodways, Pennell suggests, were distinctive because there was an unparalleled range of ready cooked food available for sale. But London was no culinary land of Cockayne. Its diversity of foods and eating establishments produced forms of social differentiation by taste as well as cost. The majority of London eating establishments were demotic, catering to working people who went there more or less out of necessity, not leisure, snatching a bite to eat in the course of their labours, or seeking a temporary escape from their master or mistress's house. The wealthier sort of the mid-eighteenth century, by contrast, demonstrated their social position through domestic eating in new and fashionable dining rooms.

The allocation of water, Jenner argues, was similarly complex, for water was a comparatively scarce commodity which was acquired only through considerable expense of time or money. In the sixteenth century, he suggests, there was a moral economy of the conduit. Mayors and aldermen sought through the maintenance and regulation of public conduits to guarantee a supply to all citizens. However, such public supplies came under considerable strain because of the increase in London's population and the city's physical expansion over the pipes feeding the conduits. One response to this situation was the appearance in the late sixteenth and early seventeenth centuries of private commercial water companies which provided limited supplies of piped water to private houses in return for an annual rent. By the late 1630s over a tenth of houses in the City had piped supplies, a percentage that grew over the next century. Whereas previous historians have simply hailed this as an example of technical progress, Jenner describes how its impact must be understood in the context of the relationship between householders and waterbearers, and emphasizes contemporary resistance to the idea of trading in water. Indeed, he suggests, the spread of piped water may have reduced the elite's commitment to maintain free public supplies, leaving some of their poorer neighbours worse off. However, rather than portraying this simply as an example of the decline of the civic community, Jenner stresses that it is best understood as one aspect of a wider shift in London culture by which independent commercial organizations came to play a greater role in everyday life. By 1700 London was not only a *polis* of citizens, it was also a *polis* of shareholders.

Histories of London frequently begin by commenting on how difficult it is to write the history of this vast and complex city. The following essays focusing on *polis* and police, gender and sexuality, senses of space and place, material culture and consumption, will not make such a project any easier. In fact, by examining broader historiographical themes which are not peculiar to early modern London, they depart from conventional approaches to early modern British urban history which seek to encompass the history of a particular place within one study. By on the one hand abandoning any claim to *comprehensiveness*, and on the other trying not to construct hierarchies of causation that give primacy to the economic or any other single factor, this collection is a contribution to the cultural, economic, political and social history of London between 1500 and 1750.

NOTES

1 *Londinopolis*, dedication 'To the Renowned City of London'.

2 Beier and Finlay, *London*, pp. 5–6.

3 R. Porter, *London: A Social History* (Harmondsworth, 1994); F. H. W. Sheppard, *London: A History* (Oxford, 1998); S. Inwood, *A History of London* (Basingstoke, 1998). The historiography of London is surveyed in H. J. Creaton, *Bibliography of London History to 1939* (1994).

4 Many of these are reviewed in V. Harding, 'Early modern London 1550–1700', and L. Schwarz, 'London 1700–1850', in P. L. Garside, ed., *Capital Histories: A Bibliographical Study of London* (Aldershot, 1998).

5 Rappaport, *Worlds*, esp. chap. 3; J. Boulton, 'Wage labour in seventeenth-century London', *EcHR*, 49 (1996); L. D. Schwarz, 'The standard of living in the long run: London 1700–1860', *EcHR*, 38 (1985).

6 J. Landers, 'Mortality and the metropolis: the case of London', *Population Studies*, 41 (1987); *id.*, *Death in the Metropolis: Studies in the Demographic History of London 1670–1830* (Cambridge, 1993). The most important recent work on sixteenth- and seventeenth-century London demography since R. Finlay, *Population and Metropolis* (Cambridge, 1981) and R. A. Finlay and B. Shearer, 'Population growth and suburban expansion', in Beier and Finlay, *London*, is V. Harding, 'The population of London 1550–1700: a review of the published evidence', *LJ*, 15 (1990), and J. I. A. Champion, *London's Dreaded Visitation*, Historical Geography Research Series 35 (1995).

7 For example, R. B. Shoemaker, *Prosecution and Punishment: Petty Crime and the Law in London and Rural Middlesex c. 1660–1725* (Cambridge, 1991); E. A. Reynolds, *Before the Bobbies: The Night Watch and Police Reform in Metropolitan London 1720–1830* (Basingstoke, 1998); J. M. Beattie, *Crime and the Courts in England 1660–1800* (Oxford, 1986); *id.*, 'London juries in the 1690s', in J. S. Cockburn and T. A. Green eds, *Twelve Good Men and True* (Princeton NJ, 1988); T. Henderson, *Disorderly Women in Eighteenth Century London: Prostitution and Control in the Metropolis 1730–1830* (1999).

8 S. Brigden, *London and the Reformation* (Oxford, 1989); D. Hickman, 'From Catholic to Protestant: the changing meaning of testamentary religious provision in Elizabethan London', in N. Tyacke ed., *England's Long Reformation* (1998).

9 For example, R. Brenner, *Merchants and Revolution* (Cambridge, 1993); K. Lindley, *Popular Politics and Religion in Civil War London* (Aldershot, 1997); T. Harris, *London Crowds in the Reign of Charles II* (Cambridge, 1987); M. Knights, 'A City Revolution: the

remodelling of the London livery companies in the 1680s', *English Historical Review*, 112 (1997); G. S. de Krey, *A Fractured Society: The Politics of London in the First Age of Party 1688–1715* (Oxford, 1985); N. Rogers, *Whigs and Cities: Popular Politics in the Age of Walpole and Pitt* (Oxford, 1989), Parts I–II.

10 See, for example, A. Foster, 'Churchwardens' accounts of early modern England and Wales: some problems to note, but much to be gained', in K. L. French, G. G. Gibbs and B. A. Kümin eds, *The Parish in English Life 1400–1600* (Manchester, 1997), esp. pp. 78–82. See also D. Keene and V. Harding, *A Survey of Documentary Sources for Property Holding in London before the Great Fire*, LRS 22 (1985).

11 Finlay and Shearer, 'Population growth and suburban expansion'; Harding, 'Population of London'; D. Keene, 'Medieval London and its region', *LJ*, 14 (1989).

12 St Dunstan's Stepney had at least 47,000 inhabitants in the 1690s: J. Boulton, 'London widowhood revisited: the decline of female remarriage in the seventeenth and early eighteenth centuries', *Continuity and Change*, 5 (1990), p. 327. Edinburgh's population was between 40,000 and 47,000. Dublin's population was approximately 51,000 in 1695, though it had trebled in size by 1760: H. Dingwall, *Late Seventeenth Century Edinburgh* (Aldershot, 1994), chap. 1; P. Fagan, *Catholics in a Protestant Country: the Papist Constituency in Eighteenth Century Dublin* (Dublin, 1998), chap. 1.

13 *The Model of a Design to Reprint Stow's Survey of London* (1694).

14 H. Inalcik and D. Quataert eds, *An Eonomic History of the Ottoman Empire* (2 vols, Cambridge, 1994), II, p. 652; J. L. McClain, J. M. Merriman and U. Kaoru eds, *Edo and Paris: Urban Life and the State in the Early Modern Period* (Ithaca NY and London, 1994), esp. p. 13.

15 D. Maclean, 'London in 1689–90', *Transactions of the London and Middlesex Archaeological Society*, new series, 6 (1929–33). p. 333.

16 Quoted in C. B. Estabrook, *Urbane and Rustic England: Cultural Ties and Social Spheres in the Provinces 1660–1780* (Manchester, 1998), p. 1.

17 Maclean, 'London in 1689–90', pp. 325, 333.

18 D. Cressy, *Literacy and the Social Order* (Cambridge, 1980), p. 129 and chap. 6; R. Trumbach, *Sex and the Gender Revolution* I (Chicago, 1998), p. 258.

19 For example, A. Johns, *The Nature of the Book* (Chicago, 1998), chap. 2.

20 E. A. Wrigley, 'A simple model of London's importance in changing English society and economy 1650–1750', *P&P*, 37 (1967).

21 E. A. Wrigley, 'Urban growth and agricultural change: England and the Continent in the early modern period', *Journal of Interdisciplinary History*, 15 (1985); Boulton, *Neighbourhood*; J. P. Ward, *Metropolitan Communities: Trades, Guilds, Identity and Change in Early Modern London* (Stanford CA, 1997).

22 A. Bryson, *From Courtesy to Civility* (Oxford, 1998), pp. 131–40; A. Bray, *Homosexuality in Renaissance England* (second edition, 1988), chap. 4; M. Pelling, 'Appearance and reality: barber-surgeons, the body and disease', in Beier and Finlay, *London*.

23 For critiques of Porter's account see T. Hitchcock, 'Roy Porter: reluctant postmodernist', *Journal of Urban History*, 24 (1998), and D. Keene, *Reviews in History*, (1997), http://www.ihrinfo.ac.uk/ihr/reviews/porter1.html. For earlier accounts, S. E. Rasmussen, *London: the Unique City* (revised edition, 1937); R. J. Mitchell and M. D. R. Leys, *History of London Life* (1958).

24 Cf. K. Wrightson, 'The enclosure of English social history', in A. Wilson ed., *Rethinking Social History: English Society 1570–1920 and its Interpretation*, (Manchester, 1993), pp. 61–3.

25 For example, French *et al.*, *The Parish*.

26 S. Porter, *The Great Fire of London* (Stroud, 1996), chap. 3; E. McKellar, *The Birth of Modern London* (Manchester, 1999).

27 For example, J. Scott, 'Radicalism and Restoration: the shape of the Stuart experience', *HJ*, 31 (1988).

28 C. Nicholson, *Writing and the Rise of Finance* (Cambridge, 1994); L. D. Schwarz, 'London apprentices in the seventeenth century: some problems', *Local Population Studies*, 38 (1987); Earle, *Middle Class*, pp. 218–19.

29 Ward, *Metropolitan Communities*; M. Berlin, '"Broken all in pieces": artisans and the regulation of workmanship in early modern London', in G. Crossick ed., *The Artisan and the European Town 1500–1900* (Aldershot, 1997); Henderson, *Disorderly Women*, chap. 6; S. E. Brown, 'A just and profitable commerce: moral economy and the middle classes in eighteenth-century London', *Journal of British Studies*, 32 (1993); P. Claus, 'Languages of citizenship in the City of London 1848–1867', *LJ*, 24 (1999).

30 J. Barry, 'Provincial town culture 1640–1780: urbane or civic?', in J. Pittock and A. Wear eds, *Interpretation and Cultural History* (Basingstoke, 1991); R. Sweet, 'Freemen and independence in English boroughs *c*. 1770–1830', *P&P*, 161 (1998).

31 Cf. P. Griffiths, 'Family and community in late medieval and early modern towns', *Journal of Urban History*, 25 (1999). On consumer culture before the 'consumer revolution' of the eighteenth century, I. W. Archer, *The History of the Haberdashers' Company* (Chichester, 1991).

32 M. Nutkiewicz, 'A rapporteur of the English Civil War: the courtly politics of James Howell 1594?–1666', *Canadian Journal of History*, 25 (1990), pp. 32–5.

33 J. D. H. Thomas, 'James Howell: historiographer royal', *Brycheiniog*, 9 (1963), p. 86.

34 S. Wiseman, *Drama and Politics* (Cambridge, 1998), chap. 7; V. Pearl, 'Puritans and poor relief: the London workhouse 1649–60', in D. Pennington and K. Thomas, eds, *Puritans and Revolutionaries* (Oxford, 1978); P. Lake, 'Popular form, puritan content? Two puritan appropriations of the murder pamphlet from mid-seventeenth-century London', in A. Fletcher and P. Roberts eds, *Religion, Culture and Society in Early Modern Britain* (Cambridge, 1994), esp. pp. 326–30; M. Jenner, '"Another *Epocha*"? Hartlib, John Lanyon and the improvement of London in the 1650s', in M. Greengrass *et al.* eds, *Samuel Hartlib and Universal Communication* (Cambridge, 1994).

35 W. Dugdale, *History of St Paul's Cathedral* (1658). Howell spent several pages decrying the lamentable condition of the cathedral: *Londinopolis*, pp. 399–402.

36 J. Graunt, *Natural and Political Observations* (1662), reprinted in P. Laslett ed., *The Earliest Classics* (Folkestone, 1973); *The Petty Papers*, ed. Marquis of Lansdowne (2 vols in one, 1927), esp. I, pp. 26–40, 171–200; P. Buck, 'Seventeenth-century political arithmetic: civil strife and vital statistics', *Isis*, 68 (1977).

37 D. Defoe, *A Tour through the whole Island of Great Britain* (2 vols in one, 1974 Everyman edition), I, pp. 314–67 and *passim*; W. Maitland, *History of ... London* (1739).

38 P. Clark and P. Slack eds, *Crisis and Order in English Towns 1500–1700* (1972); P. Clark and P. Slack, *English Towns in Transition 1500–1700* (Oxford, 1976).

39 A. L. Beier, 'Social problems in Elizabethan London', *Journal of Interdisciplinary History*, 9 (1978); P. Clark, 'A crisis contained? The condition of English towns in the 1590s', in Clark ed., *The European Crisis of the 1590s* (1985). This image of late Elizabethan London developed the account of G. Unwin, *Industrial Organization in the Sixteenth and Seventeenth Centuries* (1904).

40 V. Pearl, 'Change and stability in seventeenth-century London', *LJ*, 5 (1979); Rappaport, *Worlds*; Archer, *Stability*.

41 For example, J. A. Walter, 'A "rising of the people"? The Oxfordshire Rising of 1596', *P&P*, 107 (1985); D. Levine and K. Wrightson, *The Making of an Industrial Society: Whickham 1560–1765* (Oxford, 1991).

42 E.g., R. Wells, *Wretched Faces: Famine in Wartime England 1793–1803* (Gloucester, 1988).

43 For example, R. M. Dunn, 'The London weavers' riot of 1675', *Guildhall Studies in London History*, 1 (1973); T. J. G. Harris, 'The bawdy house riots of 1668', *HJ*, 29 (1986); M. Goldie, 'The Hilton gang and the purge of London in the 1680s', in H. Nenner ed., *Politics and the Political Imagination in Later Stuart Britain* (Rochester NY, and Wood-bridge, 1997); N. Rogers, 'Popular protest in early Hanoverian London', *P&P*, 79 (1978); G. Rudé, *Paris and London in the Eighteenth Century* (1970).

44 P. Slack, *Poverty and Policy in Tudor and Stuart England* (1988), chap. 8; A. Wear, 'Caring for the sick poor in St Bartholomew's Exchange 1580–1676', in W. Bynum and R. Porter eds, *Living and Dying in London*, Medical History Suppl. 11 (1991). Jeremy Boulton's research is showing that parish relief in late seventeenth and early eighteenth-century London was not always as generous or as amicably distributed as some have suggested: see his 'Going on the parish: the parish pension and its meanings in the London suburbs, 1640–1724', in T. Hitchcock *et al.* eds, *Chronicling Poverty: The Voices and Strategies of the English Poor 1640–1840* (Basingstoke, 1997), and his contribution in Chapter 10 below.

45 P. Earle, *The Making of the English Middle Class* (1989); H. Horwitz, '"The mess of the middle class" revisited: the case of the "big bourgeoisie" of Augustan London', *Continuity and Change*, 2 (1987); M. Hunt, *The Middling Sort: Commerce, Gender and the Family in England 1680–1780* (Berkeley CA, Los Angeles and London, 1996).

46 Porter, *London*, chaps 6–7; J. Brewer, *Pleasures of the Imagination* (1997), chap. 1; P. Borsay, *The English Urban Renaissance* (Oxford, 1989). Cf., however, Borsay's revision of his arguments: *id.*, 'The London connection: cultural diffusion and the eighteenth-century provincial town', *LJ*, 19 (1994).

47 P. G. M. Dickson, *The Financial Revolution in England 1688–1756* (1967); Earle, *Making of the Middle Class*, chap. 5.

48 K. O'Brien, 'Imperial Georgic 1660–1789', in G. MacLean, D. Landry and J. P. Ward eds, *The Country and the City Revisited: England and the Politics of Culture 1550–1850* (Cambridge, 1999).

49 The language of crisis is important in the political historiography of the late seventeenth century, for example G. De Krey, 'The first Restoration crisis: conscience and coercion in London 1667–73', *Albion*, 25 (1993).

50 For a very different attempt to square this interpretative circle, P. D. Halliday, *Dismembering the Body Politic: Partisan Politics in England's Towns 1650–1730* (Cambridge, 1998), chap. 1.

51 For example, Clark, 'Crisis contained?', p. 56; Archer, *Pursuit*, p. 203.

52 For example, D. E. Underdown, 'The taming of the scold: the enforcement of patriarchal authority in early modern England', in A. Fletcher and J. Stevenson eds, *Order and Disorder in Early Modern England* (Cambridge, 1985).

53 Gowing, *Domestic*, chap. 1.

54 M. D. George, *London Life in the Eighteenth Century* (1925); Henderson, *Disorderly Women*; T. Hitchcock, '"Unlawfully begotten on her body": illegitimacy and the parish poor in St Luke's Chelsea', in Hitchcock, King and Sharpe, *Chronicling Poverty*; A. Wilson, 'Illegitimacy and its implications in mid-eighteenth-century London: the evidence of the Foundling Hospital', *Continuity and Change*, 4 (1989).

55 For example, D. T. Andrew, *Philanthropy and Police* (Princeton NJ, 1989); S. Lloyd, '"Pleasure's golden bait": prostitution, poverty and the Magdalen Hospital in eighteenth-century London', *HWJ*, 41 (1996); T. Hitchcock, 'Paupers and preachers: the SPCK and the parochial workhouse movement', in L. Davison, T. Hitchcock, T. Keirn and R. B. Shoemaker eds, *Stilling the Grumbling Hive: the Response to Social and Economic Problems in England 1689–1750* (Stroud, 1992).

56 For example, J. M. Beattie, 'London crime and the making of the "Bloody Code" 1689–1718', and R. B. Shoemaker, 'Reforming the city: the reformation of manners campaign in London 1690–1738', in Davison *et al.*, *Stilling the Grumbling Hive*.

57 A. Wilson, 'The politics of medical improvement in early Hanoverian London', in A. Cunningham and R. French eds, *The Medical Enlightenment of the Eighteenth Century* (Cambridge, 1990), pp. 5–10.

58 For a superb example of this approach, C. Hamlin, *Public Health and Social Justice in the Age of Chadwick* (Cambridge, 1998).

59 See the debate between A. Mayne and D. Englander, 'The nature of slums', *Urban History*, 22 (1995).

60 F. J. Fisher, 'The development of the London food market 1540–1640' (1935) and 'The development of London as a centre of conspicuous consumption in the sixteenth and seventeenth centuries' (1948), reprinted in his *London and the English Economy 1500–1700* (1990).

61 For example, J. W. Scott, *Gender and the Politics of History* (New York, 1988), chaps 5–6; E. Higgs, 'Women, occupations and work in the nineteenth-century censuses', *HWJ*, 23 (1987).

62 P. Earle, 'The female labour market in London in the late seventeenth and early eighteenth centuries', *EcHR*, 42 (1989); T. Meldrum, 'Domestic Service in London, 1660–1750: Gender, Life Cycle, Work and Household Relations', London School of Economics Ph.D. thesis (1996); J. M. Bennett, '"History that stands still": women's work in the European past', *Feminist Studies*, 14 (1988); A. Vickery, 'Golden age to separate spheres? A review of the categories and chronologies of English women's history', *HJ*, 36 (1993).

63 C. Muldrew, *The Economy of Obligation: The Culture of Credit and Social Relations in Early Modern England* (Basingstoke, 1998).

64 We do *not* claim that one point of view is inherently superior to another or that these criticisms necessarily invalidate the forms of knowledge produced by positivistic economic history. This book advances an alternative approach to urban history.

65 On Boswell as an exemplary eighteenth-century inhabitant of London, Brewer, *Pleasures of the Imagination*, pp. 30–4. For poor women migrants, P. King, 'Female offenders, work and life cycle change in late eighteenth-century London', *Continuity and Change*, 11 (1996).

66 For example, J. R. Farr, '"On the shop floor": guilds, artisans, and the European market economy', *Journal of Early Modern History*, 1 (1997); *id.*, 'Cultural analysis and early modern artisans', in Crossick, *Artisan and the European Town*; D. Sabean, *Power in the Blood: Popular Culture and Village Discourse in Early Modern Germany* (Cambridge, 1984).

67 Harris, *London Crowds*; M. Knights, 'London's "monster" petition of 1680', *HJ*, 36 (1993); K. Lindley, *Popular Politics*, pp. 29–30; *id.*, 'London and popular freedom in the 1640s' in R. C. Richardson and G. M. Riddle eds, *Freedom and the English Revolution* (Manchester, 1986).

68 D. Freist, *Governed by Opinion: Politics, Religion, and the Dynamics of Communication in Stuart London* (1997). Cf. P. McDowell, *The Women of Grub Street* (Oxford, 1998).

69 For example, S. Pincus, '"Coffee politicians does create": coffee houses and Restoration political culture', *Journal of Modern History*, 67 (1995).

70 On the 1450s, W. Scase, '"Strange and wonderful bills": bill-casting and political discourse in late medieval England', *New Medieval Literatures*, 2 (1998).

71 K. Wrightson, 'The politics of the parish in early modern England', in P. Griffiths, A. Fox and S. Hindle eds, *The Experience of Authority in Early Modern England* (Basingstoke, 1996).

72 For example, J. F. Merritt, 'Religion, Government, and Society in Early Modern Westminster *c.* 1525–1625', University of London Ph.D. thesis (1992), chap. 2; K. Lindley, 'Whitechapel Independents and the English Revolution', *HJ*, 41 (1998); P. Seaward, 'Gilbert Sheldon, London vestries, and the defence of the Church', in T. Harris, P. Seaward and M. Goldie eds, *The Politics of Religion in Restoration England* (Oxford, 1990); M. Goldie and J. Spurr, 'Politics and the Restoration: Edward Fowler and the struggle for St Giles Cripplegate', *English Historical Review*, 109 (1994); S. M. MacFarlane, 'Social policy and the poor in the later seventeenth century', in Beier and Finlay, *London*.

73 G. Gibbs, 'New duties for the parish community in Tudor London' in French *et al.*, *The Parish*. For the application of a similar methodology on a national scale, B. Kümin, *The Shaping of a Community: The Rise and Reformation of the English Parish c. 1400–1560* (Aldershot, 1996).

74 *Londinopolis*, p. 32.

75 For the losses of the early seventeenth-century London wood turner Nehemiah Wallington from theft, P. S. Seaver, *Wallington's World: A Puritan Artisan in Seventeenth Century London* (1985), p. 120.

76 J. Brewer, *Sinews of Power* (1989), esp. chap. 4; T. Hitchcock, 'Sociability and misogyny in the life of John Cannon', in T. Hitchcock and M. Cohen eds, *English Masculinities 1660–1800* (1999).

77 Shoemaker, 'Reforming the city', pp. 104–6. Cf., however, P. Griffiths, 'Meanings of nightwalking in early modern England', *Seventeenth Century*, 13 (1998).

78 Theft too featured in this economy of makeshifts – and eighteenth-century London women's economic vulnerability meant that they were more likely to be prosecuted for

theft than women in rural society: J. M. Beattie, 'The criminality of women in eighteenth-century England', *Journal of Social History*, 8 (1975).

79 A. L. Erickson, *Women and Property in Early Modern England* (1993); Gowing, *Domestic*, chaps 1–2; Shoemaker, *Prosecution*, pp. 207–16.

80 N. G. Brett-James, *The Growth of Stuart London* (1935), p. 25; N. Green, *The Spectacle of Nature* (Manchester, 1990), pp. 75–6.

81 Stressed in M. S. R. Jenner, 'Early Modern English Conceptions of "Cleanliness" and "Dirt" as Reflected in the Environmental Regulation of London *c.* 1530–*c.* 1700', Oxford University D.Phil. thesis (1991), chap. 3.

82 R. O. Bucholz, *The Augustan Court* (Stanford CA, 1993).

83 On the different work cultures of these trades see Harald Decleulaer, 'Guildsmen, entrepreneurs and market segments: the case of the garment trades in Antwerp and Ghent (sixteenth to eighteenth century)', *International Review of Social History*, 43 (1998).

84 C. Wall, *The Literary and Cultural Spaces of Restoration London* (Cambridge, 1999); M. Ogborn, *Spaces of Modernity: London Geographies 1680–1780* (1998).

85 These developments thus return to some of the questions explored by Simmel, by the Chicago school of urban sociology and in writings on urban space and the street by members of the Frankfurt school such as Walter Benjamin.

86 See, for example, D. Cosgrove and S. Daniels eds, *The Iconography of Landscape* (Cambridge, 1988).

87 Cf. T. Meldrum, 'Domestic service, privacy and the eighteenth-century metropolitan household', *Urban History*, 29 (1999).

Part I

Polis and police

Chapter 2

Popular politics in the sixteenth and early seventeenth centuries

Ian W. Archer

In recent years political historians of early seventeenth-century England have remarkably transformed our understanding of the political sophistication of those below the elite. The political education of the middling groups took place through their experience of local office and the administration of the law, and the introduction of religious division into their communities broadened political horizons as men and women became aware of wider struggles of which they were a part. The commons made their views known in the increasing number of contested elections and in cruder forms of political expression like libels.[1] But we still need to know more about the local dynamics of this popular politicization, the evidence for which is often drawn from widely scattered communities at different points in time, and we need to know more about its sixteenth-century antecedents. We know rather more about the process of transmission of political ideas from London to the provinces than we do about the circulation of news within the capital. Although excellent work is appearing on the popular politics of the Civil War period, more needs to be done in relating political action to its cultural roots. Keith Lindley has reconstructed patterns of alignment within Civil War London, and produced a brilliant narrative of political action, but he has less to tell us about why Londoners took up the positions they did.[2] This is perhaps because of the limitations of some of the social historical writing on the years before the Civil War, which has been concerned with a debate over the reasons for London's stability and has concentrated on social and governmental structures at the expense of popular mentalities. Perhaps because they have been too accepting of an 'urban' historical agenda prioritizing themes such as growth, economy, social structure and institutional sophistication, the historians of pre-Civil War London have been slow to draw on the work of those historians who have been reassessing the role of ideology in politics.[3]

This chapter will look both at the circulation of news within the capital and at several of the various strands of popular political discourse in the sixteenth and early seventeenth centuries. It has been influenced by the notion that culture is best understood as a process, that people are constantly drawing upon a variety of different cultural forms, adapting them in the process, to meet the needs of specific situations.[4] The discussion will focus upon the political vocabularies and forms of political expression associated with citizenship and notions of civic honour, aristocratic populism, obedience and religion. These discourses were variable and often contested, subject to varying appropriations to meet specific political needs. Attempts to identify a stable 'popular political culture' are therefore flawed. But the task of exploring the dynamics of the various forms of appropriation is fraught with peril. In the years before the Civil War it is very rare for the historian to have available the views of a sufficient range of actors at any particular political 'moment' to make possible the kind of exercise in 'thick description' which has proved so profitable elsewhere, and therefore one runs the risk of making explanatory connections as arbitrary (and possibly more so) as those of any contemporary prejudiced elite commentator. Likewise, because of the indirectness and fragmentary nature of the sources for popular opinions, we can rarely be sure about which component of the city population is represented and therefore whether any individual political action is strictly comparable with any other political action. When the populace is loyalist at one moment and dissident at another, are we dealing with the same people, or with different sections of the community? I shall try to show how the clash between Londoners and the governments of James I and Charles I in the 1620s drew on different cultural traditions, but I do not want to suggest that the synthesis then realised was common to all Londoners or anything more than a temporary conjunction brought about by a particular set of circumstances. Different political contexts would involve different forms of appropriation from different social groups.

In acknowledging the variety of possible responses, I should emphasize some of the limits to the parameters of the present discussion. First, I have assumed what for many will seem a narrow definition of politics, looking at the understandings of national political issues by Londoners rather than at the micro-political struggles for control over resources that were waged in the capital's parishes, wards, guilds and families. This reflects the fact that I have discussed elsewhere London's local politics perhaps at the expense of a proper discussion of the impact of ideological conflict.[5] Second, the group that will most clearly come into focus in this chapter are the citizens, that is, the three-quarters or so of the city's adult male population who enjoyed the political and economic benefits of the freedom. This is not to say that the attitudes and processes to be described were necessarily exclusive to citizens, simply that citizenship provided an identity which accelerated politicization, both because of the opportunities it provided for institutional expression and because of the languages of 'freedom' it entailed. Third, this is a piece primarily about male politics. Women were not, of course, entirely imprisoned within the terms of the patriarchal political discourse which sought to confine them to the household sphere, and they might occasionally make forthright political interventions, but it is significant that much of the discourse to be discussed in this chapter was gendered in such a way as to preclude feminine involvement. Thus women were excluded form the political rights associated with citizenship (although widows might keep apprentices, they did not exercise the political privileges of citizenship), and the language of citizen honour was strongly associated with the assertion of masculine identity. Significantly, then, it was in the religious sphere that women intervened in the political spaces normally occupied by men.[6]

Londoners were often presented as self-interested and parochial. Coming to the capital from Cambridge in the 1560s, Thomas Whythorne was struck by the fact that 'there was no other talk ... but of gain and riches'. Their chroniclers were satirized as writing of 'nothing but Mayors and Sheriefs' and the typical alderman as self-importantly discoursing of 'the annals of his mayoralty and what good government there was in the dayes of his gold chain'.[7] But these remarks may have more to do with the assertion of cultural superiority on the part of the gentry than they do with the reality of the situation. The newsmongers in St Paul's Walk and at the Royal Exchange were dependent on merchants for news of developments overseas at a time when diplomatic representation was skeletal. Moreover, the ubiquity of lawyers in City government ensured that political discourse at the Guildhall did not remain cast within a materialistic mould. In arguing against Sir Edward Darcy's leather-sealing patent in 1593 the leather sellers grasped its constitutional implications, having hired the legal advice of Nicholas Fuller, the scourge of patentees and the Court of High Commission alike. Londoners were among the most forward in insisting on the call of Parliament to meet the Crown's financial needs in 1626–27 and they were in the forefront of the principled objection to ship money in 1635. This evidence rather calls into question the patronizing assumptions of the gentry commentators about the political sophistication of the citizenry.[8]

The degree to which one accepts the notion of the limited political horizons of Londoners depends on how far we see the worlds of city and court as separate entities. The court was not physically segregated from the city. Whitehall could not accommodate all the Crown's servants, who therefore lived in town houses, increasingly located in the West End but at the beginning of our period still often within the walls. Courtiers and government officials were regular visitors to civic functions like the feasts of the lord mayor and the livery companies. The social worlds of many Londoners straddled the division between city and court. Thomas Norton, city remembrancer and 'parliament man', moved between the Inns of Court, the Guildhall and the crafts whose parliamentary business he promoted, as well as enjoying relationships with a good cross-section of Elizabeth's Privy Council. Humphrey Mildmay, a regular visitor to the capital in the 1630s, socialized with members of the civic elite as well as with his fellow gentlemen; the theatre entrepreneur turned benefactor Edward Alleyn was apparently at ease with the Earl of Arundel as well as with his fellow Southwark vestrymen; John Taylor, the water poet, was a 'cultural amphibian', a waterman by trade but enjoying the patronage of the great. The relationships forged through the patronage of artisans and tradesmen by courtiers and officials could be mobilized with considerable dexterity when it came to securing some benefit for the trade.[9] The worlds of city and court interpenetrated in ways which made it difficult for the Crown to contain political speculation. 'What news at court?' a member of the King's guard was asked as he entered a shop in Bow Lane in 1546, and his answer led to an altercation about the fate of the radical preacher, Dr Crome. Drinking establishments were places where information was exchanged and where political gossip was passed around. Typical of the government's anxieties was the instruction from the aldermen in the tense months after Wyatt's rising that innholders should 'give a good ear to all such talk as their guests ... shall have'.[10]

Speculation precisely by whom? It is extraordinarily difficult to determine levels of political awareness among non-elite groups. Were libels set up in Paul's churchyard and in the Royal Exchange because they were targeted at the members of the elite who frequented those places, or was the intended audience wider? When contemporaries spoke of such-and-such a view being prevalent among the 'commonalty' or 'about the town', whom did they mean? What was the social composition of the 'multitude of people at the doore' of the House of Commons in 1601 'who say they were commonwealthe's men' seeking redress against monopolists?[11] It seems wrong in view of the extraordinary complexity of London society to jump to conclusions about the socially exclusive nature of politicization based on some of the conventional lines of social division. The statute of 1543 by which 'no women, nor artificers, prentices, journeymen, servingmen of the degree of yeoman or under, husbandmen nor labourers' was allowed to read the Bible articulates contemporary assumptions about degree, but was at odds with the social realities of a much broader audience for print.[12] Although there can be no doubt that the division between rich and poor was acutely felt in the capital, nevertheless the persistence of residential intermingling meant that social interaction between richer and poorer neighbours was not inconceivable, as the bequests by the elite to humbler neighbours by name in their wills testify. The speed of both upward and downward social mobility in the capital also meant that wealthier citizens usually had poorer kin.[13] The liverymen, the wealthier members of the guilds to whom the right to participate in elections for the lord mayor, sheriffs and members of Parliament was confined, were not as socially exclusive as first appearances may suggest. There were over fifty guilds enjoying liveried status by the later sixteenth century; they ranged from relatively humble crafts like that of the coopers to associations of wholesalers and luxury retailers like the mercers, and the number of liverymen grew from about 2,000 in 1500 to 4,000 in 1640.[14] Apprentices were not a culturally homogeneous group: some 10 per cent in the mid-sixteenth century were recruited from gentle backgrounds and some, the Leveller leaders among them, had the benefit of a grammar school education, potentially enabling them to participate in cultural forms we normally think of as specific to the elite.[15] Women in the metropolis enjoyed a degree of independence which impressed foreign visitors, and they engaged in forms of collective action which put paid to the notion that they were confined to the domestic sphere.[16]

The best evidence for the wider circulation of ideas across the conventional social boundaries comes from the early decades of the Reformation. A wealthy goldsmith like John Barret harboured poorer Lollards in the 1520s and evangelized his apprentices. Heretical circles like that centring on Anne Askewe in the mid-1540s straddled city and court, and she received money from London apprentices while in the Tower. There is a succession of humble lay divines like the illiterate Whitechapel bricklayer John Harrydaunce, who preached to crowds a thousand strong in 1536–38, or the cordwainer who spouted scripture in St Paul's in July 1549, or William White, the baker prominent in the Plumbers' Hall gathering of semi-separatists uncovered by the authorities in 1566. The roll call of the London victims of the Act of Six Articles in 1540 or of the Protestant martyrs in Mary's reign shows that heretical notions spread across the social spectrum. That women could be stirred to independent action by the force of religion is shown by the crowds of women who besieged Grindal in his palace in 1566 demanding that he withdraw proceedings against the godly city ministers.[17]

It is one thing to show the circulation of dissident ideas and the passage of information between city and court, quite another to determine the cultural matrix it entered. What were the underlying assumptions of citizen politics? The most basic element of the political consciousness of Londoners was xenophobia, foreign visitors commenting on a hatred of 'all sorts of strangers' which was clearly greater than that they encountered on their travels elsewhere. Although hostility to aliens was often reinforced by ideological and economic conflicts, there does not seem to have been very much discrimination between different groups of foreigners. The slightest provocation to the inhabitants could lead to major disturbances, and brawls between embassy servants and locals tended to escalate into full-scale confrontations and stoning of embassies. Evil May Day when in 1517 Londoners had rioted against aliens lived on in the consciousness of people and magistrates: in 1586 Recorder Fleetwood uncovered a plot 'in all things like unto Evil May Day as could be devised'; there was an attempt to stage the disturbance in the play *Sir Thomas More* in the tense year of 1593; in 1625 the bitterness of the trade disputes which flared up when news of the Amboina massacre reached the city terrified the Dutch 'so far forth as to fear some ill may day'.[18]

Xenophobia was given added edge in early modern London because of the economic threat represented by foreign immigrants, who numbered between 4,000 and 5,000 throughout the period. In their hostility to aliens many Londoners drew on another set of loyalties, namely the civic values which their freedom of the City entailed. The freedom (enjoyed by up to three-quarters of the City's inhabitants from 1550) brought valuable economic and political privileges. There were persistent anxieties throughout the sixteenth century about the erosion of the benefit of the freedom by grants of freedom by redemption, by the chipping away of the City's control over key offices of economic regulation through the pressure of courtiers, and by the evasion of regulations designed to limit the competition represented by non-free labour in the City and its environs. Rulers were judged according to their willingness to promote the interests of citizens. Failure to maintain the City's privileges would discredit them in the eyes of those over whom they ruled. In 1528 a panel of common councillors castigated the aldermen for their surrender to Wolsey over the control of the office of the common beam, which 'yf it be well pondered ys noo small rebuke and sklaunder to the governers of this Citie and the Citezyns of the same'. Several companies were divided by accusations that the rulers showed undue favour to the strangers, but by and large the maintenance of the freedom was one of those issues which had considerable potential to unite the inhabitants of the capital. The periods of greatest anti-alien agitation, like the 1510s and 1520s, 1567–72 and 1586–93, saw the combination of real or threatened physical violence against aliens with lawsuits and parliamentary campaigns to tighten the restrictions on aliens, and the citizens could count on the backing of some of their more outspoken clergy.[19]

The politics of the freedom were thus often defensive, focused on 'bread and butter' issues, and articulated by corporate bodies which owed their privileges to chartered grants from the Crown. But as David Harris Sacks has suggested the language of freedom at the heart of civic consciousness could itself be appropriated to more radical ends. In struggling against monopolistic grants acquired by courtiers or members of the civic elite, artisans and shopkeepers might suggest that their opponents were bringing them into bondage. The artisans who contested Darcy's leather-sealing grant in 1593 argued not only that they risked perjury because his patent was contrary to the charters of the city they had sworn to uphold but also 'what bondage he would procure her maiesties subiectes unto if forced to bring leather to the place appointed'. It was a radicalizing rhetoric the potential of which was more fully realised by the Levellers. When Lilburne attacked the 'Prerogative Patentee Monopolizing Companies' in 1646 he did so in terms of their offence to the City freedom: 'their Brotherhoods are so many conspiracies to destroy and overthrow the laws and liberties of England and to ingross, enhance, and destroy the trades and franchises of most of the freemen of London'.[20]

The corollary of pride in the city was a profound ambivalence in the city's attitudes towards the court and the values of gentlemen. London's rulers were shrewd enough to realise (and they were constantly reminded of the fact in the rituals of the Lord Mayor's Day) that their fortunes depended on maintaining good relations with the Crown. There were few things more terrifying than the prospect of the withdrawal of royal favour such as Mary's threat to move Parliament to Oxford in 1554 as a mark of her lack of trust of the Londoners in the light of their behaviour during Wyatt's rising. But there were many areas where value systems clashed. Attempts to enforce a proper moral order within the city were compromised by the court's traffic in reprieves of convicted criminals, by the hostility of courtiers to the methods of Bridewell, and by their predatory attentions on citizens' wives 'put to the squeak' when they met at city feasts. Many Londoners felt that the aliens were able to flourish because of their 'gret favour amonges the states and gentilles of this realme'. Citizens were suspected of overcharging during the large gatherings of gentlemen in parliaments; they were seen as militarily ineffective; their base origins meant that they could not properly serve the monarch. London's magistrates found the brawls of rival groups of aristocratic serving men and the outrageous activities of gentry *roués* as corrosive of public order as the disturbances of apprentices, and possibly they were more frequent. Their views are echoed in the more popular voice of John Taylor, the water poet, who had no time for the swaggering loudmouths he had encountered on the river.[21]

The clearest evidence of the friction between court and city comes from the apprentices, whose frequent clashes with the serving men of gentlemen demonstrate the status uncertainties of downwardly mobile younger sons. It is extraordinary how quickly large crowds were mobilized to defend the honour of an apprentice insulted by a serving man, and it is possible that the generalized terms of the conflicts (apprentices were insulted as 'scum' or 'rogues') served to generate apprentice solidarity around a grievance which initially had more resonance for those from a gentle background.[22] That these were basically conflicts about the claim of Londoners to honour is confirmed by an examination of the cultural tastes of the citizens. They were brilliantly satirized in the play *The Knight of the Burning Pestle*, where the staging of an advertised play, *The London Merchant*, is interrupted by a citizen grocer objecting to plays with 'new subjects purposely to abuse your betters' and calling instead for something 'in honour of the commons of the city'. He proposes tales such as Dick Whittington, Heywood's *2 If You Know Not Me* or his *Four Prentices of London*. What these plays offered was the praise of noble citizens who had risen from humble origins, and escapist romances incorporating tales of apprentice gallantry. The appeal of the themes is confirmed by the enduring popularity of works like *Amadis de Gaul*, the Palmerin cycle, Richard Johnson's *Nine Worthies of London* and *Seven Champions of Christendom*. The message was that it was possible for men of humble birth to achieve true nobility and that there was nothing ignoble about apprentice status.[23] A desire to participate in the martial culture was also felt by members of the civic elite. During the 1580s archery competitions were sponsored by the 300-strong Arthurian Society of Archers led by the customs official, Thomas Smythe, and promoted by Richard Mulcaster, headmaster of the Merchant Taylors' School. From 1585 'certain gallant, active and forward citizens' began voluntary training in the Artillery Garden, imitating the militia companies of Antwerp, and they became the nucleus of the Honourable Artillery Company, refounded in 1610, soon including many of the godly elite among its 500 members. Stow's continuator describes in the early decades of the seventeenth century the enthusiasm for voluntary training undergone by city adolescents practising 'all the points of war which they had seen their elders teach, having got themselves pikes and pieces fit for their handling'. These values were articulated in some of the apprentice petitions of 1641–42, *The Valiant Resolution* addressing the apprentices as 'fruitful in noble and heroic spirits'.[24]

However, it is important not to push the division between city and court too far. First, because another feature of citizen values is respect for, or perhaps idolization of, key aristocratic figures. Londoners showed peculiar loyalty to some of the key aristocratic 'losers' of the sixteenth century. The execution of Edward Stafford, third Duke of Buckingham, 'grieved the city universally' in 1521, and his grave at Austin Friars became a site of pilgrimage, with mourners claiming that he was 'a saint and holy man' and that 'he died guiltless'. Mistaken reports of the Duke of Somerset's acquittal at his trial for treason in December 1551 caused the enormous crowds gathered outside Westminster Hall to give out 'a great cry'. After his execution Londoners dipped their handkerchiefs in his blood, and they brought them out again to taunt his rival the Duke of Northumberland upon his humiliating return to the capital in August 1553. In 1601 apprentices plotted to rescue Robert Devereux, second Earl of Essex, from the Tower; his hangman was beaten up; Hayward, the parson of St Mary Woolchurch, who had preached in denunciation of the rising, found his sermons boycotted by the earl's admirers, and there was an extraordinary proliferation of libels and ballads which the government could scarcely control.[25] One could see this phenomenon as simply a form of displaced criticism of the prevailing regime. To express sympathy for Buckingham was a means of undermining Wolsey, whose rule was increasingly unpopular in the capital; Somerset was the beneficiary of the popular loathing of Northumberland; and the Earl of Essex's following in the city was a function of the growing unpopularity of the *regnum cecilianum* which was reflected in the libels littering the city streets. This was undoubtedly a contributory factor, but probably not the whole story. The reasons for Buckingham's popularity in the capital are obscure (he was hated on the Welsh marches), but is intriguing that John Lincoln, a key mobilizing force behind the anti-alien disorders of Evil May Day in 1517, was a member of his household. Somerset was widely criticized for his populism, pushing the politics of paternalist publicity to unacceptable lengths, and attempting to mobilize his popular support in October 1549 against a *coup* by his fellow councillors. Essex, although not a champion of the poor, was undoubtedly a populist, criticized for 'committing himself in his recreations and shooting matches to the public view of so many thousand citizens which usually flocked to see him', his military prowess cried up in inflammatory sermons by his chaplains and in the engravings which so angered the Queen that they were banned by proclamation. In the eyes of the citizenry aristocratic virtue consisted in an amalgam of sympathy for the poor, militarism and distance from those holding the reins of government, and through civic chivalry they were able to participate vicariously in the prevailing honour culture.[26]

Another complicating factor in the relations between city and court was the fact of the basically loyalist framework of citizen values. It is easy enough to document the ways in which the City elite was incorporated in the rituals of dynastic power. The lord mayor and aldermen joined others of the King's leading subjects at the rites of royal passage: christenings, coronations, weddings and funerals. Their presence was required to provide endorsement for key acts of royal power, in particular in the theatre of punishment with which subjects were advised of the penalties of dissidence. But the populace was also implicated to a far greater extent than has perhaps been realised in these events. David Cressy has documented for us the development of a rich cycle of loyalist celebration in the sermons, bonfires and bells commemorating the monarch's accession and the providential deliverances from the armada and gunpowder treason. These forms of celebration had a long pedigree: key events like the capture of the King of France at the battle of Pavia in 1525, victory in Scotland in 1544, peace with France and Scotland in 1550 were likewise the occasion for bonfires, bells and street parties. Royal entries to the capital provided set pieces for loyalist demonstrations, with the liveried crafts lining gravelled city streets richly hung with tapestries, the royal progress being punctuated by elaborate pageants of civic toadying. But they were supplemented by the crowds which turned out more spontaneously to witness the monarch's movements in the vicinity of the capital: 'the feldes full of pepull, gret nombur'. The rituals of the court were far more popular than has been appreciated: special scaffolds were erected for the citizens at court tournaments (the number of spectators may have been as high as 12,000), and many of the so-called 'court' sermons (including key set pieces like Dr Scory's denunciation of papal abuses in February 1559) took place in the open-air public preaching place in Whitehall with a capacity of 5,000, and their contents seem to have been widely publicized. Executions were also often highly public events, albeit, as we shall see, ones fraught with peril for the authorities. Ten thousand supposedly gathered for the execution of the Duke of Northumberland on 21 August 1553; when the Babington conspirators were executed on 20 September 1586, we are told, there was 'no lane, street, alley, or house in the suburbs of London or in the hamlets bordering the city out of which there issued not some of each sex and age', and many women and children who did not see the executions nevertheless filled the fields to watch the burning of the victims' entrails. It is worth stressing that these crowds were far larger than any which are reported as having assembled in riots before the Civil War.[27]

We have isolated a number of strands in the popular political conscious-ness of Londoners, but it is more difficult to determine whether they reflect the experiences of different sections of the populace, or whether they amount to a coherent political culture. One might argue that civic chivalry was the property of a particularly assertive sub-group of gentle-born apprentices, but I have tried to suggest that its resonance for Londoners was rather wider. Or, one might question the designation of something called 'popular culture' as loyalist because bonfires and bells were often orchestrated from above, or because Londoners who greeted Mary Tudor so rapturously in July 1553 apparently turned against her once the plans for the marriage to Philip of Spain had emerged. But there was an element of spontaneity in some of the loyalist demonstrations (not least in the street parties of July 1553), and loyalty to the Crown was perfectly compatible with criticism of those who exercised power on the Crown's behalf, just as rapturous applause for militaristic aristocratic heroes like Essex could be combined with contempt for aristocratic hooligans and court fops. What does emerge clearly is that, however loyalist the crowds were, however far they accepted the principles of an unequal social order, they cannot be described as deferential, because they had clear notions of their own about the terms on which power should be exercised. In 1593 the leather sellers who attacked Darcy's patent pointedly reminded the Lord Treasurer of the words of the Queen's father, Henry VIII, quoted by the chronicler Edward Hall, 'that his mynde was never to aske anythinge of his comens that might sownde to his dishonor or to the breach of his Lawes'. The Crown's rhetoric could be appropriated to critical and subversive ends.[28]

That critical and subversive spirit emerges in the contested nature of justice in the capital. Legal values, it has been argued, permeated popular culture.

Many Londoners would have been involved in law enforcement, whether serving as constables, participating in the watch or serving as jurors. The law was the medium through which many disputes were followed, companies spending large amounts in the harassment of non-free labour in the law courts. Experience of the law was an element in the popular evaluation of reputation, as people sought to establish their reputation through service in local office like the constableship, while insulting those who had been subject to legal sanctions: terms like 'carted whore' or 'Bridewell bird' were the common currency of abuse. Even when attacking authority the lower orders would appeal to legal sanctions. As a joiner complained in 1513, it would be better for the commons to elect 'a poer man to be maier of this citie then for to have any riche ether maier or shiref and if the seid poer man do not wele in his office then set a pair of galous at his gate & hange hym' (revealing also perhaps in its assumption that it would be easier to hang a poor man than a rich man). Likewise, in 1595 it was rumoured that apprentices had set up a pair of gallows at the gate of the unpopular lord mayor, Sir John Spencer.[29] But these examples also make it clear that some of the commons had very different notions from their rulers about the practice of justice. Apprentice solidarity revealed itself in the rescue of those whom the authorities sought to discipline for disorders protesting at grievances they felt to be legitimate, or in the sanctions they applied to those who had punished their fellows. We have already seen from the reactions to the executions of Buckingham, Somerset and Essex how the crowd could not be relied upon to perform its scripted role. There were similar problems over the government's efforts to discipline religious dissidents, whether out of ideological sympathy for the victims or a sense that the punishments had been inappropriately applied. Popular sympathy for the Protestant Robert Barnes in 1540 was such that, according to one observer there might have been a tumult if a suitable leader had emerged; a crowd 1,000 strong feted martyrs brought up to the capital from Colchester in 1555; the execution of a Brownist in 1593 had to be postponed because of the 'great multitude of puritanes' then present; in 1595 'the cry of the people' would not allow the body of the Catholic martyr Robert Southwell to be cut down so that he could be disembowelled while still alive as the penalties demanded, 'so great an impression his death did make with them' and so unpopular was the priest-killer Middlesex JP Richard Topcliffe, who officiated; in 1637 Burton, Bastwick and Prynne, playing the crowd to brilliant effect, found their way to the pillory strewn with flowers and herbs, and handkerchiefs were dipped in their blood.[30]

These latter examples demonstrate the corrosive force of religious argument on the loyalty of the populace. There is no doubting the fact that, whatever position we take over the question whether the Reformation was a popular movement, forces were unleashed which could not fully be mastered.

Religious polemicists in this increasingly religiously divided society conducted their arguments in terms designed to appeal to a wide audience. The early Reformation interludes denounced the papacy using tactics drawn from popular culture: associating their enemies with beasts and devils, and making full use of inversionary, scatalogical and pornographic devices.[31] Although one may question the degree to which the populace fully internalized Protestant theology, the reformers succeeded in creating a people who identified themselves as Protestant by the force of their anti-popery. But the anti-Catholic militancy this entailed often took forms which embarrassed the authorities. On the night of 3–4 January 1569, as news broke of the arrest of English shipping by the authorities in the Netherlands, anti-popery fused with virulent xenophobia. The lord mayor reported 'gret sturryng this night in the streates as well of merchant strangers as inglishe'. When royal officials entered the house of the Spanish merchant Antonio Guaras to seize his goods the images they removed were carried through the streets in a carnivalesque procession and burned in Cheapside, bystanders threatening that 'all foreigners and those that owned images should be burned'.[32] Likewise, the vicissitudes of Cheapside Cross, an idol in the midst of the City in the eyes of the godly, demonstrate the subversive side of godly activism. In 1581 the images on the lower register of the cross were defaced by 'certain young men' who were never identified, and the City fathers dragged their feet over the Queen's demands for the repair of the cross in subsequent years. In 1626 the cross was repaired in the preparations for Charles I's ceremonial entry, but as soon as the work was complete the cross was smeared with dirt, apparently by apprentices stirred up 'by some calvinistical sot'.[33]

The power of the pulpit was such that the government sought to control the content of sermons. At Paul's Cross, 'the very ark and watch tower of this realm', or at the Spital sermons in Easter week, presided over by the lord mayor and aldermen and often with councillors in attendance, enormous crowds might assemble, the 'holl cete boythe old and yonge boyth men and wemen'. Thomas Cromwell struggled to wrest control over the Paul's Cross preachers from the conservative Bishop Stokesley in the 1530s; all preaching was suspended in late 1548 as the pulpits rang with the clash of competing religious opinions; Archbishop Cranmer himself ascended the pulpit on two successive occasions during the rebellious summer months of 1549 to push the official line that the disturbances had been provoked by popish priests; Bishop Aylmer assembled his clergy to give them instructions to avoid treating of the Anjou marriage in derogatory terms in 1579; the early years of the war with Spain from 1585 saw the pulpits sounding a militant anti-Catholic note; in 1593 preachers were warned off dealing with Henri of Navarre's conversion to Catholicism (he was a key ally at the time); Robert Cecil checked the sermon preached by Hayward, a replacement for a less reliable candidate, at Paul's Cross in the aftermath of the Essex revolt; James I instructed his preachers to speak out against the insolence of women in 1620.[34]

But, for all the efforts to 'tune the pulpits', they never succeeded in establishing a hegemonic discourse. In so far as the Church provided legitimation for the regime and for the prevailing distribution of power, it did so conditionally, reminding every layer of society from the top downwards of its responsibilities. This might involve very powerful social critiques like those mounted by the commonwealthmen of the 1540s and 1550s, but so long as they remained generalized they were tolerated. The problem was that they did not remain generalized, and that preachers all too often fell to 'particularizing', naming names, turning their fire on individuals, or citing specific cases, or drawing attention to grievances that were all too raw, sometimes reading out bills or petitions which they had been handed by members of their congregations. Dr Bele's Spital sermon in 1517 stirred up the apprentices on the eve of Evil May Day. The lord mayor was denounced at Paul's Cross for an act of injustice by George Closse in 1586. Richard Stock denounced the City authorities for unfair taxation of the poor in 1601. John Everard, lecturer at St Martin in the Fields, censured the aldermen for their management of the Court of Orphans in 1618. Another preacher found himself in serious trouble for his attack on Lord Chancellor Bacon and his 'catamites' in 1619.[35]

The circumstances of religious conflict in which each side diabolized its opponents rendered the authorities more vulnerable to criticism from one side or the other. In 1535 the rector of St Leonard Eastcheap, Leonard Baschurch, wrote a tract, *Rex tamquam tyrannus opprimit populum*. In 1541, once the direction of royal policy had turned, the godly merchant taylor Richard Hilles, admittedly from the security of exile in Frankfurt, was denouncing Henry VIII as a tyrant. In 1538 a slanderous bill was presented to the King excoriating the aldermen as 'high heretykkes otherwise high Ranke traytors'. From the Protestant camp the mercer polemicist Henry Brinklowe lambasted the aldermen in 1543 for 'being fully bent with the false prophets ... the bishops ... to persecute and put to death every godly person'.[36] Loyalty to the Crown became entwined with the fulfilment of specific religious agendas. In dealing with the problem of a female ruler, for example, the preachers provided a justification in providentialist terms. In so far as Elizabeth was constructed as the divinely chosen deliverer of her people from popish thraldom, so her duty to promote the Gospel and wage war on the Antichrist was stressed. This matrix of loyalist argument was paradoxically corrosive of the sinews of obedience because it placed so many of the Queen's subjects at odds with her own policies. It was a problem which manifested itself in London in the autumn of 1579 as preachers denounced the Queen's proposed marriage with a French Catholic prince, the Duke of Anjou; there were 'murmurings and mislikings among the busier sort'; libels were fixed on the lord mayor's door; and the government's vicious clamp-down on John Stubbs's tract against the marriage merely fanned the flames of opposition. This was one occasion when the force of public opinion turned the direction of royal policy, for Elizabeth claimed that the public opposition was the reason for the suspension of negotiations in the midwinter of 1579-80.[37]

Royal marriages were often the occasion of clashes between religious loyalties and the claims of political obedience. The popular reaction in the capital to the projected marriage between Prince Charles and the Infanta provide an excellent example of the ways in which the various strands of popular political culture we have been looking at could interact. The marriage combined fears about the growth of popery with raw xenophobia, and it was promoted by a court which was popularly perceived as corrupt. When news of the marriage proposal for Prince Charles became public in 1617 a series of outspoken attacks on it were made from the city pulpits, but James failed to make any effort to explain his policy publicly. When the King himself attended a Paul's Cross sermon in March 1620 it was expected that a statement would be made, but instead the occasion was designed to announce a new pro-gramme of repair of St Paul's Cathedral. By December 1620 the King found it necessary to ban all discussion of the marriage by the preachers, but he could not stem the tide of criticism. In February 1621 John Everard, probably the most troublesome preacher of the capital, was imprisoned in the Gatehouse for an intemperate attack on the cruelty and tyranny of the Spanish at a Paul's Cross sermon, but he offended again in August 1622 'for sayeng somewhat he should not have don'. The preachers encouraged speculation about James's policy, and repeated proclamations were issued against 'lavish and licentious speeches in matters of state' in December 1620 and again in July 1621.[38] When Charles and Buckingham embarked on their madcap expedition to Madrid to woo the Infanta, we are told, 'the world talks somewhat freely as if it were done so that they may be married at a mass which could not be done so handsomely here'. James's determination that the Privy Council should 'provide to stay the amasement of the people' was scarcely met by the prayers offered at Paul's Cross for the success of the expedition, and the preachers were 'hardly held in and their tongues ytch to be talking'.[39] Among the populace, the Spanish ambassador was the target of repeated xenophobic attacks. Libels against him circulated widely; in February 1621 he retreated from the city 'to avoide the feare and furie of shrove tuesday'; he was abused in his litter in the streets by apprentices in April 1621; in 1623 the ambassador complained that he and his household were virtually under siege, and when negotiations were broken off the embassy was stoned.[40] The intimacy of James with the Spanish ambassador and the apparently increased prominence of Catholics at court simply con-firmed the suspicions of Londoners about the corruption of the court. They had been fed on a rich diet of court scandals; they blamed the court-sponsored

Cockayne project for their economic woes; and they had seen courtiers waxing rich on patents. During the 1620s the terms 'court' and 'courtier' appear increasingly in the political discourse of Londoners with negative connotations.[41]

Buckingham and Charles were able to tap into the immense fund of loyalist sentiment on their return from Madrid in 1623, when the city burst out in spontaneous expressions of joy. In spite of the rain, 100 bonfires were counted between Charing Cross and Temple Bar, the street parties recalled those on the occasion of the arrest of the Babington conspirators in 1586 and the service of thanksgiving in St Paul's was similar to that which Elizabeth had attended to celebrate the defeat of the armada.[42] But it was loyalty to a specifically Protestant and martial monarchy. As Charles's war effort collapsed in incompetence and incoherence, and as the Crown failed to make the effort to explain its policies, so the cult of Elizabeth revived, often in conjunction with aristocratic populism. By 1633 no fewer than thirty-three of the ninety-seven churches within the City had acquired memorials to the late Queen laying stress on her role as the defender of Protestantism. Several parishes revived the practice of ringing their bells on her accession day during the 1620s. Elizabeth was incorporated into the commemoration of providential deliverances in the sermon cycle endowed at St Pancras Soper Lane, while at St Mildred Bread Street the defeat of the armada was linked with the foiling of the gunpowder plot in new stained-glass windows provided by a wealthy parishioner. At St Antholin's a new gallery built in 1623 incorporated the badges of English monarchs from Edward the Confessor onwards, but the sequence ended with the Elector Palatine.[43] There are also indications that those aristocrats who embodied the traditions of Elizabethan Protestant militancy (a group dubbed the Patriots by Tom Cogswell) sought to mobilize the forces of civic chivalry. The Devereuxes were praised in works like Gervase Markham's *Honour in his Perfection* and Thomas Scott's *Robert Earl of Essex his Ghost sent from Elizian to the Nobility, Gentry and Commonalty of England*. In 1626 William Gouge, the godly preacher from the Blackfriars, preached to the Honourable Artillery Company invoking the hallowed memory of 'the valorous earl of Essex', and ballads commemorating the second earl as a paragon of chivalric virtue enjoyed a renewed popularity. The cultivation of this Essex tradition was to prove a powerful force in the popular mobilization for the Parliamentary forces commanded by the third earl in the 1640s.[44] Here were forms of loyalism embodying dissentient voices.

There can be little doubting the depth and extent of popular politicization in the capital in the 1620s. When collections were made for Bohemia in 1620 it was reported that 'the rich proceed with caution, but the common sort with a strange heartiness and zeal', and there was an uncharacteristically enthusiastic response to the call for volunteers in 1624. The mariners on the river Thames were reluctant to man ships licensed by the Crown to carry ordnance to the Netherlands in March 1621. Middleton's virulently anti-Spanish play *A Game at Chesse*, an allegory of the negotiations ('our famous play of Gondomar'), broke box office records in August 1624, 'frequented by all sorts of people old and younge, rich and poore, masters and servants, papists and puritans', an audience estimated at 30,000, or one-tenth of the capital's population! The messages of providential deliverance and the need for vigilance against backsliding into popery were hammered home through sermons, polemical tracts, engravings and even stained-glass windows. London crowds made their feelings clear in their repeated rioting against the Spanish ambassador and in the extraordinary scenes which greeted the returning prince in October 1623. A few weeks after the prince's return they executed providential justice on the victims of the 'fatal vesper': when the floor of a chapel in which Catholic vespers were being celebrated collapsed, they fell upon the survivors with shocking brutality.[45] The disasters of the war years saw resentment focused increasingly on the Duke of Buckingham. The profusion of libels against the duke in the later 1620s appealed across the social spectrum, some using a classical frame of reference and probably aimed at the more educated, others apparently sung in taverns. Mutinous sailors directed their wrath at the duke and his client, Sir William Russell, treasurer of the navy in 1627–28. When the King signed the Petition of Right the crowds showed their approval in a blaze of bonfires, but one group of apprentices tore down the pillory on Tower Hill, threatening to make a bonfire to burn the duke. When Buckingham was assassinated later in the year Londoners again made their sentiments felt, flocking to the Tower to fete his assassin.[46]

Whether these crowds acted out of the same motives is doubtful. The marriage could be opposed out of religious conviction or raw xenophobia, nor did one need to be a godly zealot to identify Buckingham as the fount of the country's ills. There were elements of carnival misrule in the attacks on Gondomar and on the victims of the fatal vesper with which godly divines and sober citizens felt uneasy. But it is striking how the different elements of popular political discourse we have identified in this chapter contributed to the antagonism between Londoners and the priorities of James's and Charles's government in the 1620s: Protestantism, xenophobia, civic chivalry and the defence of the integrity of the civic community all intersected in growing disillusionment. Londoners remained loyal to the Crown, but they had constructed their grounds for loyalty on a very different basis from that insisted upon by Charles I.

This chapter has demonstrated the vitality of popular political engagement in the century before the Civil War. Although historians have long recognised the power of popular xenophobia and 'bread and butter' issues in mobilizing the populace, they have underestimated the degree to which these issues could interlock with others more significant in the framework of national politics. The discourses associated with citizenship, so often deployed in an apparently localist framework to protect economic privileges, could take on more radical implications when the predator was seen to be groups acting under the protection of the Crown or the city elite. Xenophobia could become a more focused and subversive force when associated with anti-popery, as it clearly was in the successive crises over royal marriages in 1554, 1579 and 1617–23. This chapter has also made clear the ways in which popular Protestantism acted as a solvent on traditional loyalties. Protestants insisted on obedience, but their construction of obedience as due to the godly monarch imposed limits on their loyalty, limits which were increasingly tested under the early Stuarts. Moreover, the vitality of popular Protestantism in the capital and the regularity with which religious issues fused with political ones must call into question the conventional chronologies of the emergence of a 'public sphere'. It is becoming a commonplace that it was in the 1640s that the explosion of public interest in political matters heralded the creation of a public sphere of political discourse. But because of the teleological assumptions related to the development of a 'rational' political discourse which are built into traditional accounts of the public sphere, the religious content of much political argument in early modern England has been neglected. It was in the post-Reformation decades that the entrenchment of religious divisions among the populace resulted in the wider public discussion of religious issues and their frequent politicization.

NOTES

1 R. Cust, 'News and politics in early seventeenth-century England', *P&P*, 112 (1986); *id.*, 'Politics and the electorate in the 1620s', in R. Cust and A. Hughes eds, *Conflict in Early Stuart England* (1989); D. Underdown, *Revel, Riot, and Rebellion: Popular Politics and Culture in England 1603–60* (Oxford, 1985); *id.*, *A Freeborn People: Politics and the Nation in Seventeenth Century England* (Oxford, 1996); P. Croft, 'Libels, popular literacy and public opinion in early modern England', *Historical Research*, 68 (1995).

2 K. Lindley, *Popular Politics and Religion in Civil War London* (Aldershot, 1997); D. Freist, *Governed by Opinion: Politics, Religion and the Dynamics of Communication in Stuart London 1637–45* (1997).

3 The main culprits are Archer, *Pursuit*, and Rappaport, *Worlds*. The exception is S. Brigden, *London and the Reformation* (Oxford, 1988), and see now D. J. Hickman, 'The Religious Allegiance of London's Ruling Elite 1520–1603' (London University Ph.D. thesis, 1995).

4 T. Harris, *London Crowds in the Reign of Charles II: Propaganda and Politics from the Restoration until the Exclusion Crisis* (Cambridge, 1987), chap. 1; R. Chartier, 'Culture as appropriation: popular cultural uses in early modern France', in S. L. Kaplan ed., *Understanding Popular Culture: Europe from the Middle Ages to the Nineteenth Century* (1984).

5 K. Wrightson, 'The politics of the parish in early modern England', in P. Griffiths, A. Fox and S. Hindle eds, *The Experience of Authority in Early Modern England* (1995); Archer, *Pursuit*, chaps 3–4; cf. P. Griffiths, 'Secrecy and authority in late sixteenth- and seventeenth-century London', *HJ*, 40 (1997).

6 Below, p. 30; B. Capp, 'Separate domains? Women and authority in early modern England', in Griffiths *et al.*, *The Experience of Authority*; S. Mendelson and P. Crawford, *Women in Early Modern England* (Oxford, 1998), pp. 380–94.

7 *The Autobiography of Thomas Whythorne*, ed. J. M. Osborn (Oxford, 1961), p. 119; T. Nashe, *Works*, ed. R. B. McKerrow (5 vols, Oxford, 1958), I, pp. 294, 317; J. Earle, *Microcosmographie or A Peece of the World discovered in Essayes and Characters* (1628), sig. G9.

8 BL, Lansdowne MSS 74/48, fo. 137; 74/49, fo. 140v; *Proceedings in Parliament 1610*, ed. E. R. Foster (2 vols, 1966), II, p. 158; *CSPVen., 1625–26*, pp. 468, 603; *CSPVen., 1632–36*, pp. 314–15.

9 R. M. Smuts, 'Cultural diversity and cultural change at the court of James I', in L. L. Peck ed., *The Mental World of the Jacobean Court* (Cambridge, 1991); M. A. R. Graves, *Thomas Norton: the Parliament Man* (Oxford, 1994); P. L. Ralph, *Sir Humphrey Mildmay, Royalist Gentleman* (New Brunswick NJ, 1947); W. Young, *A History of Dulwich College* (2 vols, 1889); B. Capp, *The World of John Taylor the Water Poet 1578–1653* (Oxford, 1994), pp. 1–15, 92; I. W. Archer, 'The London lobbies in the later sixteenth century', *HJ*, 31 (1988).

10 Brigden, *London and the Reformation*, pp. 365, 501, 557.

11 *Proceedings in the Parliaments of Elizabeth I*, ed. T. E. Hartley (3 vols, Leicester, 1981–95), III, p. 391.

12 34 and 35 Henry VIII c. 1; J. Barry, 'Literacy and literature in popular culture: reading and writing in historical perspective', in T. Harris ed., *Popular Culture in England* c. *1500–1850*, (1995).

13 V. Pearl, 'Change and stability in seventeenth-century London', *LJ*, 5 (1979); Boulton, *Neighbourhood*; R. G. Lang, 'Social origins and social aspirations of Jacobean London merchants', *EcHR*, second series, 27 (1974).

14 S. Thrupp, *The Merchant Class of Medieval London* (Chicago, 1948), pp. 41–7; Pearl, *London*, p. 50.

15 Rappaport, *Worlds*, pp. 82–3.

16 'The London Journal of Alessandro Magno 1562', ed. C. M. Barron, C. Coleman and C. Gobbi, *LJ*, 9 (1983), p. 144; *Thomas Platter's Travels in England 1599*, ed. C. M. Williams (1937), p. 170; Capp, 'Separate domains?'.

17 Brigden, *London and the Reformation*, pp. 97–8, 103–5, 273–4, 358–9, 370–7, 411–17, 446, 608–12; P. Collinson, *The Elizabethan Puritan Movement* (1967), pp. 116, 118; PRO, SP12/39/66.

18 T. Wright ed., *Queen Elizabeth and her Times* (2 vols, 1838), II, p. 308; J. Clare, *'Art Made Tongue-tied by Authority': Elizabethan and Jacobean Dramatic Censorship* (Manchester, 1990), pp. 30–7; *The Letters of John Chamberlain*, ed. N. E. McClure (2 vols, Philadelphia PA, 1939), II, p. 602; K. Lindley, 'Riot prevention and control in early modern London', *Transactions of the Royal Historical Society*, fifth series, 33 (1983), pp. 111–12.

19 Archer, *Pursuit*, pp. 20, 131–40; G. Gronquist, 'The Relationship between the City of London and the Crown 1509–47' (Cambridge University Ph.D. thesis, 1986), pp. 67–78; CLRO, Jour. 13, fo. 22r–v; BL, Additional MS 48019, fos 225v–230; *Acts of Court of the Mercers' Company 1453–1527*, ed. L. Lyell and F. D. Watney (Cambridge, 1936), pp. 481–5.

20 D. H. Sacks, 'The corporate town and the English state: Bristol's "little businesses" 1625–41', in J. Barry ed., *The Tudor and Stuart Town: A Reader in English Urban History 1530–1688* (Harlow, 1990), pp. 297–333; *id.*, 'Parliament, liberty and the commonweal', in J. H. Hexter ed., *Parliament and Liberty from the Reign of Elizabeth I to the English Civil War* (Stanford CA, 1992), pp. 103–5; BL, Lansdowne MSS 74/42, fo. 118v, 74/48, fo. 137; J. Lilburne, *London's Liberty in Chains Discovered* (1646), pp. 40–1. Lilburne's civic consciousness and his exploitation of the ambiguous meanings of 'freemen' (all inhabitants or the body of citizens?) in the London context are worthy of further exploration.

21 Brigden, *London and the Reformation*, p. 546; Archer, *Pursuit*, pp. 232–4; *Mercers' Acts of Court*, pp. 183–4, 450, 577, 583; Chamberlain, *Letters*, II, pp. 35, 39; PRO, STAC5/A27/38; Capp, *John Taylor*, pp. 103–6.

22 Archer, *Pursuit*, pp. 3–4: C. Brooks, 'Apprenticeship, social mobility and the middling sort 1550–1800', in J. Barry and C. Brooks eds, *The Middling Sort of People: Culture, Society and Politics in England 1550–1800* (Basingstoke, 1994), pp. 80–1; P. Seaver, 'Declining status in an aspiring age: the problem of the gentle apprentice in seventeenth-century London', in B. Y. Kunze and D. Brautigam eds, *Court, Country and Culture: Essays in Honour of Perez Zagorin* (Woodbridge, 1992), pp. 129–47.

23 M. Spufford, *Small Books and Pleasant Histories: Popular Fiction and its Readership in Seventeenth Century England* (Cambridge, 1981), pp. 224–37; A. Barton, 'London comedy and the ethos of the City', *LJ*, 4 (1981); A. Gurr, *Playgoing in Shakespeare's London* (Cambridge, 1987), pp. 102–4; Earle, *Microcosmographie*, sig. G9–G11v.

24 R. Leitch, 'Richard Robinson and the Literature of London *c.* 1576–1603' (Cambridge University M.Phil. thesis, 1997); W. Hunt, 'Civic chivalry and the English Civil War', in A. Grafton and A. Blair eds, *The Transmission of Culture in Early Modern Europe* (Philadelphia PA, 1990); J. Stow, *The Annales or Generall Chronicle of England* (1615), p. 744; Strype, *Stow*, II, p. 254.

25 Brigden, *London and the Reformation*, pp. 152–5, 516–78; CLRO, Jour. 25, fo. 312v; HMC, *Hatfield House*, XI, pp. 50, 52, 53, 55–6, 57–8, 76, 77–8, 88–9, 91, 132, 148, 156, 321–2; XII, p. 201; Stow, *Annales*, pp. 783, 794.

26 Brigden, *London and the Reformation*, pp. 498–9; T. Birch, *Memoirs of the Reign of Elizabeth from the Year 1581 till her Death* (2 vols, 1754), II, pp. 81, 96–7; H. Wootton, *Reliquiae Wottonianae* (1651), p. 48; *Acts of the Privy Council of England*, ed. J. R. Dasent (32 vols, 1890–1907), XXX, pp. 619–20; HMC, *De l'Isle and Dudley*, II, p. 435; Stow, *Annales*, p. 788.

27 D. Cressy, *Bonfires and Bells: National Memory and the Protestant Calendar in Elizabethan and Stuart England* (1989); *Greyfriars Chronicle*, pp. 32, 47, 66; Machyn, *Diary*, pp. 42, 180, 186–7, 202, 227, 229, 262–4; R. M. Smuts, 'Public ceremony and royal charisma: the English royal entry in London 1485–1642', in A. L. Beier, D. Cannadine and J. M. Rosenheim eds, *The First Modern Society: Essays in English History in Honour of Lawrence Stone* (Cambridge, 1989); P. M. McCullough, *Sermons at Court: Politics and Religion in Elizabethan and Jacobean Preaching* (Cambridge, 1998), pp. 42–4, 48, 59–60, 90; A. Young,

Tudor and Jacobean Tournaments (1987), pp. 74, 83, 85–6; *Holinshed's Chronicles of England, Scotland, and Ireland* (6 vols, 1807–09), IV, pp. 914–17, 922.

28 BL, Lansdowne MS 74/42, fo. 118v; cf. C. Holmes, 'Parliament, liberty, taxation, and property', in Hexter, *Parliament and Liberty*.

29 CLRO, Rep. 2, fo. 151v; PRO, SP12/252/94.

30 J. Sharpe, 'The people and the law', in B. Reay ed., *Popular Culture in Seventeenth Century England* (1985); Gowing, *Domestic*, pp. 104–5; Brigden, *London and the Reformation*, pp. 317, 605; *The Letters and Dispatches of Richard Verstegen* c. 1550–1640, ed. A. G. Petti, Catholic Record Society, LII (1959), pp. 223, 282, 293; S. R. Gardiner ed., *Documents relating to the Proceedings against William Prynne 1634 and 1637*, Camden Society, new series, XVII (1877), pp. 86, 90; *CSPVen., 1636–39*, p. 242.

31 P. W. White, *Theatre and Reformation: Protestantism, Patronage and Playing in Tudor England* (Cambridge, 1993), pp. 28–9, 34–40, 49–51, 58–9.

32 *CSPSpan., 1568–79*, p. 148; PRO, SP12/49/9.

33 Stow, *Annales*, p. 694; *CSPVen., 1625–26*, p. 337; *CSPD, 1625–26*, p. 337.

34 Brigden, *London and the Reformation*, pp. 232–8, 444; Machyn, *Diary*, p. 131; *Greyfriars Chronicle*, pp. 60, 61; *Memoirs of the Life and Times of Sir Christopher Hatton*, ed. H. Nicolas (1847), pp. 152–3, 200–1; Stow, *Annales*, p. 713; *Verstegen Letters*, pp. 177, 182; HMC, *Hatfield House*, XI, pp. 52, 55–6, 76, 154–5; XII, p. 201; Chamberlain, *Letters*, II, pp. 286–7, 289.

35 R. H. Tawney and E. Power eds, *Tudor Economic Documents* (3 vols, 1924), III, pp. 82–4; *Holinshed's Chronicles*, IV, pp. 888–91; HMC, *Hatfield House*, XII, p. 672; *CSPD, 1611–18*, p. 519; Chamberlain, *Letters*, II, p. 243.

36 Brigden, *London and the Reformation*, pp. 278, 357–8, 408–9; CLRO, Rep. 10, fo. 16v; H. Robinson ed., *Original Letters relative to the English Reformation*, Parker Society (2 vols, 1846), I, pp. 200–5.

37 *John Stubbs's Gaping Gulf with Letters and other Relevant Documents*, ed. L. E. Berry (Charlottesville VA, 1968); *Memoirs of Hatton*, p. 132; B. Worden, *The Sound of Virtue: Philip Sidney's Arcadia and Elizabethan Politics* (1996), pp. 109–11.

38 Chamberlain, *Letters*, II, pp. 77, 140, 331, 339, 350, 449, 451; J. F. Larkin and P. L. Hughes eds, *Stuart Royal Proclamations* (in progress, Oxford, 1973–), I, pp. 495–6, 519–21.

39 Chamberlain, *Letters*, II, pp. 480, 482–3, 486.

40 Lindley, 'Riot prevention', p. 112; Chamberlain, *Letters*, II, pp. 356, 360–1, 363.

41 Chamberlain, *Letters*, II, p. 39; *Liber Famelicus of Sir James Whitelocke*, ed. J. Bruce, Camden Society, old series, LXX (1858), pp. 63–8; T. Birch, *The Court and Times of Charles I* (2 vols, 1848), II, p. 130.

42 Cressy, *Bonfires and Bells*, chap. 6; Chamberlain, *Letters*, II, pp. 515–16.

43 Cressy, *Bonfires and Bells*, pp. 134–8; A. Barton, *Ben Jonson, Dramatist* (Cambridge, 1984), chap. 14; Stow, *Survey 1633*, pp. 819–910; T. Cogswell, 'The politics of propaganda: Charles I and the people in the 1620s', *Journal of British Studies*, 29 (1990).

44 T. Cogswell, *The Blessed Revolution: English Politics and the Coming of War 1621–24* (Cambridge, 1989), chap. 2; J. S. A. Adamson, 'Chivalry and political culture in Caroline

England', in K. Sharpe and P. Lake eds, *Culture and Politics in Early Stuart England* (1994), p. 167; R. McCoy, 'Old English honour in an evil time: aristocratic principle in the 1620s', in M. Smuts ed., *The Stuart Court in Europe: Essays in Politics and Political Culture* (Cambridge, 1996), pp. 133–55; J. S. A. Adamson, 'The baronial context of the English Civil War', *Transactions of the Royal Historical Society*, fifth series, 40 (1990).

45 *HMC Twelfth Report*, app. 1, p. 108; Chamberlain, *Letters*, II, pp. 454, 577–8; Cogswell, *Blessed Revolution*, pp. 281–307; A. Walsham, 'Impolitic pictures: providence, history, and the iconography of Protestant nationhood in early Stuart England', in R. N. Swanson ed., *The Church Retrospective* (Woodbridge, 1997); *id.*, 'The "Fatall Vesper": providentialism and anti-popery in late Jacobean London', *P&P*, 144 (1994).

46 A. Bellany, '"Raylinge rymes and vaunting verse": libellous politics in early Stuart England 1603–28', in Sharpe and Lake, *Culture and Politics*; *CSPVen., 1626–28*, p. 607; *CSPVen., 1628–29*, pp. 11, 127, 283, 337.

Chapter 3

———◆———

Reordering rituals: ceremony and the parish, 1520–1640

Michael Berlin

In 1584–85 Thomas Bentley, gentleman and one time churchwarden of St Andrew's Holborn, a large parish on the north-west fringe of the city, set down 'some monument of antiquities [of] worthy memory' gathered from parish records dating back to the reign of Henry VI.[1] He noted each important physical change to the church over the previous century. The register records how the pre-Reformation fabric of the church had been built up over many decades by the parishioners through funds gathered by voluntary contributions at church ales, plays, archery contests and 'drinkings' when 'ye church-wardens & many women also used yerely as Hop Monday, Good Fryday & such like dayes to gather in boxes ye devotion of good people towards ye mayntenance of ye churche workes'.[2] Bentley displayed an orthodox conservatism in which he praised the 'great devotion & zeal of the people in old time towards the house of the Lord', yet accepted the ultimate abolition of 'superstition and idolatry' in the early years of Elizabeth I. The register records in detail the great changes in church furniture during this period. In the first two years of Edward VI the 'monuments of superstition' were defaced, the altars pulled down, the interior of the church whitewashed and the scripture in English and the royal coat of arms set up, while the rood was removed and the cross, censor and chalice were sold. All this was reversed under Mary; in the first year of her reign the register records that 'idolatry is set up again', with the scriptures being washed out and the rood with images of Mary and John resurrected. Finally, after Elizabeth's accession, Bentley records that 'in the first and second year of her majesty's all the altars and superstitious things in the church set up in Queen Mary's time were now again to God's glory hulde down & little by little all the reliques of Rome turned out of the church'.[3] Over the course of Elizabeth's reign more changes occurred, not all of which Bentley entirely approved of. Private drinkings after the election and the rendering up of accounts were said to be an innovation of 1563–64.[4] During the next two decades the rood loft was torn down (1571–72), galleries were built specifically for the poor (1577–78), the font was removed and long tables were purchased for catechizing youth (1583).[5] Bentley appears to have disapproved of the tendency for church officers to engage in private drinkings and to enhance the amenities of the vestry at the expense of the church stock. Expenditure on the sidesmen's drinkings he considered 'ill husbandry', while he reckoned the enlarging and re-edifying of the vestry house 'very ill husbandry'.[6] Paying for wine and bread at communions out of church stock, a tendency in other city churches, was to him an attempt to 'defraud the poor' of the parish.[7] Bentley's account ends with the introduction in 1584 of church celebrations on Queen Elizabeth's birthday and coronation day, which were solemnized with prayers of thanksgiving by an assembly of parish poor; fifty-two poor women of the greatest age in the parish celebrated her birthday, praying for the Queen's long life and prosperous estate, and each receiving spice cake, wine and 2*d*. Twenty-seven young maidens of the parish similarly celebrated the twenty-seventh anniversary of her coronation with prayers of thanksgiving in return for alms.[8]

Bentley's register is thus a unique source for tracing the transition from pre-Reformation parish rituals to the more circumscribed ceremonials of the later sixteenth century. His account tells what was perhaps an exemplary story: a gradual shift away from outdoor annual celebrations involving mixed groups of parishioners to socially restricted forms of ceremonial, circumscribed by a reformed liturgy and centred around new commitments of parish government. These included the distribution of relief to the parish poor, who were now to be more distinctly identified from their neighbours by separate seating, the invocation of a national church settlement under the authority and direction of the state, and the private drinkings of parish elites when they met to administer parochial affairs.

The activities and material objects which Bentley painstakingly noted constituted central ritual elements of everyday life. The body of the church provided the critical ritual space where all stages of the life cycle were marked out. Contemporary Western society may be said to be characterized by a studied informality in which explicit rituals play a peripheral role in the internal dynamics of human interaction. This rejection of formality nevertheless has deep roots in Western society, roots which can be traced to the rejection of elements of medieval Catholic religious liturgy by Protestant reformers of the sixteenth century. That era witnessed an upheaval in the forms of symbolic action by which the most basic messages of human existence were manifested. An important point to remember is that we are not dealing with a society in which ritual and ceremony can be understood in modern terms as some exterior representation of human social organization. Instead, in order to give full weight to the contemporary significance of these acts, and the responses to changes in ritual, such as recorded by Bentley, it must remembered that ritual constituted a basic facet of what it was to be human.[9]

The significance of the changes in ritual practices like those which Thomas Bentley described has featured in some of the most contentious debates in the history of London and other early modern towns over the past three decades. Early modern English urban history has been dominated by arguments about how far population growth, economic and social change and religious upheaval created instability.[10] During the 1970s historians characterized London as undergoing a period of upheaval in which an expanding population, many at the margins of poverty, created the conditions for social conflict, crime and unrest. The response of urban governments was seen as ultimately inadequate. Power in the city became entrenched in narrow elites who sought to protect their position, through amelioration of poverty and the enforcement of social discipline. At the same time the vast majority were excluded from any effective say in the running of the towns. In London participation in the formal structures of civic life was thus narrowed, and the parishes, wards, livery companies and the city corporation came to be dominated by an economic and social oligarchy. Charles Phythian-Adams has argued that at the same time urban society was marked by a shift from integrated ritual celebrations to more hierarchical forms of display, which he termed ceremonial, and has maintained that this was one manifestation of a narrowing of the basis of urban government, of the growth of oligarchic rule and of the polarization of urban society.[11]

A major critique of the view that London, along with other towns, underwent a social crisis was presented by Valerie Pearl. She sought to demonstrate that, far from being narrow and unresponsive, metropolitan government was characterized by a very large body of active participants, as much as 75 per cent of the adult male population.[12] The images of crime and disorder painted by Elizabethan and Jacobean pamphleteers which haunted urban magistrates were, she argued, projections which had little basis in reality. But this critique was open to the charge of exaggerating the position of the so-called 'crisis school' who wrote in much less apocalyptic terms than Pearl suggested. Although many of her objections are plausible, it is possible to detect behind them some of the larger ideological contests of the late 1970s and early 1980s. By denying the extent of poverty, polarization and unrest her arguments sought to challenge not just this view of urban life but also the 'sociological theories' which lay behind what she characterized as 'the philosophy of "doom and gloom"'.

Elements of this critique were expanded by Steven Rappaport and Ian Archer.[13] Rappaport argued that the very large number of freemen of the City, with rights to participate in civic elections, the activities of overlapping assemblies of wards, precincts, parishes and livery companies, formed networks of Burkean 'little battalions', which acted as a powerful buttress against social disintegration. Ian Archer, meanwhile, offered a nuanced account of the workings of guild, ward and parish in which social crisis was averted but never banished and in which coercion and social discipline existed side by side with deference and paternalism. Both these studies see levels of popular participation in parish government as a litmus test of the city's cohesiveness and social stability. Historians have stressed the pluralism and openness of parish government, the degree of popular participation in parish meetings, where large numbers of householders freely elected their neighbours to serve in the various offices associated with local government.[14]

Parish life and parish rituals have also figured prominently in a parallel debate about the nature of the English Reformation. For an earlier generation, epitomized in the works of A. G. Dickens, the impetus to reform came from a growing majority of lay activists, dissatisfied with the supposedly decayed religious forms of the medieval period, who wrought change in parish and cloister. The most important recent studies of the Reformation, by contrast, have seen it as carried out against the wishes of the majority, who abandoned traditional religion only with reluctance.[15] Other researchers have demonstrated a very high level of religious commitment by the laity to organizations such as parish fraternities in the years before the onset of reform.[16] Case studies have revealed a halting implementation of liturgical change and a very significant level of passive local resistance to the imposition of the new faith.[17] Large numbers, though unwilling to rebel against the Henrician and Edwardian onslaughts, proved notably reluctant to abandon the symbols and local traditions associated with Catholicism.[18] The rituals of parish life were the focus of this resistance to change.

The parish was a crucial nexus of urban existence. If the household was the basic unit of social life, then the parish was the next rung up where the private and the familial blended into the wider public world. The individual 'entered' and 'left' the world through the parish church, as the life cycle was punctuated by ritual acts which helped to mark the passage from the cradle to the grave. At church services the formal arrangement of parishioners, ranked according to gender, status and seniority in the parish, provided a static demonstration of social divisions within the community. Parishes were thus microcosms of the social structure of urban society in which horizontal divisions of wealth and economic differentiation were sanctioned within vertical corporate institutions. They tended to be dominated by a hierarchy of office holders, the more substantial inhabitants of the parish, who in many cases also held positions of authority in the livery companies, wards and the City corporation.[19] Parishes thus provided, in Laura Gowing's phrase, 'institutional frames for local knowledge'. The public performance of penance for moral offences at the church porch, or in front of the congregation in time of divine service, sought to both stigmatize and reintegrate those found in breach of communal social and sexual norms.[20] The institutions of the parish provided a basic means of defining communities, of formulating rules for the inclusion and exclusion of individuals and groups.

Local festive traditions gave parishes their own unique identity. Prior to the Elizabethan settlement certain parishes had long maintained customs associated with their particular patron saints, and groups of parishioners constituted themselves into informal festive communities for the celebration of specific folk customs. Henry Machyn's diary, which recorded events of the city between 1550 and 1563, described archery contests to raise funds for the parish and parochial processions, with banners, the sacrament, and accompanied by the clergy. These religious processions, especially at Corpus Christi and Ascensiontide, were a notable feature of the revival of Catholic ceremony under Mary.[21] The parishioners of St Olave's Silver Street celebrated St Olave's Day 1557 with 'a stage play of [goodly matter]' beginning at 8 p.m. and lasting till midnight, when 'they made an end with a g[ood song]'.[22] The neighbourhood around St Gabriel Fenchurch Street was the scene for the yearly setting of a maypole and for the performance of may games.[23] Parishoners from peripheral suburban parishes like St Clement Dane's, St Mary Islington and Hackney processed to St Paul's Cathedral in May.[24]

Despite this diversity certain generalizations about the trajectory of change can be made. In the late sixteenth century parishes increasingly functioned as units of local government, with greater responsibility for administering the policies of central government and the City corporation, especially with regard to poor relief. These gave parochial officials greater power over the lives of their communities and shifted their activities away from traditional celebrations of parish life like church ales to raise funds for the upkeep of the church fabric, towards the more formal exercise of power. As parishes assumed new functions parochial ritual was reduced, gradually but decisively, to ceremony.[25] This tendency was by no means a uniform process; indeed, some traditional celebrations were continued well after the formal liturgical basis of such observances had been officially removed, while other traditions, like the decoration of church interiors at Christmas with holly and ivy, may have undergone something of a revival in the early seventeenth century, along with an enhanced concern for the fabric of the church.[26] But by this date the provision of such festive amenities was but one small part of the duties of parish officials.

Fully to understand this change in parish life it is necessary to outline the constituent elements of the parochial community and their relation to parish government. Participation in the collective business of the parish revolved around the position of the householder, who was not merely the head of a family living in a particular parish, but an established resident who was capable of paying the traditional local taxes known as scot and lot.[27] Lodgers and inmates, though they might be heads of families themselves, were thus excluded from this formal definition.[28] It was to the householder that the City directed its orders for the supervision of the city's youth and the prevention of disorder at festival times by servants and apprentices under their care. House-holders of St Margaret Lothbury were held accountable for any church windows broken by their children or servants on pain of a fine. (If they failed to pay they were to be deprived of their place in church and, if obstinate, referred to the Bishop of London.)[29] The householder was eligible, if free of the City, to be appointed to hold office in the parish, and all householders, whether free or unfree, were expected to finance the various activities of the parish.[30]

The role of the individual householder in parish government was regulated through the parish's chief executive, the vestry. This was made up of the churchwardens and a group of the most prominent parishioners, acting in consultation with the incumbent. It had wide executive powers, subject to higher ecclesiastical authority, ranging from the collection and rating of taxes, the upkeep and disposition of parish property and the administration of charitable bequests, to the settlement of disputes between parishioners and the relief and moral control of the poor in their localities. The vestry acted as a self co-opting body, drawing its membership from all those substantial parish-ioners who had served in parish office. A *cursus honorum* existed which combined service in parochial office with service in adjacent ward and precinct. Service as a constable thus made the parishioner eligible for membership of the vestry.[31] Individuals could choose to pay a fine in lieu of this service, and such payment equally qualified them for membership of the vestry.[32] Over the late sixteenth and early seventeenth centuries the more substantial inhabi-tants of the parishes tended to consolidate their power by appointing so-called select vestries, which came to claim a prescriptive right to limit the rights of the inhabitants as a whole to take part in parochial government.[33]

Generally, larger, more populous parishes increasingly restricted access to elections and the smaller parishes maintained more open procedures. In the large extra-mural parish of St Dunstan in the West, for example, as late as 1587 it was routine that each year at Christmas all householders 'should come and give their voices for the election of all manner of church officers whatsoever and that if any had any cause to complain of any that were in office the year before, he should be heard'. Complaints were to be considered only if placed in writing on the table in the vestry house, an obvious barrier to less literate parishioners.[34] But by 1600 the more 'worshipful and discrete' of St Dunstan's sought to limit their numbers in the face of the 'disquietness and hindrance' caused by the 'discent of meaner sort of the multitude ...'.[35] A similar trans-formation occurred slightly earlier at St Martin in the Fields.[36] Up to 1547 the churchwardens were chosen by the whole body of the parishioners, but between 1547 and 1583 the wording in parish documents describing election procedures becomes ambiguous as to who was allowed to vote. By 1583 it is clear that the choice of churchwarden rested with a group of so-called 'masters of the parish' who composed the vestry. In the small intramural parish of St Peter Cornhill the elections alternated each year between the vestry, made up of anywhere between seventeen and thirty parishioners, and the parson, who signified his choice by 'pricking' from amongst five names submitted to him by the vestry.[37]

The reasons for this tendency to concentrate parish government in the hands of the few are made clear in the Bishop of London's instruments for the creation of select vestries. When, in 1600, the more substantial inhabitants of the St Dunstan in the West parish successfully petitioned for a select vestry they claimed that 'through the admission of all sorts of parishioners unto their vestries there falleth out great disquietness and hindrance to good proceedings by the discent of the inferior and meaner sort of the multitude of the inhabitants theyre being greater in number and more ready to cross the good proceedings'.[38] Though formulaic, such requests reveal the difficulties faced by parish elites in decades when population growth was stretching the formal constitution of the local community. Growing numbers brought social differentiation and a desire on the part of the wealthier members to distance themselves from the increasing 'multitude' of their poorer neighbours. When the thirty select vestrymen of St Saviour's in Southwark justified the exclusion of the bulk of the parish's 1,500 householders from meetings, they maintained that 'if the multitude should from time to time be privy to the stock of the parish, many of the meaner sort would neglect their labour and choose to live on the common stock'.[39] Similarly, the request for a select vestry at St Benet's Paul's Wharf complained of 'confusion and disorderly carriage of many things by reason of the general meeting which consisted of far greater number of the poorer and weaker sort where overswayed by numbers of hand and voices the men of the better understanding who had borne office or else were fit to bear offices'.[40]

The creation of select vestries was by no means a ubiquitous phenomenon. Many parishes, perhaps because of their smaller size and greater homogeneity, maintained open meetings for the election of officers.[41] But even where select vestries were not appointed, it would appear that important decisions rested with a limited group of the 'more worshipful and discrete'. St Andrew Holborn was governed by the wardens and a group of twelve so-called assistants, 'creditable men and of ye best householders', without a formal select vestry.[42] Whether with or without this formal grant of a select vestry some sort of limitation on parish pump democracy was necessary where increasing numbers forced parish elites to close ranks.

Social differentiation amongst parishioners was symbolically demonstrated and enacted at church services by the careful arrangement of seating according to a system of precedence which combined considerations of social status, seniority in parish office, age, gender and wealth. Though the traditional separation of the sexes in church seating was initially continued and reinforced by religious reform, it gradually gave way to rented family pews, the spread of which may been encouraged by the godly's emphasis on the household.[43] Proximity to the centre was accorded to those at the top of the parish hierarchy: resident aldermen and other notables, churchwardens and 'auncient' vestrymen.[44] Pew rents were graded according to the position of pews, those nearest to the chancel paying most.[45] Competition between those who felt that they had right to special placing in church inevitably ensued, and the Elizabethan period marks the beginning of that most characteristic of post-Reformation parochial conflicts, the disputed pew.[46] Special provision was made for those who were wealthy enough to pay fines rather than serve in parish office.[47] Separation by age and gender may have helped to reinforce the internal division of households by arranging groups according to their different roles in the private sphere. Special seating was provided for subordinate sexual age groups: unmarried women and maids, poor widows and young male servants and apprentices.[48] As population expanded adjustments were made to seating, with galleries being constructed and allocated to specific groups such as prominent parishioners who had fined out of parish office or poor pensioners in receipt of parochial relief.[49] The segregation of the 'deserving poor' was a way of demonstrating their subservience and dependence on their wealthier neighbours. Churchwardens continually sought to update the placing of parishioners in pews to take account of the changing social composition of the congregations and to ensure the due order of precedence remained intact.

This social segregation was reinforced by the maintenance of discipline at church services by specially appointed officials, the clerk and sidesmen. The clerk at St Margaret New Fish Street was instructed to ascertain 'what servants do sit covered with their caps on, or do sleep or talk during the sermon', and to admonish them 'with a wand to correct their stubbornness'.[50] At St Botolph's Without Aldgate pensions were granted to women for 'governing and observing the maids' and to a man for 'ruling the apprentices sitting over the belfry', while in St Olave Jewry the clerk was to correct the 'great sluggishness and diverse unreverent behaviour [which] is used in the church by servants and children in divine service'.[51] At All Hallows the Great the parish employed a common sergeant to carry a black staff for disciplining servants at services.

The desire for order and discipline during church services extended to all the activities of parish government. At meetings of parish vestries similar rules about good order applied. In St Martin Ludgate the churchwardens were to sit at the upper end of the table, 'as other churchwardens and wardens of the companies doe in other places'.[52] The emphasis on maintaining the state and dignity of proceedings mirrored the ceremonialism of the livery companies. This was no accident, as parish officials were often from the same group of householders who held office in the livery companies. Accordingly, several of the rules and customs of the vestries echoed those proceedings of the courts of the livery companies. At some vestries gowns were required to be worn by vestrymen on pain of fine, while the wearing of cloaks was forbidden.[53] Vestries set down rules for behaviour: 10s fines were imposed at St Andrew Holborn for 'interuptors, revilers and revealers of secrets' and a 5s fine was stipulated for 'withstanders and breakers of good orders'.[54] Fines were also imposed for the failure of vestrymen to attend meetings when duly summoned and on those who refused to take up office in the parish (the rate of fines periodically adjusted to take account of the numbers choosing to fine rather than serve).[55] In all these matters the emphasis was, like the procedures for the livery companies, placed on the need to maintain decorum and good order and to minimize the possibility of open conflict.

There were some indications that the problems of the parishes made the holding of parochial office seem less and less attractive. Parishioners chose to fine out of office rather than serve, a tendency which was at work in the livery companies and the civic corporation as well as in the parishes. The numbers choosing to fine rather than serve appear not to have caused much concern for most of the later sixteenth century. But in the early seventeenth century, especially during the periodic attacks of the plague, the problem of finding suitable candidates for parish office came to forefront of the vestries' concerns.[56] Fines had to be increased on those unwilling to serve in the more onerous parochial offices such as scavenger and constable. At St Benet's Pauls Wharf in 1611–12 the vestry had to raise the fines to £3 for scavenger and £36 for constable after several men had refused office and it was complained of 'distaste and discontent ... by reason of the daily suit of most men to be spared from executing the said offices'.[57] A similar attempt at the better enforcement of the system of fines had to be put into effect at St Dunstan in the West in 1599 because, it was alleged, 'many inconveniences and disorders have of late arisen by the taking of fines and the dispensing withall of such persons of the better sort as of late have been chosen constables and scavengers' of which the alderman of the adjacent ward had complained that 'thereby the service of Her Majesty and of this honourable city is greatly neglected and not performed as in duty and right apperteineth'.[58]

The general tendency for parish government to be dominated by wealthy elites can be seen in the growth of private dinners and other acts of conviviality which attended the various meetings of the vestry. In the Elizabethan period, parochial officials increasingly gathered in private 'drinkings' and dinners, often in taverns. The contrast with the relatively socially integrated gatherings of pre-Reformation church ales and other festivals described above could not be more stark. The annual rendering up and auditing of accounts was one such occasion when vestrymen were entertained at the expense of that year's churchwardens, who supplemented the cost with allowances out of the church stock. In 1570 a group of parishioners in St Margaret Pattens reached an agreement by which each man promised to provide gifts of money and food for a dinner at the rendering up of the parish accounts for the term of their natural lives; Edward Rede, pewterer, promised 20s yearly 'of his liberality and goodwill' to provide a buck 'therewithal to make merry', Henry Outhwaite, baker, promised bread, John Edwards, vintner, promised two gallons of wine, and Thomas Griffin, fruiterer, promised apples.[59] In 1629 the vestry of St Dunstan in the West attempted to revive an annual audit dinner for serving and former parish officers to which the readers of the Inner and Middle Temple customarily donated two bucks, 'for a neighbourly meeting'. The vestry noted with regret that the dinner had only recently been forborne 'out of the private respect of same particular persons' who refused to come to the gatherings because the rising cost of victuals had pushed the cost of preparing the bucks to four or 5s per 'man and wife'. To meet the increased expense they agreed to increase the allowance out of the church stock to 40s per buck 'upon consideration whereof and for the maintaining and increase of neighbourly love and friendship occasioned by those meetings'. Such attempts at fostering better social relations did not prevent the better sort of the parish from formally excluding the multitude from parish meetings by means of a request for a select vestry in 1636.[60] The important thing about such acts of conviviality was that they were essentially gatherings of office holders and their circle who, supplemented out of church funds, provided for neighbours from the same social group.

A similar occasion for commensality among parish elites was the ecclesiastical visitation usually held on a biennial or triennial basis some time at the end of January or the beginning of February. The visitation by the Archdeacon of St Paul's of St Botolph Aldgate was the occasion for a dinner of parish officers, ex-officers, their wives and 'bidden guests' (including ecclesiastical officials) held at a tavern near the church where the archdeacon's officials sat for the inspection of churchwardens' presentments. These meals could be quite lavish, with several courses (sirloin, mutton, breast and loin of veal, capons, sack, wine, oranges and lemons and cheese in one account) and as many as thirty-two people attending. The expense of these affairs was met by the churchwardens themselves, who received an allowance out of parish funds.[61] Visitation meals were sometimes held at the house of a prominent parishioner; at St Dunstan in the East dinners were held at the house of William Webb during and after the year of his mayoralty.[62] The consecration of a new burial ground was another occasion for lavish display in the presence of the Bishop of London and his entourage; at St Botolph Aldgate the vestry arranged an elaborate meal at Sir Allan Apsley's house for the consecration of the parish's new burial ground in Rosemary Lane in 1615. Two 'messe' of meat consisting of sixteen dishes to the messe were provided for the bishop's table, with eight 'messe' for the vestrymen and the bishop's servants. To pay for this meal there was to be a parish collection of £40, with any surplus going to the repair of pews.[63] On occasion meals were provided as part of charitable bequests, similar to the sometimes lavish memorial dinners of members of the livery companies. The godly-influenced bequest of Henry Syvedell, which gave £5 out of tenements in Thames Street to the parish of St Martin Ludgate to provide sermons on the anniversaries of Elizabeth I's accession, the defeat of the Armada and the failure of the Gunpowder Plot, also included money for a supper for the preacher, the churchwardens, the two chief constables and two of the 'auncientest' of the parish to be held after the sermons, 'as well for the continuence of brotherly love and kind neighbourhood amongst them as also for the churchwardens pains to be taken in and about this business'.[64] Dinners for parish officers and their wives together with their vestrymen and others from this social group underscored the sense in which they saw themselves as the natural rulers of the parish, the 'worshipful and discreet'. They contrasted with the more socially mixed gatherings based on voluntary contributions at traditional church ales.

Perhaps one of the most important events in the parish calendar was the annual perambulation or rogation of parish boundaries. Every year on the so-called Rogation Days – the Monday, Tuesday and Wednesday before the feast of the Ascension (30 April–3 June) when a small procession led by the incumbent, the churchwardens and one or two of the parish 'auncients' accompanied by a group of local children walked a circuit starting from the church around the outward boundary of the parish, stopping at various recognised places where boundary marks were located. At these points psalms would be sung (103, 104), an appropriate epistle read ('cursed be he that transgresseth the bounds of his neighbours') and prayers recited in thanksgiving and for the preservation of Elizabeth. As Keith Thomas has pointed out, the perambulation was the only pre-Reformation parish procession to survive in the Royal Injunctions of 1559.[65] The symbolic forms of the old religion such as the carrying of crosses and banners were removed, but the perambulation retained its importance as a ritual designed to preserve and enhance notions of community by its delineation of the formal limits. It also provided an opportunity for yet more commensality among office holders, who would round off the occasion by retiring to the nearest tavern.

Its importance in a rural setting had been centred on the customary offerings of prayers for good weather and a successful harvest. In the crowded metropolis its significance was somewhat different. The circuitous route through the built-up city carried the perambulation through main streets as well as down back alleys, through gardens, even through or beneath private dwellings if they straddled the route. The declaration of boundary marks was necessary in order to demonstrate publicly the limits of parochial jurisdiction at a time when the parish was shouldering greater responsibility for the assessment of taxes and the relief of the poor as the city grew in population and area of settlement. The presence of parochial children, who were rewarded for attending with small gifts of 'points' (bits of lace or ribbon attached to wands), money and food is interesting. By ritually implanting parish boundaries on the memories of the young inhabitants the exercise was designed to fix them for future reference and to safeguard parochial property rights. At St Botolph Aldgate the curate gave the assembled children points 'signifying to them that there was a right of way for the parishioners always to go circuit the bounds of the parish', and at St Bartholomew Exchange the points were given to them 'to remember the circuit'.[66] The children involved would come from established local families rather than the very poor and would thus be likely to remain in the area as adults; at St Peter Cornhill they were all the children of serving vestrymen.[67] This perhaps makes sense when it is recalled that in legal inquisitions into disputes over property marks elderly inhabitants would be called upon to give evidence based on personal memory. Moreover, the recipients of points seem predominantly to have been boys, for they were expected to be more likely to be called upon to give such testimony.

The perambulation of St Botolph Aldgate was recorded in particular detail by the parish clerk in the parish's Memoranda Book and his descriptions provide a picture of the annual event over several years.[68] St Botolph Aldgate was a large extramural parish which was particularly subject to the full effects of London's population growth. The city's eastern expansion meant that each year the perambulation was forced to take an ever more difficult route through newly enclosed back gardens which had been established on the traditional path. The perambulation was thus forced to break down pales and pass through private gardens, chalking up the parish's initials S.B.A. on newly erected brick walls. This involved the procession in encounters with enclosing neighbours which could turn ugly. In 1600 the perambulation tried to enter Edward Beckes's garden at the lower end of Hog Lane and was resisted by Beckes and his wife. Beckes was reported to have said to his wife, 'Let us rather die together this day,' than allow them through. When the alderman's deputy for Portsoken (the ward in which St Botolph's was located), the constable and churchwardens ordered Beckes and his wife to keep the peace and allow them to pass through the garden, Beckes responded by striking out at them, hitting the curate and forcing the solemn procession to retreat and change course. The next year the perambulation was more successful in asserting its right to pass through Beckes's garden and after effecting an entry it stopped to distribute points to the accompanying children and especially remind them of the parish's right of way.[69] The determination of the parish officers to assert their right of way on perambulation was perhaps influenced by the difficulties they experienced in frequent legal disputes over purprestures on parish lands. The most detailed descriptions of the perambulation were entered in the parish Memoranda Book in October 1596, a time when the vestry set up a committee to look into encroachments on parish property and was engaged in a protracted dispute over a wall built on part of the newly acquired second burial ground. The St Botolph's perambulation also became involved in confrontations with officials of the Tower of London when the procession passed near the Tower postern. The touchiness of the Tower's officials, who challenged the perambulation's right of way with a contingent of armed men, was a frequent source of dispute with civic processions if they passed too near the boundary of the liberty of the Tower on the western side of Tower Hill. The limits of the Tower of London's jurisdiction were a key area of boundary disputes between civic processions and royal officials: a mayoral procession which passed near the Tower liberty occasioned a large-scale riot by apprentices in June 1595–96. The smaller and decidedly less well armed parochial officials had frequent encounters with the Underporter and Headborough of the Tower liberty. The perambulation of the parish was usually rounded off with a return to the church for a short service of thanksgiving before the parish officers retired to a nearby tavern. In the case of St Botolph's this might be the Maiden Head in East Smithfield or the Blue Bell, where in 1597 the parish officers 'friendly they spent their money and dined there'.[70]

One reason why the officials of parishes like St Botolph's were so concerned to delineate the formal boundaries of the parish was that they were increasingly concerned to demonstrate publicly the geographical limits of their responsibility for poor relief and the extent of the area in which they had the right to collect poor rates. As we have seen, an increasing proportion of parish business was taken up with the relief as well as the moral supervision and control of the poor. Parochial ceremony thus took on aspects of ritualized subjugation which influenced the form of charitable bequests. Doles were usually given out after divine service, at which the recipients were forced to pray in thanksgiving for the generosity of their benefactors. The Protestant emphasis on charity as a duty to God by the elect tended to turn the poor into objects of the charity of the rich.[71] On Sundays at St Bartholomew by the Exchange alms were distributed to the poor immediately after the reading of the gospel, who were to sit in special pews at the upper end of the chancel, 'there not only to praise God for his benefits in moving the hearts of godly persons to give relief but also to be ready at hand to receive the same'.[72] Pensioners were to be examined on their religious knowledge before receiving aid. Pensions were to be withheld for ignorance of the creed as well as failure to attend services, bad behaviour in church or evidence of immorality outside it. At the distribution of alms under the 1612 bequest of Robert Dow (or Dove), Merchant Taylor, in St Botolph's Without Aldgate, the parish clerk was to exhort the recipients to come to church to serve God every Sunday and holy day on pain of loosing their pensions, after which the poor were to kneel down, 'and humbly, with heart and hand lift up to God', recite the Lord's prayer and say, 'God reward all good benefactors, and bless the Worshipful Company of Merchant Taylors.'[73] Similar directions in other charitable bequests could be reproduced many times. The Reformation brought a concern for greater discrimination in charitable giving and the ceremonial parts of bequests seems to have been part of this process by which only the 'deserving poor' would be eligible for relief.

A concurrent development in the preoccupation with the monitoring of the behaviour of the 'deserving poor' was the disciplining and control of the recalcitrant poor. To this end many parishes set up whipping posts, stocks and 'cages' (small temporary prisons) for the punishment and detention of vagabonds apprehended within the parish boundary.[74] Parishes instituted special searches by their constables to apprehend vagrants within the locality. In preparation for the coronation of James I the constables of the precinct of St Katherine's by the Tower set about a wholesale moral 'cleansing' of the area involving the rounding up and punishment of all suspicious persons, rogues, beggars and lewd women.[75] St Katherine's may have been particularly vigilant because of it proximity to the tower and its liminal status as extramural area. The constables' accounts and memoranda book record yearly payments for the whipping and carting of women as well their punishment by 'ducking and cucking'.[76] Such ritual public punishments were part and parcel of the inherited framework of Elizabethan parochial government which had existed in the fifteenth century and in that sense were nothing new.[77] But London's population growth combined with a renewed emphasis on banishing the sin of idleness in reformed theology must have meant that policing the margins between the deserving and the undeserving poor was a prime aim of parish government.

How well did parochial ceremony fulfil the aim of promoting 'amity and love of neighbours'? Did it promote social stability, as Rappaport and Archer have maintained, or did it foster greater social divisions within the parish? What do the changes noticed thus far over the period, the transition from communal ritual to hierarchical ceremony, tell us about the quality of civic life in the parish and the nature of urban society as a whole in this period? Parochial ceremony undoubtedly filled some of the gaps left in the ritual year by the reformation of the liturgy. It also may have helped to promote the sense of 'neighbourliness' which earlier customs had sought to embody. The records of St Margaret Pattens record the reconciliation of disputes amongst parishioners; in one instance 'undecent and uncomely words' between two parishioners were resolved by the vestry with the promise that 'strife is remitted and forgiven from the beginning of the world until this present day'.[78] Perhaps the agreement to provide money for a buck, wine, bread and fruit for an annual audit dinner reached by four of the vestry at that time lubricated the process of reconciliation. Settlements were further ensured by the payment of bonds for good behaviour (20s at St Margaret's) and a 40s fine to the poor box.[79] Another way in which parishes helped to lessen the effects of social conflict was in the frequent provision of emergency relief to orphaned pauper children, who might be nursed, clothed and apprenticed to Christ's Hospital at the expense of the parish. Such periodic poor relief was, however, dispensed without the ceremonial discipline required at the performance of charitable bequests. The importance of these small acts of humanity in the amelioration of suffering is impossible to overestimate and must have done much to add to the stability of urban society, though as poverty increased in the later sixteenth century the ability of parishes to provide such personal small-scale relief may have been severely limited as parishes participated in city-wide schemes which involved compulsory levies on householders.

It would thus be wrong to see the parochial system as completely breaking down in the face of a growing crisis in urban society in this period. However, the growing number of poor, the periodic attacks of plague, the policies of civic government to combat the effects of these problems, and the divisive effects of puritan rhetoric clearly had a profound impact on the nature of parochial institutions. The parish was transformed from a 'ritual unit' into a unit of local government. Parish elites increasingly took power away from the rest of the inhabitants and treated church property as their own, using church stock as a source of revenue to be disposed of as they saw fit. It would be tempting to make a correlation between the trend toward oligarchy and one or other of the religious tendencies of late Elizabethan Protestantism. Certainly during the religious conflicts of the 1640s closed vestries came to be associated with the defence of Laudian innovations in ceremony.[80] But there is little evidence that the ceremonial closure of ranks can be directly linked with doctrinal factionalism.

These trends did not go unchallenged at a local level. When in 1607 the parishioners and subsidy men of St Saviour's Southwark petitioned Parliament against the select vestry of thirty men who they alleged had against all law and equity usurped the right of the commonalty to a say in the running of the parish they attacked the way in which the select vestry treated the parish as a select dining club: 'They call themselves Vestrymen, Masters, and Governors of the parish. They spend thirty pounds a year, or thereabouts, in feasting themselves and their wives, ... they benefit themselves with leases of the church lands, to the great hinderance of the poor ...'.[81] Interestingly the parishioners compared their usurped rights to the popular elections to the House of Commons, the Common Council of the City, Convocation, and other assemblies 'in cities, boroughs and parishes of England'.[82] Hierarchical government in the parishes thus was related to that which pertained in the city and the nation as a whole, an association that was to be made in the 1640s. It was bound to create as much conflict as consensus. Many of the select vestries were, like the system of government of the liveries and that of the city, subject to attempts to make them more open to popular participation during the political upheavals of the Civil War.[83] Most importantly for the themes of this chapter, however, is the way in which the private dinners and restricted assemblies of the vestries were seen as part of the way in which the parishes were dominated by a hierarchy of wealth and privilege. The circumscribed ceremonials of the parishes of Elizabethan London may have acted as a force for stability, but they also symbolically and actually reordered parochial society.

NOTES

1 GL MS 4249. Bentley is discussed in C. M. Barron, *The Parish of St Andrew Holborn* (1979), p. 31, and Archer, *Pursuit*, pp. 84, 94, 95.

2 GL MS 4249, fos 221, 222v.

3 *Ibid.*, fos 227, 228, 229v.

4 *Ibid.*, fo. 230v.

5 *Ibid.*, fos 232, 234.

6 *Ibid.*, fo. 234.

7 *Ibid.*, fo. 235. Cf. E. Freshfield ed., *The Vestry Minutes and other Records of St Christopher le Stocks* (1886), p. vii.

8 GL MS 4249, fos 238 ff.

9 A good definition of ritual is provided by Edward Muir, *Ritual in Early Modern Europe* (Cambridge, 1997). See also P. Burke, *Popular Culture in Early Modern Europe* (New York, 1978).

10 Many of these studies take their inspiration from P. Clark and P. Slack eds, *Crisis and Order in English Towns 1500–1700* (1972).

11 C. Phythian-Adams, 'Ceremony and the citizen: the communal year at Coventry, 1450–1550', in Clark and Slack, *Crisis and Order*.

12 Valerie Pearl, 'Change and stability in seventeenth-century London', *LJ*, 5 (1979).

13 Rappaport, *Worlds*; Archer, *Pursuit*.

14 Pearl, 'Change and stability'; Frank Freeman Foster, *The Politics of Stablity: A Portrait of the Rulers in Elizabethan London* (1977).

15 C. Haigh, *The English Reformations: Religion, Politics and Society under the Tudors* (Oxford, 1993); Eamon Duffy, *Stripping the Altars: Traditional Religion in England 1400–1580* (New Haven CT and London, 1992); K. Wrightson, 'The politics of the parish', in P. Griffiths, A. Fox and S. Hindle eds, *The Experience of Authority in Early Modern England* (Basingstoke, 1996). A good summary of recent thinking about the impact of the Reformation is provided by R. Tittler, *The Reformation and the Towns in England: Politics and Political Culture c. 1540–1640* (Oxford, 1998).

16 C. M. Barron, 'The parish fraternities of medieval London', in C. Harper-Bill and C. M. Barron eds, *The Church in Pre-Reformation Society: Essays in Honour of F. R. H. du Boulay* (1985); G. Rosser, 'Communities of parish and guild in the late Middle Ages', in S. J. Wright ed., *Parish, Church and People: Local Studies in Lay Religion* (1988).

17 Beat A. Kümin, *The Shaping of a Community: the Rise and Reformation of the English Parish 1400–1560* (Aldershot, 1996); Alexandra F. Johnston and Sally-Beth Maclean, 'Reformation and resistance in the Thames/Severn parishes: the dramatic witness', in K. L. French, Gary G. Gibbs and Beat A. Kümin eds, *The Parish in English Life* (Manchester, 1997).

18 The most systematic account of the transformation of popular customs in early modern England is Ronald Hutton, *The Rise and Fall of Merry England: The Ritual Year 1400–1700* (Oxford, 1994). The changing ceremonial cycle of London is discussed in L. Manley, *Literature and Culture in Early Modern London* (Cambridge, 1995), chap. 5, and M. Berlin, 'Civic ceremony in early modern London', *Urban History Yearbook* (1986). See also David Cressy, *Bonfire and Bells: National Memory and the Protestant Calendar in Elizabethan and Stuart England* (1989).

19 Foster, *Politics of Stability*, p. 29 ff.

20 Gowing, *Domestic*, pp. 39–41.

21 Machyn, *Diary*, pp. 132, 287, 62–3 (St Peter's Cornhill, 1554), 103, 132 (St Giles Cripplegate, 1556). For the use of parish processions as a element of Marian revivalism see S. Brigden, *London and the Reformation* (Oxford, 1989), pp. 383–4.

22 Machyn, *Diary*, p. 145.

23 Kingsford, *Stow*, I, p. 200. See also Machyn, *Diary*, p. 20. Machyn's record of Fenchurch Street maypole noted that on the same day, 26 May 1551, 'the lord mayre by conselle causyd yt to be [taken] down and broken'. For other local celebrations of May customs in Machyn see *Diary*, p. 89 (giants, hobbyhorses and morris dancers at St Martin's in the Fields, 1555), p. 137 ('a go[d]ly May-game', Fenchurch Street, 1557), p. 201 (St John Zachary, 24 June, but described as a 'May-game'), p. 283 ('a grett May-polle by bochers and fysher-men, fulle of hornes' at Cuckold Haven, 1562).

24 *Ibid.*, pp. 63, 89, 138.

25 Cf. the conclusions of Charles Phythian-Adams, *Local History and Folklore* (1975), who regards the parish as a ritual unit, a concept to which I am obviously indebted. See also P. Burke, 'The repudiation of ritual in early modern Europe' in his *The Cultural Anthropology of Early Modern Italy* (Cambridge, 1987).

26 *VCH, London*, I (Ecclesiastical History), pp. 321–5. Some churchwardens' accounts record payments for holly and ivy at Christmas throughout the period under study. See GL MSS 4570, fo. 91 (holly, ivy and frankincense, St Margaret Pattens); 6836, fos lv, 3v (payments for holly and ivy at Christmas as well as birch at midsummer, St Helen's Bishopsgate).

27 The following discussion of the householder is indebted to A. M. Dingle, 'The Role of the Householder in Early Stuart London', University of London M.Phil. thesis (1974). For a systematic account of the workings of parish government see Archer, *Pursuit*, chap. 3.

28 Pearl, 'Change and stability', p.17.

29 GL MS 4352/1, fos 14–14v.

30 *Ibid.*, p. 81.

31 GL MS 3016/1, fo. 121.

32 *Ibid.*, fo. 125.

33 The creation of select vestries is discussed in Foster, *Politics of Stability*, p. 43 n, and A. Argent, 'Aspects of the Ecclesiastical History of the Parishes of the City of London 1640–1649 (with special reference to the parish clergy)', University of London Ph.D. thesis (1984), esp. chap. 1.

34 GL MS 3016/1, fo. 2.

35 *Ibid.*, fo. 43.

36 S. and B. Webb, *English Local Government from the Revolution to the Municipal Corporations Act: The Parish and the County* (1906) p. 184 *infra*.

37 GL MS 4165/1, fos 47, 53, 68.

38 GL MS 3016/1, fo. 43.

39 Cited in Christopher Hill, *Society and Puritanism in Pre-revolutionary England* (1964), p. 434. See also Archer, *Pursuit*, pp. 73–4.

40 GL MS 878/1, fo. 1.

41 For example, GL MSS 2590/1, fo. 19; 4352/1, fo. 13.

42 GL MS 4249, fo. 5v.

43 Margaret Aston, 'Segregation in church', in W. J. Sheils and D. Wood eds, *Women in Church*, Studies in Church History, 27 (1990).

44 At St Lawrence Jewry pews were constructed for resident aldermen as well as the Recorder of London in 1570; the 'great stone' used for the sepulchre was to be removed for this purpose (GL MS 2590/1, fo. 34). At St Dunstan in the East the church was re-edified and special pews were constructed in anticipation of the mayoralty of William Webb (GL MS 4887, fo. 296). At St Dunstan in the West pews were provided for judges from the neighbouring Inns (GL MS 3016/1, fo. 169). J. F. Merritt, 'Puritans, Laudians, and the phenomenon of church-building in Jacobean London', *Historical Journal*, 41 (1998), p. 941, notes the construction of new pews in the programmes of refurbishing churches in the early seventeenth century.

45 GL MS 4887, fo. 180.

46 C. Hill, *Economic Problems of the Church* (Oxford, 1956), pp. 175–82.

47 The vestry of St Dunstan in the West agreed in 1628 that the churchwardens should 'place in the galleries of the said Church so many of the auncientest and better sort of the parishioners which have not borne office ...' (GL MS 3016/1, fo. 125).

48 GL MSS 1175, fo. 25; 4072/1, pt 1, fos 20v, 25v.

49 GL MSS 3016/1, fo. 125; 1172/1, fo. 8v; 2590/1, fo. 93.

50 GL MS 1175/1, fo. 40v.

51 GL MSS 1454, Roll 96; 4415/1, fo. 13v; 819/1, fo. 12. Cf. St Martin Ludgate, where pensioners were allowed 1s weekly to 'look to the boyes' during sermons as well as keeping watch at the vestry door 'for unrewly fellows' (GL MS 1311/1, fo. 110).

52 GL MS 1311/1, fo. 97.

53 GL MSS 819/1, fo. 11; 1175/1, fo. 51; 3016/1, fo. 169.

54 GL MS 4249, fos 12–12v. See also P. Griffiths, 'Secrecy and authority in late sixteenth- and seventeenth-century London', *HJ*, 40 (1997).

55 GL MS 1175/1, fos 8v, 25, 30, 33, 55v.

56 Dingle, 'Role of the Householder', pp. 159, 236.

57 GL MS 877/1, fo. 40.

58 GL MS 3016/1, fo. 33.

59 GL MS 4570, fo. 450.

60 GL MS 3016/1, fos 129, 187.

61 GL MSS 9234/1, fos 12, 20; 9234/2, fo. 90; 9234/5, fo. 22; 9234/7, fos 49, 165.

62 GL MS 4887, fos 305, 309, 322.

63 GL MS 9234, fo. 37.

64 GL MS 1311/1, fos 113v–114. His will stated that he was ready to 'inherit the joys prepared in heaven for God's elect servants'.

65 Keith Thomas, *Religion and the Decline of Magic* (Harmondsworth, 1973), pp. 71–5.

66 GL MS 9234/5, fos 260–260v. See also E. Freshfield ed., *Accomptes of the Churchwardens of the Paryshe of St Christofer's in London 1575 to 1662* (1885), pp. 50, 52, 53, 54, 55, 60, 78, 80 (St Christopher's le Stocks); J. E. Cox ed., *The Annals of St Helen's, Bishopsgate, London* (1876), p. 222. Cf. the remarks of Sir John Hawkins's *History of Music*, quoted in John Brand, *Observations on Popular Antiquities in England and Wales* (1900), p. 114: 'in order to perpetuate the memories of their boundaries, and to impress the remembrance thereof in the minds of young persons, especially boys; to invite boys therefore, to attend this business, some little gratuities necessary; accordingly, it was the custom, at the commencement of the procession, to each a willow wand, and that at the end thereof a handful of points, which were looked on by them as honorary rewards long after they ceased to be useful, and were called tags'.

67 GL MS 4165/1, fo. 30v.

68 GL MSS 9234/1, fos 56, 77v; 9234/2, fos 56v, 62, 74; 9234/4, fos 162–162v; 9234/5, fos 77, 227; 9234/6, fo. 247; 9234/7, fos 101–2; 9234/8, fos 85–6, 260–260v.

69 GL MS 9234/5, fos 85–6.

70 GL MSS 9234/3 fos 61–61v (encounter with tower officials); 9234/5, fo. 227 (meal at the Mayden Head); 9234/6, fo. 247 (meal at the Blue Bell). Parish officers also partook of meals at taverns when they went about their daily affairs; an account of expenses of the building of 'parish houses' at St Botolph Aldgate records the cost of 'suppers' when an agreement was made (9236, fo. 12). At St Margaret Pattens the churchwardens held a breakfast at a tavern when a lease was sealed (4570, fo. 216).

71 Hill, *Society and Puritanism*, pp. 282–3.

72 E . Freshfield ed., *The Account Books of the Parish of St Bartholomew Exchange in the City of London 1596–1698* (1895), p. 5.

73 The benefaction is detailed in Strype, *Stow*, II, pp. 361–5. It laid particular emphasis on the behaviour of the recipients 'for as much as the Poor these days are given unto too much idleness and little labour to get'. That Dow may have had some personal experience of the potential insolence of social inferiors may be inferred by the punishment meted out to a Widow Tompkins who was sent to Bridewell in 1598 'for casting certain foul bowls of beastlynesse' against Dow's back door (GL MS 9234/7, fo. 137).

74 GL MSS 4165/1, fo. 106; 6836, fos 91v, 135. (St Helen's Bishopsgate provided stocks and a whipping post.) See also the examples listed in W. F. Cobb, *The Church of St Ethelburga the Virgin ... The Churchwardens and their Accounts* (1905), p. 11; E. Pendrill, *Old Parish Life in London* (Oxford, 1937), pp. 201–3.

75 GL MS 9630, fo. 12.

76 *Ibid.*, fos 8, 11, 16 ('ducking and cucking'), 21, 26.

77 M. Spufford, 'Puritanism and social control', in A. J. Fletcher and J. Stevenson eds, *Order and Disorder in Early Modern England* (Cambridge, 1987).

78 GL MS 4570/1, fo. 438.

79 *Ibid.*, fo. 440.

80 Keith Lindley, *Popular Politics and Religion in Civil War London* (Aldershot, 1997), chap. 3.

81 The petition is reprinted in full in Strype, *Stow*, II, p. 11, and discussed in Archer, *Pursuit*, pp. 73–4.

82 Strype, *Stow*, II, p. 11.

83 Hill, *Society and Puritanism*, p. 423; Lindley, *Popular Politics and Religion*, pp. 55–60.

Chapter 4

Thief-takers and their clients in later Stuart London

Tim Wales

One January morning in 1696 the sheriffs of London entered Newgate in search of coin clippers. They came 'with drawn swordes and a great Attendance, some thiefe-takers some serjeants', and searched the pockets and trunks of Thomas Carter and David Davies. They found money there (some of which Davies claimed had been left with them by his sister for safe keeping). Who were these thief-takers who partnered the sheriffs and City officers and who, according to Davies, had secured him and rifled his pockets in 'most rude and barbarous manner'? Davies had his own answer and named names: '[Du]n, St Ledger Rouse Jenkins with several others formerly Convicts but now knowne by the name of Theife [takers].' And amongst those who deposed against Carter and Davies were Anthony St Leger, Bodenham Rewse and James Jenkins, all significant figures in the trade of thief-taking.[1]

The events of that morning bring one close to the main themes of this chapter. I shall describe the work of thief-takers in the late seventeenth century to explore the relationship between private activity and public authority in the policing of the capital. Davies was right to associate thief-takers and convicts, for several thief-takers had a background in, and all had connections with, criminal networks. Much of their trade lay in brokering the return of stolen goods to their owners, a trade which involved ambiguous relations with thieves. It was claimed that 'the Practice of pretended Thief-takers, was, to compound felonies for the Thieves, to prevent their Prosecutions, and to harbour them, and receive their stoll'n Goods'.[2] Such a description captures the position of thief-takers as brokers while underplaying the complexity of their role and the extent of popular and 'official' tolerance of such practices. During the 1690s, however, the state made greater use of thief-takers and their knowledge of criminal networks in its pursuit of coiners and plotters.

Indeed, it is due to the participation of thief-takers in the prosecution of clippers and coiners in the 1690s that we can identify them and their shifting penumbra of associates. Looking at court records, one can see major thief-takers acting in a variety of cases and roles. But the density of detail is provided by individuals who appear acting against coiners in pre-trial depositions, on recognizances to prosecute, and as witnesses listed on indictments. We can pick out eleven leading thief-takers in the 1690s (alongside other lesser figures): Rewse, Jenkins, St Leger, Anthony Dunn, John Gibbons, John Bonner, John Connell, Robert Saker (or Seagers) , Richard Summers, John Anderson and Caleb Clarke. They and their clients and associates are my principal protagonists.

Thief-takers are a shadowy group, who are known best from a small number of high-profile individuals like Jonathan Wild, the self-styled Thief-taker General of Great Britain and Ireland, or Stephen McDaniel and John Berry, who notoriously set up innocent people for rewards dependent upon their conviction. Recent research has gone far towards providing an account of thief-taking more sensitive to the continuities in its practices over several centuries and its immediate social and judicial contexts.[3] Such work shows how thief-taking prospered in a system where the detection of felonies was largely a private matter. Thief-takers filled a void, providing services that a public watch patrolling the streets did not. Much of their story over the 250 years for which we can discern their existence exhibits continuities based on structures of prosecution and law enforcement, and on the priorities of victims of theft. Indeed, if one focuses on thief-taking less as a form of privatized policing than as a set of relations between police and policed, such continuities stretch well beyond the formation of new police forces after 1800 to today's symbiotic relationship between police and criminal, where the police seek information and the criminals influence. Dick Hobbs's work on the relationship between detectives and working-class culture in the East End of the 1980s is highly suggestive here. He presents a picture of the obtrusive presence of detectives, spending time in pubs making contacts, who at once take bearings from local culture and owe more to it than to official prescription. Detectives are informal resources of information and play a game in which their expertise and influence are bargained for information.[4] Much of this is fairly consistent with thief-taking in early modern London; some of it can be directly paralleled from the records.

   These striking continuities show thief-takers at different points in time responding to the demands of potential clients and exploiting institutional arrangements to their advantage. Incentives offered by rewards, the development of police offices, and the changing balance of power within the court as defence counsel exposed testimonies to sharper scrutiny all impacted on practices of thief-taking.[5] Indeed, the role of thief-takers as entrepreneurs responding to shifts in demand renders them a good illustration of social and judicial changes.

A sharpened consciousness of crime was apparent in the 1690s when metropolitan and national authorities turned to the services of thief-takers more frequently. In what follows, the relationship of thief-taking to popular and official understandings of crime and justice will be emphasized. The national and metropolitan political contexts of thief-taking will be explored. I also hope to contribute something to the developing history of relations between police and policed.[6] Throughout thief-takers are seen as brokers between their very different sets of clients; their responses to the priorities of each group will be examined. I will first identify different elements in the demand for thief-takers and then discuss several leading figures and their networks. Finally, I will explore how thief-takers positioned themselves between their sets of clients, establishing themselves as figures of authority and credibility in different spheres of legality and criminality.

A New Dictionary of the Terms Ancient and Modern the Canting Crew (1699) defined thief-takers as those 'who make a Trade of helping People (for a gratuity) to their lost Goods and sometimes for interest or Envy snapping the Rogues themselves, being usually in fee with them, and acquainted with their Haunts'.[7] This trade grew with the great expansion of London's population and the diversification of its economy in the later seventeenth century. For many victims of theft, the priority was to get their property back or some financial recompense from the thief rather than to prosecute. In 1663 the Recorder of London noted how shoplifters would compound with shop-keepers, and that shopkeepers, if they could not get the goods from the thief, would extract the cost from the next shoplifter they laid hands on. The shop-keeper's priority was restitution. A more dramatic scale of compounding is suggested by William Sutton's claim in 1692 that he had been forced to pay £400 on bonds given by his wife 'in composition of Robberyes Felonies Thefts & other Crimes comitted by her'.[8] This was an area of activity that lay outside the formal mechanisms of prosecution, which inevitably leaves little trace in records. There were advantages for all parties in reaching a financial composition: whether a criminal making monetary recompense to avoid the rigours of the law, or victims paying a fee to get their goods back. Brokering the return of stolen goods was, as *The Life of Mary Frith* (1662) put it, 'A Lawless Vocation yet bordering between illicit and convenient, more advantagious by far to the injured than the Courts of Justice and benefits of the Law.'[9]

Newspaper advertisements also point up the frequent preference for resti-tution over prosecution. Many in London, as in eighteenth-century Yorkshire, called for the return of goods described as lost but which must often have been stolen: otherwise some people were remarkably careless with their purses, horses, jewellery and bonds.[10] In May 1696, for example, £109 in gold and silver was 'lost' near Bushey on the Watford road, for which a twenty-guinea reward was offered, and '4 Lockets, with a Gold Inamelled Ring set with a Ruby Stone cut long and square, Table fashion, all set upon a black Ribond' were 'lost' between St Albans Street and Hatton Garden.'' This emphasis reflected a concern with social restitution; a desire to evade the expense of prosecution and a hard-headed recognition that getting one's goods back for a fee was often the best that one could hope for in a situation where inter-mediaries were passports to criminal circles.

Newspaper advertisements and handbills were part of the practices of thief-taking; private citizens sought to enlist or sidestep the services of a thief-taker by offering a reward and contacts to whom goods or information should be sent. Thief-takers also advertised their services: Jonathan Wild publicized his 'Lost Property Office' as a front for the return of stolen goods. There are only hints of this development in the 1690s. In 1696, for example, the thief-taker James Jenkins offered a two-guinea reward, 'or if Bought or Pawned their money again with Content', for the return of a gold oval picture-case stolen from a lady's closet.'² By Anne's reign, John Bonner was advertising his services in a more direct way:

> This is to give notice that those who have sustained any loss at Sturbridge Fair last, by Pick Pockets or Shop lifts: If they please to apply themselves to John Bonner in Shorts Gardens, they may receive information and assistance therein; also Ladies and others who lose their Watches at Churches, and other Assemblies, may be served by him as aforesaid, to his utmost power, if desired by the right Owner, he being paid for his Labour and Expences.'³

By the 1690s rewards offered by private citizens were supplemented by statutory rewards. Indeed, the most significant new opportunity for thief-takers was the offer of rewards of £40 for the successful prosecution of highwaymen (from 1693), and of clippers and counterfeiters (from 1695). A further statute (1699) offered a certificate of exemption for burglars and house-breakers (converted into a £40 reward in 1706). These rewards, especially those offered for the prosecution of coiners, were to have a major impact on the profits of thief-taking. Informing for profit had long been acceptable in the prosecution of breaches of socio-economic regulations, and this principle was extended to the pursuit of felons by parliamentary ordinance during the 1650s and through *ad hoc* rewards offered by proclamation after the Restoration.'⁴

Such developments belonged to a general intensification of the demand for informers in the later seventeenth century, a time of major plots, real and imagined, which gave informers opportunities to save their necks or to pocket a reward. Post-Restoration anxieties about political and religious dissidence also encouraged the use of spies by both local loyalists and central govern-ment, most notably by Charles II's security chief, Sir Joseph Williamson.'⁵

London saw two great waves of informing: the harrying of Nonconformists by John Hilton and his associates between 1682 and 1686 and the campaign for moral reformation in the 1690s. In these different campaigns private informers and their connections in public office pushed forward prosecutions more aggressively than would have been possible under the formal mechanisms of policing.[16]

Political fears encouraged the use of informers, as well as a general concern with crime. This was in part a response to the problems of the metropolis and to concern with the defence of the currency. Finally, it represented a redrawing of the image of crime in the light of models borrowed from images of political and religious dissent. Crime in London had long concerned the national authorities, but fears sharpened and expanded towards 1700, changes that are revealed in the new responsibilities of provost marshals. When Gilbert Thomas received his commission as provost marshal in Middlesex, Westminster, Southwark and Surrey in 1664 his remit was, conventionally enough, to deal with murder, robbery and vagrancy, but also to pursue the new threat of Quakers, who, it was felt, plotted against the government and circulated seditious books. In 1666 Thomas was writing to the Earl of Arlington, evaluating the evidence of spies and informers.[17]

Later seventeenth-century regimes placed greater emphasis on serious crimes against property – highway robbery, burglary, housebreaking and clipping and counterfeiting the coinage. There was an intensified engagement with the 'problem' of order, but also a shift in how it was defined, for these crimes were regarded as the acts of *criminal gangs*.[18] Official perceptions became preoccupied with the idea of gangs: an extension no doubt of themes lifted from earlier rogue literatures, but also something new. Highwaymen were a particular concern from the 1660s: proclamations and warrants were issued to the keeper of Newgate to organize horse patrols (1678, 1689, 1693). A royal proclamation against highway robbery in 1690 targeted fifteen 'persons notoriously known to be persons who daily commit such offences in despite and defiance of law and are some or most of them indicted or accused upon oath and are of them known to be of one Party and Knot do keep company the one with the other and all of them fly from Justice'.[19] (The phrase 'one party and knot' is suggestive, as it reflects broader shifts in perceived threats to the social and political order – fears about sectarians banded together in opposition to the state.)

This shift was directly related to anxieties about crime – highwaymen or coiners were sometimes linked with political conspiracy. These claims were on occasion made by men and women who introduced accusations of treasonable plotting to add colour to their attempts to escape the gallows feeding the authorities facts; the highwayman James Whitney tried to save his neck by claiming that he had information about a plot to assassinate William

III. In such and other ways highwaymen could become political characters. Some of them declared allegiance to King James; a number of them turned to this way of life after the King's army was disbanded by his successor, thus confirming other anxieties connecting crime with demobilization. Other criminals flatly declared their political position: a coiner locked up in Newgate threatened to shoot the warden of the Mint if King James ever came back.[20]

Concern with coining shows a similar mix of motives. Clipping diminished the silver content of the currency. This was a 'problem' in the period 1670–90 and a 'crisis' in the war years thereafter. The difference between the actual and the face value of silver rose from 16 per cent to 49 per cent between 1689 and 1694.[21] This concern also had political dimensions, ranging from the symbolism of an offence which was treason in the 1690s to the Jacobite affiliations of some coiners and clippers. The broader symbolic association of coining with political dissidency explains why a major drive against coining was also launched in the 1680s at the height of the reassertion of authority during the Tory reaction.[22]

The career of William Chaloner in the 1690s is a case study in the political nature of much coining activity. He attempted to infiltrate his own man into the Mint to act as an agent against clippers, and proposed methods to Parliament to improve the currency. He also accused a secretary of state of treasonable plotting with Jacobites, but was himself a forger. The authorities' pursuit of him and his associates – including Thomas Carter and David Davies, who had sheltered Fenwick conspirators – takes up many pages of the depositions collected by the warden of the Mint, Isaac Newton. These stories describe a grey area where conspiratorial politics and crime intersect: Chaloner attempted to accuse leading political figures of treason and to barge in on the Mint, while simultaneously creating a place for himself inside criminal networks.[23] Coining also confirmed perceptions of criminal gangs, vulnerable to the temptations of rewards and the activities of thief-takers.

Other perceptions of disorder in the 1690s also encouraged thief-taking. The Reformation of Manners campaign provided one such source. As well as a deep concern with a rising tide of theft in the 1690s, magistrates were also motivated by a long-standing desire to reform manners and a fear of the poor at a time when 'problems' raised by poverty were sharpened by a run of bad harvests, currency manipulation, and the damage to overseas trade by French commercial raiding.[24] The 1690 proclamation should also be read in terms of an intensification of the threat of the disorderly poor: the Black Guard of youths, for example, who haunted wharves, or the grand jury's 1694 complaint about the great influx of people lacking 'visible estates or honest way to mainteyne themselves ... [who] turn Robbers on the highway, Burglarers, pickpockets'.[25] A campaign for moral reformation, triggered by providentialist interpretations of the events of 1688, merged with concerns about rising

London crime. Significantly, the Tower Hamlets Society – the first Reformation society (among whose numbers were two men who later became leading thief-takers) was formed in response to the 1690 proclamation against highwaymen – it urged the suppression of brothels, 'the nurseries of the most horrid vices, and sinks of the most filthy debaucheries ... [and] (as we suppose them) the common receptacles, or rather, dens, of notorious thieves, robbers, traitors and other criminals, that fly from public justice'.[26]

Prompted by these concerns, leading government officials employed thief-takers in rising numbers. In 1667 Thomas Martin, who was charged with housebreaking at Surrey Assizes, petitioned for a reprieve. He claimed that the Lord Chief Justice, who knew both of his close ties with highwaymen and that he had recently been framed by some of them, had ordered him to apprehend highway robbers. A month later he presented the judges with his warrant from the Duke of Albemarle to take thieves, hoping thereby to boost his case for a pardon.[27] In the early 1670s Sir William Morton, justice of the King's Bench, wrote to Sir Joseph Williamson about his running of thief-takers and leaning on suspects to turn King's evidence in property cases. In 1669 he asked Williamson to add the names of seventeen highwaymen to a royal proclamation appearing in the *London Gazette*: others were not to be named until a few days later as, Morton wrote, 'I have emissaries out to take them others'.[28]

Morton and Williamson discussed individual cases, but their concern was general. In 1672 Morton requested £290 for expenses in his pursuit of highwaymen.[29] His activities show how far the central authorities shared a crime-consciousness that led almost inevitably to the employment of thief-takers. Mint officials developed relationships with individual thief-takers. The 1680s also saw moves to strengthen the hand of the Treasury Lords and the Mint in granting rewards and overseeing prosecutions. Mint officials also developed a stake in direct detection; they employed a clerk to the warden as a taker of coiners.[30] The pursuit of coiners also shows the same manipulation of pardons to elicit information. In 1683 Henry Guy at the Treasury wrote to the Attorney-general, forwarding a J. P.'s petition for a warrant to apprehend a fugitive clipper in order to make maximum use of this potential 'grass'. In London the scale of both prosecutions and the involvement of thief-takers rose to new levels in the 1690s. In 1693 the Mint warden wrote that he had 'deputed (newly) severall Trusty persons to prosecute such Criminalls upon notice given Thereof to my Office in the Mint in the Tower'.[31] The appointment of Isaac Newton as warden resulted in a rise in the use of thief-takers; in 1696 he referred to 'my Agents' and 'My Agents & Witnesses' – these 'agents' were freelance thief-takers, a point confirmed by the names of witnesses appearing before Newton and his use of thief-takers as expert advisers.[32] Rewards had a further appeal for the authorities, as they were a way of encouraging private initiatives in law enforcement. A sermon of 1694 blasted 'that soft pernicious tenderness that sometimes, certainly, restrains the hand of Justice, that slackens the care and vigilance of Magistrates, keeps back the Under-Officers, corrupts the Juries (for Passions and Affections bribe as well as Gifts) and with-holds the Evidence, both from appearing and from speaking out, when they appear'.[33]

Statutory rewards may, at one level, have had rather limited impact on the activities of thief-takers. The impact of the statute against highwaymen was apparently muted. Rewards for coiners and clippers almost certainly did make a difference in the short run, as 1696 saw a peak of prosecutions that dropped after the great recoinage. The sheriffs of London and Middlesex spent £3,235 7s 6d in one year (1695–96) to catch highwaymen, clippers and coiners – perhaps eighty rewards paid out on convictions.[34] However, rewards alone would not have generated the structures of thief-taking, which, in any case, were already established. Statutory rewards cumulatively swelled the profits of thief-taking, and the short boom of the mid-1690s may even have attracted new recruits. But the key element of thief-taking, without which nothing was possible, was knowledge of criminal networks.

The different markets for thief-takers' services inevitably shape the ways that they appear in extant records. One of their principal services was providing an 'extra-legal' alternative to the courts, and we would not expect to find signs of this in court files. Coining provides evidence of thief-takers and their associations. By contrast, the appearance of thief-takers as witnesses in theft cases is scattered, and they are not very visible in prosecutions of highway robbery, burglary or horse theft. This disparity reflects the requirements of evidence: the methods used to track a thief were of less relevance than testimonies of the crime itself. But in coining cases, thief-takers were central to the evidence needed for a conviction: they searched houses, uncovering incriminating evidence.[35] Nevertheless, with one exception, a Mint official, no leading prosecutors of coiners prosecuted only that offence.

Thief-takers usually worked in pairs or groups: Anthony Dunn and Anthony St Leger often worked together; Bodenham Rewse and James Jenkins also. However, thief-takers worked together in shifting patterns. When St Leger was accused of taking a bribe, Rewse and Jenkins acted as his sureties. In 1699 Richard Summers, John Anderson and Robert Saker were the target of a counter-suit for forcible entry and assault, prompting John Bonner, Caleb Clarke, Nathaniel Whitebread and John Hooke to stand as their sureties. These associations were doubtless riven by tensions: for example, Bonner sued Connell for riotous assault in 1701.[36] But group solidarity is more striking, even if it only expressed the need for mutual support in cases of counter-suits or the sharing of spoils. Above all, the avoidance of open conflict was essential when thief-takers' livelihoods depended on maintaining a semi-respectable front. A turf war could (literally) be fatal.[37]

Given the fluidity of networks, it is artificial to distinguish sharply between thief-takers and their associates. Leading figures do stand out, but others could reasonably be described as thief-takers. Two types of associate are particularly interesting: constables and defendants who also appeared as prosecutors. The constable's warrant was one way of ensuring the legality of the thief-taker's search. But certain figures appear as regular prosecution witnesses and associates, including Richard Portlock, constable of St Paul's Covent Garden and an associate of Bonner, John Hooke, constable of St Sepulchre's Middlesex, who acted with Saker, Summers and Rewse, James Cooper, constable of Bread Street ward, and connected through campaigns to reform manners and prosecute clippers with Rewse and Jenkins. Hooke and Cooper continued these connections even after they left office, and Cooper operated in Middlesex (outside his formal jurisdiction) as well as in the City.[38]

Indicted criminals who may have been protected or blackmailed by thief-takers appear for a few sessions as informers against various accused and then disappear from the records. Others, like Joseph Hatfield, James Frimley and William Buxton, were as likely to be prosecuted as to give evidence for the prosecution case. Hatfield was frequently indicted for theft and was associated with John Connell.[39] William Buxton of Whitechapel was a witness against counterfeiters and was also accused of the same offence. (On one occasion he was cleared by Bonner.) In 1701 he was accused of running a house where youths gambled and drank all day, and settled 'theire scores' by picking pockets. He was a minor thief-taker and in 1698 was anticipating Wild's use of advertisements: 'Supposed to be stolen and dropped in the yard of one William Buxton in Church-Lane near Whitechapel at the Globe, by a person unknown, 3 pieces of Camblets and 2 Pieces of Grogram. If the person that lost them gives an account of their Marks, and pays the Charges, they may be had again.'[40] Buxton is a good example of how thief-takers were able to extend their reach inside criminal networks, providing information and contacts (and, in the case of Hatfield and Connell, pooling stolen goods).

The careers of several thief-takers show how the particular circumstances of the 1690s offered a route into the trade. Anthony St Leger and Anthony Dunn swapped information for a pardon and then became thief-takers: Dunn was prosecuted at the Old Bailey on five counts of felony or burglary between 1686 and 1692, and St Leger on four occasions between 1687 and 1692. Both men appear in the gang targeted by the 1690 royal proclamation, while Dunn informed against his accomplices in an Islington burglary in 1691.[41] In 1692 St Leger was pardoned for a burglary in the house of the Master of the King's Horse because he had been 'very instrumental' in discovering his accomplices. Dunn and St Leger were also bracketed together on a pardon of convicts in

Newgate 'for suspicion of several felonies' in January 1693, and, in June the same year, they petitioned the Treasury (with the support of the recorder and mayor), seeking payment for bringing clippers and coiners to book. This team seems to have broken up at some point in the later 1690s (though never being an exclusive partnership); yet both remained active thief-takers. In 1698 Dunn was awarded £80 out of the proceeds of the Malt Lottery tickets for chasing burglars; in 1703 St Leger received a reward from the Leicestershire and Wiltshire sheriffs for the conviction of highwaymen.[42]

Bodenham Rewse, a Bloomsbury embroiderer, and James Jenkins, a jeweller living off the Strand, fell into thief-taking through their activities as Reformation of Manners informers. They acted as the Tower Hamlets Society's hired men, arresting prostitutes and informing against bawdy houses, building up their knowledge of criminal networks and establishing contacts. The pair, usually working together, were the most active prosecutors of the Reformation of Manners campaign between 1693 and 1695. They then began to track larger and more profitable fry, especially clippers and coiners. Rewse is a good illustration of the political ties of thief-takers, through his participation in the capture of Jacobite conspirators after the assassination plot. (He later purchased the position of Newgate under-keeper.) As Faramerz Dabhoiwala demonstrates, Rewse and Jenkins were not just men who moved from moral crusading to chasing thieves; from the very beginning they worked for cash.[43]

John Gibbons was a minor government office holder and coffee-house keeper who stumbled into thief-taking in the conspiratorial atmosphere of the 1680s. He was a footman to the Duke of Monmouth in the early 1680s, and helped to capture hired assassins who killed Monmouth's friend, Sir Thomas Thynne, in 1682, and received a share of a £200 Crown reward published in the *London Gazette* and a £500 reward offered by Thynne's heir. He was also implicated in the conspiracies around his master in the early 1680s, being twice imprisoned, on one occasion reported as saying that he hoped to be one of those to kill the King, and that he had scouted for a suitable spot to carry out the act.[44] This poacher turned gamekeeper after the Glorious Revolution, when he was appointed a messenger of the royal chamber, where he worked under the secretaries of state, following orders and arresting suspects. He picked up £894 in rewards for Jacobites in the fall-out from the assassination plot, and scooped a share of secret service funds tracking conspirators across the country with Anthony Dunn. His official position made him a man of authority amongst thief-takers. When Dunn and St Leger arrested Mary Adams's brother, she was advised that 'Gibbons had a great interest in Mr. Dun and Mr. St Leger and could command them to use their endeavours to take evidence against her brother [off] and that there must be money to do it'. His coffee house was a hive of activity, evident in the charges bought against him for corruption. A retiring City marshal advertised it as a meeting place where 'he will settle all affairs that he had in his hands while holding that office'.[45] The charges brought against Gibbons in 1698 included blackmail, handling counterfeit money, taking bribes to tip suspects off, and that, corresponding 'with a great many Clippers and Coyners [he] used to receive several sums of money from them as contribucon for coniving at them and was wont to solicit for any of them when they were in restraint'. His downfall was rooted in conspiracy. It seems to have been a by-product of the government's pursuit of Chaloner, while testimony came from the circle of Edward Ivie, alias Jones, whose role in the 1680s plots was that of a government agent who had testified at the Earl of Shaftesbury's treason trial in 1681.[46]

Gibbons's career shows a thief-taker positioning himself as broker between the worlds of authority and crime: he had an official position, ran a coffee house which was a site where plans and plots were hatched, and built up connections with criminals and magistrates. He was a source of information and protection for coiners and highwaymen, and all in all he had the muscle to extort cash from his 'penconers'. To the authorities he was a necessary evil. Indeed, as early as 1696 he was accused, with Dunn and St Leger, of compounding with coiners (though a warrant for his arrest was issued as late as eighteen months after). Meanwhile the under-secretary, James Vernon, was unenthusiastically contemplating using his services: 'He has an old intimacy with the coining trade,' he wrote, and 'he has been one of their scouts, and if he be concerned with them in point of profit, I am afraid he will betray anyone else rather than them. But he is a tool [he continued] with so devilish an edge, that I dare not venture upon him without an allowance, and yet I think something of this nature ought to be done.'[47]

Combining evidence of patterns of demand for thief-taking with the experiences of leading thief-takers, we can see how they established their credibility within networks where officers and criminals acquired knowledge of each others' activities. Their success in claiming influence with the authorities put them in a strong position with their contacts 'on the ground'. A key figure here was the London Recorder, Sir Salathiell Lovell, who was said to smack of corruption through his ties with thief-takers. Whether he lined his pockets with bribes is not known, but that he clearly worked closely with thief-takers is clear. Lovell backed Dunn and St Leger's 1693 petition and presented himself as a powerful fighter of crime; in 1702 he described his nine years of 'trouble & fateague in the discovery and Conviccon of such offenders [i.e. coiners] and other Criminalls than any person in the Kingdome'. His legal (and political) power was boosted in 1693 through his elevated role in the pardoning process, presenting his recommendation to the Cabinet after each sessions.[48] It is not difficult to see how his authority and influence brought him into close contact with thief-takers.

Knowledge and reputation mattered greatly to thief-takers; the flow of information and clients depended as much on their prominence as on criminal and government contacts. Their status as brokers to some extent detached them from the criminal world; ordinary people had access to their services, knowing how to open contact with them. The self-presentation of thief-takers is visible in records, where they appear as mediators. The Jacobean thief-taker, John Pulman, immersed his client Robert Handes in the murky depths of criminal cultures: Handes reported how he 'spent money with Pullman at sondry tymes in company because I would see as many villaines as I could to see & heare &c in their meetinges'.[49] Above all, it was important for a thief-taker to establish himself as a reliable hunter of thieves and goods.

These two elements are neatly twinned in a 1720 trial report. Elizabeth Cole lost her purse while crossing the Thames and without a second thought asked the waterman 'if he knew any Thief Taker?' We then follow the pair walking to the Old Bailey home of one Murrel, a thief-taker, who stressed both his respectability and high profile in criminal networks, telling Cole that 'there was no Occasion for a Thief-Taker, he would be Thief-Taker himself; for he would send for them to his House, whither he was sure they would come, and then have a Constable and secure them'. We should keep in mind, of course, that Murrel was seeking to make an impression in the courtroom, and that the Old Bailey was a key site for thief-takers, a place to establish their competence before magistrates, police and people.[50]

Their frequent appearances at Old Bailey sessions made thief-takers familiar figures amongst jurors.[51] In one case Gibbons was accused of unduly using his influence with the grand jury: one Anthony Hildyard claimed that Gibbons dropped into his cell on the morning of his trial and:

> told him what services lay in his power and that he had been with the Grand Jury the day before where they dined and also that morning & acquainted them with the evidence and that he had known the Deponent [i.e. Hildyard] some years and pulling out some papers he shewd the Deponent one of them, the Import of which was to put the Grand Jurymen in mind of the Deponent and said that he designed to send those papers to the Grand Jurymen for that purpose.[52]

This courtroom influence could invest thief-takers with considerable power in trials that were short and without the pleas of defence counsel. Hay and Snyder have demonstrated how the balance of power in court that tipped towards the prosecutor could be exploited by experienced thief-takers. Coining trials are a good example of this: here thief-takers were experts who presented a case with some knowledge, but they were also highly suspect as they prosecuted for profit a crime where the law's severity was often regarded as out of proportion to the offence. Newton complained that 'the new reward of forty pounds per head has now made the Courts of Justice & Juries so averse from believing witnesses & Sheriffs so inclinable to impannel bad Juries that my Agents & Witnesses are discouraged & tired out by the want of success & by the reproach of prosecuting & swearing for money'.[53] In trials where judgement of the personalities involved was still a consideration, thief-takers had influence so long as they could win juries over.

Other business places for thief-takers included alehouses and coffee houses. The thief-takers Clarke, Hooke and Anderson were all victuallers – Anderson offered a £10 reward in 1699 after a wounded highwayman escaped from his West Smithfield alehouse. Robert Saker was a distiller.[54] These places were sites for bargaining; the Cole case was typical, as Murrel's base was a tavern. Wives also helped their thief-taker husbands to settle into local networks; it was Mrs Murrel who first spoke to Elizabeth Cole. They frequently acted as go-betweens, mainly with other women. For example, St Leger's wife negotiated with Mary Adams, who was trying to win her brother's acquittal. Adams reported that she 'was twice at St Leger's house, and the second time St Leger's wife opened a trunk full of plate and showed it to the deponent and showed her also a parcel of rich Flanders lace and other things of value which made the deponent wonder should be found in so mean a house' – an exhibition, no doubt, of the thief-taker's qualifications.[55]

Mary Connell also acted as her husband's working partner, picking up a share of an £80 reward in 1697 for the conviction of counterfeiters. She was listed as a witness when her husband chased a £100 reward for the conviction of an arsonist, and she was also accused of extorting money from Mary Harding, whom she discovered concealing stolen clothes from the back of a waggon. Stopping at a tavern on the journey to the magistrate's parlour room, Connell told Harding over a drink that:

> Shee was imployed by the waggoner who lost the Cloath to helpe him to it againe, who was to give her Eight pounds for her paines, and this informant [i.e. Harding] being putt in fear by the aforesaid Menaces, shee did then give Mary Connell Four Guineas in Gold, and about a week afterwards Mary Connell sent for this informant to the Dogg tavern in Drury Lane, and there by Threatnings and Canting upon her sometimes gieving her Sweet words and sometimes Sower, did then extort from this informant againe the Further Somme of Four Guineas more in Gold, saying I'le make it upp you shall never here noe more of it.[56]

This is more than a simple story of extortion: Connell was clearly dealing with receivers of stolen goods, an offence that was usually perceived and prosecuted as a crime of women. Similarly, the prominence of women in coining offences helps to explain the participation of Saker's wife in setting up a counterfeiter.[57]

On occasion, neighbours tipped thief-takers off about coiners, but in many other cases coiners were themselves well known in criminal circles. There is evidence of coiners who were connected with highwaymen and other thieves, unsurprisingly perhaps, given their access to specie and coin, and the mutual aid and protection offered by such associations. It was these coiners and clippers who confirmed the worst fears of the authorities about criminal gangs. Jack Gibbons was associated with coiners and the highwaymen Cogswell and Brady. In 1695 Anthony Dunn and William Atton deposed that they had gone with a magistrate's warrant to search the house of Katherine Reynolds, alias Butler, for Thomas Peirce, a highwaymen, and that they turned up broad money, clipped money, a set of scales and brass weights. In 1699 Dunn hunted for coining tools belonging to Thomas Moore, another highwayman.[58] This partial glimpse of coiners' networks is confirmed by the past operations of their pursuers: Dunn and St Leger had both been highwaymen and burglars, while Rewse and Jenkins had spent years rounding up prostitutes and becoming familiar with London's street life.

The power derived from the thief-takers' mediatory role was vividly displayed in the bribery charges against Gibbons, Dunn, St Leger and the Connells. But recorded interactions between thief-takers and suspects were more usually characterized by bargaining and trading, especially when it was the thief-taker's knowledge that was being tapped. Thomas Hunter's story is a good illustration of such practices. He robbed a clutch of goldsmiths, on one occasion fleeing with his booty with a crowd hot on his heels crying 'Stop, thief.' Hunter also ransacked a goldsmith's shop in Lombard Street, who used Saker to retrieve the bulk of his lost goods from the thief's 'receiver', Richard Lewis. Lewis (and his accomplice, Volt) met up with Hunter at the Dog tavern:

> where Sommers, the Thief-Taker, came to them and read aloud the Paper which Mr Fordham had sent abroad concerning his loss, and thereupon Sommers asking them (and particularly Hunter) whether they knew anything of it, they answered no ... But to remove all suspicion of it from themselves, they immediately went to Mr Segar's in the Old Bailey where having stayed a little while talked of the matter, saying they knew nothing of it.

Summers had seen the goldsmith's handbill and called in at the alehouse, presumably knowing that he would find the three men there. They denied any involvement in the crime, and later repeated their claims to Saker. But Volt was arrested for another robbery and, doubtless concerned that he might turn King's evidence, Lewis revealed the true facts of the case to Saker, who swapped money for Fordham's goods. (Hunter's share of the spoils was twelve or fourteen guineas.) Hunter appears quite contrite in *The Ordinary of Newgate*'s description of these events: asked what amends he could make to his long line of victims, 'he answer'd that he was sorry he could not help them to their Goods again; but said that Mr Fordham had recover'd the greatest part of his from Mr. Segars, the Thief-taker'.[59]

The process of detection usually involved the participation of 'middlemen' like Saker. As brokers between magistrates, criminals and victims, they helped to shape the day-by-day workings of the law. They comfortably conversed with magistrates yet rubbed shoulders with thieves. 'Middlemen' were frequently corrupt and even prepared to trade in human lives, but they did provide a valuable service: stolen property was returned; information was passed on to magistrates about criminal networks; thieves received help to offload their booty. In return, thief-takers received money, and a measure of protection and patronage from magistrates. To be effective, they had to offer a knowledge of criminal worlds to magistrates and more than 'the dangers of Inquisition or Examination or Fees of silence' to thieves who provided information and expected to profit from it.[60] So it was that thief-takers manipulated policing and prosecution processes for or against criminals, balancing promises to thieves of part of a reward or help selling stolen goods with the ever-present threat of framing or revealing them.

The demand for the services of London thief-takers rose towards the close of the seventeenth century: the city continued to grow, concern about crime and the preservation of property shot up, and the press both expressed this concern and provided mechanisms through which thieves and lost goods were tracked down. This demand was also fuelled by anxieties about political conspiracies, the coinage, and changing ideas about the nature of criminal activity that stressed its organized and collective character. And placed squarely in the middle of so many of these seemingly different contexts and concerns was the figure of the thief-taker: a point of contact between Jacobite plotters and criminal networks, the Royal Mint and seedy alehouses, the justice and the thief and, of course, the criminal and his victim.

NOTES

This chapter is the result of collaborative research between Professor John Beattie and myself. It was originally intended to produce a joint essay, but, while we are in considerable agreement, there are sufficient differences in emphasis to justify separate pieces. He discusses thief-takers in his *Urban Crime and the Limits of Terror: Policing, Prosecution and Punishment in London 1660–1750*. I am very grateful to him for all his encouragement and advice. I would also like to thank Robert Tittler, Cynthia Herrup, Tim Hitchcock, John Morrill, Heather Shore, Susan Skedd and the editors for their assistance.

1   PRO KB2/1: Dns Rex *v.* David Davies and Thomas Carter.

2   *A Short State of the Case of Joseph Billers* (1709?), p. 4.

3   G. Howson, *Thief-taker General: The Rise and Fall of Jonathan Wild* (1970); R. Paley, 'Thief-takers in London in the age of the McDaniel gang *c.* 1745–1754', in D. Hay and F. Snyder eds, *Policing and Prosecution in Britain 1750–1850* (Oxford, 1989); A. Johnstone and R. Tittler, '"To catch a thief" in Jacobean London', in E. B. DeWindt ed., *The Salt of Common Life: Individuality and Choice in the Medieval Town, Countryside and Church,*

Studies in Medieval Culture 36 (Kalamazoo MI, 1995); J. M. Beattie, *Crime and the Courts in England 1660–1800* (Oxford, 1986), pp. 55–9.

4   D. Hobbs, *Doing the Business: Entrepreneurship, Detectives and the Working Class in the East End of London* (Oxford, 1988), pp. 183–216.

5   Beattie, *Crime and the Courts*, pp. 50–5, 58–9; *id.*, 'Scales of justice: defence counsel and the English criminal trial in the eighteenth and nineteenth centuries', *Law and History Review*, 9 (1991); L. Radzinowicz and R. Hood, *A History of the Criminal law and its Administration since 1750* (5 vols, 1948–86), II, pp. 318–25, 333–7; Paley, 'Thief-takers', pp. 317–26.

6   T. Henderson, *Disorderly Women in Eighteenth Century London: Prostitution and Control in the Metropolis 1730–1830* (1999), esp. pp. 104–65, is an important example of this approach.

7   B.E., *A New Dictionary of the Terms Ancient and Modern of the Canting Crew* (1699), sig. M1v.

8   PRO SP29/97, fo. 188; LMA DL/C/146, fo. 287.

9   *The Life and Death of Mary Frith, Commonly Called Moll Cutpurse* (1662), pp. 43–4.

10 J. Styles, 'Print and policing: crime advertising in eighteenth-century provincial England', in Hay and Snyder, *Policing and Prosecution*, esp. pp. 68–75. My discussion is based on the *London Gazette* (1696) and all papers in the Burney Collection, 1698–1700.

11 *London Gazette*, 14–18 May, 1–4 June 1696.

12 Howson, *Thief-taker General*, pp. 74–80; *London Gazette*, 8–11 June 1696.

13 Quoted in J. Ashton, *Social Life of the Reign of Queen Anne: Taken from Original Sources* (1919), p. 422.

14 J. Beattie, 'London crime and the making of the "Bloody Code"' in L. Davison, T. Hitchcock, T. Keirn and R. B. Shoemaker eds, *Stilling the Grumbling Hive: The Response to Social and Economic Problems in England 1689–1750* (Stroud, 1992), pp. 52–3.

15 A. Marshall, *Intelligence and Espionage in the Reign of Charles II 1660–1685* (Cambridge, 1994).

16 For Hilton: M. Goldie, 'The Hilton gang and the purge of London in the 1680s', in H. Nenner ed., *Politics and the Political Imagination in Later Stuart Britain* (Woodbridge, 1997). For the Reformation of Manners see F. Dabhoiwala, 'Prostitution and Police in London *c*. 1660–*c*. 1760', Oxford D.Phil. thesis (1995), pp. 141–74; R. B. Shoemaker, *Prosecution and Punishment: Petty Crime and the Law in London and rural Middlesex c. 1660–1725* (Cambridge, 1991), pp. 238–72; *id.*, 'Reforming the city: the Reformation of Manners campaign in London 1690–1738', in Davison *et al.*, *Stilling the Grumbling Hive*.

17 *CSPD, 1664–65*, p. 230; *1666–67*, pp. 178–9 (and see also *1664–65*, pp. 121, 264).

18 I intend to develop this point more fully elsewhere.

19 *CSPD, 1678*, p. 41; Beattie, '"Bloody Code"', pp. 52, 71–2 n. 8; PRO PC2/72, fos 23–4. The phrase 'one party and knot' also occurs in a 1669 proclamation (*London Gazette*, 15–18 November 1669).

20 L. B. Faller, 'King William, "K.J.", and James Whitney: the several lives and affiliations of a Jacobite robber', *Eighteenth Century Life*, 12 (1988); P. K. Monod, *Jacobitism and the English People 1688–1788* (1989), pp. 111–13; PRO MINT15/17, nos 27, 421.

21 D. W. Jones, *War and Economy in the Age of William III and Marlborough* (Oxford, 1989),

pp. 18–9, 228–35, 240; C. E. Challis, 'Lord Hastings to the great silver recoinage', in C. E. Challis ed., *A New History of the Royal Mint* (Cambridge, 1992).

22 See esp. *CTB 1681–85*, pp. 541, 572, 731, 853–4.

23 Depositions are in PRO MINT15/17. Chaloner's career is described in F. Manuel, *A Portrait of Isaac Newton* (Cambridge MA, 1968), pp. 237–44; J. Craig, 'Newton against the counterfeiters', *Royal Society of London Notes and Queries*, 18 (1963), pp. 138, 140–3; R. S. Westfall, *Never at Rest: A Biography of Isaac Newton* (Cambridge, 1980), pp. 571–5. For his allegations of Jacobite conspiracy in high places see *CSPD, 1697*, pp. 339–41, 344, 355, 359–60, 362–3. For Carter and Davies see J. Garnett, *The Triumphs of Providence* (Cambridge, 1980), p. 155; Craig, 'Newton', p. 142; Westfall, *Never at Rest*, pp. 573–5.

24 Beattie, '"Bloody Code"', provides the best brief overview.

25 Quoted in *ibid.*, p. 62.

26 Shoemaker, *Prosecution and Punishment*, p. 249, quoting *Antimoixeia* (1691).

27 *CSPD, 1667*, pp. 446, 518.

28 *CSPD, 1668–69*, p. 242.

29 *CSPD, 1670*, pp. 50, 393; *1671–72*, pp. 131–2, 134, 144, 147, 238, 298.

30 *CTB 1681–85*, pp. 541, 548, 569–70, 572; *1685–89*, pp. 673, 731, 1216–17. For the clerks *CTB 1669–72*, pp. 952–3, 1096, 1107, 1135; *1685–89*, pp. 1369–70; *1693–96*, pp. 292, 1387–8; *1696*, pp. 29, 49.

31 *CTB 1681–85*, p. 991; PRO T1/23, fo. 30.

32 J. F. Scott ed., *The Correspondence of Isaac Newton*, IV (Cambridge, 1967), p. 209; PRO MINT15/17, no. 201 (Bodenham Rewse); Craig, 'Newton', p. 139 (Caleb Clarke).

33 William Fleetwood, *A Sermon against Clipping, Preach'd before the Right Honourable the Lord Mayor and Court of Aldermen, at Guild-Hall Chappel on December 16, 1694* (1694), p. 24.

34 *CTB 1696–97*, p. 212.

35 For example, LMA MJ/SP/1694/May/14, 26; MJ/SP/1698/January/66; *OBSP* 21–3 February 1693 [94], p. 2.

36 CLRO SF 421, Gaol Delivery recog. no. 21; 444, Sessions of the Peace recogs nos 71–4; LMA MJ/SR/1695.

37 Paley, 'Thief-takers', pp. 333–4, emphasizes these dangers. The only thief-taker known to have hanged in the 1690s, Matthew Coppinger, fell foul of Chaloner (Manuel, *Newton*, p. 239).

38 Portlock: LMA, MJ/SP/1695/July/32, 35, 40. Hooke: PRO MINT15/17, no. 443 (where he is acting with Bonner and Saker), no. 440 (with Summers and St Leger); LMA MJ/SP/1701/April/34–6 (with Caleb Clarke). For Cooper acting in Middlesex, see MJ/SP/1695/July/26; MJ/SP/1696/February/23.

39 For Hatfield see PRO ASSI35/143/2; LMA SP/1699/December/52; WJ/SP 1703/March/2; CLRO SF438; MJ/SR 1949. The most dramatic accusation against him was that he carried bribes to Lovell from Connell, and persuaded a condemned man to take the blame for another's crimes: see *British Journal*, 24 April and 1 May 1725. When the Hardings were pursued by the Connells (see below), a witness claimed that Hatfield had sold her the goods claimed to be stolen: LMA MJ/SP/1701/April/30. For Frimley see *OBSP*, December 1697, p. 3 , and LMA MJ/SP/1697/December/43.

40 LMA MJ/SR 1880 (indictments of James Peirce and John Wyld), MJ/SR 1882 (indictments of William Archer), MJ/SP/1696/September/65, MJ/SP/1697/April/23; MJ/SP/1701/April/47; *London Gazette*, 1–4 August 1698.

41 LMA MJ/CJ/1, pp. 1, 53, 60; MJ/CJ/2, pp. 7, 14, 22, 29; MJ/SP/1691/April/67.

42 *CSPD, 1691–92*, p. 110; PRO C82/2693: Newgate pardon; PRO T1/22, fos 150v–153; *CTB 1697–98*, p. 213; *Calendar of Treasury Papers, 1702–07*, pp. 167, 181.

43 *CTB 1696–97*, p. 227; LMA DL/C/156, fos 237–8; Dabhoiwala, 'Prostitution and Police', pp. 153, 155–6, 169–70.

44 Narcissus Luttrell, *A Brief Historical Relation of State Affairs* (6 vols, Oxford, 1857), I, pp. 165–6; T. B. and T. J. Howell eds, *A Complete Collection of State Trials* (33 vols, 1809–26), IX, cols 56–60; *CSPD, June–September 1683*, p. 57; *1684–85*, p. 48.

45 *CSPD, 1689–90*, pp. 326, 521, 525; *1696*, pp. 173, 181; *CTB 1702*, p. 783; PRO MINT15/17, no. 42; *The History of White's* (2 vols, 1892), I, pp. 4–5.

46 PRO MINT15/17 no. 31; *CSPD, 1698*, pp. 252–3; PRO MINT15/17 nos 42, 44, 45, 53, 54, 55, 91, 94, 96, 97, 99, 104, 151, 183, 240.

47 PRO MINT15/17, no. 97; *CSPD, 1696*, p. 406; *1698*, p. 302; G. P. R. James ed., *Letters illustrative of the Reign of William III from 1696 to 1708: Addressed to the Duke of Shrewsbury by James Vernon, Esq., Secretary of State* (3 vols, 1841), I, p. 344.

48 Howson, *Thief-taker General*, pp. 38–41; BL Add. Ms 35,107, fo. 28v (I am grateful to Paul Hopkins for this reference); J. Beattie, 'The Cabinet and the management of death at Tyburn after the revolution of 1688–1689' in L. G. Schwoerer ed., *The Revolution of 1688–1689: Changing Perspectives* (Cambridge, 1992), esp. pp. 224–6. For Lovell's claim see PRO T1/78, fo. 130.

49 Johnstone and Tittler, '"To catch a thief"', p. 259.

50 *OBSP*, 12–14 October 1720, p. 4.

51 J. M. Beattie, 'London juries in the 1690s', in J. S. Cockburn and T. A. Green eds, *Twelve Good Men and True: The Criminal Trial Jury in England 1200–1800* (Princeton NJ, 1988), esp. 234–7.

52 PRO MINT15/17 no. 45.

53 Douglas Hay and Francis Snyder, 'Using the criminal law 1750–1850: policing, private prosecution, and the state', in *id., Policing and Prosecution*, pp. 47–8; Scott, *Correspondence of Isaac Newton*, p. 209.

54 LMA MJ/SR 2031; CLRO SF444, Sessions of the Peace recogs nos. 72, 74; *Post Man*, 19–21 December 1699.

55 PRO MINT15/17 no. 42.

56 *CTB 1697–98*, p. 150; LMA MJ/SR 1949; *An Account of the Apprehending and Taking, of John Davis, and Philip Wake* (1700); LMA MJ/SP/1701/April/29.

57 PRO MINT15/17 no. 6.

58 PRO MINT15/17, no. 91; LMA MJ/SP/1695/January/1; PRO MINT15/17 no. 229.

59 *The Ordinary of Newgate his Account*, 21 June 1704.

60 *Life of Mary Frith*, p. 44.

Part II

Gender and sexuality

Chapter 5

The pattern of sexual immorality in seventeenth- and eighteenth-century London

Faramerz Dabhoiwala

Sexual immorality was a matter of perennial social concern in early modern England. Over the course of the seventeenth and eighteenth centuries it was the object of innumerable public and private initiatives: parliamentary Acts against adultery and bastardy, national campaigns for the 'reformation of manners' and hospitals for girls at risk of seduction, to name but a few. Much of contemporary fiction and drama revolved around sexual intrigue. And in daily life, too, the moral dilemmas and practical problems it raised were ubiquitous. Nowhere were these matters more prominent than in London. Yet comparatively little is still known about the sexual lives of metropolitan men and women in this period.

Oddly enough, one important reason for this is that the evidence is too rich and too varied to be easily manipulated. Only the roughest estimates can be made, for example, of illegitimacy rates in the capital, whereas for other parts of the country such calculations are often the starting point for discussions of sexual behaviour.[1] Partly by choice and partly of necessity, historians of London have therefore adopted a much greater diversity of approaches. The result has been some striking and innovative research, especially in recent years. But it has also meant that different types of sexual immorality have tended to be discussed discretely: prostitution, for example, by historians of crime; adultery by historians of family life; fornication and bastardy by historians of population. And a related consequence is that the sexual lives of the lower orders and of the upper ranks are rarely analysed together.[2]

There are, of course, good reasons for drawing such distinctions. The most obvious is that they are inherent in the sources available to us. The sexual behaviour of the middling and upper ranks is documented in diaries, letters and other personal records, as well as in the often voluminous detail of private litigation over adultery, divorce and other marital issues. Such material is rarely available for men and women lower down the social scale. They are, by contrast, well represented in records generated by various forms of socia. policy: the public policing of crime and of sexual immorality, for example, or the provision of various kinds of special hospitals, such as those for illegitimate children or penitent prostitutes. Much excellent recent work on sexual behaviour has been based on such sources, but they have their own limitations. They focus on particular types of activity to the exclusion of others; they represent behaviour in judicial and institutional categories; and they tend to ignore the middling and upper ranks of society.

More generally, the bias of our sources is a reminder that contemporaries, too, often sought to ascribe different moral standards to different degrees of people, and to distinguish different categories of sexual immorality. But although such prejudice is an important indicator of contemporary assumptions, it is not always an adequate basis for categorising actual behaviour.

A good example is prostitution. At first sight, it would seem to be a type of behaviour that was clearly defined in early modern England. 'Whores', 'harlots', 'strumpets', 'night-walkers' and keepers of 'bawdy houses' were listed as criminal offenders in every legal handbook; they were common targets of metropolitan policing; and prostitution is thus commonly described and defined through judicial records. Yet this obscures a great deal. Contemporary attempts to distinguish prostitution as a type of behaviour were not identical with our own. They focused mainly on motivation, rather than on promiscuity and payment; and they were counterbalanced by other patterns of thought that denied the very concept. Both at law and in general discourse, for example, a 'whore' was any woman who had sexual relations outside marriage, irrespective of her promiscuity, social position or remuneration; just as a 'bawdy house' was simply any place – a home, tavern or lodging-house – where men and women met to commit sexual immorality. As a result, it is often difficult in legal records to separate prostitution from other forms of sexual immorality.

Analysing prostitution as a type of criminal behaviour also obscures the extent to which it was rooted in normal, untransgressive, social and economic patterns. Many such features of sexual trade appear hardly or not at all in judicial records, depending on the vicissitudes of policing: clients, 'casual' encounters, procuring and, more generally, all those areas that escaped prosecution through secrecy or the protection of rank.[3] Moreover, if one turns to non-legal sources to fill out the picture, it becomes clear not just that 'prostitution' overlapped significantly with categories such as fornication, adultery and bigamy, but that this fluid pattern of sexual behaviour largely cut across social divisions. Amongst the lower ranks of metropolitan society it was subject to various kinds of public legal sanction. Higher up the social scale, like other vices, it was largely free from such trammels and is therefore documented in other ways: but the similarities of sexual trade across the social spectrum are infinitely more marked than any differences.

Several of these points are raised, implicitly or explicitly, in recent work on early modern sexual relations. But as yet there has been little attempt to link them together into any broader revision of Lawrence Stone's classic account of sex in this period, which separated 'Upper-Class Sexual Behaviour' from 'Plebeian Sexual Behaviour', and treated prostitution as a sub-set of the latter.[4] It remains the case that the sexual behaviour of the lower orders is usually analysed separately from that of their superiors, and prostitution separately from other forms of heterosexual immorality.[5]

This essay is an attempt to overcome these divisions, and to take a fresh look at the pattern of sexual immorality as a whole: by reading across the grain of familiar sources, and by linking together issues usually treated separately. The argument has two parts. The first shows that men and women of all ranks entered into very similar types of illicit relationships. It does so by juxtaposing a well known source for supposedly 'gentlemanly' patterns of sexual behaviour, the diary of Samuel Pepys, with evidence drawn from the opposite end of the social spectrum, amongst men and women prosecuted for immorality. The second part of the essay focuses in greater detail on the 'common' whoredom found in judicial sources, and on contemporary attempts to categorize it as a distinct form of sexual behaviour.

There were several ways of classifying sexual behaviour in early modern England. The most universal code was that of the Church, which in essence drew a simple distinction between chastity and unchastity. The latter could in theory be subdivided, most obviously into fornication, adultery and incest; but in practice – even in proceedings before the Church courts – such categories were often immaterial, and were subsumed under a general term such as 'whoredom', 'incontinence' or 'uncleanness'.[6] Nor did the Protestant tradition admit of prostitution as a separate category of behaviour. Before the middle of the eighteenth century, the term 'prostitute' was rarely used, either as a noun or as a verb; and in any case its meaning was synonymous with that of 'whore', the most common term for any unchaste woman. This orthodoxy was epitomized during the 1650s in the puritan Adultery Act, which included specific measures against bawds and brothel keepers but none against prostitutes, because implicitly they fell under its provisions against adultery and fornication.[7] Similarly, although bigamy, buggery and rape were statutory felonies, there was no clear-cut distinction at common law between other types of sexual immorality. For the purposes of day-to-day policing, 'public' or 'common' prostitution or 'whoredom' was held to be particularly culpable; but this was essentially a distinction of degree, based on considerations of public order.[8] In legal principle, sexual immorality was thus usually defined very broadly.

In reality, too, unchaste behaviour was not easily divisible into distinct types. Few sources illustrate this more vividly than the diary of Samuel Pepys, an ambitious young civil servant in Restoration London. Pepys's diary has long been regarded as a classic source for historians of sexual behaviour. They have used it primarily to explore the diarist's own state of mind, and the circumstances that influenced his constant philandering: the pressures of work, his relationship with his wife Elizabeth, and his use of sex as a means of psychological reassurance.[9] But in fact the diary's full scope is much greater, not least because Pepys's sexual and social acquaintances spanned the social scale, from the court of Charles II to the street walkers of the West End. The relationships he described were often ones of deep inequality, and his judgements are inevitably subjective and self-serving. Nevertheless, read with due care, the diary provides invaluable information on the sexual behaviour of a substantial cross-section of metropolitan society.

On occasion, Pepys was able to take sexual advantage of his power as an employer of servants, as an influential civil servant who was regularly petitioned in person by the wives of naval personnel, or simply (in the case of young girls) as a respected older man.[10] But it also appears not to have been too hard for him to find other women who were under much less of an obligation to suffer his fondling or his 'ponendo her mano upon mi cosa', yet would freely 'bear with any such thing'.[11] Indeed, more often than not, his partners appear to have been just as deliberately engaged in sexual bartering as he. Nell Payne, a former servant, was willing to be fondled for a shilling. Mrs Daniel, the wife of a naval officer, initially 'resist[ed] pretty much, sed never the minus submitted' for the sake of her husband's promotion. On later occasions, it was she who returned to claim Pepys as her valentine (which obliged him to buy her gifts), and to attempt to borrow money from him in exchange for a sexual favour. Most enduringly, Mrs Bagwell, the wife of a naval carpenter, was Pepys's occasional mistress for several years, whilst he furthered her husband's career.[12]

All of these themes recur in the best documented of Pepys's affairs, that with Betty Lane, a linen draper in Westminster Hall. Once he persevered, Pepys swiftly progressed from fondling her to doing 'what[ever] I would with her but only the main thing'; and within a few months that too had been achieved. When Betty married Samuel Martin, who worked for the navy, Pepys was thrilled – 'I must have a bout with her very shortly, to see how she finds marriage' – as it gave him licence to have intercourse with her regularly without much danger of discovery. But Mrs Martin's attitude appears to have been equally calculating. Prior to her marriage, she enjoyed being entertained and flirted with by Pepys at a succession of taverns and eating houses; and thereafter she was no less adroit at having him take her out for a good time, borrowing money from him, and continually keeping up the pressure on him to obtain preferment for her husband. Moreover, leaving aside such material considerations, Mrs Martin's libido simply appears to have matched that of

Pepys; and often it was she – 'la plus bold moher of the orbis' – who initiated their love-making.

What is especially striking is that she was connected with a host of other women with flexible sexual morals. By the time Pepys's affair with her was well established, he was accustomed to meeting at her lodgings not only Mrs Martin herself, but also her landlady, 'a pleasant jolly woman' who was willing to be entertained, to be fondled, and to receive 20s as a valentine's gift; or Mrs Burrows, a pretty widow who was even more complaisant in the face of Pepys's advances. Amongst others in the same circle were Nell Payne, the former servant; and Betty Howlett, a shopkeeper's daughter whom Pepys had long pursued, with occasional success. Mrs Martin's husband himself had 'another woman whom he uses, and hath long done, as a wife'; and her sister Doll became another of Pepys's mistresses after Mrs Martin introduced them to one another. Doll Lane had other lovers too. Only when she was unexpectedly delivered of a child did she suddenly claim to have been married throughout and only recently widowed: 'when, God knows, she hath played the whore, and is sillily forced ... to forge this story', mused Pepys.[13]

Such behaviour was not confined to the decades of the Restoration. The same pattern of sexual immorality amongst the upper and middling ranks that emerges from Pepys's diary is observable in other first-hand accounts of metropolitan life throughout the later seventeenth and eighteenth centuries.[14] Nor was it particularly socially distinctive. The types of sexual relations that men and women of the lower orders entered into were very similar, above all in their fluidity of forms. Even in the apparently most extreme case, of women prosecuted for whoring, it is often impossible to distinguish categorically between those who were 'professional' and those who engaged in sexual trade only on an 'amateur' or 'part-time' basis; or between 'prostitutes', 'mistresses' and other sexual offenders.

The associations between women taken to court as 'lewd, idle, and disorderly' whores and their 'clients', for example, often appear to be on or well over the borderline between prostitution and more personal relationships. Such was frequently the case when a servant or apprentice deserted his service to set up house with a woman, only to find her prosecuted for 'enticing' him. The brazier's apprentice John Mason, for instance, was committed to bridewell for deserting his apprenticeship; his partner Mary 'Mason' for 'deluding and Inticing' him away. Hester Cook, alias Pierce, acquired the further surname 'Sheffield' through her long-standing association with the apprentice Edward Sheffield. When they were arrested and charged with incontinence he claimed 'hee hath been marryed a yeare to her'. Prosecutions of such couples had some legal justification, as apprentices were in theory prohibited from forming sexual relationships; yet they show also how the distinction between a mercenary, deluding harlot and a loving partner could lie entirely in the disapproving eye of a guardian or parish officer. And it was not only servants and apprentices who suffered from such moral oversight. The father of Francis Thursfield managed to have his son's lover arrested and committed to Bridewell for – as he saw it – 'inticeing away Francis ... with intencone to debauch him and haveing marryed him against his will'.[15] 'Living in contentment' (as one house of correction calendar transcribed 'incontinent') or 'as man and wife', whether for a week or for several years, was no substitute for the legal security of marriage.[16]

Yet it is in fact upon the potential insecurity of marriage, and the ability of men and women to form adulterous relationships outside it, that prosecutions for 'keeping company' and 'living incontinently' shed most light. Many a supposed prostitute and married 'client' appear to have embarked upon a long-term affair, 'living incontinently' or 'in adultery' whilst he neglected his wife, beat her, turned her out of the house, or simply took up residence himself at his lover's place.[17] The resulting struggles between wife and mistress could be fierce. During March and April 1723, for example, Honour O'Connor of St James's, Westminster, waged a continuous physical and a legal battle against the widow Mary Winwood, who had taken to 'keeping company' and 'living together as Man and Wife' with her husband Derby O'Connor. Mary Winwood fought back, having Honour bound over, threatening and repeatedly assaulting her. The fight continued for several months, but by August Mrs Winwood appears to have gained the upper hand, on separate occasions being bound over as 'Mary Oconner' and giving Honour a badly bruised arm when she tried unsuccessfully to take back her husband by force. Derby himself did little except to prevent his mistress from actually stabbing his wife to death.[18]

Like Mary Winwood alias O'Connor, Mary 'Mason', and Hester Cook alias Pierce alias Sheffield, many women took the surname of their lover for their own. This practice was widely followed regardless of the marital state of either party, and it is a further indication of fluid relational patterns that were not solely dependent upon the sanction of marriage, nor very different across ranks.[19] In polite society, Pepys was not the only gentleman to be on occasion confused over the marital status of a couple, even when they were acquaintances with whom he met and conversed on a regular basis.[20] Indeed, after the death of his wife he himself lived for many years in a similar arrangement with a woman called Mary Skinner. His friends appear to have accepted this as perfectly respectable: his old acquaintance Robert Hooke, for one, referred to Mary simply as the new 'Mrs Pepys'.[21] Of course there were those who disapproved: but such relationships – and tacit acceptance of them – were to be found in all ranks. Amongst the less well-off, keepers of bawdy houses were certainly not the only landlords prepared to turn a blind eye to 'a person who lived incontinently with' another and 'lodged together ... as man and wife', although the fact might well be used against a lodger who ran into debt.[22] Similarly, it is obvious that parish officers prosecuted adulterous men only when their deserted family threatened to become a charge to the ratepayers.[23] It seems very likely, therefore, that untold numbers of couples did cohabit 'as man and wife' for extended periods, having children together and not being called to account for many years, if at all.[24]

One underlying reason why such practices were not easily controlled was that this was a society in which even the basic distinction between chaste and unchaste relationships was sometimes hard to determine.[25] In theory it was a simple matter. Sexual relations within marriage were sanctioned, all others were not. In practice, however, it was far from straightforward: for in London even the definition of matrimony could be blurred from the outset. By the later seventeenth century, most of the capital's inhabitants were married not according to the conventions of the established Church, but in irregular, 'clandestine' ceremonies, which took place without publicity or the calling of banns and were commonly conducted by shady, unbeneficed parsons in insalubrious surroundings. Clandestine marriage was especially popular because it was cheap. Yet, as contemporaries were well aware, the nature of the trade lent itself to many and frequent irregularities: sham marriages, unregistered ones, forged certificates, bigamy and other abuses.[26] All in all, there is overwhelming evidence – certainly until 1753, when the Marriage Act attempted to regularize matters – for a significant undermining of the supposedly objective, unitary standard of marriage.

Irrespective of how marriage was defined, the types of sexual relations that men and women engaged in outside it – from casual encounters to long-term partnerships – did not differ significantly by rank. Promiscuity and sexual trade were not confined to those women prosecuted at law as prostitutes. Conversely, women who engaged in prostitution were just as capable of entering into more stable types of relationship. Such equivalence of behaviour regardless of rank was a commonplace of Christian and moralist assumptions about sexual immorality. But there were also other strands of thought in early modern England, which categorized prostitution as a separate type of behaviour, engaged in by 'common' whores who were cut off from respectable society. Unlike other whores, such women were held to be necessarily poor and sexually indiscriminate. The remainder of this essay will examine the basis and the validity of these assumptions. It focuses in turn on the circumstances of sexual trade at the lower end of the social scale; on the motivation of those who engaged in it; and on their position within metropolitan society.

Anonymous sex was not hard to find.[27] Walking the streets – or, by extension, frequenting other public spaces such as parks, taverns or playhouses – was the most common way for men and women to meet, regardless of where the sexual transaction actually took place.[28] At their most basic, such encounters ended in the nearest unlit alley, park or field.[29] But usually, especially if they were willing to spend more money, men enjoyed the companionship, drink and conversation that accompanied a more leisurely copulation indoors. Some women took their clients back to their lodgings, with or without the connivance of their landlord; others made for a suitable private or public house. Indeed, as a grand jury for the City complained in 1693, it was not hard to find 'Taverns and other publick houses who doe entertain leud and disolute people who Pick up one another in the streets, and carry them to those places, where they are entertained and concealed in their debauchery and leudness'.[30] Most of the thousands of alehouses, taverns and coffee houses scattered throughout the metropolis could provide private rooms for their customers; and many appear to have had as little compunction as widow Harris of Whitechapel about 'suffering whoredome and adultery to be acted in her [ale]house she being privie to it'.[31] Such public establishments shaded into unlicensed, private houses like that of Susanna Church of St Giles, who would provide anyone with 'beds to Lye together in, she knowing they are not men with their wives'.[32] More active keepers had a live-in prostitute or two, or could 'sen[d] for men to women and for women to men' if the need arose.[33] Because of the small-scale, impermanent nature of most bawdy houses, such go-betweens fulfilled an essential function for all those men and women who did not wish to solicit publicly in the streets.

In short, a 'bawdy house' could be any number of things: a private home or a tavern or a brothel, of greater or lesser sophistication and expense. And often, little distinguished it at first sight, like the place in Westminster that Samuel Pepys visited with some friends one morning in 1662: 'went to a little house behind the Lords' house to drink some Wormewood ale, which doubtless was a bawdy house — the mistress of the house having that look and dress'.[34] Irrespective of her look and dress, it was likely to be a woman who ran the establishment. Men were certainly heavily involved in the trade, both as husbands and as independent keepers, but most bawdy houses were kept by women. Many were widows. And for many, both single and married, acting as a bawd was only a part-time supplement to a more respectable occupation: often, for example, they were victuallers.[35]

Indeed, when it came to attracting clients, drink was all-important. Whether in the form of wine, gin or Wormewood ale, alcohol was crucial to the successful operation of a bawdy house. Some keepers sold their own, with or without a licence; others fetched it from the nearest shop or tavern. Either way, pressing it upon clients at greatly inflated prices was a ubiquitous practice. Investigating the bawdy houses in Fleet Alley in July 1664, Pepys 'went in and there saw what formerly I have been acquainted with, the wickedness of those houses and the forcing a man to present [i.e. immediate] expense', and such 'impudent tricks and ways of getting money, and raising the reckoning by still calling for things, that it came to 6 or 7s presently'. The bawd Sarah Box, who allowed 'lewd disorderly persons to lye togeither knowingly' and had one lodger who 'ployd at her house as a comon whore', would not apparently allow customers to retire with the woman unless first 'they did spend their money for drink'. In other cases clients found that even 'whilst they were in Bed' a keeper 'brought them up severall quarters of Brandy', or 'severall bowles of Punch'.[36] Such ancillary services were part of the sociability that many clients sought in prostitution, and their provision was often the most lucrative aspect of the trade. As a consequence, even if a regular client like the grocer's apprentice Thomas Young could get away with 'but a shilling' for his 'knock', he might well be forced to pawn his handkerchief and the very buttons of his shirt in order to pay the much higher bill for his drink.[37] At another establishment, its resident prostitute explained that the clients 'used to sitt up and drink till late att night ... and according to the ability of the person [the keeper] had used to receive five, tenn or Twenty shillings for the use of the bed in lying with this Informant besides the benifitt of the liquer she sold'.[38]

These facts place prostitution firmly within the general pattern of female employment. The retailing of food, drink and other goods was the most important occupation of older women in London during this period, and acting as a bawd was often a natural adjunct to such provisioning. For many 'common' prostitutes, similarly, the selling of sex was not an exclusive or full-time occupation, but merely a supplement or temporary substitute for an income from domestic service or needlework. These were the only trades open to most women in their teens, twenties and early thirties, but both were badly paid and notoriously insecure. As a domestic servant a woman could earn in the region of £2 to £6 per annum plus board and lodging; in other occupations typical earnings might be around 5s per week, without such benefits in kind. Even as a stable income such sums were very low, comparable in fact to levels of poor relief in the more affluent City parishes. Yet both in service and in the needle trades most women were employed only for a few weeks or months at a time, moving from one position to another, taking other jobs in between, and spending periods of time 'out of place' and out of work. As a consequence, tens of thousands of young women throughout the capital lived on the margins of independent subsistence, relying upon irregular forms of income, credit and occasional parish grants to keep themselves going.[39] Occasional prostitution was merely a variation on this economy of makeshifts.

Yet even at this level of society, prostitutes and their clients were of an infinite variety; and the economics of the trade therefore depended primarily upon personal circumstance, upon 'the ability of the person'.[40] There is thus little point in calculating such a thing as 'the average fee' for a sexual encounter.[41] Indeed, just as to talk of a 'maximum fee' would be nonsense, so any 'minimum' too is arbitrary. It could not, for example, apply to the 'two very pretty little girls' who picked up James Boswell one night in May 1763 and were content simply with 'a glass of wine and my company'; or to the genteel 'lady of the town', Miss Watts, who was prepared to allow him 'favours' for free when he called upon her earlier that same evening.[42] More generally, as we have seen, such casual sexual trade was to be found at all levels of society, not just amongst the lower ranks: so that although prostitution was part of the economy, its limits were not definable in economic terms.

Nor, indeed, did contemporaries believe they were. Economic exchange and impoverishment were held to be the inevitable consequences of all forms of sexual immorality, rather than of prostitution in particular.[43] Even at law it was difficult to distinguish 'prostitution' from other sexual liaisons on the grounds that it involved the exchange of money and goods: for almost any relationship, of any length and in any social context, was bound to do so.[44] Both at law and more generally, attempts to define prostitution as a separate type of behaviour therefore took a different approach, based essentially on the supposed motivation of prostitutes. There were two contradictory arguments. One, a minority opinion until the middle of the eighteenth century but increasingly fashionable thereafter, was that such women were compelled against their will. The other, more conventional notion was that they were the wilful seducers of innocent men: part of a criminal subculture that preyed on respectable society.

The first view was epitomized by those like the reforming magistrate John Fielding, his fellow JP Saunders Welch, and others involved in mid-eighteenth-century charities for prostitutes, who stressed that such 'unfortunates' were often driven to the trade by circumstances beyond their control: extreme poverty, neglectful parents, molestation as a child or seduction by 'the Bawd and Debauchee'.[45] Although their rhetoric was shaped by the desire to portray common prostitutes as fit objects of philanthropy, Welch and Fielding both had considerable experience of dealing with street walkers and bawdy houses in infamous areas of the West End, and their assessment undoubtedly held true for a proportion of those involved in the trade. Prostitution out of sheer necessity was the lot, for example, of Mary Price, the twenty-three-year-old wife of a tallow chandler of St Martin in the Fields, who lodged at a tavern in Mayfair and roamed about Chelsea, Kensington and Hammersmith begging for a living and supplementing her income with casual sex. Justifying herself to a local gardener who had observed her in a field with the elderly and respected citizen of Kensington, Francis Gotobed, she confided that 'she had had many a shilling and sixpence of him and had it not been for him she should have been half starved'.[46] Likewise, it was plain to many who policed the centre of town that 'those Stroling Gilts which are whipt in Bridewel, do often Complain with Tears in their Eyes, that it is for want of Employment, and to get bread that they betake themselves to or continue in that abominable Course of Life'.[47]

Moreover, the powerful rhetoric directed at the 'bawds' and 'rakes' who were said to 'prey' upon young or otherwise vulnerable women – 'with Intent', as one mother complained, 'to make a property of [my daughter] by having her Debauch'd' – clearly had some basis in reality.[48] It drew, for example, upon the experiences of women like Isabella Cranston, who in the early 1720s had been 'decoyed' into the brothel of Sarah Jolly 'under pretence of being hired into service' and was there delivered up to the libertine Colonel Francis Charteris; or like Anne Bond at the end of the decade, who 'being out of Service, and sitting at the Door of the House where she lodged, a Woman, who was a Stranger to her, came to her, and ask'd her, if she wanted a Place? and told her, she helped Servants to Places'. The woman was Elizabeth Needham, some-time neighbour of Mrs Jolly and just as notorious a brothel keeper and bawd; and Anne Bond, too, found herself in service to Colonel Charteris. For ten days he trapped her indoors, made her sleep in his bedroom, 'offer'd her a Purse of Gold ... several times, and told her, that he would give her fine Clothes and Money, and a House to live in, and would also get her a Husband'; and then he gave up trying to persuade her, raped her and turned her out.[49]

Such tales of poverty, brutality and compulsion could be multiplied many times.[50] But that is partly because the richest surviving sources – judicial records – are inevitably biased towards cases where a woman was 'debauched' and she or her relatives sought redress at law. In fact, it is equally evident that other women acquiesced in the approaches of a bawd, and entered into prostitution with a much greater degree of choice.

Take, for example, the case of Winifred Lloyd, a middle-aged bawd who operated in the West End in the late 1720s.[51] In the spring and summer of 1729 she helped one of her regular clients, a 'Squire Janssen', to an acquain-tance and sexual intercourse with two young women. One was Hanna Smith, the fourteen-year-old apprentice of James and Mary Gerrard of Fore Street, near Bedlam, a girl with whom Mrs Lloyd 'had some former acquaintance'. Around Easter, as Hanna was walking through the park to Westminster, they met again. Taking up Mrs Lloyd's invitation to visit her at her lodgings later that day, Hanna was introduced to Janssen, who 'was very fond of this Deponent and called her pretty Girl and desired Mrs Lloyd to be kind to her and let her want for nothing and the Squire himself gave her half a Crown, and bad her come and see Mrs Lloyd often where she would be made much of'.

One evening about three weeks later, Mrs Lloyd collected Hanna and took her back to her lodgings to meet Janssen again. After he had been 'very fond' of her, 'hugging and kissing her', they went by coach to a bagnio in St James's

Street where he had sex with her and gave her 10s. Mrs Lloyd waited in a nearby tavern, had Hanna stay the night with her, and took her home the next morning. Out of the 10s she bought her a pair of shoes, a pair of stockings and a pair of clogs, and kept the rest. Hanna continued to visit Mrs Lloyd and to be 'made much of' by Janssen. The bawd 'encouraged her saying he would make a Woman of her for ever'.

Even more striking is the case of the Gerrards' maidservant Mary Macdonald, whom Mrs Lloyd managed also to 'seduce'. Well after Hanna Smith's 'debauchment', and presumably with her encouragement, she too took up Mrs Lloyd's invitation, visited her and was introduced to the kind and generous Squire Janssen. He entertained them in a tavern, 'made very much' of Mary, 'kissing her and using other dalliance', and gave her 19s. Upon Mrs Lloyd's encouragement that 'she need not be afraid for the Gentleman would not hurt her', Mary returned the next Sunday. Mrs Lloyd took her to a fortune teller who tossed some coffee grounds and 'told her she had had a present of Mony from a Gentleman, and that he would give her a great deal more, sufficient to make a Woman of her, and that if she this Deponent refused it she would never thrive'. So Mary met Janssen in the park, agreed to go along with him, and spent the night with him. He gave her five guineas, and Mrs Lloyd, appropriating the money effortlessly, 'commended [her], telling her she was now made a Woman of'.

These matters only came to light some weeks later: not because of any scruples on the part of Hanna Smith or Mary Macdonald, who continued to consort with Mrs Lloyd, but, typically, because their employer became suspicious that the bawd 'had seduced away her maid servant'. From the point of view of the women themselves Mrs Lloyd appears as a trusted friend, one who commiserated with Hanna Smith on the pain of sexual intercourse – 'O,' she told her, 'when he first lay with me I cryd out Murther, but if you was forty years old it would not hurt you' – and one who offered them the attractions of a good time, of outings to taverns, of 'being made much of', of being kissed and hugged, of 'having ... so many kind Invitations', of being wined and dined by a gentleman, and being bought new clothes. Her ability to befriend young, securely employed women, and their willingness to go along with her, thus appear to have depended less on any deception than on the attraction of the companionship and the life-style that she offered. To her, and to them, being 'made a Woman' was clearly as much a social as a sexual achievement, a passage into independence as well as adulthood.[52] And for countless other women, sexual trade was even more plainly a matter of calculated choice. Like Ann Carter of Ratcliff, who saw it not as the final resort of a desperate woman but as the exchange of money for 'the Satisfaction of her Body ... according to Contract'.[53] Like Anna Harrison, who scraped a living in the 1690s as a lowly maidservant, all the while dreaming of moving in with a prosperous widower, or of making her fortune by keeping a coffee house; but meanwhile supplementing her income by casual sex with acquaintances, touching them for food, drink, clothes and money in return for hurried intercourse.[54] Or like Philippa Wheeler, whose life story was recounted under cross-examination by her husband, imprisoned in Newgate in the winter of 1675:

> This Examinant saith that true it is hee was marryed to one Phillip[pa] Fettiplace at Highgate in the yeare 1666: And lived with her as man and wife about 3 quarters of a yeare. And this Examinant further saith that the aforesaid Phillip left this Examinant and went with one Esquire Poulton to Greenwitch and lived with him there about 5 weekes untill the aforesaid Poulton and shee had spent the money they made of this Examinants goods which shee had taken from him, and then the said Phillip came to this Examinant againe and lived with him about 3 weekes. And this Examinants occasions calling him into the cuntry to receive some money, after hee had staid there about 9 dayes, hee had word sent him that the aforesaid Phillip was seen in one Madam Delynes house, whoe lived in the Haymarket neere St James, whoe was reputed to keepe a notorious Bawdihouse, and there the aforesaid Phillip continued about the space of 6 weekes, and some short tyme afterwards the aforesaid Phillip shipt herselfe to Virginia where shee hath continued for 7 yeares or thereabouts this Examinant not hearing from her in all that tyme, but this Examinant further saith that twoe persons comeing from Virginia told this Examinant that the aforesaid Phillip Fettiplace alias Wheeler was dead.[55]

In fine, the motives of those involved in sexual trade differed very widely. In some cases, the balance was heavily weighted towards compulsion rather than choice. But for most women of lower rank, as for those higher up the social hierarchy, sexual trade simply grew out of, and fitted into, their existing social and economic circumstances: it did not constitute a radical break with them. In that sense, very little distinguishes their stories from those of a century later, when much fuller sources for the background and attitudes of metropolitan prostitutes first become available. Then, too, most poor prostitutes differed very little from other women of their class; they turned to prostitution, generally in their late teens and early twenties, as a temporary measure, 'the best of a series of unattractive alternatives'; within the trade, they could be successful, and they were as likely to take advantage of their clients as the reverse.[56]

Much of this reality – that women could choose to engage in prostitution, that many of them were assertive and self-confident, and that they were able to outwit both their clients and those who sought to police them – was evident to contemporary observers. It contradicted the view of prostitutes as helpless victims of social and economic circumstances, and it underpinned the alternative attempt to distinguish prostitution as the predatory behaviour of a criminal subculture. The prostitute as seductress of innocent men was as misleading a stereotype as the prostitute as victim, but once again such rhetoric had some basis in fact.

It was articulated most forcefully with regard to the 'seduction' of clients who were sons, servants and apprentices. For parents and masters were not only responsible for the moral well-being of young men in their care, they were also vulnerable themselves if they failed in their vigilance. A single lapse could be bad enough: the mother of fifteen-year-old William Ross of Wapping was understandably outraged when he was picked up by a prostitute 'who Enticed him to lye with her, and Cald for Liquor which came to twelve shillings and then engaged him to sell a Ring for twelve shillings which was worth 20s'.[57] But more serious were cases where falling in with bad female company induced a young man to steal and embezzle systematically from his parents or master. Visiting the coffee house of Mary Hambleton in Little Drury Lane one Sunday afternoon early in 1695, the tailor's apprentice Edward Fursse and his friend sat in the cold until 'one Hester Ascue asked them to goe into the back roome and [said] she would make a fire'. In the back room another woman appeared, and 'with the said Ascue kept them company and enticed them to the carnal knowledge of their bodyes behaving themselves very lewd and impudently'. 'After this,' Edward confessed, he 'used to frequent the said ill house very often,' sleeping with Mrs Hambleton as well as with her two prostitutes. Consequently, over a period of two months, he was persuaded to bring them from his master's goods

> half an Ell of Canvase, the covering of a pair of Stayes, $^1/_4$ of canvass and a hank of coulered stiching silk [which] he disposed of to [the] two lewd women with the privity of [the] said Hambleton; and the said Hambleton herself had $^1/_2$ an Ell of Canvass and desired this Deponent to bring her bone buckerome and velvet for a cap and to lend her money to pay her rent and had in money of him at two several times twelve shillings and six pence besides moneys spent and at several other times in the whole at least one pound and ten shillings.[58]

Such disasters could be nipped in the bud through determined action. William Hyatt followed his servant to the lodgings of the infamous Mary Draper in Gravel Lane; 'after shee had denyed him ... uppon search hee was found under her bed', and Hyatt had the woman arrested.[59] Countless other masters, however, could act only after the fact: from William Muggleton, whose apprentice lay twice with a woman and thus wasted 4s 6d of his money, to the haberdasher Philip Pym, who claimed to have lost £80 worth of goods through the 'entertaining', 'keeping company' and 'seduction' of his servant Rowland Holt.[60] Even the 'Artsmasters' of Bridewell itself (to whom poor boys were bound as apprentices) were not immune from similar despoliation.[61]

More direct robbery took a variety of forms. Street walkers commonly used their apparent sexual availability as a front for the more lucrative business of pickpocketing. Sometimes the theft was perpetrated in the aftermath of sex, but often no such effort was required. Men who allowed themselves to be fondled by a woman they had just picked up frequently found themselves left standing on the street or sitting in a tavern minus watch, money and woman. To perpetrate such thefts, street walkers often operated in pairs or in larger groups, and had arrangements with the keepers of particular public houses for the smooth operation of their scam.[62] Depending upon the drunkenness of the victim and his general vulnerability, tactics ranged from accosting him in the street and leading him gently to a tavern to more direct muggings like that of John Pargiter in June 1698, who 'was besett with divers persons ... and Mary Smith ... Embraced [him] and said unto him My Deare Come and goe along with me; divers others were about him and some said he should not goe home tonight', and when he disengaged himself he found he had been robbed.[63] Some bawdy houses, too, had the pickpocketing of clients down to a fine art. And some, through their trade in stolen goods, were part of extensive criminal organizations.[64]

Even apart from such connections, many who were involved in prostitution relied as a matter of course on loose networks of co-operation. In the eyes and the language of aggrieved parents, masters, and pickpocketed clients, all this amounted to a clear-cut divide between honest and respectable society and those who inhabited it, and a separate, predatory culture of thieves and prostitutes.[65] This was also how prostitution was portrayed in recurrent campaigns for moral reform, especially by those in socially declining neighbourhoods who felt their own claims to respectability to be under threat from the poorer, less orderly individuals increasingly surrounding them.[66] More generally, of course, such a dichotomy between honest and dishonest society underpinned the wider discourse of crime and social order in early modern England.

Yet, as we have seen, this perception of prostitution was undercut in several ways. Its concept of 'common' prostitution was defined far more in social than in sexual terms: as the whoredom of the idle and disorderly poor, and the natural concomitant of their other vices, rather than as a distinctive form of sexual relations. Thus it was not the activity of prostitution that was carefully described in every seventeenth-century legal handbook, but the character of 'the dissolute person, as the Strumpet': included, like 'the rogue', as one of the standard categories of thriftless poor.[67] In reality, of course, not all prostitutes were dishonest or disorderly, any more than all of them were impoverished. And conceptually, too, distinctions between honest and dishonest society had always been blurred, especially in fiction and in religious discourse, by popular ideas about the ubiquity of sin and of whores: clandestine as well as open, from 'Women of Fashion, who intrigue', through 'Good-natured Girls' and 'Kept Mistresses' to ordinary street walkers. Instead of a clear divide between respectable and disreputable groups, society was thus just as commonly perceived as infiltrated throughout by whoredom. Finally, even the basic notion that prostitutes were personally culpable for their actions was increasingly challenged from the early eighteenth century onwards by more wide-ranging interpretations, based on poverty, parental neglect and libertine rapacity.

In addition to these conflicting and changing ideas about the nature of whores, there was the problem of male complicity. Even if rhetorically the clients of prostitutes could be explained away, either as archetypal rakes and whoremongers who were already part of a dishonest subculture, or as innocent youths enticed into it, in practice it was impossible in any meaningful way to separate them from the rest of society. Those prosecuted at Westminster quarter sessions in the course of 1713, for example, included a typical cross-section of respectable occupations: a hatter of Piccadilly, a tallow chandler, a trunk maker, a victualler, an upholsterer, a soldier, a carpenter, a cabinet maker, a drawer in a public house, footmen, periwig makers, gentlemen and two visitors from Chesterton in Warwickshire.[68]

Most importantly of all, it was not just through their clients that prostitutes were connected with the reputable world around them. They themselves, too, were drawn from the same ranks, with husbands and 'friends' who were (again at random from 1713) attorneys, bakers, barber-surgeons, blacksmiths, brass button makers, braziers, bricklayers, butchers, carpenters, cooks, cordwainers, excisemen, file makers, gentlemen, glaziers, grocers, grooms, haberdashers, hat dyers, 'hot pressers' from Fashion Street, japanners, jewellers, joiners, mercers, painters, pin makers, plasterers, sailors, salters, sawyers, scriveners, sergeants, shoemakers, soldiers, tailors, trunk makers, victuallers, watermen, weavers and wig makers.[69] In short, women who engaged in prostitution were not, as a group, socially or economically distinct from respectable society. They were part of wider metropolitan communities. Their activities involved, and were shaped by, close contact with the other members of those communities; and even their sexual behaviour was not always easily distinguishable from that of the men and women around them. This was as much so amongst the bottom ranks of metropolitan society as it was amongst its elite, irrespective of the bias of the law and of the hierarchical patterns of thought that underpinned it.

The argument of this essay has been simple. Contemporary attempts to distinguish 'common' prostitution as a separate type of behaviour had some basis in fact. But they were never more than partial and competing descriptions of reality, and they were always challenged by other patterns of thought that stressed the indistinguishability of all whores. In truth, too, the types of illicit relations that men and women of all ranks engaged in were very similar, even if their material and social circumstances varied considerably. Thus adultery, prostitution and other forms of sexual immorality were part of one interconnected pattern of social and sexual relations: they cannot properly be understood in isolation.

NOTES

I am grateful to Hanna Pickard for her help with this essay.

1 See Richard Adair, *Courtship, Illegitimacy and Marriage in Early Modern England* (Manchester, 1996).

2 For prostitution see Randolph Trumbach, 'Modern prostitution and gender in *Fanny Hill*: libertine and domesticated fantasy', in G. S. Rousseau and Roy Porter eds, *Sexual Underworlds of the Enlightenment* (Manchester, 1987); Archer, *Pursuit*, chap. 6; Paul Griffiths, 'The structure of prostitution in Elizabethan London', *Continuity and Change*, 8 (1993); Tony Henderson, *Disorderly Women in Eighteenth-Century London* (1999). For marriage and adultery see Lawrence Stone, *Uncertain Unions: Marriage in England 1660–1753* (Oxford, 1992) and *Broken Lives: Separation and Divorce in England 1660–1857* (Oxford, 1993). For fornication and bastardy see Adrian Wilson, 'Illegitimacy and its implications in mid-eighteenth-century London: the evidence of the Foundling Hospital', *Continuity and Change*, 4 (1989); Nicholas Rogers, 'Carnal knowledge: illegitimacy in eighteenth-century Westminster', *Journal of Social History*, 33 (1989); Tim Hitchcock, '"Unlawfully begotten on her body": illegitimacy and the parish poor in St Luke's Chelsea', in *id. et al.* eds, *Chronicling Poverty* (Basingstoke, 1997).

3 Of course policing need not always be biased towards the 'lower' reaches of the market: cf. Archer, *Pursuit*, p. 213.

4 Lawrence Stone, *The Family, Sex and Marriage in England 1500–1800* (1977), chaps 10–12.

5 For homosexual relations see Alan Bray, *Homosexuality in Renaissance England* (1982); Randolph Trumbach, 'London's sodomites: homosexual behaviour and Western culture in the eighteenth century', *Journal of Social History*, 11 (1977); *id.*, 'Sodomitical assaults, gender role, and sexual development in eighteenth-century London', in Kent Gerard and Gert Hekma eds, *The Pursuit of Sodomy* (New York, 1989); Rictor Norton, *Mother Clap's Molly House* (1992).

6 'A Sermon against Whoredome and Uncleanness', in *Certain Sermons or Homilies Appointed to be Read in Churches* (1683 edition); John Godolphin, *Repertorium Canonicum* (third edition, 1687), p. 473; Martin Ingram, *Church Courts, Sex and Marriage in England, 1570–1640* (Cambridge, 1987), p. 239.

7 *Acts and Ordinances of the Interregnum, 1642–1660*, ed. C. H. Firth and R. S. Rait (3 vols, 1911), II, pp. 387–9.

8 Michael Dalton, *The Countrey Justice* (sixth edition, 1635), p. 189; E[dmund] W[ingate], *Justice Revived* (1661 edition), pp. 26–7; W[illiam] Shepherd, *A Sure Guide for His Majesties Justices of Peace* (second edition, 1669), p. 419; Godolphin, *Repertorium Canonicum*, p. 474.

9 J. H. Wilson, *The Private Life of Mr Pepys* (New York, 1959); Stone, *Family, Sex and Marriage*, pp. 552–61; M. H. Stein, in Pepys, *Diary*, X, pp. 176–80.

10 Pepys, *Diary*, e.g. III, p. 191; VI, pp. 155, 187, 202; VII, pp. 104, 172, 364; VIII, pp. 276, 280, 293, 315; IX, pp. 55, 143–5, 274, 277, 282, 307, 328, 337 (servants); VII, pp. 338–9, 395, 418–19; VIII, pp. 46, 53 (Betty Howlett-Mitchell); VII, pp. 168, 345, 392, 396; VIII, pp. 12, 14, 71, 128; IX, p. 158 (Elizabeth Burrows); I, pp. 237, 239 (Diana Crisp); VI, pp. 307; VII, pp. 4–5, 153; VIII, p. 114 (Frances Tooker).

11 *Ibid.*, e.g. VI, pp. 297, 310, 318–19, 332, 334–5 (Judith Penington); VII, p. 389; VIII, pp.

166, 234; IX, p. 194 (Margaret Penn); VII, p. 2; VIII, p. 29; IX, pp. 170, 172, 188, 189–90, 218 (Elizabeth Knepp); quotations from IX, p. 218.

12   *Ibid.*, IX, p. 188 (Nell Payne); VI, p. 335; VII, p. 417; VIII, pp. 233, 244, 282; IX, pp. 132, 248, 306 (Mrs Daniel); IV, p. 222 to IX, p. 221, *passim*; Arthur Bryant, *Samuel Pepys: The Years of Peril* (Cambridge, 1936), p. 372; *id.*, *Samuel Pepys: The Saviour of the Navy* (Cambridge, 1938), pp. 166–7, 386 (Mrs Bagwell).

13   Pepys, *Diary*, IV, pp. 203, 234, 263, 317; V, pp. 17, 216–17, 219, 242, 262, 285–6, 302, 338; VI, pp. 1–2, 35, 68, 71, 141; VII, pp. 49–50, 61–2, 75, 128, 134, 142–3, 232, 262, 284, 319, 322–3, 337, 342, 345, 359, 386, 406, 413; VIII, pp. 3, 39–40, 58, 64, 102–3, 110–11, 120–1, 128, 177, 224, 236, 255–6, 317–18, 323, 375–6, 393, 422, 429, 435, 440, 461, 478–9, 498, 601; IX, pp. 78, 99, 118, 121, 126, 136, 165, 208, 220, 249, 514, 527 (Betty Lane-Martin and her circle); quotations from IV, p. 317; V, p. 215; VI, p. 71; VIII, pp. 64, 128; IX, p. 514.

14   See e.g. *The Diary of Robert Hooke M.A. M.D. F.R.S. 1672–80*, ed. Henry W. Robinson and Walter Adams (1935); William Byrd, *The London Diary (1717–1721) and other Writings*, ed. Louis B. Wright and Marion Tinling (New York, 1958); *Boswell's London Journal 1762–1763*, ed. Frederick A. Pottle (New York, 1950); Giacomo Casanova, *History of my Life*, trans. Willard R. Trask (12 vols, Baltimore MD, 1997), IX–X.

15   CLRO SF 211, recog. 73; BCB XII, fo. 336; BCB XVI, fo. 17; LMA WJ/SR/1812, HCC.

16   LMA WJ/SR/2211, HCC 21 April; BCB XII, fo. 225. Cf. LMA WJ/SR/1822, HCC William Fish and Margaret Coffin; MJ/SR/2640, recog. 137; BCB XII, fo. 317.

17   See e.g. CLRO LMCB/1, fos 60v, 68r–v, 98, 145, 149; BCB XV, fo. 233; LMA MJ/SR/1413, recogs 1, 2, 3; MJ/SR/1808, recogs 62, 68, 72; MJ/SR/1823, inds 84, 92; MJ/SR/1815, recog. 143, ind. 28; MJ/SR/1820, recog. 158; WJ/SR/1822, recog. 86; WJ/SR/2013, HCC Elizabeth Wheeler; MJ/SR/2016, recog. 194; WJ/SR/2216, recog. 56; MJ/SR/2214, recog. 169; MJ/SR/2640, recogs 120, 121. For prosecutions brought by wives against adulterous husbands see e.g. BCB XVI, fos. 215, 240–1; LMA MJ/SR/1616, recog. 192; MJ/SR/1815, recog. 19; MJ/SR/1823, recog. 63; CLRO SF 397, recog. 61; SF 476, recog. 59. For prosecutions brought against adulterous wives and their lovers (and not involving bastardy) see e.g. CLRO SF 292, recog. 50; SF 395, recogs 70, 104; LMA WJ/SR/1602, recog. 110; MJ/SR/1820, recogs 18, 190; MJ/SR/1837, recog. 58; MJ/SR/2005, New Prison calendar no. 32.

18   LMA WJ/SR/2401, recogs 12, 13, 68, 70, 110, *ignoramus* ind. Mary Winwood; MJ/SR/2409, recog. 265; MJ/SP 1723 August/11. By 1735, Honour O'Connor was widowed: WJ/SR/2643, recogs 384, 387, ind.

19   Cf. *Reflections Arising from the Immorality of the Present Age* (1756), pp. 56–7 n.

20   Pepys, *Diary*, VI, pp. 204, 206, 212, 213, 234, 273; VII, pp. 74, 237–8 (Abigail Williams, mistress of Lord Brouncker).

21   *Ibid.*, I, p. xxxix; *Diary of Robert Hooke*, p. 262.

22   CLRO CSP April 1695, deposition of Mary Button; BCB XVI, fo. 266; [Daniel Defoe], *Augusta Triumphans* (1728), pp. 14–15.

23   E.g. LMA WJ/SR/1602, recog. 97; MJ/SR/1825, recog. 113; MJ/SR/2214, recog. 169.

24   E.g. LMA WJ/SR/1822, HCC; MJ/SR/2205, recogs 115, 117, 118; MJ/SBB/713, p. 7; LMA DL/C/151, fos. 22r–24r; BCB XVI, fo. 215; CLRO SF 472, recogs 15, 17, 18, 19. Cf. Rogers, 'Carnal knowledge'.

25 Cf. R. M. Smith, 'Marriage processes in the English past: some continuities', in Lloyd Bonfield *et al.* eds, *The World We Have Gained* (Oxford, 1986), and the literature cited there.

26 Roger Lee Brown, 'The rise and fall of the Fleet marriages', in R. B. Outhwaite ed., *Marriage and Society* (1981); Lawrence Stone, *Road to Divorce: England 1530–1987* (Oxford, 1990), chaps 4–5; Jeremy Boulton, 'Itching after private marryings? Marriage customs in seventeenth-century London', *LJ*, 16 (1991); R. B. Outhwaite, *Clandestine Marriage in England 1500–1850* (1995).

27 For contemporary surveys see *The Wandring Whore* (1660–63); [John Dunton], *The Night-Walker* (1696–97); [Edward Ward], *The London-Spy Compleat* (fourth edition, 1709); *Hell upon Earth* (1729); 'Father Poussin', *Pretty Doings in a Protestant Nation* (1734), revised and reissued as *Satan's Harvest Home* (1749); [John Cleland?], *The Case of the Unfortunate Bosavern Penlez* (1749); *A Congratulatory Epistle from a Reformed Rake* [1758].

28 Even prostitutes resident in bawdy houses would often ply in the street, or 'stand at the door to pick up men as they pass by': LMA MJ/SR/2205, recog. 95; Pepys, *Diary*, IV, p. 164; V, 219; VI, p. 63; [Cleland?], *Case of ... Penlez*, pp. 12–13.

29 See e.g. LMA MJ/SR/1825, recog. 19; MJ/SR/2409, HCC; WJ/SR/2896, HCC; *Boswell's London Journal*, pp. 263–4. Cheapest of all was a quick 'manual abortion': *Congratulatory Epistle*, p. 10; Pepys, *Diary*, IX, p. 297.

30 CLRO CSP January 1693, grand jury presentment.

31 LMA MJ/SR/1402, recog. 106.

32 LMA MJ/SR/2640, recog. 48.

33 CLRO CSP April 1705, deposition of Jane White. Cf. *Lorenzo Magalotti at the Court of Charles II*, ed. and trans. W. E. Knowles Middleton (Waterloo, Ontario, 1980), p. 125; Casanova, *History of my Life*, IX, pp. 189–90.

34 Pepys, *Diary*, III, p. 49. Cf. *ibid.*, VII, p. 100.

35 See e.g. PRO KB 9/887–9; KB 9/918–20; KB 10/2 (Hilary and Michaelmas 1681); KB 10/4 (Hilary to Michaelmas 1687).

36 Pepys, *Diary*, V, pp. 219–20, 225–6; *Lorenzo Magalotti*, p. 125; Lodewijk van der Saan, 'Verscheyde Concepten en Invallen' (1694–1704), Universiteitsbibliotheek Leiden, MS BPL 1325, fos 147–9; CLRO CSP October 1700, deposition of Sarah Curtis; LMA MJ/SR/1818, recog. 54; MJ/SR/2214, prosecution recogs 47, 49, recogs 39, 125; *Boswell's London Journal*, pp. 240–1.

37 CLRO MC6/550, deposition of Thomas Jones.

38 CLRO CSP April 1705, deposition of Jane White; CLRO SF 489, ind. Mary Coleman, Newgate calendar.

39 For female employment see M. Dorothy George, *London Life in the Eighteenth Century* (Harmondsworth, 1966), chap. 3, pp. 145–6, 425–8; Peter Earle, 'The female labour market in London in the late seventeenth and early eighteenth centuries', *EcHR*, 62 (1989); L. D. Schwarz, *London in the Age of Industrialisation* (Cambridge, 1992), chaps 1–2; Tim Meldrum, 'Domestic Service in London 1660–1750', University of London Ph.D. thesis (1996). For poor relief see S. M. Macfarlane, 'Social policy and the poor in the later seventeenth century', in Beier and Finlay, *London*. For basic subsistence levels and living expenses see e.g. Saunders Welch, *A Proposal ... to Remove... Common Prostitutes*

from the Streets of this Metropolis (1758), p. 38; George, *London Life*, pp. 169–70; Macfarlane, 'Social policy', p. 256; Peter Linebaugh, *The London Hanged: Crime and Civil Society in the Eighteenth Century* (1991), pp. 190–2, 242.

40 For street walkers negotiating for anything between a handkerchief and several guineas see BCB XVI, fo. 419; LMA MJ/SR/2016, recog. 252; *Congratulatory Epistle*, p. 10.

41 *Pace*, for example, Griffiths, 'Structure of prostitution', pp. 46–7.

42 *Boswell's London Journal*, pp. 256, 263–4. For an example of a 'lewd woman' paying a man to lie with her see CLRO LMCB/2, fo. 75.

43 Laura Gowing, 'Gender and the language of insult in early modern London', *HWJ*, 35, (1993).

44 See e.g. LMA MJ/SR/1825, recog. 21, ind. 12, New Prison calendar Susanna Neale.

45 Welch, *Proposal*; John Fielding, *A Plan for a Preservatory and Reformatory* (1758); J[oseph] Massie, *A Plan for the Establishment of Charity-Houses* (1758); [Jonas Hanway], *A Plan for Establishing a Charity-House* (1758).

46 LMA DL/C/151, fos 320–8; DL/C/249, fos 56–63, 116–17 (quotation from fo. 56v). For Francis Gotobed's substantial standing in the parish see *Middlesex County Records: Calendar of the Sessions Books 1689 to 1709*, ed. W. J. Hardy (1905), p. 40.

47 Thomas Bray, 'A General Plan of a Penitential Hospital for the Imploying and Reforming Lewd Women', Karpeles Manuscript Library, Santa Barbara CA.

48 LMA MJ/SR/3080, HCC 10 August 1758; MJ/SBP/16, ind. 122.

49 *London Journal*, 6 April 1723, p. 3; WPL E.2576, no. 103, cited in Trumbach, 'Modern prostitution', p. 76; *OBSP*, 25 February 1730, p. 17; *OBSP*, supplementary pamphlet devoted to the trial of Charteris (1730), quotations from p. 4.

50 See e.g. CLRO SF 246, recog. 40, ind. Dorothy Brumstone; SF 394, recog. 16; SF 395, recog. 21, ind. Sara Young; SF 397, recogs 37, 38; LMA WJ/SR/2401, prosecution recog. Mary Goddard, recogs 7, 8, *ignoramus* ind. Elizabeth Male and Mary Hall.

51 The following account is based on LMA WJ/SP July 1729/1–3; WJ/SR/2523, recogs 23, 24, 25, Gatehouse calendar nos 5, 6. Cf. e.g. Pepys, *Diary*, I, p. 250; LMA MJ/SR/1402, recog. 106; WJ/SR/1713, prosecution recog. Mary White, recogs 79, 123, HCC Hannah Groom, Elizabeth Huffington.

52 Cf. Faramerz Dabhoiwala, 'The construction of honour, reputation and status in late seventeenth- and early eighteenth-century England', *Transactions of the Royal Historical Society*, sixth series, 6 (1996), pp. 210–11.

53 *OBSP*, 1 July 1730, p. 12.

54 Van der Saan, 'Verscheyde Concepten', fos 148v–149.

55 CLRO CSP November 1675, deposition of Richard Wheeler; SF 246, ind. Richard Wheeler, Newgate calendar.

56 Judith R. Walkowitz, *Prostitution and Victorian Society* (Cambridge, 1980), chap. 1.

57 LMA MJ/SR/2214, prosecution recog. 50, recog. 45.

58 LMA MJ/SP/1695 April/2.

59 BCB XII, fo. 238; PRO KB 9/918, *certiorari* ind. 6; KB 29/324, rotulus 78.

60 BCB XIV, fo. 256; CLRO SF 207, recogs 27, 29, ind. Elizabeth Allibone and Daniel

Towse. Cf. PRO, KB 9/889, information 50; LMA WJ/SR/1602, recogs 34, 39; CLRO LMCB/1, fo. 140v.

61 E.g. BCB XX, fos 203, 207, 209.

62 See CLRO CSP December 1695, deposition of Richard Roberts.

63 CLRO CSP July 1698, deposition of John Pargiter.

64 See e.g. *OBSP*, 16 January 1730, pp. 9–10; 8 April 1730, p. 7; 28 September 1730, pp. 17–19; 14 October 1730, pp. 17–18.

65 Cf. R. Campbell, *The London Tradesman* (1747), p. 315.

66 *Antimoixeia: or, the Honest and Joynt-Design of the Tower Hamblets for the General Suppression of Bawdy-Houses* (1691); *The Vices of the Cities of London and Westminster* (Dublin, 1751), pp. 14–15; Robert B. Shoemaker, 'Reforming the city: the Reformation of Manners campaign in London 1690–1738', in Lee Davison *et al.* eds, *Stilling the Grumbling Hive* (Stroud, 1992), pp. 108–9.

67 Dalton, *Countrey Justice*, pp. 100–1; William Sheppard, *A Grand Abridgement of the Common and Statute Law of England* (4 parts, 1675), III, pp. 27–32.

68 LMA WJ/SR/2207, recogs 9, 12, 15; WJ/SR/2216, recogs 37, 39, 41, 43, 47, 48, 51, 53, 58, 59, 62, 63, 64, 65, 67, 134.

69 CLRO SF 552, recog. 17; SF 556, recogs 13, 14, 16, 19, 24, 25, 36, 37, 39, 40, 41, 45, 46, 47, 49, 62, 63, 64, 65, 72, 75, 79; LMA MJ/SR/2205, recog. 76; MJ/SR/2214, recogs 23, 28, 46, 166, 334, 336; WJ/SR/2207, recogs 2, 14, 24, 40; WJ/SR/2216, recogs 52, 54, 61.

Chapter 6

Wives and marital 'rights' in the Court of Exchequer in the early eighteenth century

Margaret R. Hunt

U rban historians have long suspected that city women were more independent and less likely to passively accept the blandishments of tradition than their rural counterparts. Research into women and the law now appears to be confirming this view. As Robert Shoemaker has shown, eighteenth-century urban Middlesex women were more likely to prosecute by recognizance and to act as witnesses in court than rural women.[1] Laura Gowing's work on late sixteenth- and seventeenth-century defamation and marital separation suits in ecclesiastical courts suggests that urban, and especially London, women's greater propensity to sue was of long standing.[2] Nevertheless, we do not know whether urban women were *actually* more assertive, nor whether their readier access to courts simply encouraged them to air grievances there which their country cousins would have managed in less traceable ways. Still, it seems that some eighteenth-century people did feel that city women were more assiduous in defence of their rights and less easily taken advantage of than other women.[3]

This assumption surfaces in 1705 in an Exchequer suit about a disputed marriage brokerage fee. John and Elizabeth Spinkes accused another couple, Anthony and Joanna Hilton, of taking advantage of Elizabeth Spinkes's (then Elizabeth Prichard's) naivety, misrepresenting John's wealth and prospects to her, and locking her up during the betrothal negotiations in order to extort from her a fee for brokering the alliance. It is the Hiltons' response to this claim that is most interesting. They asserted that they did not 'believe that the said Elizabeth would suffer herself to be locked up or be anywise governed by these defendants ... for that she is (as these defendants believe) of the age of forty years and upwards, *hath lived most if not all of her life in London, and [is] not easily to be imposed on by any person*' (emphasis mine).[4]

The reputation of London women notwithstanding, there remains considerable doubt among historians as to whether the generality of pre-modern

*women really exercised much individual agency. The dearth of records gener-
ated by women themselves and the abundance of conservative moralizing
about them have encouraged the belief that married women, in particular,
were too cowed, confined and oppressed to control their own destinies to any
appreciable degree. Thus, as recently as 1989, Roy Porter suggested that most
women of the period were so trapped at home that they became virtual
ciphers.* [5] *Two developments have combined to overturn such assumptions.
First, copious evidence is coming to light about early modern women's (and
especially urban women's) activities outside the home as consumers, wage
earners, petty retailers, and political and religious agitators.* [6] *Second, evidence
is accumulating on women plaintiffs, defendants and witnesses in a number
of legal venues. Clearly women did act on their own behalf in public forums,
and they did so in far larger numbers than we used to think.* [7] *The story that is
now taking shape is not a simple one however. Ambiguity, complexity and
constraint are everywhere in the records, and particularly evident whenever
women talked about – and sought redress from – exploitative behaviour by
men.* [8]

*Malcolm Gaskill has written that court records 'provide practical contexts
in which popular mentalities can be explored not just as abstract structures,
but as ideas in action'.* [9] *Cases involving female litigants or concerned with
marital difficulties reveal something about the 'abstract structures' married
and unmarried women used to order their experience and about how those
ideas were transformed into actions. The courtroom is a place where notions
of 'right' or 'entitlement' intersect more primitive feelings: ravaged dignity,
psychic devastation, desire for revenge, and intolerable feelings of loss
(including material loss). This chapter utilizes the records of one London-
based court, the Court of Exchequer, to explore the ways some London women
and their families constructed notions of 'right' within marriage as well as a
sense of 'having been wronged' by their husbands.* [10] *Elaine Hobby has urged
us to discover the ways early modern women sought 'to turn constraints into
permissions, into little pockets of liberty or autonomy.'* [11] *Here we focus on
those grudgingly awarded 'permissions' and 'little pockets of liberty' just
when they are on the point of turning into something else: a sense of how
marriage 'should' operate that some women were willing to defend publicly in
a court of law.*

SMITH *V.* AMSON: SETTING THE STAGE

The June 1723 nuptials of James Smith, a London dealer, and Elizabeth, a
goldsmith's daughter, were inauspicious. The couple had not gained the
consent of Elizabeth's widowed mother, Anne Amson, and she, for her part,
was so grieved and so suspicious of her son-in-law that she refused to receive

the couple in her home. However, her daughter begged her to relent, so after a few months Anne decided that 'tho' [the marriage] was to [her daughter's] ruin ... there was not other remedy but patience and resignation to the will of God', and she reluctantly permitted the couple to move into two 'well-furnished' rooms in her house in the City. But proximity only bred greater contempt. According to Anne, James Smith grew quarrelsome, 'morose' and abusive towards her and her daughter. Angry that he had not received all of Elizabeth's dowry, Smith treated '[Anne Amson] and her Character with abundance of scurrility', and launched several suits against her for the money. He also threatened his wife, then pregnant, 'with breaking her bones or [words] to the like effect and thereby put her in bodily fear of her life', so much so that she and her mother obtained a warrant for his arrest if he did not desist. When the couple separated Smith refused to pay anything towards the upkeep of his pregnant wife, and continued to make Elizabeth's life miserable – on one occasion he broke into Anne's house, flourished a knife at his wife, and 'used her so inhumanely' that she jumped out a window and 'had like to have lost her milk[,] the ... Child she has had by the Complainant [Smith] then sucking at her breast'.

Unsurprisingly Smith's perception of events was quite different. He claimed in a suit in the London Court of Exchequer, brought barely sixteen months after the marriage, that his mother-in-law had conspired from the beginning 'to cross [our] Measure and put an end to [our] happiness'. According to him, she persuaded the couple to live with her 'by feigned affection and subtle contrivances', mainly to 'procure [for] herself the advantage of the help and assistance of [Elizabeth] in the management of her [i.e. Anne's] ... [business] affairs'. She then incited her daughter to 'refuse to converse with or admit ... [Smith] into bed with her'. Smith also alleged that his mother-in-law had tried to wreck his reputation and trade by publicly reporting that he was 'a Broken Merchant and a Bankrupt and not worth a Groat and was a runaway', prompting him to sue her for defamation. Finally, Anne persuaded some business partners of her daughter's to arrest Smith for debt.[12]

It is a common fallacy that eighteenth-century marriages were virtually indissoluble, that abusive husbands were above the reach of the law, and that incompatible couples were chained together for life. In fact the sources reveal that troubled and crumbling marriages constituted a significant proportion of legal business in the early modern period. The small but steady stream of middling and elite men and women who sued for legal separation in diocesan ecclesiastical courts and sometimes in the Court of Arches[13] were but one small part of this phenomenon. A much larger number of individuals or couples found lawyers to negotiate private articles of separation or, if they lacked money, simply abandoned the marriage. Others turned to common law courts, borough courts and local courts of request, initiating suits for conjugal support, unpaid dowries, 'criminal conversation' damages and defamation. In the central equity courts (Chancery and Exchequer) men sued marriage brokers for misrepresenting the assets of their wives before marriage, while wives and their kin sued husbands for dissipating their separate estates or jointures, or failing to support them. Wives, relatives or neighbours often went to JPs or magistrates to 'swear out the peace' against abusive husbands, and families took revenge on violent sons-in-law (and husbands upon in-laws who failed to pay portions) by having them imprisoned for debt. The suits did not stop with the death of one or other of the principals. People bickered in probate and equity courts over the estates of husbands or wives from whom, in life, they had been estranged. Widowers frequently sued the family of their dead wife for debts, personal property or portions. Their in-laws retaliated by suing husbands for the living expenses and medical or funeral bills of their estranged wives. The result is a mountain of information, but one that historians, until recently, have either ignored or – blinded by the belief that early modern marriages were somehow sacrosanct – have failed to see as thematically connected.

WOMEN LITIGANTS IN EQUITY

The status of wives under English law is often summed up by the dictum 'man and wife are one and that one is the husband', and until recently most historians assumed that there was little else to say. It is true that the common law was unkind to married women. But, as Amy Erickson has demonstrated, it was only one of at least five different systems of law operating in the eighteenth century, some of which did permit married women to sue their husbands, to possess movable property, to pursue a trade, and even to demand a separation with alimony.[14] Most responsive to married women's claims were ecclesiastical and equity law, the second of which forms the basis of this chapter.

The most important equity courts were Chancery and Exchequer. The scale of business in these courts was immense. There were between 200,000 and 250,000 equity cases brought in Chancery and roughly 40,000 in Exchequer between 1700 and 1800 (the two followed nearly identical procedures and handled similar cases).[15] A longitudinal study of Chancery by Henry Horwitz found that women made up 14·4 percent of plaintiffs in 1627, a figure that had risen to 21·2 per cent by 1818/19.[16] The total number of eighteenth-century litigants is difficult to measure because of the regular participation of co-plaintiffs and co-defendants, but, assuming an average of 1·6 plaintiffs per case, and taking 18 per cent as a benchmark for the proportion of women plaintiffs, an estimate of 69,000 women plaintiffs in the two courts in the eighteenth century is not too far off the mark. This figure may be roughly broken down by marital status into perhaps 34,000 married women (most acting as co-plaintiffs with their husbands), 23,000 widows and 12,000 spinsters.[7] Plaintiffs are, of course, only half the story. Less attention has so far been paid to defendants, but it is reasonable to assume that there were at least as many female defendants as plaintiffs (actually there were almost certainly more),[8] and that their marital status did not differ radically from that enumerated above for plaintiffs. It is likely, then, that the total number of women litigants, both plaintiffs and defendants, in the central equity courts in the eighteenth century exceeded 135,000. The vast majority of these cases have never been seriously examined by historians.

The figures give some idea of the scale of women's involvement in the central equity courts. However, we should be clear about what they actually mean. Marriage-related litigation was *not* the most common type of litigation undertaken by women; the data show that women were at least as likely to sue over inheritance, mortgage foreclosure, tithes, debts or trade disputes. More-over, marriage litigation was a broader phenomenon than wives suing husbands (or vice versa). A range of people at the periphery of any marriage (fathers, mothers, brothers, sisters, friends) participated in litigation over trusts or jointures, conjugal maintenance, dowries, marriage brokerage, spousal abuse, marital finances, the estates and debts of deceased wives or husbands, separations and adultery. In fact widows engaged in marriage litigation more frequently than wives: often they were parties to suits over marriage portions (Smith *v.* Amson is one such case), or they found themselves having to cope with the legal detritus of an abusive and difficult relationship after a husband had died.

Nonetheless it *was* significant that wives sued on their own account in equity courts, though it is probable that less than 5 per cent of married women litigants actually did so, and a still smaller percentage took legal action against their own husband. Generally women who sued their husband utilized the legal fiction of the *prochein amy*, meaning that a close relative or friend acted as titular plaintiff in their place.[9] Married women also sued when their husbands were 'beyond the sea' (often this simply meant that the pair had separated). These two strategies probably resulted in a few thousand cases in the eighteenth century, a tiny percentage of the total volume of Chancery and Exchequer business.[20] But while they were not numerous in statistical terms these cases matter because they symbolize equity's willingness to take seriously problems that sprang from the intersection of gender, money and marriage. There were other courts willing to hear marriage-related litigation (most notably the ecclesiastical courts), and people used common law courts and other venues to prosecute marriage-related vendettas. But because equity courts were cheap, employed the vernacular tongue, handled a wide range of family matters, and could block actions in other courts, and because they were capable of recognizing that husbands and wives might have separate and antagonistic interests, they quickly became the venue of choice for settling many kinds of marital disputes.

In the sixteenth century female litigants in equity had been drawn largely from the upper gentry or aristocracy.[21] But by the early eighteenth century the range of women, and especially London women, who resorted to the equity courts had broadened considerably. Middle- to high-income litigants continued to predominate (this remains true in most civil jurisdictions to this day). But the fact that filing a bill cost between £3 and £6 in the early eighteenth century, and that both Exchequer and Chancery permitted plaintiffs and defendants to petition for admission *in forma pauperis*, thus exempting them from most court costs, seems to have encouraged significant numbers of poor people (again, most notably Londoners) to bring their grievances there.[22] Among *in forma pauperis* litigants could be found female servants, sometimes banding together to sue a deceased master's executor for an unpaid legacy, destitute widows, portionless spinsters, abandoned and runaway wives, sailors' widows, and a variety of petty tradeswomen.[23] Costs were also kept down by the fact that nearly three-quarters of cases nation-wide and an even larger proportion of London cases were dropped early in the process, usually during the pleading stage before depositions were filed and costs began to mount.[24]

TALES OF THE EXCHEQUER

The high proportion of cases that were dropped reflected plaintiffs' motives for initiating a suit in Exchequer in the first place. For some this was but one step in a campaign to encourage their adversaries to come to an out-of-court settlement; for others it was an effort to stop or suspend an action initiated in another court; for still others the main aim seems to have been to embarrass the other party by publicly airing the intimate details of a private dispute. That so many cases did not proceed to judgement, though good for the litigants' purse, does pose problems for the historian. Most cases break off *in medias res* at the point where one or the other of the parties gave up the fight and disappeared, agreed to settle, concluded that the matter had been sufficiently publicized or resolved to pursue the dispute elsewhere. The material provides an intimate view of eighteenth-century life, but narrative closure eludes us. It is rare to discover what the court thought about a particular individual's claim, and we have few clues as to what the final outcomes were.

Yet these cases are still recognizably stories. In recent years, and especially since the publication of Natalie Zemon Davis's *Fiction in the Archives* (1987), historians have developed a sharp interest in the stories people tell in legal contexts.[25] Storytelling requires the narrator to impose imaginative order on to a stream of fragmented impressions and memories. To tell a story in the highly charged atmosphere of the courtroom (in the case of Exchequer a story that was *read* in court, as oral testimony was rare) presented unusual narrative challenges. Pressures to be compelling and believable were unusually strong. The adversarial character of Exchequer – indeed, of any court – encouraged storytellers to speak in moral absolutes and to shape narratives around generally accepted behavioural norms, which had been – they alleged – systematically flouted by the other party. The resulting stories are manifestly full of lies, omissions, temporal transpositions and eccentric interpretations of events. Yet Exchequer cases remain an exceptional source for uncovering the value systems both women and men brought to marriage.

Exchequer differs from some other courts studied by historians in recent years in that the richest materials are not the depositions, which, in any case, are very few in number. More revealing are the 'bills', filed by plaintiffs through their counsel, and the 'answers', supplied by defendants to subpoenas issued by the court. (Taken together they are referred to as 'pleadings'.) Both bill and answer sought to organize the disputed events into a compelling narrative, and were much more carefully crafted than most court depositions. Litigants told their story to a paid advocate in relative privacy and without undue time pressure. Litigant and counsel could draft alternative versions, shape the presentation, and smooth out and conceal the question and response structure, as well as the outbursts, recriminations and confusion that colour many depositions. Finally, unlike many depositions, pleadings display a clearly recognizable beginning, middle and end, generally chronologically arranged.

But whose story do these records tell? Exchequer pleadings were mediated texts, structured by legal protocol and saturated with the idiosyncratic vocabulary and syntax of the law. At the same time pleadings drew heavily on the language and narrative disposition of the litigant. In the case of Smith *v.* Amson it is reasonable to suppose that the mother-in-law, Anne Amson, spoke of her daughter's marriage in phrases very like those that appear in her pleading: 'tho' [the marriage] was to [her daughter Elizabeth's] ruin ... there was not other remedy but patience and resignation to the will of God'; that she did defame her son-in-law by calling him 'a Broken Merchant and a Bankrupt and not worth a Groat'; and that it was she who enlarged upon the story of Smith breaking into her house and assaulting Elizabeth with the colourful, if inconclusively worded, claim that her terrified daughter 'had like to have lost her milk the ... Child she has had by [Smith] then sucking at her breast'. It also seems likely that it was Anne Amson who transformed her statement from a bare recollection of events into a story about her basic decency and her son-in-law's fundamental depravity: how she relented and forgave her daughter for marrying without her consent, the generosity she extended to the young couple, the base way James Smith repaid her and her daughter. We can be sure that her lawyer encouraged her in this exercise; he certainly gave these elements a prominent place in the narrative. But it is hard to believe they are not, in the first instance, Anne Amson's own.

In fact, neither litigants nor their lawyers had an especially large repertoire of tales to tell about marriage. This may owe something to narrow conceptions of what judges wanted to hear. But more fundamentally it was a response to three interconnected factors. First there was the relatively patterned way in which many marriages broke apart: throwing together at close quarters two incompatible people tended then, as now, to breed a wearisomely small range of scenarios. Second, there was the overdetermined character of eighteenth-century marriage, constituting as it did the main, and sometimes the *only*, permissible mode of organizing sexuality and reproduction, intergenerational property transfer, gendered power relations, residence arrangements, status, and domestic production and consumption. And finally there was the stress of sustaining patriarchal relations in the face of widely divergent temperaments, intellects, leadership skills and capacities for compromise on the part of wives and husbands. It is often the case that the most difficult human interactions have the greatest tendency to devolve into cliché. The demands placed upon marriage required the most simplistic and repetitive of legitimating narratives, from 'they lived happily ever after' (the stuff of romances) to 'she was an adulterous whore and so the marriage foundered' (a staple in the consistory courts).[26] But it is time to try to inject more complexity into this picture.

THE HUSBAND'S SIDE

The husband in an Exchequer cases almost always represented himself as having entered upon marriage with reasonable expectations, only to find an unloving, disobedient wife who, aided and abetted by her family, refused to make peace or live with him. James Smith in Smith *v.* Amson complained that his wife stopped speaking to him, refused to sleep with him, declined to move out of her mother's house and live separately with him, and resisted his efforts to seek a reconciliation. He claimed that he pleaded with her in vain 'to consider better of her past Conduct, return to her duty and forget the unnatural impressions her mother had made on her in prejudice of [his] Love and well intended Inclinations toward her'.[27] In 1724 Henry Gould complained that, following a row, his wife 'without any just cause or Reason' and 'without his Consent went away and hath absented herself from this Defendant ever since'.[28] In 1698 Gideon Harvey complained that his wife 'thought fit to ... withdraw herself from this defendants house and company notwithstanding she was ... desired and entreated by this defendant ... to stay with him at his house'.[29] These husbands knew that their wives were bound by law, religion and custom to allow them sexual access and to obey their wishes (these principles lay at the heart of traditional conceptions of marriage), and they made their wives' conscious resistance central to their suits.

Another key theme of men's stories was fraud, especially with regard to the marriage portion. In many marriages there was skirmishing even *after* the ceremony about the size of the portion, with husbands seeking to raise the amount and in-laws to lower it – or to claim that a portion had never been part of the bargain. In 1719 William Milton of London sued his mother-in-law, Ann Sell, an Audley End widow, claiming that they had agreed on a marriage portion of £50–£100. Sell responded that she had never consented to the marriage and was in any case not 'of any ability to give any marriage portion', as Milton well knew, '[she] having then several children and no other subsistence than what she got by keeping ... [a] small victualling house'. More damning, she claimed that he had no 'pretence of asking any portion he being at the time of his courtship only a common gager in the excise of beer and ale' who, shortly after the marriage, was 'turned out of his employment and left destitute'.[30]

Another accusation frequently made by men was that their wives had carried away trade goods, money and other possessions. The details they supply suggest strongly that women *did* often try to retain items that they considered their own, or that could be easily sold, pawned, or hidden with friends or relatives.[31] What is interesting is that men generally sought to conceal or underplay the fact that the items in question came from the woman's own trade or were things she had brought with her to the marriage; women, on the other hand, always emphasized the items' origins. Clearly husbands and their lawyers feared that common law rules about women's property passing to husbands on marriage might become diluted in the more 'woman-friendly' atmosphere of equity, while women and *their* lawyers welcomed the opportunity to publicize the injustice of applying coverture in too heavy-handed a fashion.

A wife's freehold or copyhold property posed a more strictly moral problem. Under common law, when a woman property owner married, the 'fruits' (i.e. rents or agricultural produce) of the land became the absolute property of her husband. However, he could not permanently alienate land without his wife's permission. But what if a husband was in danger of being imprisoned for debt or would suffer a serious blow to his credit unless his wife agreed to liquidate their joint real-estate assets? As his wife and helpmeet was she not morally obligated to consent to the sale? Evidently husbands thought so. Equally clearly wives who were concerned about their own and their children's financial security often did not. Separate settlements, consisting of money or property kept, generally in trust, for the benefit of women or their children either during the marriage (the separate estate) or after a husband's death (the widow's jointure or other trusts), complicated matters still further.

The original intent of separate estates and jointures since the late Middle Ages had been to provide a permanent livelihood for women and their children, safe from grasping or feckless husbands and their creditors. But they raised similar problems to real property: at what point should a woman's duty to her husband in the present outweigh future provision for herself or her children? Husbands in Exchequer cases thought that it should be fairly early in the process, and drew upon rising contemporary antipathy to separate settlements to bolster their position.[32] By contrast, wives and their kin often went to extraordinary lengths to maintain control of jointures and separate estates, even when the marriage threatened to collapse under the strain. Marriage, as these men encountered it, was a volatile, morally ambiguous institution in which their authority was questioned at every turn.

THE WIFE'S SIDE

Most marriages had broken down irreparably by the time the litigants reached court, so that there was little inducement for women to voice the kind of ostentatiously conventional views of matrimony and gender relations that we so often find in other public venues. Instead women depicted themselves as the victims of men who thought nothing of sacrificing justice, equity and family duty to the lure of financial gain. Thus Anne Hearne's 1703 suit against her estranged husband Edward claimed that she had been left a 'substantial estate' of £800 by her first husband, thus making her an excellent marriage prospect. In consequence 'several persons of good rank and quality and of good substance and estate aged between forty and fifty years' asked for her hand, but Anne, 'not knowing her Destiny, refused them all'. All, that is, except for Edward Hearne, who boasted of a great fortune, and whom Anne consented to marry in the 1680s, 'not knowing of [his] mean and low Condition till after such marriage had taken effect'. It quickly became evident that Hearne had married her for her money, for 'no sooner [had Hearne] got [her] ... fortune into his hands but he grew very outrageous beating and bruising [her] in a very outrageous manner in so much that [she] hath often despaired of her life'. Anne was forced to live with relatives and:

> So soon as ... Edward Hearne had got as many of [Anne's] effects ... into his hands as he possibly could which he quickly did do to upwards the value of one thousand pounds [he] ... never came near your Oratrix since or allow[ed] one farthing ... for her subsistence so that [she] ... must have starved in all this time being about Eleven years had it not been for the charitable kindness and benevolence of her Friends and Relations.[33]

Deceived, exploited and spurned: this is a generic story, well known in contemporary drama, fiction and law, about a young heiress who is seduced by a heartless fortune hunter, maltreated, and then abandoned once everything of value, from her virginity and self-respect to her fortune, has been wrested from her.[34]

The formulaic character of Anne Hearne's complaint – as well as some of its tactical limitations – are revealed in Edward Hearne's answer. Hearne claimed that he never tried to induce Anne to marry him by boasting about the worth of his estate; instead *he* was prevailed upon to marry *her*. Moreover she exaggerated the value of her fortune: it consisted only of £200 and 'certain Grocery Wares ... valued at three score pounds'. The couple parted because of Anne's 'indiscreet and extravagant courses' and 'turbulent temper'. and her 'embezzling her [*sic*] ... Stock in trade',[35] leaving him with a £60 debt. Far from being inhumane and cruel, as his wife was claiming, he left only when 'misfortunes in trade' made it necessary for him to go abroad; he had given his wife money for her maintenance in his absence and he had spent much more 'to defend several vexatious and unnecessary suits commenced against him by [his wife's] relations ...'. In short, Anne was a middle-aged shopkeeper rather than a 'gentlewoman heiress'; she, not he, began the courtship; her so-called 'fortune' was negligible, and, far from being blameless, she was an extravagant termagent with a horde of litigious relatives.[36]

Women's tales generally represented men as cruel, more interested in money than in love, prone to claim financial benefits to which they were at best marginally entitled, and unwilling to support their wives before and after the separation. The last of these, 'maintenance', as it was generally called, was especially important because it was one of the few clear female 'rights' in marriage. In the 'social contract' between husband and wife, the responsibility to maintain the wife was the *quid pro quo* for her obedience and sexual services. Mary Duncan, who sued her sailor husband William in 1716 when he revoked a power of attorney empowering her to collect a portion of his wages, charged him with intent 'to impoverish and bring her and her poor family to utter ruin'.[37] Mary Flat, defending herself in 1701 from one of her deceased husband's creditors, capped a sad tale of abuse (Thomas Ellis 'was this Defendant's former husband to her great sorrow') by claiming that she separated from Ellis with only the clothes on her and her daughter's backs, for he had not left them 'anything whatsoever to Maintain them[selves] with'.[38] Anne Amson justified her refusal to pay her estranged son-in-law the marriage portion on the grounds that her daughter had been left

> bereft of all manner of assistance from the Compl[ainan]t and she and her Child she hath by him must necessarily have come to the parish for their respective maintenances had not this Defendant [Anne] out of Compassion ... maintained [them] ... ever since the Compl[ainan]t left her they or either or them not having had one penny directly or indirectly from the Compl[ainan]t [since about thirteen months before].[39]

Such pre-emptive or, as in this case, defensive appeals to wives' 'right to maintenance' are ubiquitous in Exchequer marriage cases.

In theory a woman's possessions became her husband's the instant the knot was tied. But women in Exchequer cases accused husbands of pushing this doctrine to such an extreme that it threatened to defeat the law's larger purpose –the well-being of families. Their stories are awash with men who grab their wife's wages or trading profits, leaving both wife and children to starve, who pawn or sell their wife's possessions, exploit her labour (being forced to do hard and dangerous work while heavily pregnant is a recurrent complaint), try to squeeze money or loans from in-laws using physical violence, and appropriate their wife's separate estate and jointures. The impression women and their relatives sought to convey in their suits was of domestic patriarchy run amuck.

THE MARITAL ECONOMY OF WOMEN

If even a quarter of what was said about them was true, the men in these cases demonstrated woefully little concern for their families' welfare. Contemporaries would not, for the most part, have recognised them as 'good husbands'. At the same time one suspects that what was most unusual about them was the extremity of their actions – and perhaps the extent of the resistance they encountered from their wives and in-laws – not their core assumptions about male supremacy, which would have been shared to some degree by most men of the time, and by at least some women.[40] These cases have value not because these fractured families were 'normal' (they were not) but because they reveal, in a highly stylized fashion, fault lines which lay at the heart of many more marriages than the ones that ended up in court.

These relationships were destroyed by fundamental disagreements about what was and was not acceptable in marriage. Specifically some wives were far less committed to male supremacy than their husbands, especially if it cost them their future security, personal possessions, access to their own money, or the right to their own trading profits. The law of coverture was possibly enhanced in this period by the growing prestige of the common law and the courts' willingness to enforce its often arcane rules. But the London evidence suggests that many women had their own ideas about how marriage and property should be organized, ideas that enjoyed less general assent than the various patriarchal alternatives espoused by most husbands but which were not lonely fantasies either. It was these perceptions of 'right' that fuelled women's powerful defences of their interests in the courts and elsewhere.

Equity cases brought by London women and their relatives rely upon four suppositions or principles, which recur so frequently as to suggest that they possessed real normative value. The first was the notion that, in the event of marital collapse, either by death or by separation, women were entitled to goods or a sum of money at least equivalent in value to what they had brought to the marriage. While the common law made no provision for ensuring that husbands set such sums aside (a marriage settlement might, but they were negotiated only in a minority of marriages), women themselves, many husbands, and, crucially, the bureaucrats and lawyers who administered probate and equity, agreed that if possible women should not lose their money for ever once they married.[41] In law this principle applied narrowly to the administering of wills and estates and to disputed jointures after a husband's death, but it had its corollary within marriage in that many women felt justified in demanding a say in the management of the family finances commensurate with what they had brought to the marriage. The other side of the coin was that wives sometimes objected to husbands who tried to control or monitor the spending of what they (the women) saw as joint assets. Thus, in one seventeenth-century Chancery case, a woman was represented telling another that 'what was her Husbands was her own, and why should she account for [how she spent] her own': in so doing, she neatly converted coverture and the common law principle of a wife's legal nullity into a justification of independent management of a share of the marital assets.[42] This may be an isolated case, but it resonates with scores of other disputes over money in relation to marriage.

The second principle of what I will call the 'female marital economy' was the right to maintenance. As we have seen, this was held up as a true 'right', based on common law, though, as Amy Erickson points out, it was very hard to enforce in actual common law courts.[43] Enforceable at law or not, the right to maintenance had great moral power, and the Exchequer records provide much evidence about the ways London women actually used the 'right' to mount day-to-day challenges to their husbands' authority.

Two rather typical early eighteenth-century cases from opposite ends of the social spectrum illustrate well women's tactical use of the maintenance argument. In 1710 Mary Hart and her husband Samuel, a London merchant, fell out over his failure to provide her a 'decent livelihood', and his endeavours, as his wife put it, 'by all ways and means possible to grasp all the profits of the [joint tenancy and her separate] Estate' and 'to alien[ate], mortgage and encumber the same to raise up moneys to support his expensive ways of living'. The couple separated and Samuel launched several suits to claim the money. Efforts by his solicitor to effect a reconciliation initially failed because Mary 'was averse thereto and did Revile and Reproach her said Husband to a very high Degree', causing Samuel to withdraw from the negotiations. However, Mary later applied to her husband's solicitor, complaining that she was 'afraid [her husband] would spend his whole estate and ruin [her] and her children', and persuaded him to draw up papers putting the entire estate into a trust for the benefit of the couple's eldest son with annual (separate) allowances for herself and her husband, as 'that would be the best way to preserve the said Estate and put it out of her ... husband's power to sell or dispose thereof'.[44] This was a significant intervention and, like many such cases, demonstrates the high degree of legal sophistication some women attained while in pursuit of what they deemed to be their own.

But women did not have to have a knowledge of the law to appeal to the right to maintenance. In 1701 James Salter, a Whitechapel coachman, sued his uncle, William Bland, from whom he had purchased, on instalment, an old hackney coach and three horses. Salter proved unable to meet the payments and being 'illiterate and inexperienced in these matters' was persuaded by Bland to sell everything back, he (Salter) understanding this to be 'a sort of mortgage' whereby he could continue to use the coach and horses to make his living. When Bland locked the stable door against him Salter sued, only to discover from Bland's answer that his (Salter's) own wife had asked Bland to take the coach and horses 'for that her husband had no profit by them but on the contrary that they impoverished him so that she could not have a shilling of her husband to buy her children bread ...'.[45]

The third 'principle' of the female marital economy was the belief that it was unjust for a husband to use violence or threats to extract more money than he was entitled to from his wife or her relatives. Financial disputes were only one of many pretexts for wife beating but it is clear that many men did use physical violence to extort portions or other monies from in-laws, or to seize women's separate estates or trade goods if they were *feme sole* traders.[46] Exchequer wives' antipathy to wife beating, at least when it was linked with financial extortion, was probably encouraged by ambivalent attitudes towards marital violence in the judiciary and the culture at large. While status superiors were assumed to have the right – indeed, the responsibility – to physically discipline their inferiors, grievous bodily harm inflicted on a wife by her husband sufficiently defeated the purpose of marriage that, from at least the fifteenth century, magistrates were willing to require men to post bonds for their better behaviour. In addition, from an early date men could be prosecuted for murder if they beat their wives to death.

Cases brought by London women and their relatives across a number of venues routinely introduced allegations of spousal violence and cruelty to demand legal separation, gain judicial relief from attacks upon wives' jointures and separate estates, bolster maintenance claims, justify disobeying a husband's direct command to return to the marital home, and avoid paying portions. Anne Amson forcefully articulated both a woman's right to be free from extreme cruelty *and* her right to maintenance when she and her lawyer insisted in court that 'she is not obliged either to maintain [James Smith's] ... wife and Child for nothing or to turn [them out of her house and expose them] to the insults or ill usage ... with which [her husband] ... hath lately threatened her ...'.[47] In other words, Smith should maintain his wife financially even if she refused, out of fear, to live with him. This was far indeed from the common law view of marriage.

The final 'principle' deals a death blow to our received notions about early modern wives' supposed legal incapacity. Although it was well established that women could not testify against their husbands in common law courts, London women were perfectly aware that the common law was not the only law in town. They also knew that while *they* could not sue their husbands at common law, their relatives and friends were under no such disability. Henry Gould's wife 'threatened [that] she would be the ruin of him' and 'see him in gaol',[48] and her father made good her threats by initiating suits against Gould in both the common law and the equity courts. Women and their families also swore the peace against abusive husbands,[49] sought to have them imprisoned for debt and brought them up before the ecclesiastical courts. At some earlier point in time, presumably during the litigious seventeenth century, a surprising number of London women and their relatives had come to view abusive or extortionate behaviour by husbands as actionable just like any other hurt. Neither the courts nor wives applied the same standards to husbands as they did to other people (a definitional problem that, even today, undermines efforts to eradicate family violence), and many women's efforts to use the law must have got nowhere in either instrumental or jurisprudential terms. Still, it is quite evident that the law had come to be seen as an important weapon in the arsenal of victimized wives, and that it had taken its place alongside the more traditional remedies (magic, intervention by relatives and neighbours, the solace of religion) as a source of real power. The women in these cases believed they had a 'right' to go to law, either on their own or by proxy, even if the source of their distress was their own husband.

PATRIARCHAL POWER AND CLANDESTINE ACTION

The marital economy of women informed and perhaps inspired litigation, but it also helped legitimize clandestine and extra-legal activity by wives. In 1710 Richard North, a Westminster joiner, sued one of his wife's friends over £30 his wife, Alice, had lent her. His bill states that Alice, 'intending to secrete and conceal' the money and turn it 'to her own use[,] without [his] consent hath contrived [with her friend] to prevent ... [him] from recovering it'.[50] Wives also tried to hold on to profits from their own trade. In 1704 Horace Merry sued several of his wife Anne's friends, alleging that she had embezzled £650 worth of 'his' trade goods. In the defendants' answer it became clear that Anne had traded as a milliner before her marriage, and that the disputed items were the profits and stock in trade of her independent business. As one of the defendants put it, the business 'was left to the sole and separate dealing and management of Ann', and following her marriage Merry was in 'no way concerned in the said Trade of Milliner ...'. Clearly Anne felt entitled to profits arising from her own labour, and with her friends' support she went to considerable lengths to stop her goods and receipts falling into her husband's hands.[51]

Women who separated from their husbands resorted to similar stratagems to protect their property. In 1710 Elizabeth Tobin of the Charterhouse gave or lent (a disputed point) £20 to Anne Ellis to induce her to separate permanently from her husband and move in with her, 'enjoin[ing Anne] not to give her said husband any part of the money or acquaint him with it'.[52] The actress Charlotte Charke boasted of how she kept her estranged husband from pocketing her earnings by giving and taking 'All receipts ... in the Name of the Widow Gentlewoman, who boarded with me, and I sat quiet and snug with the pleasing reflection of my security'.[53]

Patriarchal power within marriage was less effective in the eighteenth century than has often been presumed. Wives operated at a grave disadvantage; men were perfectly able to make their lives unendurable. Yet despite the disproportionate legal, ideological and practical advantages men enjoyed, they did not always succeed in besting wives who were smarter, better connected, or more politically and legally astute, and who were every bit as capable of articulating ideological justifications for what they did. This is possibly evidence of those 'crises of masculinity' that Anthony Fletcher, among others, sees as a periodic feature of gender relations.[54] However, these cases more likely reflect a combination of long-standing disenchantment with the more extreme manifestations of male supremacy, a legal environment that permitted women and their supporters to act such disenchantment out in public, and enough day-to-day conflict of interest and diversity of opinion among women *and* men to frustrate the full application of patriarchal custom.

Exchequer cases clearly demonstrate this diversity of interests. Fathers, mothers, brothers, sisters, neighbours and friends all feature prominently in marital conflicts and the resulting suits, and there is good evidence that they sometimes succeeded in thwarting husbands' violent and mercenary designs. Husbands' pursuit of their interests also competed with the interests of other householders. Few men were enthusiastic about spending money to support other men's wives, as women and their relatives knew well. This explains why it was rare for women to appeal for maintenance, in or outside the courtroom, without describing in graphic language how close they were to being thrown upon the parish.

WOMEN'S AGENCY REPRISED

Early modern marriages often show a gap between law and practice, between supposedly normative ideals (often enshrined in the common law) and the ways people actually behaved and accounted for their actions. Most men, at least outwardly, endorsed the idea that they should support their wives because this duty lay at the heart of paternalist justifications of male supremacy; for their part women often claimed (though seldom in the context of Exchequer suits) that they were happy to hand over their assets to their husbands. Yet a significant number of men and women seem to have been unable or unwilling to stick to these principles in practice. Resort to the law was often represented by litigants as a last-ditch attempt to return people to their duty, but in practice husbands and wives in troubled marriages could not agree about the nature of that duty, and the courts were unable to bridge the divide.

These London wives did not have an easy time of it, but they had principles and more of them than we might expect were willing to act on them. Coverture was a cold doctrine, and many women tried to bypass it. Women developed an emotional attachment to their clothes, to gifts from kin, and to possessions obtained through their own hard work, and they took steps to avoid giving them up. Wives felt demeaned, controlled and immobilized by having always to turn to their husband for money, so some of them organized secret or semi-secret financial networks and sources of supply. Finally, despite their protests to the contrary, many London women were neither dutiful nor obedient, and they were very willing to use the authority and prestige of the courts to alter the balance of power between themselves and their husbands. A good wife was supposed to bend herself, body and spirit, to her husband's will. But many women could not stomach the indignity and the loss of control that this implied, and some of them did not even try.

How important is it that these were *London* women? London and Middlesex cases make up a very large proportion of Exchequer and Chancery business, and marital cases do seem to have come disproportionately, though by no means exclusively, from metropolitan, as opposed to provincial, litigants. Public and institutionalized airing of marital conflict was more common in London than anywhere else in England. Nowhere else were so many law courts, lawyers, printing presses, newspapers, coffee houses, executions, pulpits and scandal-prone aristocrats concentrated in one place, and it is possible that this worked to relax Londoners' reticence about bringing their marital problems out in the open. Convenience and cost may have played an even more important role. Londoners, including distressed wives, turned to the equity courts because they were close at hand, relatively cheap, and took seriously everyday domestic and neighbourhood conflicts over money. Those women 'not easily to be imposed on' who lived in London, and who could beg or borrow a few pounds, enjoyed a level of access to the law courts that was unmatched anywhere else in Britain.

Equity court records are a treasure trove of insubordinate women, thrusting their stories forward with a level of self-possession and a wealth of detail found in few other eighteenth-century sources. But the equity courts represented only one outlet for dissatisfied or desperate wives: the more informal solutions many sought, and which some, at least, surely found, have left few traces in the historical record. It must be stressed once again that those seeking legal redress were *not* a tiny minority. Significant amounts of this sort of litigation survive for both the seventeenth and the eighteenth centuries across dozens of legal venues. But it would be foolish to suggest that just any woman, Londoner or no, could go to law. Illness, poverty, illiteracy, emotional paralysis, lack of confidence and isolation from potential supporters all lessened the likelihood that women would find their way to court and probably inhibited the search for other solutions as well. Female agency was real; so were the inward and outward barriers to its exercise.

CONCLUSION

In 1711, six years after John and Elizabeth Spinkes brought the marriage brokerage case with which this chapter opened, Elizabeth sued for legal separation in the London consistory court. In her complaint she claimed that John had brutally abused her, threatened repeatedly to kill her, confined her to a madhouse, and appropriated her separate estate. She assembled a clutch of witnesses to the abuse, including her brother-in-law, female neighbours who had overheard her screams and tried on a number of occasion to intervene, and the master of the madhouse where she had been confined, who said that her problem was deep distress, not insanity. From the opposing side John and his witnesses testified that Elizabeth was unchaste, disobedient and a drunk, and that she had misled her husband about the size of her fortune. The Spinkeses' maidservant also claimed that Elizabeth had employed a White-chapel fortune-teller to predict her husband's death and make a magical preparation to hasten that day. In spite of these allegations the court ruled in Elizabeth's favour, awarding her a separation and annual alimony of £28. (John, a physician, was alleged to make between £200 and £300 each year.)[55]

Elizabeth Spinkes was a London woman, past the bloom of youth, with a prior reputation for strength of character. She lived close to the courts, was an experienced litigant,[56] and enjoyed support from relatives and neighbours. We cannot know which of these factors proved most salient in her case. What *is* clear is that at some point in time she turned irrevocably against her husband. John Spinkes had caused her permanent injury, used intolerable means to get his hands on her money, locked her up, and behaved in ways that made a mockery of marriage. Not only did she become convinced that she no longer owed John obedience, devotion and wifely discretion but, along with her supporters, she succeeded in persuading the court to her point of view.

Exchequer cases reveal a world in which male supremacy was less confident, marriage less secure and women more resourceful than they are generally assumed to have been. Equity courts, and non-criminal law more generally, have only recently begun to attract significant attention from social historians,[57] and much lies ahead. Standard claims about the hegemony of the common law and coverture must be thoroughly reassessed, and in some cases retired. We need to develop a clearer sense of how seventeenth- and eighteenth-century lay people (as opposed to lawyers) experienced the law, and to look closely at the development and dissemination of more instrumental attitudes toward litigation and the courts. As this chapter shows, equity courts offered a venue for *some* women to assert and defend perceptions of right and wrong that were quite different from what we think of as normative for the early modern period. More research is needed in order to figure out how their sometimes unorthodox stances on marriage fitted into larger gendered systems. *Was* it the case that metropolitan women were 'not [as] easily to be imposed on' as other women? We do not know the answer to this question yet, but when we do it could make us view both London and London's women in a very different light.

NOTES

1 R. B. Shoemaker, *Prosecution and Punishment: Petty Crime and the Law in London and Rural Middlesex c. 1660–1725* (Cambridge, 1991), pp. 207–16.

2 Gowing, *Domestic*, pp. 13–14, 34, 142.

3 This was, of course, the main reason why country girls were preferred as servants.

4 PRO E 112/847 Suit 1466 (Spinkes *v.* Hilton).

5 R. Porter, 'Does rape have a historical meaning?', in R. Porter and S. Tomaselli eds, *Rape* (Oxford, 1989), p. 231. To be fair Porter is here partly recapitulating the positions of earlier scholars; elsewhere in this article he displays greater optimism about the possibilities for female agency.

6 See P. Earle, 'The female labour market in London in the late seventeenth and early eighteenth centuries', *EcHR*, second series, 62 (1989). An excellent overview that offers much new evidence about women's public lives is S. Mendelson and P. Crawford, *Women in Early Modern England, 1550-1720* (Oxford, 1998).

7 See, among others, S. D. Amussen, *An Ordered Society: Gender and Class in Early Modern England* (Oxford, 1988); M. L. Cioni, *Women and Law in Elizabethan England with Particular Reference to the Court of Chancery* (New York and London, 1985); A. Erickson, *Women and Property in Early Modern England* (London and New York, 1993); Gowing, *Domestic*; G. L. Hudson, 'Negotiating for blood money: war widows and the courts in

seventeenth century England', in J. Kermode and G. Walker eds, *Women, Crime and the Courts* (London, 1994); M. Hunt, 'Wife-beating, domesticity and women's independence in eighteenth-century London', *Gender and History* 4 (1992); Shoemaker, *Prosecution and Punishment*; T. Stretton, *Women Waging Law in Elizabethan England* (Cambridge, 1998).

8 For an important recent debate about the implications for women's agency see M. Chaytor, 'Husband(ry): narratives of rape in the seventeenth century', *Gender and History* 7 (1995); G. Walker, 'Rereading rape and sexual violence in early modern England', *Gender and History* 10 (1998).

9 M. Gaskill, 'Reporting murder: fiction in the archives in early modern England', *Social History* 23 (1998), p. 4.

10 Cases cited here are drawn from a sample of 450 London and Middlesex Exchequer pleadings drawn at rough five-year intervals from the period *c.* 1700 to 1725. Exchequer rather than Chancery materials are used because Exchequer court pleadings are indexed and filed by county while Chancery pleadings are not. It may safely be assumed that the character of marital litigation and the rate of participation by women differed little if at all across the two courts.

11 E. Hobby, *Virtue of Necessity: English Women's Writing 1646-1688* (London, 1988), p. 8.

12 PRO E 112/1019 Suit 2485 (Smith *v.* Amson).

13 See Hunt, 'Wife-beating', for a fuller discussion of the London consistory courts. On the Court of Arches see L. Stone, *Uncertain Unions: Marriage in England 1660-1753* (Oxford and New York, 1992).

14 Erickson, *Women and Property*, pp. 5–6.

15 Both Chancery and Exchequer also had a common law side.

16 H. Horwitz, *Chancery Equity Records and Proceedings 1600-1800: A Guide to Documents in the Public Record Office*, PRO Handbook 27 (1995), pp. 36–7.

17 The estimate of 1·6 plaintiffs per suit is based on my enumerations for the period 1714–16; it is probably low for the eighteenth century, since by 1818/19 Horwitz finds an average of 1·81 plaintiffs per suit. The 18 per cent figure is between Horwitz's 1627 and 1818–19 percentages of female plaintiffs. Though speculative it also accords well with my study of London Exchequer cases brought between 1714 and 1716, where I found that about 17 per cent of cases involved women plaintiffs. The number of cases featuring female litigants is not commensurate with the percentage of female plaintiffs and defendants among total litigants, because cases often had co-plaintiffs and co-defendants; however, it is suggestive. I have further broken the 18 per cent down as follows: 50 per cent wives, 33 per cent widows and 17 per cent spinsters. These figures are based again on my own enumerations for the early eighteenth century, adjusted somewhat against the likelihood that the number of spinsters and widows suing in the courts was growing over the course of the eighteenth century (see Horwitz, *Chancery Equity Records*, p. 37).

18 There were procedural incentives to name people who were fairly peripheral to the dispute as co-defendants, thus many cases name more defendants than plaintiffs.

19 The clerks' indexes show these cases in the following form: 'Duncan by Rowley *v.* Duncan', so it was a very transparent fiction.

20 There are other peculiarities. Occasionally one finds a woman plaintiff or defendant

who pretends the case is being brought in the name of her husband when there is actually no husband to be found. See for example PRO E 112/980 Suit 256 (Barry *v.* Peters). Rather more common are male defendants who claim that they have nothing to do with the dispute (usually it is a trade dispute) in which their wife is embroiled. See for example E 112/980 Suit 308 (Hamilton *v.* Herring)

21 Cioni, *Women and Law.*

22 See esp. PRO E 225/425 (Clerk's Papers). It is unclear precisely which costs were waived for *in forma pauperis* litigants. I am grateful to Amanda Collins for researching this question for me.

23 See for example Frances Robings, Jane Steele and Mary Powys *v.* Sir Richard Blackmore in PRO E 185/17 (the *in forma pauperis* petition) and E 112/985 Suit 624 (the bill of complaint). Like many 'pauper' litigants these women were illiterate. Litigants of this sort often sued for fairly small sums of money – well under £20. See PRO E 185.

24 Horwitz, *Chancery Equity Records*, p. 25. My own figures for London Exchequer litigants suggest that 85 per cent of cases were dropped during or immediately after the pleading stage and only about 8 per cent of suits generated interim or final decrees.

25 N. Z. Davis, *Fiction in the Archives: Pardon Tales and Their Tellers in Sixteenth Century France* (Stanford CA, 1987). See Gowing, *Domestic*, pp. 42–8, 232–62, and Gaskill, 'Reporting murder', for nuanced discussions of narrativity in early modern English trials. Cf. P. Brook and P. Gewirtz eds, *Law's Stories: Narrative and Rhetoric in the Law* (New Haven CT and London, 1996).

26 Consistory courts heard suits for legal separation, mostly on grounds of adultery or cruelty. Though repetitive, adultery narratives were not quite as simplistic as they seem. For some of their ramifications see Gowing, *Domestic*, pp. 188–206.

27 PRO E 112/1019 Suit 2485 (Smith *v.* Amson).

28 PRO E 112/1019 Suit 2488 (Breamer *v.* Gould).

29 PRO E 112/705 Suit 1653 (Harvey by Butler *v.* Harvey).

30 PRO E 112/1019 Suit 2509 (Milton *v.* Sell).

31 This theme had surfaced long before in legal separation cases. See Gowing, *Domestic*, p. 213.

32 See Erickson, *Women and Property*, pp. 107–19, 122–4, for an excellent discussion of marriage settlements.

33 PRO E 112/826 Suit 163 (Hearne by Rogerson *v.* Hearne).

34 See for example E. Haywood, *The Mercenary Lover: or The Unfortunate Heiresses. Being a True, Secret History of a City Amour* (London, 1726). I am grateful to Cameron McFarlane for bringing this and similar titles to my attention.

35 Hearne means *his* stock in trade, of course, and under common law it *was* his, regardless of who operated the business. The possessive pronoun confusion perhaps reflects a certain residual uneasiness on Hearne's or his lawyer's part about who had the best moral right to the property in question.

36 PRO E 112/826 Suit 163 (Hearne by Rogerson *v.* Hearne).

37 PRO E 112/980 Suit 303 (Duncan by Bowley *v.* Duncan and Steer).

38 PRO E 112/705 Suit 1660 (Cliffe *v.* Flat).

39 PRO E 112/1019 Suit 2485 (Smith *v.* Amson).

40 For the cultural centrality of male beliefs about the need to control women, and the way they routinely shaded into violence, see A. Fletcher, *Gender, Sex and Subordination in England, 1500-1800* (New Haven CT and London, 1995), p. 192; Gowing, *Domestic,* pp. 225-6.

41 Erickson, *Women and Property,* pp. 137-8 (see also pp. 162-3).

42 T. Ivie, *Alimony Arrainged* [sic]*, or the Remonstrance and Humble Appeal of Thomas Ivie, Esq; from the High Court of Chancery, to his Highness the Lord Protector of the Commonwealth of England, Scotland, & Ireland, &c. Wherein are Set Forth the Unheard-of Practices and Villanies of Lewd and Defamed* [sic] *Women, in Order to Separate Man and Wife* (1696), p. 11.

43 Erickson, *Women and Property,* pp. 124-5.

44 PRO E 112/847 Suit 1442 (Hart *v.* Baker). By the time this suit was filed Samuel Hart was dead and his widow had become embroiled in an action concerning the non-payment of solicitors' fees.

45 PRO E 112/712 Suit 2036 (Salter *v.* Bland).

46 *Feme sole* traders were married women who, according to the custom of some towns and cities (including London) were permitted to trade and have their own credit as single women on condition that their husbands did not meddle in the business. See M. R. Hunt, *The Middling Sort: Commerce, Gender and the Family in England 1680–1780* (Berkeley and Los Angeles CA, 1996), pp. 138–41.

47 PRO E 112/1019 Suit 2485 (Smith *v.* Amson).

48 PRO E 112/1019 Suit 2488 (Breamer *v.* Gould).

49 See for example PRO E 112/1019 Suit 2485 (Smith *v.* Amson); E 112/826 Suit 142 (Adcock *v.* Thomson).

50 PRO E 112/847 Suit 1409 (North *v.* Nightingale).

51 PRO E 112/837 Suit 859 (Merry *v.* Stone). Horace Merry sought to mislead the court by representing Anne Merry as a former servant whom he employed in his milliner's trade and eventually married. See Gowing, *Domestic,* pp. 211, 213–14, for other cases involving conflicts over the wife's trade profits or moneys she had brought into the marriage.

52 PRO E 112/847 Suit 1418 (Tobin *v.* Ellis). For a more detailed discussion of this case see M. R. Hunt, 'The Sapphic strain: English lesbians in the long eighteenth century', in J. M. Bennett and A. M. Froide eds, *Singlewomen in the European Past 1250–1800* (Philadelphia PA, 1999), pp. 285–6.

53 C. Charke, *A Narrative of the Life of Mrs. Charlotte Charke (Youngest Daughter of Colley Cibber, Esq.)* (1755), p. 76.

54 Fletcher, *Gender, Sex and Subordination,* pp. 297–346.

55 Lengthy portions of the London consistory court case are reproduced in M. R. Hunt, '"The great danger she had reason to believe she was in": wife-beating in the eighteenth century', in V. Frith ed., *Women and History: Voices of Early Modern England* (Toronto, 1995), pp. 81–102. The original case records of Spinkes *v.* Spinkes are in LMA DL/C/154 (Libels, Allegations and Sentences), DL/C/632 (Depositions) and DL/C/42 (Acts of the Court).

56 Elizabeth Spinkes alleged in her consistory court suit that John Spinkes locked her up in the madhouse in order to induce her to testify in yet another suit at Chancery involving her marriage settlement. I have not been able to find the records of this case.

57 See among others Gowing, *Domestic*; C. W. Brooks, 'Interpersonal conflict and social tension: civil litigation in England 1640–1830', in A. L. Beier, D. Cannadine and J. M. Rosenheim eds, *The First Modern Society: Essays in English History in Honour of Lawrence Stone* (Cambridge and New York, 1989), and C. Muldrew, *The Economy of Obligation: The Culture of Credit and Social Relations in Early Modern England* (New York, 1998).

Chapter 7

'The freedom of the streets': women and social space, 1560–1640

Laura Gowing

The Englishwomen have great freedom to go out of the house without menfolk ... many of these women serve in the shops. Many of the young women gather outside Moorgate and play with young lads, even though they do not know them ... [1]

Alessandro Magno was not the only sixteenth-century tourist to comment on the peculiar freedoms of London women; it was a commonplace that the city's social and working conditions ran counter to many of the restrictions that hedged or safeguarded women in more tightly-knit, less mobile communities. By the seventeenth century London women were established in popular literature as the epitome of pride and independence, mad fashions and haughty demeanour, and ballads warned men: 'Let no city-girl your freedom beguile, / She'll cheat you with modest behaviour, / Who sits like a rabbit trust up for to boil / and swears she's a maid by her Saviour'.[2] A particular kind of urban femininity was being constructed around the social and cultural shifts of high migration, economic pressures, changing civic cultures, an expanding domestic service sector, and changing patterns of consumption.

Conventional narratives of urbanization and modernity trace the city of spectacle and anonymity, in whose streets women were a disorderly presence, to the post-industrial period. Elizabeth Wilson sees the modern city as a challenge to patriarchal structures: in the industrial city, she argues, women found both new freedoms and particular vulnerabilities. But the dynamics that Wilson traces are not exclusive to the forming of modern urban life. The dangers and the pleasures of urban femininity were already being worked out well before the seventeenth century.

In early modern societies as in modern ones, gender and space were intricately related. Doreen Massey's delineation of the relationship between gender, space and place describes 'spatial control, whether enforced through the power of convention or symbolism, or through the straightforward threat of violence', as 'a fundamental element in the constitution of gender in its (highly varied) forms'.[3] Popular concerns, expectations and fantasies about city space both reflected and intensified prevailing gender ideology; gender relations were constituted by uses of space, and played their own part in determining spatial practices.

As well as relationships, the negotiations of urban space helped form identities. Female subjectivity has frequently been dependent on ideas of containment and restriction, privacy and enclosure. Here Susan Hanson and Geraldine Pratt's understanding of the relationship between space and subjectivity is helpful: it is negotiated, they argue, through 'the traffic between symbolic and concrete spaces', between mental space and physical space.[4] The interplay between imagined and actual space helped define the gendered self.

There is also the physical body to contend with. The feminist philosopher Elizabeth Grosz writes of the city and the body as mutually defining. The city's architectural arrangements contribute to the social and cultural constitution of the body; the city is defined by the particularities of its use.[5] For both women and men, early modern urban life involved particular concerns around the physical body: clothes, bodily functions, personal space had their own urban rules. More specifically, the place of the female body in the city was shaped by a host of representations, ideologies and subjective experiences. The public presence of women on the streets was persistently identified with sexual disorder. Economic anxieties made women's place in the urban market place problematic. Civic rituals highlighted the exclusion of women from the urban community. And in a crowded city, a nudge of the elbow or a shove in a shop doorway could mean a loud and long dispute. Women's awareness of embodiment, Gillian Rose suggests, is often linked with a sense of space as not their own; in an urban environment where space and territory were so hotly contested, this was surely a key experience of feminine subjectivity.[6]

In the early modern city, gendered space was defined not merely through particular configurations of space and time, but also through a sense of the city itself. The city was consistently imagined through gendered personifications, which had their own impact on gendered spatial practices. The early modern image of the city invoked tensions around space, place and gender. Traditional tropes of the feminine city related to the walled city, subject to attack and siege. Early topographies and histories of London imagined 'her' as a heroic matron; later, Thomas Dekker's characterization of London after the 1602 plague construed the city as a predatory, deceptive harlot: 'Thou art the goodliest of thy neighbours, but the proudest; the wealthiest, but the most wanton. Thou hast all things in thee to make thee fairest, and all things in thee to make thee foulest: for thou art attired like a bride, drawing all that look upon thee, to be in love with thee, but there is much harlot in thine eyes.'[7] Lawrence Manley has argued that the Tudor and Stuart characterization of the city as feminine stressed the city's bonds of loyalty, like a wife, to the kingdom, and worked to limit the implications of the city's independence. It also construed her as fickle and lewd.[8] These figurings of the city and femininity surely worked both ways: civic culture was inflected by gender ideologies, but imagining the city as a fickle wanton had its own impact on ways of thinking about women and sexuality in the metropolis.

Urban culture was undergoing its own redefinitions. The emerging self-consciousness of the Elizabethan city was reflected in literature, drama and ritual. Histories and geographies of the city traced its history and the character of its parts; pamphleteers like Dekker and Nashe described its trades and its idioms; city comedies constructed plots around the dynamics of civic space and neighbourhood life.[9] Gender had a defining part in these imaginings of space and place. In literature, drama and street talk, women proved a focus of specifically urban anxieties about public and private space, sexual honesty and economic activity. Excluded from the civic freedoms to which respectable men aspired, their use of the opportunities of urban life was frequently construed as disorderly. Persistently, urban women were envisaged as predators in a predatory city. Popular ballads warned men of city women: their sexual looseness, their expensive tastes, their cunning. Rarely did they warn women of city men.[10] The sexualization of urban space was key to the concrete and symbolic tensions of the early modern metropolis.

CITY WOMEN

Elizabeth Wilson has argued that women find a special freedom in modern cities, where the rigid controls of patriarchy are more easily evaded than they are in smaller, more kin-based communities.[11] Well before industrialization, many of the circumstances of women's lives in sixteenth- and seventeenth-century London bear this out. In contrast to most other early modern cities, before 1640 women did not outnumber men in the London population; but even before the service boom of the later seventeenth century, young women were migrating to the cities in large numbers and from a wide range of origins, and the vast majority of women living in London, like men, had been born outside it.[12]

Like their male counterparts, female migrants often arrived in their teens and settled near others from their home villages. They relied on networks of kin and friends from home to help them in finding service and settling their marriage choices. Young single women, in particular, probably courted and socialized more freely than they would have done under parental regulation at home, at least until their masters and mistresses complained. They married rather later than the small proportion of young women who lived with their parents, and they did so after several years of work and independent earning.[13] In a world where reputation was paramount, some women found the anonymity of the city allowed them to escape their past and remake life anew: some left masters, others husbands; some abandoned newborn infants. The mobility of city life was double-edged. It meant also that women whom nobody knew very well could be readily accused, 'thou hadst a bastard in the country', or 'you were carted out of the place where you lived before'.

London women took a significant part in the public life of their communities. They used the legal system, for example, more often than women outside the city: both at the sessions and at the Church courts – where, by the early seventeenth century, they constituted the majority of litigants – they made complaints, pursued disputes and testified.[14] The political and religious developments of the 1640s and 1650s opened up some new opportunities for women as active users of urban space; but already by 1640 an understanding of the potential, risks and tensions of the urban female experience was in place.

LIVING SPACES

The most familiar axis of social space for early modern commentators, as for most gender historians, was public versus private. The equation of public with male, female with private, was by the sixteenth century an ancient, well established trope with both biblical and classical authority. However, it was (and remains) open to several readings.

The historical model of 'separate spheres', which dates a transformation in gender relations to a reinforcement or reconstitution of the distinction between male/public and female/private to between 1650 and 1850, has been challenged in both its chronology and its terms. Firstly, it has become quite clear that the period before 1650 did not see a 'golden age' of shared public worlds and more equal gender roles in politics, economy or housework.[15] The chronologies of the withdrawal of middle-class women from productive labour in the late seventeenth century and the definition of working women's labour as low-skilled, low status and poorly paid, both key to the narrative of separate spheres established by Alice Clark in 1919, have been shown to be complex, provisional and continuous or cyclical.[16] Moreover, there are some problematic elisions of meanings in the model of separate spheres. One of these is the confusion between public or private *issues* and *events* and public and private *spaces*. Public events might take place in private spaces; women's participation in one kind of public realm did not give them a place in others. Nor is the relationship between separate spheres and the distribution of power clear. In the field of politics, early modern women participated in a wide range of political activities, and claimed a variety of public voices, but, as Amanda Vickery has argued for the eighteenth century, their place in the public sphere should not be confused with access to institutional power.[17]

The axis of public and private was also not straightforward for early modern commentators. Sixteenth-century prescriptive authors related it to the distinction between 'outside' and 'inside': the walls of the ordered household were to ensure the regulation of women's speech, their chastity and their subordination to their husbands. But the household thus created was not a private one. The very construction of this image of domestic relations was predicated on the public, political implications of domestic life and conjugal relations. In practice, of course, few women could follow these rules: working women had to move between private and public, outside and inside every day.

The management of domestic space was unlikely to create a private, self-contained interior. The household was embedded in the community and its boundaries were often permeable and insecure; historians have sometimes doubted whether privacy was ever possible in early modern houses.[18] In London, the density of housing and the fragility of buildings meant that little that went on inside houses could be entirely hidden. Prosecutions for fornication and adultery record neighbours spying through holes in walls, half-open doors and torn hangings. But despite (perhaps because of) the thinness of walls and the lack of corridors between rooms, eavesdropping was an established offence, not a regular pastime. The concept of privacy was a powerful one in early modern domestic and neighbourhood relations, and it was related to issues of gender in ways that were more complex than those explained by the model of separate spheres.[19] The word 'private' was frequently associated with illicit sex; locking a door was good ground for suspicion. Privacy was no guarantee of honesty. The records of neighbourly intervention in marital violence also seem to suggest that the household was open to public scrutiny. Both Susan Amussen and Margaret Hunt have argued that seventeenth-century domestic relations were regulated by neighbourly concern: men's violence was a public rather than a private affair, and publicity worked as a form of control.[20] However, it is also possible to read the testimonies of wives and neighbours as suggesting that intervention in family disputes very often had to be asked for by the victims of domestic violence or their servants or friends.[21] There is, of course, no evidence for the amount of marital violence that was not interrupted, commented on or prevented. In theory, the private walls and doors of the household safeguarded a woman's reputation. In practice they might facilitate suspicions of dishonour and the practice of male violence. As a concept, privacy surely held ambiguous meanings for women.

Within the early modern house, the organization of social and domestic space confounds attempts to align 'public' and 'private' space with masculine and feminine worlds. While the ordering of domestic rooms in ordinary medieval and Tudor houses established a graduated series of increasingly closed spaces, from the public street through the shop to the private parlour, the simple equation of masculine spaces with public, feminine with private, did not apply.[22] Traditional patterns of use of domestic space, however, did make some areas of the house, at some times, specifically female: most obviously, the parlour at its transformation into the female space of childbirth and lying in.

The seventeenth century saw some shifts in the organization of domestic space. The archaeologist Matthew Johnson has argued that the shift from a hall-based house to single-function rooms was accompanied by an increased gender differentiation of domestic space. Like the enclosure of fields, closure in houses reflected a redefinition of social relations. The new domestic arrangements both reflected and produced gender and class relations that were structured around segregation and privacy, rather than open interaction and confrontation. This increased stress on segregation, and the identification of women with the more private spaces within the house, might correspond, Johnson suggests, to the anxieties about women's threat to male authority that David Underdown has characterized as a crisis in household order.[23] Such a model fits fairly neatly, too, with Alice Clark's chronology of changes in women's working patterns, which dates the increased segregation of male and female labour to the late seventeenth century.[24] Relating these chronologies to subjective experiences of space, however, is problematic. Any reconstruction of spatial practices from floor plans, even when augmented by more qualitative evidence like probate inventories, is bound to be tenuous: the result tends to reflect, at best, the prescriptions of those who built spaces and boundaries, rather than the experiences of those who constituted them by everyday use. In urban areas, with their denser housing, the shift to single-function rooms may have happened at a different pace, and with different implications. Early seventeenth-century building plans suggest that the shift from a hall-based house took place earlier in London than elsewhere in the country: already by the sixteenth century the ground or first-floor hall was replaced by other spaces, cooking was confined to the kitchen, and the upper-floor chambers were bedrooms.[25] At the same time, denser population must have meant that, in many crowded houses, some rooms remained firmly multifunctional through the seventeenth century. The rooms in most common use – notably the shop and the kitchen – remained at least bipermeable; the shop was entered directly from the street, the kitchen generally opened on to a yard. In these circumstances, any endeavour to mark a firm distinction between the working and living spaces of apprentices, servants, women and men was unlikely to succeed. The urban shift in room use seems neither so marked nor so clearly related to patterns of gender conflict as Johnson's model suggests. Nevertheless, the cultural context of enclosure, the purposes of marking boundaries and the relationship of those boundaries to gender relations remain significant.

Equally important to Londoners' perceptions of gendered domestic space was the provisionality of the household's boundaries. In practice households were permeable and potentially unstable. Lodgings were a vital sector of the capital's housing structure, with men, women, servants or couples renting rooms for weeks or years, and living as a fairly ambiguous part of the household: shared stairways, yards and kitchens meant that the boundaries of the house and those of the family unit were not necessarily congruent. The house, though, was a moral unit: landladies and landlords, held responsible in the courts for immorality in their houses, were quick to accuse lodgers of whoredom and 'dishonesting' their houses. In 1610 Margaret Smith of the quayside parish of St Benet Paul's Wharf fell into dispute with her lodger, Anne Fanne; she told friends that 'when Anne Fanne came into her house she took her to be an honest woman but afterward she thought her to be a whore for that diverse men resorted to her whom she did not like ... and ... for that cause she had rid her house of her'. She told Anne herself: 'thou art a whore thou hast dishonested my house for I did see Hopkins and thee together he with his breeches down'.[26]

The lack of privacy in houses and the tenuous boundaries of city space made for particular experiences of neighbourhood relations. Words spoken in one shop could be heard across the street, those in a room might be heard by someone next door: two women sharing a house near Lombard Street in 1617, each in a separate downstairs room, had a noisy argument, clearly heard by a clothworker working in the same house and another woman upstairs.[27] Much poor housing was clustered around yards, a convenient central space across which conversations or insults could be publicly exchanged. Agnes Franklin, an armourer's wife of St Andrew Holborn, testified in 1615 that with a group of women in an upper chamber of her house she had heard Henry Smith, the minister and preacher of household order, standing by her window in his yard, call Eleanor Hedge, who was standing inside her window about ten yards away looking into the same yard, a whore.[28] The verbal abuse that culminated in suits for defamation took place most often on the borders of houses, in shared yards or alleys, or on doorsteps, and it frequently called on a communal ideal: the honesty of the neighbourhood, parish or street. In the alleys where the poorest inhabitants lived, windows and doors were even closer; and alleys, whose gates were meant to be closed at night, constituted a particularly closed kind of neighbourhood with its own reputation and disputes. Yards could constitute the same sort of community, with a group name: 'there is not an honest woman in all the yard where thou dwellest,' accused a man in Goodman's Yard, in Whitechapel, in 1615.[29]

Modern discussions of gender and architecture have stressed the extent to which women's spatial lives are shaped by buildings designed for masculinity. But early modern building practice was often more informal. Near Cheapside in 1617 a woman sewing in her garret was disturbed by the loud voice of her neighbour, complaining that Elizabeth Shorey – the neighbour on the other side – had put a window into her wall.[30] Elizabeth Shorey's window suggests the impact women might have on a built environment where houses were frequently being subdivided, extensions or windows added to walls, and penthouses built on to the street. Women did not live passively in rigidly organized spaces: they adapted the rooms and walls within which they lived and caused them to be rebuilt. Indeed, women's agency over their neighbourhood environment was frequently at the heart of conflict: what provoked the predominantly female defamation suits at the Church courts often turns out to have been disputes over building rights, access to water or light, or shop space. While defamation disputes in rural areas were most likely to take place outside the house, in alehouses, fields, market places or on highways, the vast majority of London cases took place in the house of at least one participant, just outside it, or in the same street.

The precise location of defamation suits makes the charged meanings of neighbourhood and domestic space even more apparent. In London, as outside, a prime place for insults and verbal abuse was the doorstep. As the threshold between public and private, household and community, doorsteps carried considerable symbolic weight. They were a good place for attacking and defending honour; and in a culture that understood the walls of the house as the guarantee of female chastity, they marked a special boundary for women. For many women, doorsteps were also a primary workplace, where they sewed, made lace, knitted or nursed babies. Their complaints against men who made water near their doors, children running up and down the street, or neighbours 'railing' near by registered a sense of territory. Standing or sitting at their doors, women also embodied the authority of neighbourhood morality. Oral reputation, a crucial measure of credit in a society of low literacy, was brokered to a considerable extent amongst women: their words about sexual behaviour served to condemn not just women, but men, casting doubt on their morals, reliability, business activities and honesty. The boundaries of the house, marked as they often were by women's work and social lives, had a moral power as well as a physical one. In this way, women's sense of physical space and their disputes over it were closely tied both to their working lives and to their roles in neighbourhood relations.

CITY SPACE

The evidence of neighbourhood disputes over personal or family territory gives the impression that women's sense of their own space, if not centred entirely on the house, was focused on a fairly circumscribed area: the street, yard or alley, the water pump or well, the shop or doorstep. But women also lived, worked and walked around a much larger space: the city itself. If women's experiences were shaped around the places of parish, street, alleys and yards, in London they were also shaped by a gendered sense of the city itself – both as women and men imagined it, and as they found it. Londoners shared the sense of an urban world in which gender determined how space was used and what it meant. They did not all share the same perceptions of space: women and men worked with their own mental maps, delineating for them the strange and the familiar, the welcoming and the threatening

In the early seventeenth century, Joane Granger and William Dawson had stalls selling fruit, artichokes and cucumbers in the parish of St Clement Dane's. They had a long established rivalry, competing to serve the same customers, and in the late summer of that year they had a public argument by their stalls, William telling Joane to 'keep her own parish and not take away his customers' and she responding 'that the street was as free for her as for him'.[31] Was it? Certainly, the sixteenth-century literary and religious advice that ordered wives to 'keep to the indoors' and their husbands to 'look to the outdoors' could not reasonably be applied to the majority of working couples. William Dawson's complaint was not that Joane Granger was working outside her house, but that she was working outside her parish, and the substance of his words could have been addressed to another man as well as a woman.

Two contexts, though, made a difference. The first was the restrictions on women's work in cities, by which authorities confronted and regulated the informal, marginal selling and reselling in which many women engaged in markets and on streets, and the second was the fact that William went on to accuse Joane of living 'like a queane' and 'a drunken whore'. The combination of anxieties about women's work and women's workplaces, and a discourse of sexual morality that constructed disorder as primarily sexual and predictably feminine, made for a very particular traffic between concrete and imaginary spaces. If women in cities were less subject to the most familiar figures of patriarchal order – fathers, husbands, parish officials who knew them – they also ran up against the other characteristic associated with women in urban contexts: the identification of femininity and female sexuality with disorder. Women's presence in certain spaces and times could be readily construed as disorderly.

Of necessity, most London women had active social and work lives around the city. Servants and wives frequently ate outside the house, and did business and drank in alehouses. The daughters, wives and servants of craft households spent much of their days running errands and selling goods in open markets. Servants' daily work could take them on extensive circuits around the city. Mary Denton, a servant examined on suspicion of theft in May 1627, answered the question 'what company had been with her lately' with a report of her recent movements:

the Thursday morning next she went to my lady St Albans' man in Blackfriars but saith she spoke not with him only she spoke with a footman ... demanded whither she went from thence saith she wente to Cole Lane and thence left word with a coachmaker's man but who he was she knoweth not ... and being demanded why she tarried so long this morning being out 3 hours or thereabouts she answered she could not come sooner from about her business.[32]

Joan Dessall, servant in an aristocratic Westminster household in 1634, testified to a very similar social and work life, with long periods in the house interspersed with visits to the market, taverns, and a range of wider social contacts:

the Sunday ... she stayed at her mistress her house and was not out of doors but at night once to the market for an artichoke and with my lady's maid and two of her servants at the inn the sign of the Cock in Tothill Street where they stayed not half an hour. And the same night betwixt nine and ten of the clock she went out of her mistress's fore door to one Mr Adite in Petty France to ask for one Mr Rogers who lodged there and had lately been her master ... and so came away home.[33]

Nevertheless, such movements could also be construed as suspicious or disorderly. Printed diatribes characterized London women's mobility as urban disorder, reading women's free use of the streets as evidence of dishonesty. 'Would matrons walk or wives discreet / with silver shining brows / From street to street? No, rather they / would keep within their house,' ran one attack on London's ills. 'And strumpets stately in attire / Like ladies must resort / To places where themselves think best / Without all kind of doubt: / They customed are about the town / and shall be borne out.' Here neither unchaste nor chaste women have a public right to be on the streets: the chaste are to remain within the house, the unchaste are to be driven out of the city. Donald Lupton's London and the Countrey Carbanadoed proffered a series of characterizations of London's quarters, tracing en route a map of gender roles and gendered images. Cheapside wives 'hold that a harsh place of Scripture, that women must be no goers or gadders abroad' and 'cannot endure to be shut up'; the Exchange is a 'like a beautiful woman, absolutely good, if not too common'; and in Turnbull (now Turnmill) Street, the most notorious district for prostitution, 'Here are lasses that seem to hate enclosures, for they would lay all open.'[34] The mobility of urban women was specifically identified with sexual immorality: only enclosure could keep women private and chaste. The 'open' and the 'common' carry a special weight in the city, investing familiar concern for female chastity with a special, civic significance: the logical conclusion of the reciprocity of urban community is that women are common too.[35]

Street talk reflected and manipulated prescriptions for female behaviour. Jane Boven, returning to her house in St Sepulchre after being sworn to testify at the Consistory Court in 1611, ran into Alice Fulham, against whom she had been asked to witness. Alice asked 'where she had been prancking that day'.[36] It was reported of Frances Andrews, plaintiff in a suit for marital separation in 1623, that she 'liveth loosely and carelessly in and about the city not befitting an honest woman'.[37] Women's presence in alehouses, frequently accepted without comment, was sometimes the focus of complaint. Alice Collet of Stepney, challenged by her neighbour for washing on a Sunday, replied that 'it was better to do so than to go from alehouse to alehouse'.[38]

Understandings of women's place in city space varied most of all by time. A vocabulary of disorder, focusing on night walking, increasingly identified women's presence on the night-time streets as symptomatic of social and sexual disorder.[39] The ballad 'News from the Tower-Hill: or, a Gentle Warning to Peg and Kate, to Walke no more Abroad so Late' warned of the recent 'great abuse' of women gadding about the streets at night, tempting men.[40] Neighbourhood social life might go on late into the evening: Elizabeth Jacob, a chandler's wife, reported sitting at the door of her house in Crown Court, off Chancery Lane, around eleven or twelve at night with Dorothy Mytton and a group of other men and women, 'talking neighbourly together'.[41] Yet, farther afield, women risked or courted propositions, or were accused of night walking. Francis Kenninghall, noticed by the constable walking in Smithfield at 9.00 or 10.00 p.m., responded to his questions, 'Honest men may walk at all hours.' There is little evidence that women asserted the same.[42] The burden of popular literature and legal action was to clear the late-night streets of suspicious women, to safeguard honest men.

The urban community was constructed around rituals of space, time and season, participation in which was determined by gender, age and social status. After the Reformation, the ceremonies of late medieval London – midsummer shows, candle-lit processions – were overtaken by solidly civic rituals, celebrating, in Michael Berlin's words, 'the secular, privatized values of civic honour and pecuniary worth'.[43] The ceremonies of good order which punctuated city life through the late sixteenth and seventeenth centuries emphasized masculine virtues and men's participation; and, accompanying as they did a new concern with civic building and urban space, they may have made for a noticeable reinforcement of the masculinization of public space and communal ritual. Certainly the spatial marking out of good order roused women as well as men to vocal opposition. When meetings of the Middlesex sessions moved from the Old Castle tavern in St John Street to the new session house, Hicks Hall, at the foot of St John Street, Grace Watson, an apothecary's wife living there, appeared at the session accused of 'giving reviling speeches against Sir Baptist Hicks touching the building of the sessions house'.[44]

Processional routes circled the city, creating maps of civic display. In counterpart to this largely masculine progress of honour was a typically female progress of dishonour: the processions of 'carting'. Walking at a cart's tail or riding on it, criminals were led around the city's public spaces to mark their shame; both men and women were carted, but women were often ordered to do so naked, or wearing blue mantles or hoods to mark them out as bawds, carrying white rods to denote fornication, or holding a distaff for scolding.[45] Like the celebratory processions, their progress centred on the city's broadest street, Cheapside. In 1579 Joan Sharpe, Edith Bannister and Clemence Belton, who had abandoned infants in the Royal Exchange, were ordered to be 'tied unto a cart's tail and whipped with rods naked in Newgate Market Cheapside Leadenhall and in the borough of Southwark having several proclamations openly made at every of the said four places declaring their several offences'.[46] Others were carted from or to their own house door, through the market place or from the session house; each progress marked a particular use of civic space for public shame.

More informal rituals marked out gendered urban space in a less orderly fashion. Whilst the majority of disorderly or riotous assemblies involved women as well as men, other collective uses of city space were clearly gendered. For women, Bernard Capp has argued, meetings in the street, in the well and at church might constitute 'a semi-separate domain outside the family structure and beyond male control'. Men's and women's leisure involved different spaces and different games. Henry Machyn records, on Easter Monday 1557, twelve men shooting a wager in Finsbury Field, while the wives of his parish played at barley-break.[47] Shrove Tuesday, in turn, was associated with attacks by apprentices and craftsmen on bawdy houses such as Mrs Leake's in Shoreditch.[48] A prosecution from 1613 records another kind of female use of city space: Elizabeth Taylor, Joan Jones, Elizabeth Williams, Elizabeth Crayford and Martha Greene were all committed to prison without bail 'for going a pilgrimage to Tyburn'.[49] Formal and informal, orderly and disorderly, rituals marked out space by gender.

Gendered space had economic meanings as much as political ones. Women's work in early modern cities and towns was subject to a range of circumscriptions which focused specifically on women's use of street and market space.[50] Street selling was particularly identified with women, and the sellers were regularly complained of for suspected dealing in stolen goods, using false measures, blocking the highways or trading without a licence. In 1585 the Cornhill wardmote inquest presented 'the women sellers of yarn ... for that they stop and hinder the passage in the Queen's high street and forestall the inhabitants thereabouts and besides that if foul weather happen they be very troublesome to the inhabitants most humbly craving that some place may be appointed for them by your honour and worship's discretion'.[51] Hucksters and waterbearers were the targets of similar presentments and restrictions. The promiscuous mobility of women's street selling also threatened disease, as the Cornhill wardmote made clear in 1582, presenting 'the vagrant women such as commonly goe up and downe in the streets carrying and selling of apparel whence the same cometh is not known, but suspected to come from houses which have been visited whereby the common people are in danger of infection'.[52] And, like prostitutes, the sellers were seen as enticers, as in the 1611 presentment of 'the annoyance presented by such as sell apples and other fruits at the Exchange whereby the street is obstructed with baskets and other things that coaches and carts cannot well pass and divers young women and maid servants live in that idle course of life and sit there at unlawful hours in the night time, and entice apprentices and servants to waste their monies unduly'.[53] Punishments for economic infringements might play explicitly on the iconography of sexual disorder. Henry Machyn reports seeing, in March 1561, 'a woman ride about Cheapside and London for bringing young fry of diverse kind of fish unlawful, with a garland upon her head hanging with strings of the small fish, and on the horse afore and behind her, led by one of the beadles of Bridewell'.[54]

Fishwives, fruit sellers and herb women were subject to a continuous stream of orders from the aldermen's court from the 1590s, restricting their numbers, movements and work. The mayor's order in 1595, against 'an exceeding great number of lewd and wicked women called fishwives, which swarm about in all parts of this city liberties and suburbs ... and ... greatly enhance the prices ... [and] be of such vile behaviour and condition as is not fit any longer to be suffered', called for a 'perfect reformation of their intolerable abuses'. Officers of the wards were instructed, accordingly, to 'make diligent search and enquiry' for all those selling fish and fruit, enquiring their age and 'whether they be wives widows or maidens'. The results in most wards were one or two, but ten in Bishopsgate, twenty in Cripplegate and forty-two in Farringdon Without, and a Common Council Act decreed that there should be only 160 such sellers, all of them to be wives and widows of freemen, 'of honest fame and behaviour and every of them to be of the age of thirty years at the least'.[55] Markets were always pressed for space, and mobile sellers always the target of such regulations; in 1632 Common Council was still attempting to disperse the herb women 'who have used to sit and stand in Cheapside'.[56] Ian Archer has argued that the polarized social conditions of the 1590s prompted a thrust of disciplinary activity against petty traders, fishwives and hucksters, rather than profiteering wholesalers: thus economic tensions might bear most forcefully on those who were already working on the margins of the market – women.[57] Women were more frequently the objects of attack largely because their work was more mobile and marginal both to trade organization and market space. But the means of reforming market abuses, and the language that City authorities resorted to, betray the persistent association of women's street selling with 'lewdness', disorderly youth and dishonesty in all its senses.

Official initiatives against women's street work might be echoed at a much more informal level by violence and disruption. Men used a register of gestures – nudging, poking, spitting, or 'hemming' – against women working in streets, alleys and yards. Elizabeth Cliffe, for example, deposed in 1567 that, at home in her own house in Holborn, she had seen one of the men who lodged there spit several times upon the head of a maidservant who had come into their yard to do the heavy washing at their well.[58] Women's outdoor work was the target not just of literary attacks, such as in the city comedies, but actual ones. The marginalization of women's work also made for social and economic competition amongst women. In the markets, with their rigid – if informal – hierarchies of place, this could be particularly acute. Mrs Griffin and Katherine Fayermanners fell into a dispute in 1591, alongside a group of market women selling butter in Cheapside. Griffin told Fayermanners to 'get her down to the lower end of the market like a whore as she was and a thief', and Fayermanners called on the market women with them: 'You honest women why did you let that whore and that thief to stand amongst you? Down with her she may stand beneath at the cart's arse well enough for she is a whore a filth and an arrant thief.'[59]

The most apparently male-dominated spaces of the city were open to working women, and also problematic to them. The Royal Exchange was built specifically for merchants to meet in, to avoid the unpleasantness and trouble – according to John Stow – of 'walking and talking in an open narrow street ... being there constrained either to endure all extremities of weather, viz. heat and cold, snow and rain, or else to shelter themselves in shops' (as women did).[60] It was not planned for women's transactions and conversation, and in 1590 women were presented for selling apples, oranges and other fruit at the Cornhill gate and 'abusing themselves in cursing and swearing to the great annoyance and grief of the inhabitants and passers-by'.[61] Women used it nevertheless; but the confident male strolling that its architecture encouraged seems to have left their use of it ambiguous. Within the first ten years after its completion the Exchange, whilst functioning as an effective symbol of the city's prosperity and security, had become also a dangerous and troublesome civic space, ill lit and beset on Sundays, holidays and at night by football players, 'lewd boys', 'rogues' and 'whores'.[62] The results for women were various. Prostitutes used the Exchange at night; illegitimate mothers abandoned their newborn babies there; during the day it remained a recognisably male space, so that women walking through it might be accosted, as Margaret Marr was in 1574, by two men, an acquaintance and a stranger. Thomas Slater and his friend pressed her to drink with them, asked who the father of her (illegitimate) child was and why she had 'chosen such a father to your child, that is not able, to keep you to lie home'; she confessed 'that in carrying home ... Edmund Alden's work to him ... he did overcome her so with fair words, that at last she yielded unto his request and so was begot with child by him'. Her story, at least in the second-hand version that was reported by Thomas Slater in court, presents a consistently problematic understanding of city space, in which she is unable to deliver work or cross the Exchange without men's verbal or physical intervention.[63]

If the use of public buildings was hedged about with restrictions, London's fields should have been a uniquely free common space. Men and women, though, used them differently. In Finsbury fields, Moorfields and Spitalfields, the Elizabethan copperplate map of London shows men shooting with guns or bows and arrows, or walking with dogs, women carrying washing or laying it out to dry. Already the fields are marked out for men's leisure and women's labour, and the maps show these taking place simultaneously. Susan Fidgett met her suitor in the fields in 1592, while she was drying clothes and meeting 'with other young folks'.[64] But there was also another, far more notorious, axis of pleasure and labour there: that of illicit sex and specifically prostitution. Insults in the city made repeated and particular reference to this understanding of what the fields were for. In Chick Lane near Smithfield in 1631 Jane Goldsmith told Elizabeth Baker she was 'a quean who was begotten with child in the green fields'.[65] In Grace Jellis's shop in St Botolph Aldgate Richard Munford took her by the arm into the street and told her, 'Yonder is the man that was in the haycock with Gammar Holmes when she lost her shoe,' and 'that [Holmes] had not lost all her baseness in the haycock she had brought some of it into East Smithfield.'[66] 'Go into the fields,' George Harwood taunted Margaret Ellis in 1636, 'and play the whore with the boys and be brought home at 12 o'clock at night with the constable.' In Newgate market in 1615 David Jones told Anne Austen 'to go into St George's Fields again and have her clothes turned up above her navel'; and in a footpath on the way to Islington in the same year Elizabeth Clay told Frances Dan, 'I have heard say that thou hast had a bastard and that thou were delivered thereof in Moorfields.'[67]

Insults worked a fantasy on the real life of the fields, but one that had some truth to it. In 1574 a thirty-year-old married woman confessed that she had been in the back side of Islington fields with a young girl when they were approached by a man. He asked her 'what wench that was'; she said, 'an honest poor wench', and he answered, 'Well, I pray thee send her after me.' He gave the girl 'fourpence for her labour', and she was left infected with syphilis.[68] Thomas Thornton, walking in Lincoln's Inn Fields on a summer evening in 1631, met Sidney Russell, a stranger to him, and 'seeing ... her alone in the habit of a gentlewoman conceived her to be a light person and offered her the courtesy of a pint of wine.' (He was alleged, after 'some dalliance', to have made a clandestine marriage with her.)[69] The conjunction of men's pleasure and women's work, then, composed the sexual reputation of the fields as well as its more respectable one; if the fields meant sport to men, they had more complex and risky meanings for women, who, if they mentioned the fields as they witnessed in court, took care to explain why they were there and where they were going.

Women's use of the streets, fields and civic spaces of early modern London was neither simple nor free. The rhetoric of enclosure and the identification of female mobility with sexual and economic disorder shaped female identities and women's use of space. In this context, women's part in street life could be self-conscious and anxious. Agnes Modye, in the throes of a tearful lovers' quarrel with Robert Buckley at Pie Corner in 1574, tried to stop him arguing with her in the street, saying she 'was loath to stand in the street'; but he 'said he cared not who saw him stand in the street' and walked off, leaving her crying out so loud that 'one standing by her in the street bid her hold her peace'.[70]

SEX AND THE CITY

Sexuality – usually at the heart of any discussion of women and disorder – was central to perceptions of gendered space and time; and in particular, prostitution, on which most official regulation of sex in public spaces concentrated. While before 1546 the regulation of London prostitution had focused on restricting it to Southwark, by the late sixteenth century no single place could be identified with prostitution: officials concentrated instead on tracking it down right across the city, focusing on the most notorious areas – Clerkenwell, Aldersgate and Bishopsgate.[71] In the intensely (though frequently unsuccessfully) regulated city streets of the 1580s–1640s, the shadow of illicit sex and prostitution could be seen or imagined everywhere.

The inhabitants of city parishes tended to accuse their neighbours of illicit sex very much on their own ground. Those of St Bartholomew's, near Smithfield, referred to Long Lane, to Charterhouse Lane or the famous Turnbull Street, all within their parish. A woman in Chancery Lane accused another of 'laying her tail under every rogue at the Whitefriars', just the other side of Fleet Street. Most consistently associated with sexual disorder were the places just outside the city walls and the liberties: 'St Katharine's whore', one Newgate woman called another.[72] A woman from one of the peripheral parishes, St Botolph without Aldersgate, accused another of being whore to an oatmeal man 'in Old Street at the town's end', neatly signalling the significance of the limits of the city – perhaps especially significant for those who lived on its borders.[73]

Such references relied on established notoriety: the place names they used did not have to be known for sex, but they had to have an identity in the popular knowledge of city places. The woman who accused another of being cured of the pox in Black Horse Alley in 1616 presumably knew, and knew her audience knew, precisely which of the five Black Horse Alleys in the city she meant.[74] Charing Cross, Whitefriars, Newgate Market, Somerset House, 'the glasshouse' (a glass factory by the Tower), Highgate, Primrose Hill – all these were established enough places in the popular imagination to be meaningful. Insults made reference to a map of immorality (Turnbull Street, Bridewell, Bankside). But the popular map of the city did not necessarily coincide with other imaginary cities. Turnbull Street was notorious in literature, in street talk and in the courts; however, while popular literature and drama highlighted Cheapside as an area of disorder and sexual misconduct (*A Chaste Maid in Cheapside* is meant to be an oxymoron), its inhabitants were not especially likely to be accused of whoredom or prosecuted for keeping bawdy houses. The more recently developed areas of east London, some of them well reputed for prostitution, rarely featured in the language of insult: despite the number of bawdy houses detected in Whitechapel, it was not used in insults. Stepney and Whitechapel women were accused instead of whoredom in Leadenhall, having bastards in Newgate, being caught in a ditch at Bankside in Southwark. Stepney itself, a newly built-up area whose housing was clustered largely around the long, narrow Wapping High Street, seems not yet to have developed a popular culture of place which inhabitants could use against each other: the City they lived outside gave them their main terms of reference. Like the authors who laid out maps of London characters and quarters, giving each its own characteristics, ordinary women and men worked with mental maps of the city in which concrete and imaginary space worked together.

If insults were about imagining sex and place, they were also about constructing sexual histories. In her Cheapside shop in 1573 Christian Redmore, a butcher's wife, shared with her ex-servant these words about Ralph Kybley and another of her servant's previous employers, Mary Lawne: 'Raff Kybley is a bawdy knave and a whoremaster knave, and if he come by her shop and hold but up his finger ... and saith divine monks and then she saith through the friars ... he goeth though St Martin's, and she through the friars and there they meet.'[75] It is a speech of great local specificity: Christian was standing in her shop in the Shambles, St Martin's and Greyfriars were just north of her: the sexual plot is precisely mapped on to the alleys and lanes of the quarter where she and her audience worked. In Leadenhall market, selling hides with other butchers' wives, she told a story that alleged Ralph Kybley 'this day sevennight ... stood watching at Leadenhall until Mary Lawne had sold her hides, and then they went together to the tavern'. Each time Christian spoke, she placed her allegations specifically somewhere that could be seen from her stall – imagining something that could not be seen.

Christian Redmore's words present a picture of how women and men might use the spaces of the city for illicit pleasures, making secret signs to arrange meetings and creeping through alleys. But they also expose the storytelling about sex and sexual places in which women and men engaged. In this storytelling, women appear merely passive users of space and receivers of sexual pleasure; it is Ralph Kybley who is the active mover, who has but to hold up his finger. Redmore's narrative engages, too, with the city's layers of sexual fantasy and history. 'Divine monks,' Ralph Kybley says to direct his lover through Greyfriars: the words recall the place's older history, transformed from a monastery at the Dissolution into a new church and Christ's Hospital in the 1552; in 1573 its history, and the sexy image of monks, remained a powerful part of the place's identity.[76] Like the words with which other women and men insulted their neighbours, Christian Redmore's stories wrote sex into the urban map – and with it, the condemnation of sexual and spatial freedom. Imagining the spatial past was part of constructing the spatial present.

Historians of the nineteenth century have identified the eroticization of the city as a phenomenon of modernity, shaped by the emergence of modern visual and economic cultures and the developing roles of middle-class women as shoppers and consumers, working-class women as bar girls and shop girls, self-possessed, knowing users of metropolitan social spaces.[77] But the eroticization of urban space was also part of early modern culture. It limited women's freedom on the city streets; but it might also have contributed to the creation of a city of opportunities.

Many of the particular tensions around gender, sex and space that seem to have characterized the modern city thus turn out to be familiar in the early modern urban world. The late sixteenth and early seventeenth centuries were times of particular urban stress and change. Old freedoms were being eroded; new understandings of citizenship were being defined. Redefining gendered space was an important part of that process. For at least some women the 1640s were to suggest another shift in the uses of social space, their political and religious commitments opening up new ways of acting in public and new ways of being seen. However, the tensions of femininity in public space were reworked, rather than erased. Gendered uses of space were dynamic, but they worked on some persistent understandings of the relationship between disorder, sexuality and femininity.

Spatial practices always involve an interplay between the concrete and the imaginary: in the early modern city, where cultural definitions of femininity, cities, and public and private spaces crossed at so many points, and where urban identity and gender identities were in the making, that interplay was especially productive. In a changing urban culture, with a new strain of self-conscious civic identity, a sharpening concern with sexual order, and heavy pressures on housing and markets, the construction of languages, fantasies and histories to mark gendered space was both essential and potent.

NOTES

Many thanks to the participants in seminars in London, Leicester, Oxford and York in 1996–97 who discussed earlier versions of this work, and to Trish Crawford, Bob Shoemaker, Andy Wood and the editors for their perceptive and helpful comments.

1 'The London Journal of Alessandro Magno', ed. Caroline Barron, Christopher Coleman and Claire Gobbi, *LJ*, 9 (1983), p. 144. Quotations have been modernized throughout.

2 *Advice to Young Gentlemen; or, An Answer to the Ladies of London*, in *The Pepys Ballads* ed. W. G. Day (6 vols, Cambridge, 1987), IV, p. 365.

3 Doreen Massey, 'Space, place and gender' in her *Space, Place and Gender* (Cambridge, 1994), p. 180.

4 Susan Hanson and Geraldine Pratt, *Gender, Work and Space* (1995), p. 19.

5 Elizabeth Grosz, 'Bodies–cities' in her *Space, Time, and Perversion: Essays on the Politics of Bodies* (1995), p. 109.

6 Gillian Rose, *Feminism and Geography* (Cambridge, 1993), p. 146.

7 Thomas Dekker, *The Seven deadly Sinnes of London* (1606), 'Induction'.

8 Lawrence Manley, 'From matron to monster: Tudor–Stuart London and the languages of urban description', in Heather Dubrow and Richard Strier eds, *The Historical Renaissance: New Essays on Tudor and Stuart Literature and Culture* (Chicago and London, 1988).

9 John Stow, *The Annals, or General Chronicles of England* (1615); *Londinopolis*; and see Gail Kern Paster, *The Idea of the City in the Age of Shakespeare* (Athens GA, 1985), chap. 4.

10 See, for example, *The Invincible Pride of Women: or, The London Tradesman's Lamentation* and *An Answer to the London Cuckold*, in *Pepys Ballads*, IV, pp. 153, 123; Edward Hake, *Newes out of Powles Churchyard* (1579).

11 Elizabeth Wilson, *The Sphinx in the City: Urban Life, the Control of Disorder, and Women* (1991).

12 Roger Finlay, *Population and Metropolis: The Demography of London 1580–1650* (Cambridge, 1981), pp. 140–1.

13 Vivien Brodsky, 'Single women in the London marriage market', in R. B. Outhwaite ed., *Marriage and Society: Studies in the Social History of Marriage* (1981).

14 Gowing, *Domestic*, chap. 2; Robert Shoemaker, *Prosecution and Punishment: Petty Crime and the Law in London and Rural Middlesex c. 1660–1725* (Cambridge, 1991), p. 208.

15 Amanda Vickery, 'Golden age to separate spheres? A review of the categories and chronology of English women's history', *HJ*, 36 (1993).

16 Judith Bennett, 'History that stands still: women's work in the European past', *Feminist Studies* 14 (1988).

17 Vickery, 'Golden age'. On the participation of women in seventeenth-century politics see Sara Mendelson and Patricia Crawford, *Women in Early Modern England* (Oxford, 1998), chap. 7.

18 See, for example, Lawrence Stone, *Road to Divorce: England 1530–1987* (Oxford, 1990), p. 21; Archer, *Pursuit*, p. 67.

19 Anthropological work on privacy has discussed its varying meanings in different

cultural contexts: see, for example, Lidia Sciamma, 'The problem of privacy in Mediterranean anthropology', in Shirley Ardener ed., *Women and Space: Ground Rules and Social Maps* (Oxford, revised edition 1993).

20 Susan Amussen, '"Being stir'd to much unquietnes": violence and domestic violence in early modern England', *Journal of Women's History* 6 (1996); Margaret Hunt, 'Wife-beating, domesticity and women's independence in eighteenth-century London', *Gender and History* 4 (1992).

21 Gowing, *Domestic*, chap. 5.

22 John Schofield, 'Social perceptions of space in Medieval and Tudor London houses', in Martin Locock ed., *Meaningful Architecture: Social Interpretations of Buildings* (Aldershot, 1994).

23 Matthew Johnson, *An Archaeology of Capitalism* (Oxford, 1996), esp. chap. 4. David Underdown, 'The taming of the scold: the enforcement of patriarchal authority in early modern England', in Anthony Fletcher and John Stevenson eds, *Order and Disorder in Early Modern England* (Cambridge, 1985).

24 Alice Clark, *Working Life of Women in the Seventeenth Century* (third edition, 1992).

25 Frank E. Brown, 'Domestic space in seventeenth-century London', *Comparative Studies in Society and History*, 28 (1986), p. 587.

26 LMA DL/C 219, fos 231, 245. Lodging houses themselves could be the scenes of complex disputes, often amongst women: see Bernard Capp, 'The poet and the bawdy court: Michael Drayton and the lodging-house world in early Stuart London', *Seventeenth Century*, 10 (1995).

27 LMA DL/C 224, fo. 106.

28 *Ibid.*, fo. 2.

29 *Ibid.*, fo. 82.

30 LMA DL/C 225, fo. 98.

31 LMA DL/C 219, fo. 2 (1609).

32 LMA WJ/SR(NS) 18/12 (1627).

33 LMA WJ/SR(NS) 40/11 (1634).

34 Hake, *Newes out of Powles Churchyard*, sig. D8v; Donald Lupton, *London and the Countrey Carbanadoed* ... (1632), pp. 29, 27, 51.

35 See also Lyndal Roper, '"The common man", "the common good", "common women": gender and meaning in the German Reformation commune', *Social History* 12 (1987), and Paster, *The Idea of the City*, p. 156.

36 LMA DL/C 220, fo. 544v.

37 GL Consistory Court Depositions, MS 9189/1 fo. 4.

38 LMA DL/C 214, fo. 398 (1593).

39 Paul Griffiths, 'Meanings of nightwalking in early modern England', *Seventeenth Century*, 13 (1998).

40 *Pepys Ballads*, I, p. 266.

41 LMA DL/C 214, fo. 95 (1591).

42 GL MS 9056, fo. 46 (1566).

43 Michael Berlin, 'Civic ceremony in early modern London', *Urban History Yearbook* (1986).

44 LMA MJ/SBR I, fo. 579.

45 See, for example, Machyn, *Diary*, p. 299.

46 CLRO Rep. 20, fo. 47v.

47 Bernard Capp, 'Separate domains? Women and authority in early modern England' in Paul Griffiths, Adam Fox and Steve Hindle eds, *The Experience of Authority in Early Modern England* (Basingstoke, 1996) p. 129; Machyn, *Diary*, p. 132.

48 Peter Burke, 'Popular culture in early modern London', in Barry Reay ed., *Popular Culture in Early Modern England* (1985).

49 LMA MJ/GBR I, fo. 217.

50 See also Michael Roberts, 'Women and work in sixteenth-century English towns', in Penelope J. Corfield and Derek Keene eds, *Work in Towns 850–1850* (Leicester, 1990).

51 GL MS 4069/1, fo. 40 (1585).

52 *Ibid.*, fo. 33 (1582).

53 *Ibid.*, fo. 118.

54 Machyn, *Diary*, p. 253.

55 CLRO Rep. 24, fos 68, 98v.

56 CLRO Jour. 35, fo. 440.

57 Archer, *Pursuit*, p. 203.

58 LMA DL/C 210, fo. 69.

59 LMA DL/C 213, p. 103.

60 Stow, *Annals*, p. 667.

61 GL MS 4069/1, fo. 51v.

62 Frequent presentments to the Cornhill wardmote complained that these abuses made the exchange dangerous for inhabitants and passers-by: see, for example, GL MS 9056, fos 19, 21v.

63 LMA DL/C 211/1, fos 195–195v.

64 LMA DL/C 214, fos 171–2.

65 LMA DL/C 232, fo. 30v.

66 LMA DL/C 231, fos 401v, 402v.

67 LMA DL/C 234, fo. 226; DL/C 224, fo. 95; DL/C 224, fos 76v–77.

68 LMA DL/C 212, fo. 121.

69 LMA DL/C 194, fo. 17.

70 LMA, DL/C 211/1, fo. 35v.

71 Paul Griffiths, 'The structure of prostitution in Elizabethan London', *Continuity and Change*, 8 (1993).

72 LMA DL/C 218, fo. 393 (1609); DL/C 220, fo. 507v (1611).

73 LMA DL/C 222, fo. 9 (1614).

74 LMA DL/C 224, fo. 267v. Since the exchange took place in St Bride, Fleet Street, it was probably the one in that parish, but the others were less than a mile away, indicating something of the small scale of local terms of reference.

75 LMA DL/C 211, fos 261 ff.

76 St Martin's was also an ex-monastery, retaining the right of sanctuary.

77 Lynda Nead, 'Mapping the self: gender, space and modernity in mid-Victorian London', in Roy Porter ed., *Rewriting the Self: Histories from the Renaissance to the Present* (1997); Judith R. Walkowitz, *City of Dreadful Delight: Narratives of Sexual Danger in Late Victorian London* (1992), p. 46.

Part III

Senses of space and place

Chapter 8

Skirting the city? Disease, social change and divided households in the seventeenth century

Margaret Pelling

Were early modern Londoners convinced urbanites, or were they 'skirters' – town-dwellers following patterns of living which involved avoidance of, as much as commitment to, urban environments? To raise this possibility is also to reflect on the peculiarities of English urban experience and, indirectly, of English attitudes to city life. It is hardly necessary to stress that England was the first western European country to urbanize most of its population, *but* by a late and accelerated process. Before 1700 England was still a predominantly rural society, but one in which metropolitan experience was widely diffused. In early modern England we have what is in fact a paradox: that urbanization – a process which concentrates the material effects of residence in one place – was a function not so much of residence as of mobility.[1] Perhaps this fact will bear extrapolation, to suggest a mode of metropolitan living which was mobile, the effect of constant movement in and out of the city on a periodic, even daily basis. Moreover, rather than multiplying representations of urban experience, people sought it mainly in one place, London. Was it simply because London was an irresistible magnet, or was it, at least in part, because of a feeling that the undoubted attractions of London were better confined to one location, like an oversized ghetto?

By way of prelude to his account of an 'urban renaissance' beginning in the later seventeenth century, Peter Borsay comments that there was no urban planning in England for 300 years before the Restoration.[2] It is part of my argument to suggest that it is surely no coincidence that these were centuries blighted by plague. In urban terms, England had some part in inventing the notion of a metropolis, but the strangeness of the English situation lies in the contrast between London and the provinces. The real English inventions are the suburb, the garden city and the suburban lawn. If England did, during the 'urban renaissance', evolve a stable style of urban living, it was arguably short-lived, and probably always a matter of providing a suitable backdrop for the urban play, rather than a truly urban infrastructure. On this reading, it becomes significant that, even at their most urbane, the English did not build palaces in towns, but rather (as Borsay notes) inns which looked like palaces – that is, urban accommodation which provided status and comfort, but on a temporary basis.[3]

This essay also reflects on assumptions apparently underlying the flourishing field of British urban history. This field is remarkable for the care taken with issues of definition. The sizes and typologies of towns, contrasts between them, the waxing and waning of towns, their regional interrelationships, and religious and economic factors affecting them, are all the subject of careful scrutiny. As a result we have many effective demonstrations of how towns may legitimately be seen as more than the sum of their parts and as important to what was still a non-urbanized society. However, it is possible to wonder whether the price of establishing these points is too great an emphasis on the structural and the functional. These aspects are combined in a focus on residence, in which it is easy for the physical fabric of towns to serve as a proxy for human activity. So we are often presented with too dehumanized a picture, one which uses with too little question the quasi-scientific, quasi-objective vocabulary of classical economic analysis. An obvious example, in spite of recent pleas for the virtues of small towns, is the persistent use of the word 'growth' – a term adapted from the natural world, but allowed to remain unaffected by the knowledge that in the natural world all growth is self-limiting. (For early modern people, it was urban growth which was, or ought to be, self-limiting.[4]) Unlimited growth, it seems, is still equated with success. A post-Malthusian variant of this is when great cities like London are given credit for being a 'brake' on population growth.[5]

I would quarrel with this vocabulary as being both teleological and repressive of issues of human agency and the complexity of human responses. This perspective may arise from my experience as a medical historian, because medical historians are always debating pitfalls and methods of approach.[6] By the same token, however, they are at least inoculated against uncritical, Whiggish notions of human agency, and also against producing a polarized account, negative instead of positive, which is not only simplistic but also breeds its own backlash. So while I would claim that urban history has a tendency to be positivistic, I am not wanting simply to paint the town black, still less to add a black border of 'filth-and-disease' in the old style. Rather, I am suggesting that we should reflect more on the ambiguous nature of urban experience – to spend (to extend the metaphor) fewer resources on the scenery, and more on the play itself, its characters, their entries, exits, lives, loves and deaths. Nor should we allow literary historians to have any monopoly of the speeches of characters.

This essay will begin with perceptions of the natural and human attributes of towns conducive to ambivalence on the part of urban dwellers. It will then turn to evidence of vigilant seasonal and 'semi-detached' patterns of living by middling elites, with emphasis on plague and smallpox as socially divisive, and as intensifying the 'skirting' mentality already in place. Such patterns emerge as pre-dating the settled styles of suburban living familiar from later periods, and as dividing households remaining in the city as well as those able to retreat from it. Finally, I will suggest that these changes were powerful enough to erode major social institutions such as service and apprenticeship, which were uniquely dependent upon a compulsory sharing of household space.

Attitudes to towns in the early modern period were heavily influenced by biblical and classical conventions about comparisons between the active and the contemplative life, politicians and exiles – what later became the contrast between public men and private gentlemen. However, as Martin Butler and Andrew McRae have shown for the town and the country respectively, socio-economic change could effect major shifts in literary expression.[7] It was standard in the western European tradition to praise a town not so much for its built attributes as for the advantages of its site – in Hippocratic terms, its airs, waters and place. Charles Phythian-Adams quotes a grace sung in medieval Winchester: 'The ton is god and wel iset / The folk is comely on to see; / The aier is god both inne and oute / The site stent under an hill; / The riveres renneth all aboute; / The ton is rueled apon skille'.[8]

Several of these apparently natural attributes were only ambiguously natural, since water and place, for example, were vital elements in defence, transport and manufacture. Nonetheless, literature in praise of cities dwelt on nature's gifts as well as the works of man.[9] However, there appears to have been a bias towards the natural in the English mentality, which exceeded traditional emphases on natural adornment, and which was detected by Continental representatives of Renaissance cities. As Polydore Vergil put it, the English, 'accordinge to their aunciente usage, do not so greatlie affecte citties as the commodious nearenes of dales and brookes'.[10] Similarly, at the literary level, More's *Utopia* was unusual among depictions of ideal societies in its integration of town and country. The more open character of English towns was sometimes attributed to the lesser need for strong defensive structures like walls.[11] For the English, it could be surmised, an integral part of towns was those elements that did not so much adorn them as deny them supremacy and provide a means of escape – their gardens and rivers, and the meadows, lanes, springs and woods that surrounded them, and which provided the fresh air which was so valued.

This was not some lingering remnant of the call of the wild or northern European tribalism. I am not suggesting that in some atavistic way the English were non-urban. A sense of crowding and the urge to find a new Eden possibly motivated exploration of the New World, but Eden was rarely wild and it could be recreated.[12] The wild areas – the so-called wastes, fens and wild woods – were shunned as dangerous, unhealthy and unproductive. English settlers in the New World cut down forest in order to improve the health of settlements, and looked to cultivation to temper extremes of climate. Given the distribution of malarious fever in south-east England, Londoners had good reason to dislike, and to modify, low-lying, marshy areas as much as the exhalations of polluted rivers.[13] The forcible adaptation of nature to man's use and benefit was of course a major strand in seventeenth-century political and social thought, but pride in London's well-cultivated setting was of long standing.[14]

Similarly, although current historiography stresses the forces of attraction exerted by towns in socio-economic terms, it is not usually mentioned that towns were a refuge from the cold. Although the Little Ice Age was not as severe as used to be thought, it was probably cold enough to influence behaviour, and contemporaries were aware that built environments baffled cold winds and that a pile of people created a level of warmth greater than the countryside.[15]

I shall be taking most of the forces of attraction to towns as read, but another factor is the positive value placed on populousness. Acknowledgement of the extent to which contemporary comment about towns was based on observation of local conditions need not preclude recognition of the influence of fears about depopulation. This created a vocabulary of decline that was generally understood. Contemporaries were capable of deploring excess population in the wrong place, or of the wrong kind – too many poor people, the desertion of the countryside for the towns, pestered suburbs, the 'teeming' Irish, towns overweighted with women, or cities too great to be governable. However, it is difficult to find expressions of fear of over-population as such. There was a vague but real sense that population had fallen rather than risen during human history, and a belief that an increasing population of the ruled reflected credit upon rulers and safeguarded national defence. These notions were current in the sixteenth century, although not precisely quantified until the 'political arithmetic' of the mid- to late-seventeenth.[16] With respect to London, John Graunt recorded the contemporary urban myth that by the mid-seventeenth century London's population was thought to be measurable in millions: while this impression owed something to Londoners' sense of a crowded society, the context seems also to have been the feared extent of plague losses. Such observations convey the ambiguity of London's pre-eminence: London was perceived as destroying many of those coming there from the country, but its populousness was also a source of reassurance.[17]

That cities needed lungs – open green spaces within or just outside them – is a view usually attributed to Enlightenment improvement or nineteenth-century sanitary reform. Similarly, the nice as opposed to the nasty notion of a suburb is supposed to be a relatively late development, mainly because of industrialization, but partly because of the association of the early modern suburb with poverty, overcrowding, slack regulation and offensive trades.[18] In spite of meticulous local studies like Jeremy Boulton's of Southwark, the broad-brush account of G. Sjoberg and others positing a prosperous centre and a periphery increasing in disadvantage in proportion to its distance from the city's heart is still the model of early modern towns.[19] The fairly consistent inability of English people to live in city centres with any conviction would doubtless be seen, like the nice suburb, as a product of Romanticism and the industrial revolution. With respect to London, this generalization partly depends on how we interpret the earlier drift westward towards Westminster, which was certainly in part an anti-urban tendency.[20] I would argue that London's shape, and still more the Londoner's pattern of life, pre-dating major physical change like that necessitated by the Fire, resulted from a tug of war which reached stasis not in wide open spaces far from the capital, or indeed in the New World, but in the villages, meadows, orchards and streams of what later became the Home Counties.

Concern about London's expansion is usually attributed to fears about disease, 'pestering' and political unrest, but to these fears about the monster being created should be added a lament for what was being destroyed, in terms of London's recreation grounds.[21] Londoners expected to be able to walk or ride out of their city to take the air, listen to birdsong, eat cream, cakes and fruit, drink well or spring water, or play games on greens.[22] Not surprisingly, Pepys's diary records copious examples of these recreations – a walk in the fields and visit to the 'great cheese-cake house' in Islington; to Bow and Old Ford 'only to take the ayre', and then to Hackney to '[play] at shuffle-board, eat cream and good cherries; and so with good refreshment home'; to Barnet, to try the well waters, discovered twelve years before; to Mile End Green, for cream and cakes; taking the air in fields beyond St Pancras; 'not being fit for business', by water to Greenwich, 'it being very fine and cool and moonshine afterward', to eat a cake or two; sleeping on the grass 'by the canaille' in Westminster Park; taking the air beyond Hackney, 'drinking a great deale of milke'; being tired with business, and so driving to Mile End Green to drink 'a cup of Byrde's ale'; in 'most pleasant weather' to Hackney marshes, and round about to Old Ford and Bow.[23] His 'usual tour' was via Islington; his 'long tour' was to Islington via Hackney and Kingsland. For some, pleasure was a by-product of business, as with the simpling expeditions of London apothecaries, or perhaps the drying of clothes by laundresses on hedges and bushes.[24] That this environment was increasingly artificial, an effect greatly increased not only by drainage schemes but also by the development of pasturage, market gardens and orchards to feed London, helped to cater for recreational Londoners rather than otherwise.[25] Improvements in London later in the seventeenth century, while also expressing social segregation, were attempts to recreate these lost amenities, in terms of the parks, large gardens, pleasure grounds and nearby spas whose names recur frequently in the titles of later Stuart plays.[26]

These excursions out of London were, of course, only nominally innocent and healthy. Like gardens within towns, nearby villages and fields offered sensual pleasures, and they supplied opportunities for secret meetings, clandestine affairs, and passages of arms, especially among the young. For all ages, they offered greater freedom from surveillance and jurisdiction. Especially at night, there was the risk of criminal activity in comparatively lonely circumstances.[27] Tavern keepers, cake women, keepers of bowling alleys, fortune tellers and medical practitioners predictably multiplied in such locations in response to demand, which could include the expectation of contact with women.[28] An interesting example from around 1630 is a case involving the surgeon James Winter, whose wife was obviously also active in his business. Together they maintained a dwelling not only in Fleet Street, but also at West Green, in Tottenham parish. Winter's wife appears to have been more active in the 'country' location. The countrified aspects of this case, which involved a woman who, 'lamishe and troubled with a Fanning payne', went from Tottenham to lie in a house in West Green, included payment to the practitioners in the form of sheep and poultry.[29]

What I am trying to suggest here is a set of attitudes, and a way of life on weekly if not daily levels, which corresponds with but also refines the existing picture of a mobile population migrating to and from London on a life-cycle basis. Mentally and physically, Londoners went in and out of the capital constantly, drawn in only to retreat, in a pattern of smaller movements less traceable than life-cycle migration but nonetheless an essential part of the same picture. One example among many is John Chamberlain, who in May 1624 told a correspondent that he was off to stay in Hertfordshire, 'to injoy some part of the sweetnes of this backward spring after so long and tedious a winter'.[30] These smaller or more sporadic movements laid down patterns which later hardened, for middling and upper strata, into what we now call commuting.

This has a tendency to sound like cod Shakespeare – daisies pied and violets blue. It is time to turn to some grim realities behind this ambivalence, and to provide evidence of social process and practice. I am not wanting to ignore major causes of socio-economic change, but rather to factor in a component of cultural materialism, and to suggest that it should have explanatory power. Like many taking this approach, I will produce an updated version of older approaches – most effectively expounded by literary historians and traditions in German historiography which integrated the social and the scientific. I recognize the need to avoid both scientific positivism and biological determinism, vices of this older literature which have been criticized, as well as the vices of the history of ideas.[31] In this, for London in particular, I am influenced by F. J. Fisher, whose lead has been more admired than followed, except in respect of plague, where some links between the cultural and the material have been legitimized by general and literary historians.[32]

At the same time, it is plague as *epidemic* which has been accommodated; the social consequences of *endemic* disease, like the mind sets produced by a *constant* threat of disease, have proved more elusive. The 'urban penalty' – excess mortality – is well established on an aggregate basis, but we have little idea of what it meant for those most concerned.[33] In other modern and historical contexts it is assumed that human motivation in general, and perceptions of risk in particular, are such that centres of economic activity will attract migrants even when such places are unhealthy, and that, conversely, the poor will not live in healthy areas where economic opportunities are few. This generalization is seemingly supported by migration to the American colonies, where unhealthy but rich southern states attracted more migrants than the northern ones.[34] Nonetheless, we as historians give ample scope to *some* kinds of human decision making in respect of plague before 1650; there is then a kind of blank, before we have, in the eighteenth century, both a settled urban bourgeoisie and a coherent campaign to avoid disease.[35] It would be possible to suggest ways in which these findings can be reconciled, but I am interested in the precursor situation, forms of urban experience leading up to coherence at the levels of both ideology and the built environment.

I will now turn to evidence of seasonal residential patterns in London in the early seventeenth century among a group arguably belonging to the nascent middle class – the membership of the London College of Physicians, which varied between twenty and forty between 1550 and 1640,[36] and was drawn mainly from the parish gentry, the clergy and the commercial classes.[37] It is rare to have detailed evidence of the seasonal dynamics rather than structure of such a group, and this is possible only because the college was small and highly self-conscious about its behaviour. From 1580 (a date at which other City record keeping improves) physicians were assiduous record keepers, both for self-definition and self-justification. Although the college met to hold elections, admit new members and discuss business, its institutional life was dominated by attempts to prosecute those it saw as irregular practitioners and empirics, a task carried out primarily by the president and four censors. The college had major and minor meetings, and public and private meetings, but meetings of censors represented the least as well as the most in terms of its activity. That is, if the censors did not meet, we can assume that the college had no effective presence in London at the time. Thus, in measuring censorial business, one is acceptably approximating to college activity. What I have called 'active months' can be tabulated to show patterns of censorial activity over the ninety-year period, but they also show the seasonal pattern of the college's presence in London. The college began the period by meeting on average just over once a month; by the final two decades it was meeting at an average rate of just under twice a month. Activity displayed marked seasonal variation. It was most sustained from late September to December, with a considerable drop in January. November appears as the highest monthly peak because of a flurry in activity in the 1630s. The only years in which no meetings were held in either November or December were 1593 and 1636, both plague years. Activity normally built up again in late winter, only to fall again in spring, before a second major peak in June, which included one of the four quarter-days. The June peak was also accentuated by the 1630s. July was busier than either January or May, but was nonetheless part of the steep summer decline represented by August. The depths of the 'summer recess' were also marked by the greater lengths of time between meetings.

For the college as a group of medical practitioners, its post-winter inactivity, and even more the summer recess, present the paradox of absence from London just when need among the population, owing to seasonal patterns of disease prevalence, was likely to be greatest. This was even more so when the college shut down through plague. Plague, illness, royal business, imprisonment, or journeys of more than three miles out of London, were listed as acceptable excuses for absence in a 1584 resolution.[38] Besides plague, one other major factor both structured and justified the college's activity: the quartering of the year according to the law terms, which was related to elite patterns of seasonal attendance.[39] However, the college did not have the same justification for absence as landholders or lawyers travelling to assizes. Although it clung to the legitimacy of its absences, it was pulled in opposing directions by the fact that irregular practitioners gained ground, morally and competitively, during them. Some efforts were therefore made to counter, in particular, summer absences. The June quarter-day meeting was increasingly represented as the most important after the first, in September or October, and it was this, and the hope of launching a pre-emptive strike against the irregulars before summer, which explain the June peak. The college also tried to limit absence from London by the timing of its feasts, but could rarely manage to hold one each year; repeated attempts to hold feasts in summer proved unavailing.

As well as being complicit in the elite's regular absences from London, the college also monitored levels of disease. How it did so is not clear: early references to premonitory phenomena like unusual plagues of woodlice were not repeated in later records, although plague is frequently mentioned. However, college members, who advised their elite patients on when to avoid London, made full use not only of their professional contacts but also of the bills of mortality, which originated as an early warning system for government and the court.[40] Because contemporaries thought in terms of disease states, rather than specific diseases, so that one form of disease could worsen into plague, any excess of mortality could prompt a removal.[41] In mid-century

Graunt noted retrospectively that 'many times other Pestilential Diseases, as Purple Fevers, Small-Pox &c do fore-run the Plague a Year, two or three'.[42] Certainly the college showed an uncanny ability to foreshadow epidemics, its activity against rivals increasing not only after epidemics, on its return to London, but also just beforehand.

How significant was the college's seasonal activity, and how representative? It deliberately isolated itself from civic responsibilities, except its responsibility to repress irregular practice.[43] However, in their pattern of urban living, and in their ideology, it would be an oversimplification to see academic physicians as merely an appendage of rural elites. Physicians may have followed monarchs round the country, helped wealthy patients recruit nature and pass time on country estates, or gone abroad on military and diplomatic missions,[44] but there is also evidence of a settled, albeit part-time, way of life as middling countryside householders. Parallels could be found among groups of lawyers.[45] It is frustrating that at a college meeting in June 1598, when absenteeism was being discussed, five absent fellows were simply named and five more simply stated as 'in the country', but it is clear that this group – constituting a fair proportion of the membership – were not known to be absent for good, professional, reasons.[46] Very occasionally, during the worst plague periods, college members met at the president's house in the country; and by 1648 the social critic John Cook could denounce most college physicians as deserting London for their country houses.[47]

Although this may have been an aspect of prosperity among physicians, which contemporaries sometimes interpreted as parasitism, there is little reason to see the physician's country house as his version of the route out of London into land ownership. The analogues of this country-house ownership should rather be sought within cognate groups among middling elites like merchants, but rather earlier and for different reasons, than the phenomenon as noted by Defoe, and in accounts like Nicholas Rogers's of the 'big bourgeoisie'.[48]

Evidence confirming this pattern of residence is found in the first London directory of merchants, published in 1677,[49] which locates merchants not only in increasingly urbanized fringes like Spitalfields, Moorfields, Houndsditch and Goodman's Fields, but also in growing satellite villages, like Newington, Mile End, Hackney, Shadwell, Hogsden (Hoxton) and Islington. Some merchants compromised by also giving a central location, like one of the Barnardistons, who lived at Hogsden but 'could be spoken with' at Mr Hedges's in Broad Street, or William Burd, of Hackney Town, to be spoken with at Mr Sherwood's, also in Broad Street, or John Clark of Hogsden, who could be met at his warehouse in Olive Tree Court in Leadenhall Street.[50] Although many merchants lived closer to London than the physicians, their way of living suggests that physicians did not behave so differently from the commercial classes.

That such men were likely to maintain two houses in and around London was envisaged as early as 1665 by Richard Kephale, who specified that in time of plague unsound household members should remain in one house, and the sound in the other. Pepys was tempted by the attractions of a country house in the 1660s, but resolved instead 'to keep a coach, and with my wife on the Saturday to go sometimes for a day to this place, and then quit to another place; and there is more variety and as little charge, and no trouble, as there is in a country-house'.[51] Other sources indicate that such ambivalence about residence pre-dated the Restoration. The process of monitoring the metropolitan environment can be detected in a variety of personal records of which John Chamberlain's letters are a good example. Not surprisingly, however, correspondents like Chamberlain saw the elite as more newsworthy than the middling sort.

A source combining monitoring with glimpses of middling life both seasonal and semi-detached in terms of London residence is the 'Obituary' compiled by the lawyer Richard Smyth between 1627 and his death in 1674.[52] The basis on which Smyth decided what deaths were worth noting was a combination of period-specific factors – for example, his royalism and providentialism – and influences more characteristic of the *longue durée*, but given local meaning. Collectively, events singled out in this way could be labelled as pities, prodigies, forebodings or revenges. They include the loss of only children, the execution of husband-poisoners, deaths from medical interventions, and unusually long lives. Smyth's selection thus combines both warning and reassurance, and complicated feelings arising from a tally of deaths among friends and acquaintances. Such a selection, apparently sporadic and of its nature qualitative rather than quantitative, has behind it a recognizable form of psychological integrity.

Smyth's purposes are encapsulated in his frequent notice of sudden deaths and others preceded by only a very short illness. On the one hand sudden death was a reminder of human vulnerability, and an instruction to be always ready, to die every day one lived; on the other, Smyth was noting sudden deaths, as physicians did, as an early warning system against plague. An entry which makes this explicit is that for Ferdinando Sothern, sexton of Cripplegate parish, who died in 1665, 'having not lyen sick above a day or two, and so suspected to have died of the sickness, but not retorned'. Here Smyth is using his own data-gathering to improve on information in the bills. That Smyth and/or his legal colleagues were out of London in summer and possibly also the spring vacation is indicated by groups of deaths during these periods for which Smyth lacked specific dates or circumstances.[53]

Smyth not infrequently notes the disease or 'casualty' which was the cause of death, but it is relevant for what follows that the disease other than plague to which he attaches most significance is smallpox. As well as noting medically significant tragedies like the death from smallpox of a friend's wife in childbed (1648), he also notes the death of members of the elite like the Countess of Northumberland (1637), the Earl of Bedford (1641), Sir Robert Shirley, then a prisoner in the Tower (1656), Henry, Duke of Gloucester (1660) and Mary, Princess of Orange (1660). This recognition of smallpox as a threat to the elite coincides with increasing awareness of plague as a disease of the poor, so that smallpox became the focus for urban techniques of disease avoidance. Not surprisingly, Smyth also notes smallpox deaths close to home, like that of his cousin (1670), and, significantly, 'a young maid who came out of Gloucestershire to London with our maid to get her a service', who died at her uncle's house in the Strand in 1674. [54]

A final, and complementary, aspect of Smyth's list is its examples of Londoners half in and half out of the city. It is a possibility that part of the significance of these deaths for Smyth was the monitoring of health and the attempt to avoid death. Caution must be exercised: Mr Ravenscroft, a Cateaton Street cheesemonger, who drowned in a pond by Islington in 1649, may have caught Smyth's attention simply as an unexplained occurrence. Ravenscroft could have been a victim of violence, or a man who walked out of London in order to kill himself. Smyth notes a number of other suicides: to mark and try to interpret self-murder was a widespread contemporary instinct, and a form of monitoring of urban stresses and misfortunes. [55] Less ambiguous than Ravenscroft is Mr Meredith, a rich Smithfield citizen, who, walking in the fields, suddenly died. Interestingly, he was walking there in February – a form of exercise which could also be justified by medical theory. Traces of Smyth's own recreational activity are found not only in his regular mentions of vintners and brewers, noted by Harding, but also in his listing of innkeepers and cake women working on London's outskirts. [56]

Of those noted by Smyth as dying in the country, it is reasonable to infer that those said to have died of consumption, like a Little Britain bookseller, were in the country for their health, but for most it is impossible to know whether they were convalescing, travelling on business, staying with friends, or at a country residence of their own. There are, however, a substantial number whose place of business had apparently become separate from their place of rest, recreation and retreat. For some, the separation was simply between warehouse and place of business, and relatively limited in geographical scope if not mentally, like the distracted bookseller and printer of Cornhill who hanged himself at his Leadenhall warehouse. [57] For others, it was seemingly a case of retirement outside the city, like 'old' Oliver Markland, once innkeeper at the Castle in Wood Street, who died at Stratford [at] Bow in 1658. Others, however, had apparently set up household away from their place of business while still active, like Mr Keeling, councillor at Guildhall, who died at his house in Hackney in 1649, or, more explicitly, Mr Alexander, common

crier of the city, who was buried 'at his country house at Hadley by Barnett' in
1666, or Mr William Lorrindg, confectioner, who died at his country house in
1674.[58] Still others are simply given as resident in outlying villages, which in
the later seventeenth century included Highgate, Newington Green, Islington,
Clerkenwell Green, Hackney, Hogsden, Bethnal Green, Kingsland, Spitalfields
and Mile End Green (note all the 'Greens'). A complicated final example is
Smyth's old acquaintance Dr Edward Wattehouse, who died in 1670 on a
Monday at his house in Mile End Green, having preached in London on the
Sunday a week before. He was buried at Greenford in Middlesex, where he
had estate in land, and where he was taken ill after preaching in Finchley.[59]

The seasonal mode of living of physicians, and their habit of leaving London
when conditions for the majority were at their worst, has already raised the
issue of the social divisiveness of disease. This effect, which might have been
expected to fade with the disappearance of plague, was instead perpetuated, as
already suggested by Smyth's obituaries, by the increasing salience of smallpox,
epidemic in London from about 1630.[60] In terms of Londoners' responses
there was a certain seamlessness in the way in which specific practices evolved
during plague were continued or adapted in respect of smallpox. One such
was that condemned by Dekker in 1620: to avoid the stigma of plague on their
households, he claimed, householders moved sick servants from the main
house into garden houses at midnight, pretending that they had been there
throughout their illness, and removing the body for burial through the back
gate. Similarly, the prosperous could send plague-stricken household members
to their suburban 'garden houses' or 'pleasure houses'.[61]

With smallpox, a more obviously infectious and inevitable disease,[62] these
emergency measures developed into a new way of life for urban households.
Expedients were adopted which distanced the sick from other household
members. They could involve degrees of physical separation ranging from a
nominally enclosed household space or separate room to a specially rented
room near by. Thus Katherine Oxinden wrote to her landlord in 1634 begging
him to let her

> have a Chamber more for a time [to] lay a sick boddi in if [I] shold have ani visited
> with the smale poxe for it tis so rife that I looke everi day when one of us shale have
> it an if it be Godes plesure that it must bee so I wolde faine take the likellest corse to
> keepe the soune [sound] from the infachded [infected] which I can by no menes doo
> [at present].

Mrs Oxinden also wanted a kitchen to herself: 'wee fech water an bake
together an when wee whash we have noe remidie but too come together'.
Contemporary responses are also illuminated by the noting of behaviour
which went against the trend, as when Chamberlain noted satirically that Lady
Purbeck had smallpox and her husband was 'so kind that he stirres not from

her beds feet'.[63] The well known concern over 'divided houses' in the 1630s is *prima facie* concerned with the crowding together of rootless poor people which also served to concentrate infection.[64] However, it is also related to demand for temporary lodgings. Moreover, while the chopping up of urban properties into small units could lead to increased sharing of spaces like staircases, it is also compatible with a growing desire for separate quarters. There are several ways, then, in which divided houses may be related to contemporary perceptions of the urban burden of disease. Later developments in the use of household space, interpreted as an effect of the growth of privacy or increased prosperity, can be seen as spurred on by prudential considerations. Such developments included a reduced inclination to share sleeping space with servants and their truckle beds.[65] What is known of changing room use in seventeenth-century London is compatible with a need to reduce contamination by instituting separate spaces even under the same roof. Evidence suggests a more precise definition of public areas, and reduced access even by servants to rooms defined as occupied by the family of blood.[66]

Thus smallpox, like plague but more continuously, served as an engine of social alienation. In other respects, however, it differed from plague in the degree to which it was accommodated and even domesticated. The flight response adopted for plague could still be appropriate, but smallpox defined itself as a disease that could not be evaded, especially in London. In spite of high-profile deaths among adults like those noted by Smyth, smallpox also rapidly became established as a disease of the young, especially those coming from the country. One illustration is the behaviour of the London cleric Symon Patrick and his wife, whose son caught smallpox in August 1687. Though 'very full', the boy did so well that they did not think of removing their 'lovely' baby daughter out of the house; she later developed the disease and died, to their great sadness and self-reproach.[67]

To appreciate the complexity of smallpox as a social issue affecting patterns of residence, we should put ourselves inside the head of a parent deciding to send a child to London to enter service or apprenticeship. On the one hand were the forces of attraction of London in terms of the child gaining a place in the world. In the balance were the child's life, and the enormous investment in terms of upbringing and committed resources represented by a child ready to leave home. To some extent, sending an 'unseasoned' child to London must have appeared as a death sentence, and many seventeenth-century parents stopped sending children to London for that reason. I would *not* argue that those who continued to do so adopted a fatalistic attitude, as this is a description rather than an explanation. Instead we have a rationalization of smallpox as part of urban experience, which could include the process of growing up. As many contemporary accounts make clear, not least that of Alice Thornton, the worst thing that could happen to a child ill with smallpox was for the disease to strike inwards, rather than purging itself outwards in the form of pustules on the surface of the body. Hence a child resisting heating regimes and other measures designed to encourage this form of purgation was endangering its own life by its disobedience. Smallpox encouraged the view that there was a susceptibility in the child which had to be eliminated, and if it lost its beauty as a result, that was only part of the process of growing up and loosening familial bonds.[68] There are parallels here with doctrines relating to original sin and socialization. Smallpox thus added complexity to the existing analogies between entering adulthood and the adolescent experience of urban life. The urban seasoning process could even be given a positive gloss as an initiation rite, as it was by a mayor and historian of Winchester around 1633, who claimed that the good cleansing air of Winchester induced in some incomers a short, sharp fever; this purged them of their impurities, and they were healthy thereafter. Similarly, Graunt considered that London air was so 'medicated' and 'impregnated' that it was less susceptible than the open and freer country air to bad as well as good impressions.[69]

These rationalizations were hardly sufficient to prevent the operation of smallpox as a divisive force both in London and in its relationship with the countryside. I have argued elsewhere, using apprenticeship disputes, that smallpox was a major factor in eroding the conventions of service and apprenticeship, especially those specifying the duty of care owed to the apprentice by the master, and the tight conventions about the breaking of indentures which were predicated on masters and apprentices living under the same roof.[70] The growth of wage labour and decline of the domestic system of production organized around apprenticeship are major long-standing issues: again, I wish only to add a cultural and material factor of the kind that current historiography tends to overlook. However, it is also fair to observe that, while an account of this social change in terms of impersonal economic forces is in place, it seems to leave human experience untouched. As far as I know the literature does not tell us when or how domestic space began to exclude those not members of the family of blood, or how, at the level of the household, the domestic servant diverged from the apprentice and the employee.[71] It should be stressed that this is not to exclude the possibility, already raised, that *all* household relations might be affected by disease in a way which could be represented in spatial terms.

The apprenticeship disputes referred to, which mostly date from the mid- to late-seventeenth century, reveal something of individual decisions in the face of urban circumstances affecting households. They derive mainly from middling and upper levels of crafts and trades, where the balance of power between master and apprentice was more evenly poised, but several show the workings of a town/country divide, made explicit by one father, who 'being [as he alleged] a Countryman and willing to have peace', offered the London master an extra £5 to resolve a dispute over the costs of the apprentice's ill health.[72] Apprenticeship cases can be unusually expressive of an alienation between town and country which is in effect a chronic form of the mutual distrust engendered during plague. Thus the country's fear of the town is tellingly displayed by one father who was too frightened to receive back into his family the son who had been returned into the country to recover his health after smallpox. Several cases refer to the country as a place of convalescence; one boy returned home 'to follow the plow for his health sake'.[73]

Such events were an increasing violation of the convention that the master was obligated to care for his apprentice in sickness and in health under his own roof. A case around 1671 gives some suggestion of a social process in the making: it was alleged against a silversmith that his apprentice always lay at the Cripplegate shop; he was left there even when ill, and was left behind, still ill, when the master moved to a new house in Foster Lane.[74] This case suggests, first, an interior separation of domestic and work space, and then a further split between two separate locations.[75] In a further case of the 1660s, involving parties of high social standing, the master cited as evidence of his good treatment of the apprentice that on Saturday nights in summer he provided him with a horse so that he could ride down to the master's country house for the Sabbath day. Obviously the master, a draper, spent summer weekends or even summer months in the country. This and other cases in which an apprentice or servant was left for extended periods to mind the shop represent a regularization of the situation parodied in Jonson's *The Alchemist*, when the master of the house, Loveday, absents himself because of plague, leaving his servants in charge.[76]

In conclusion, whatever the nature of London's influence in other respects, the effects of disease were felt most acutely there and led to shifts in living patterns which were echoed in smaller centres, or affected their development. This was as much to do with consciousness of disease as with disease itself. Broadly defined as a property of places and their 'airs' as well as of people, fear of infection should be added to factors more conventionally adduced for the resort to suburbs, for what is usually seen as gentrified country living, and for the increased incidence of 'split' households, in which, even for middling groups, it became desirable to divide the household between workplace and home. A mental framework for these changes is seen in the discussion in plague tracts of whether it was moral to abandon close ties in the cause of self-preservation. Along with emphasis on self, this literature promoted a 'grading' of household obligations which encouraged separation between the family of blood and the household of contract. Smallpox and other fevers came to be associated with plague in seventeenth-century discussions, but were given added dimensions in terms of the life cycle. With smallpox, compromises could be reached in the form of servants and apprentices who were seasoned by already having had smallpox or, later, who had been inoculated.[77]

There are also other, more familiar issues on which the fear of disease arguably has some bearing. One is the change in patterns of recruitment of apprentices to London. As is well known, as the seventeenth century wore on, apprentices tended to come from nearer London, and were less frequently sent from remote counties.[78] That is, apprentices sent to London were more likely to be seasoned – already adapted to urban life. A second issue is the feminization of towns. Contemporaries tended to regard mature women especially as having some immunity to infectious disease, partly because of their role in nursing children. What role this may have had in producing unbalanced urban sex ratios, especially in large towns later in the seventeenth century – which is acknowledged to be an effect of migration – seems a problem worth investigation.[79] Thirdly, although it was hardly new to value the health of children, it may be that bills of mortality and 'political arithmetic', in giving a new visibility to the burden of mortality suffered by children, encouraged increased emphasis on the preciousness of children, as a national asset as well as to individual families.[80]

An important question arising from this, which cannot be given space here, is the relationship between the attitudes and practices described here and the sending of London children to wet and dry nurses living in fringe areas or satellite villages.[81] In an excursion in spring 1664 Pepys's stopping places included Hackney, where he had boarded as a 'little child', and Kingsland, 'by my nurse's house ... where my brother Tom and I was kept when young'. Pepys's reflection was 'Lord! how in every point I find myself to over-value things when a child', but such early experiences could nonetheless have contributed to Londoners' feelings for rural villages.[82]

A fourth issue is the effect on the sense of civic duty, particularly the requirement to take office, of civic lives divided between town and country. The plague tractates were concerned with obligations not only within the household, but between rich and poor, rulers and ruled; living half in and half out of the city may have been presented as a compromise by those liable to bear responsibility, but was probably corrosive in the long term. Improved roads and transport, usually interpreted as facilitating urbanization, were undoubtedly seized upon by contemporaries as making it easy to get away from the city more frequently.[83] A last, related, suggestion refers to that proliferation of types of towns which is said to be part of the English urban renaissance. This development could equally be seen as the result of a repulsion from cities, and a desire to recreate many of the amenities of urban living on a relatively small scale, without the burdens and threats to health of life in the metropolis. It is, after all, a notable feature of English urbanization that it consists of the growth of many small or 'moderate' towns rather than the early emergence of a number of large cities.[84] Thus urban amenities could include the natural but humanized pleasures which the English expected to find on the outskirts of towns, and which constantly drew even the most inveterate urbanites out of the metropolis.

NOTES

Versions of this chapter were given to the Seminar in Medieval and Tudor London History at the Institute of Historical Research, London, and at the 'Worlds of John Winthrop' conference at the Millersville University of Pennsylvania. I am grateful to both audiences for their responses. I also wish to thank Maxine Berg, Vanessa Harding, Mark Jenner, Jack Langton, Joad Raymond and Patrick Wallis for bibliographical information, and the editors of this volume for valuable comments.

1 P. Clark and D. Souden eds, *Migration and Society in Early Modern England* (1987); A. McRae, 'The peripatetic muse: internal travel and the cultural production of space in pre-revolutionary England', in G. MacLean, D. Landry and J. P. Ward eds, *The Country and the City Revisited* (Cambridge, 1999).

2 P. Borsay, *The English Urban Renaissance: Culture and Society in the Provincial Town 1660–1770* (Oxford, 1991), pp. 87–8.

3 *Ibid.*, pp. 210–11.

4 Giovanni Botero, *The Greatness of Cities* (1598, trans. 1606), in *id.*, *The Reason of State*, trans. P. J. and D. P. Waley (1956), pp. 276 ff.

5 See, for example, Boulton, *Neighbourhood*, pp. 1–2, and references there cited.

6 See, for example, L. Jordanova, 'Has the social history of medicine come of age?', *HJ*, 36 (1993).

7 M. Butler, *Theatre and Crisis 1632–1642* (Cambridge, 1987); A. McRae, *God Speed the Plough: the Representation of Agrarian England, 1500–1660* (Cambridge, 1996).

8 C. Phythian-Adams, 'Jolly cities: goodly towns: the current search for England's urban roots', *Urban History Yearbook* (1977), p. 30.

9 Botero, *Greatness of Cities*; B. J. Kohl, R. G. Witt and E. B. Welles eds, *The Earthly Republic* (Manchester, 1978), pp. 136–47 (on the wise choices made by men).

10 *Polydore Vergil's English History*, ed. H. Ellis, Camden Society 36 (1846), p. 4.

11 H. Rosenau, *The Ideal City* (third edition, 1983), p. 55; D. K. Keene, 'Suburban growth', in *The Plans and Topography of Medieval Towns in England and Wales*, ed. M. W. Barley, Council for British Archaeology Research Report 14 (1976), p. 77.

12 See esp. J. M. Prest, *The Garden of Eden* (New Haven CT and London, 1981); J. E. Duncan, *Milton's Earthly Paradise* (Minneapolis MN, 1972).

13 K. O. Kupperman, 'The puzzle of the American climate in the early colonial period', *American Historical Review*, 87 (1982), esp. p. 1287; *id.*, 'Fear of hot climates in the Anglo-American colonial experience', *William and Mary Quarterly*, 41 (1984), esp. p. 233; M. Dobson, 'Contours of death: disease, mortality and the environment in early modern England', in J. Landers ed., *Historical Epidemiology and the Health Transition*, suppl. to *Health Transition Review*, 2 (1992).

14 C. Webster, *The Great Instauration: Science, Medicine and Reform 1626–1660* (1975), esp. section V; Keene, 'Suburban growth', p. 81.

15 A. B. Appleby, 'Epidemics and famine in the Little Ice Age', *Journal of Interdisciplinary History*, 10 (1980); Kupperman, 'American climate', pp. 1254–5; *Vergil's English History*, p. 4.

16 M. Campbell, '"Of people either too few or too many": the conflict of opinion on population and its relation to emigration', in W. A. Aitken and B. D. Henning eds, *Conflict in Stuart England* (1960); P. Griffiths, J. Landers, M. Pelling and R. Tyson, 'Population and disease, estrangement and belonging 1540–1700', in P. Clark ed., *The Cambridge Urban History of Britain*, II, *1540–1840* (Cambridge, 2000), pp. 217–18; J. C. Riley, *Population Thought in the Age of the Demographic Revolution* (Durham NC, 1985); A. O. Aldridge, 'Population and polygamy in eighteenth-century thought', *Journal of the History of Medicine*, 4 (1949).

17 J. Graunt, *Natural and Political Observations upon the Bills of Mortality* (fifth edition, 1676), in *The Economic Writings of Sir William Petty*, ed. C. H. Hull (2 vols, New York, 1964), II, pp. 320–1, 383–4, 393–4.

18 See T. R. Slater, 'Family, society and the ornamental villa on the fringes of English country towns', *Journal of Historical Geography*, 4 (1978); MacLean *et al.*, *Country and City Revisited*, esp. Introduction, and essay by J. P. Ward; C. B. Estabrook, *Urbane and Rustic England: Cultural Ties and Social Spheres in the Provinces 1660–1780* (Manchester, 1998), esp. chap. 10. The early modern suburb could, however, be seen as a degeneration and contraction of the medieval version: see Keene, 'Suburban growth'.

19 Boulton, *Neighbourhood*. For a reassessment of the 'ideal types' of Sjoberg and of J. E. Vance see J. Langton, 'Residential patterns in pre-industrial cities: some case studies from seventeenth-century Britain' (1975), reprinted in J. Barry ed., *The Tudor and Stuart Town: A Reader* (London and New York, 1990). For applicability to London see M. J. Power, 'The social topography of Restoration London', in Beier and Finlay, *London*.

20 I will not be dealing with the phenomenon of Westminster and the West End, which has been treated elsewhere. See G. Rosser, *Medieval Westminster 1200–1540* (Oxford, 1989); J. Merritt, 'Religion, Government and Society in Early Modern Westminster *c.* 1525–1625', University of London Ph.D. thesis (1992); M. J. Power, 'The east and west in early modern London', in E. W. Ives, R. J. Knecht, and J. J. Scarisbrick eds, *Wealth and Power in Tudor England* (1978); L. Stone, 'The residential development of the West End of London in the seventeenth century', in B. C. Malament ed., *After the Reformation* (Manchester, 1980).

21 On changes in the personification of London in prosaic sources see L. Manley, 'From matron to monster: Tudor–Stuart London and the languages of urban description', in H. Dubrow and R. Strier eds, *The Historical Renaissance* (Chicago and London, 1988). Stow's account of London and its suburbs (1603) contrasts an earlier state of fruitful, wholesome beauty freely available to Londoners with a present environment of lost trees, decayed wells, enclosed fields and restricted access: Kingsford, *Stow*, I, pp. 11 ff, 127, II, pp. 72, 77–8, and *passim*.

22 For topical literary references see F. C. Chalfant, *Ben Jonson's London* (Athens GA, 1978).

23 Samuel Pepys, *Diary*, ed. H. B. Wheatley (8 books in 3 vols, 1962), Bk 2, p. 201 (1 April 1662); Bk 4, p. 146 (11 June 1664), p. 168 (11 July 1664), p. 368 (14 April 1665), p. 374 (23 April 1665), p. 389 (19 May 1665); Bk 5, p. 343 (15 July 1666); Bk 7, pp. 145–6 (17 October 1667); Bk 8, p. 298 (7 May 1669).

24 *Ibid.*, Bk 4, p. 394 (30 May 1665); Bk 5, p. 272 (11 May 1666). On botanizing by Londoners see C. E. Raven, *English Naturalists from Neckam to Ray* (Cambridge, 1947).

25 On Moorfields' changing environmental condition, mainly induced by different phases of urban development, culminating in its reclamation *c.* 1610, see Stow, *Survey*, II, pp. 76–8, 369–70; Chalfant, *Jonson's London*, pp. 130–1. On London's food supply see F. J. Fisher, 'The development of the London food market 1540–1640' reprinted in *id.*, *London and the English Economy 1500–1700*, ed. P. J. Corfield and N. B. Harte (1990); J. Chartres, 'Food consumption and internal trade', in Beier and Finlay, *London*.

26 R. H. Perkinson, 'Topographical comedy in the seventeenth century', *English Literary History*, 3 (1936).

27 See R. Ashton, 'Popular entertainment and social control in later Elizabethan and early Stuart London', *LJ*, 9 (1983). For the fears of apprentices traversing suburban spaces at night see W. J. Hardy and W. Le Hardy, *Middlesex County Records, Reports* (1928), p. 138; CLRO MC6/302.

28 See, for example, M. Pelling, 'Appearance and reality: barber-surgeons, the body and disease', in Beier and Finlay, *London*.

29 RCP Annals, 10 December 1630, p. 295. All page references are to the transcription/translation of the Annals, now available on microfilm. I am grateful to the President and Fellows of the College for permission to quote from the Annals.

30 Chamberlain, *Letters*, II, p. 557.

31 For overviews see C. Webster, 'The historiography of medicine', and M. Pelling, 'Medicine since 1500', both in P. Corsi and P. Weindling eds, *Information Sources in the History of Science and Medicine* (1983).

32 Fisher, *London and the English Economy*. As recent examples on plague see G. Calvi, 'A metaphor for social exchange: the Florentine plague of 1630', *Representations*, 13 (1986); F. M. Getz, 'Black Death and the silver lining: meaning, continuity and revolutionary change in histories of medieval plague', *Journal of the History of Biology*, 24 (1991); C. Jones, 'Plague and its metaphors in early modern France', *Representations*, 53 (1996).

33 See Griffiths *et al.*, 'Population and disease', pp. 203–9, stressing 'background' rather than 'crisis' mortality, and urban mortality as a penalty borne mainly by children.

34 See D. S. Smith and J. D. Hacker, 'Cultural demography: New England deaths and the puritan perception of risk', *Journal of Interdisciplinary History*, 26 (1996); Dobson, 'Contours of death', p. 82; Kupperman, 'Fear of hot climates', pp. 228, 232.

35 P. Slack, *The Impact of Plague in Tudor and Stuart England* (1985); A. Everitt, 'Social mobility in early modern England', *P&P*, 33 (1966); Borsay, *English Urban Renaissance*; J. C. Riley, *The Eighteenth Century Campaign to Avoid Disease* (Basingstoke, 1987).

36 For a fuller discussion of what follows on the college see M. Pelling, *The Strength of the Opposition: the College of Physicians and Irregular Practitioners in Early Modern London* (forthcoming); and references cited in note 37.

37 W. J. Birken, 'The Fellows of the Royal College of Physicians of London 1603–1643: A Social Study', University of North Carolina Ph.D. thesis (1977); *id.*, 'The social problem of the English physician in the early seventeenth century', *Medical History*, 31 (1987). M. Pelling, 'The women of the family? Speculations around early modern British physicians', *Social History of Medicine*, 8 (1995); *id.*, 'Compromised by gender: the role of the male medical practitioner in early modern England', in H. Marland and M. Pelling eds, *The Task of Healing* (Rotterdam, 1996).

38 RCP Annals, 13 April 1584, p. 25.

39 On the law terms see C. R. Cheney ed., *Handbook of Dates for Students of English History* (London, reprinted 1991), pp. 65–9; W. R. Prest, *The Rise of the Barristers* (Oxford, 1986), pp. 41–2, 58–61. For their effects on residence *c.* 1632 see BODL Bankes MS 62, fos 12, 51v. For justification in terms of health see Francis Bacon, *The Historie of Life and Death* (1638), p. 195.

40 RCP Annals, 1562 and 1563, pp. 38, 39; Griffiths *et al.*, 'Population and disease', pp. 212–14.

41 This was variously expressed, and re-cohered into a principle by Thomas Sydenham: see, for example, Chamberlain, *Letters*, II, p. 576; *The Autobiography of Mrs Alice Thornton*, ed. C. Jackson, Surtees Society 62 (1875), p. 6; John Arbuthnot, *An Essay concerning the Effects of Air* (1733), p. 218.

42 Graunt, *Observations*, p. 366.

43 Pelling, 'Compromised by gender', pp. 103 ff.

44 For references to these activities see *ibid.*

45 See the example of Paul Croke's Hackney residence: Prest, *Rise of the Barristers*, p. 41.

46 RCP Annals, 26 June 1598, p. 114. Three more were absent but named as Queen's physicians; another was absent 'but with permission', making a total of fourteen absentees. The meeting was attended by sixteen fellows.

47 *Ibid.*, 9 November 1625, p. 198; John Cook, *Unum Necessarium* (1648), p. 64.

48 Daniel Defoe, *Curious and Diverting Journies, thro' the Whole Island of Britain* (1734), esp. journeys I and V; N. Rogers, 'Money, land and lineage: the big bourgeoisie of Hanoverian London' (1979), reprinted in P. Borsay ed., *The Eighteenth Century Town: A Reader* (London and New York, 1990).

49 *The London Directory of 1677* (1878).

50 *London Directory*, sigs. B3, B8, C1.

51 Richard Kephale, *Medela Pestilentiae* (1665), p. 10; Pepys, *Diary*, Bk 7, p. 24 (14 July 1667).

52 Richard Smyth, *The Obituary*, ed. H. Ellis, Camden Society 44 (1849). For Smyth's life, and an analysis of his 'Obituary', see V. Harding, 'Mortality and the mental map of London: Richard Smyth's *Obituary*', in R. Myers and M. Harris eds, *Medicine, Mortality and the Book Trade* (Folkestone and Newcastle DE, 1998).

53 Smyth, *Obituary*, pp. 63, 7, 10, 11, 13, 15, 16.

54 *Ibid.*, pp. 26, 13, 18, 43, 52, 53, 87, 103; Stephen Bradwell, *Physick for the Sicknesse, Commonly called the Plague*, 1636 (Norwood NJ, 1977), p. 9.

55 Smyth, *Obituary*, p. 27. In general, see M. MacDonald and T. R. Murphy, *Sleepless Souls* (Oxford, 1990).

56 Smyth, *Obituary*, p. 7 (1633); Arbuthnot, *An Essay*, p. 211; Harding, 'Mortality and the mental map', p. 64; Smyth, *Obituary*, pp. 36, 39, 67, 80.

57 Smyth, *Obituary*, pp. 64, 70.

58 *Ibid.*, pp. 47, 27, 72, 104.

59 *London Directory*, p. xv; Smyth, *Obituary*, p. 86.

60 S. R. Duncan, S. Scott and C. J. Duncan, 'Smallpox epidemics in cities in Britain', *Journal of Interdisciplinary History*, 35 (1994), esp. p. 255. But cf. RCP Annals, 1561, p. 37; Simon

Kellwaye, *A Defensative against the Plague* (1593), fo. 38. On smallpox in London see Graunt, *Observations*, pp. 349, 352, 366; on its demographic significance and later decline see J. Landers, *Death and the Metropolis* (Cambridge, 1993).

61 Thomas Dekker, *Villanies discovered by Lanthorne and Candle-light* (1620), sig. I2; O. Grell, 'Plague in Elizabethan and Stuart London: the Dutch response', *Medical History*, 34 (1990), pp. 429–30. See also *The Shutting up Infected Houses* (1665), p. 11.

62 Contemporary controversies over smallpox's causation focused variously on menstrual blood, corrupt air and 'fumes from the blood': Kellwaye, *A Defensative*, fos 38–9. On the distinctness of smallpox and plague, and similarity of their causes and cures, see Thomas Sherwood, *The Charitable Pestmaster* (1641), pp. 3, 9–14; Arbuthnot, *An Essay*, pp. 177–9, 192.

63 *The Oxinden Letters 1607–1642*, ed. D. Gardiner (1933), p. 94; Chamberlain, *Letters*, II, p. 593 (1624).

64 GL *Returns of Divided Houses in the City of London (May) 1637*, transcr. T. C. Dale (typescript, [1937]).

65 U. Priestley, P. Corfield and H. Sutermeister, 'Rooms and room use in Norwich housing 1580–1730', *Post-medieval Archaeology*, 16 (1982), esp. pp. 115–16. These authors also examine shops.

66 F. E. Brown, 'Continuity and change in the urban house: developments in domestic space organisation in seventeenth-century London', *Comparative Studies in Society and History*, 28 (1986).

67 Symon Patrick, 'A brief account of my life', in *Works*, ed. A. Taylor (9 vols, Oxford, 1858), IX, pp. 507–8.

68 *Autobiography of Alice Thornton*, esp. pp. 124–5, 157–9, 222–3. For advice on the care of smallpox sufferers see Kellwaye, *A Defensative*.

69 T. Atkinson, *Elizabethan Winchester* (1963), p. 218; Graunt, *Observations*, p. 392. On city and country airs, and the 'seasoning' of children, see also Arbuthnot, *An Essay*, pp. 208–9, 216–17, 219.

70 M. Pelling, 'Apprenticeship, health, and social cohesion in early modern London', *HWJ*, 37 (1994).

71 See S. Ogilvie and M. Cerman eds, *European Proto-industrialization* (Cambridge, 1996).

72 CLRO MC6/245 (*c*. 1669). The apprentice's illness was smallpox.

73 CLRO MC6/222A–B; MC6/288B (1672); MC6/62A (1654), deposition of Mary Banks. People could of course move to, or remain in, London for health reasons: see Patrick, 'Brief account', pp. 420, 540; Bankes MS 62, fo. 49.

74 CLRO MC6/276, deposition of Mary Ricketts.

75 Some instances recorded in *Returns of Divided Houses* (1637) suggest a splitting between shop and home, though this can reflect marital status, etc.: pp. 57, 74, 109, 112, 113, 118, 172.

76 CLRO MC6/217B, deposition of Robert Blake; MC6/196A (1666).

77 See, for a county adjacent to London (Essex), J. R. Smith, *The Speckled Monster: Smallpox in England 1670–1970* (Chelmsford, 1987), esp. pp. 20–1.

78 M. J. Kitch, 'Capital and kingdom: migration to later Stuart London', in Beier and Finlay, *London*.

79 On sex ratios see Griffiths *et al.*, 'Population and disease', pp. 199, 200, 217–18; R. Finlay, *Population and Metropolis: the Demography of London 1580–1650* (Cambridge, 1981), pp. 139–42.

80 M. Pelling, 'Child health as a social value in early modern England', reprinted in *id., The Common Lot: Sickness, Medical Occupations and the Urban Poor in Early Modern England* (1998); Graunt, *Observations*, pp. 348–9; Corbyn Morris, *Observations on the Past Growth and Present State of ... London*, in T. Birch ed., *A Collection of the Yearly Bills of Mortality* (1759), esp. pp. 88–9, 106, 113–14. London was also seen as destroying adults, but more by degenerative, diet-related conditions than by epidemic, air-related diseases: Graunt, *Observations*, pp. 350–2.

81 On wet nursing in London see Finlay, *Population and Metropolis*, pp. 94–100, 144–8; Griffiths *et al.*, 'Population and disease', pp. 201–2.

82 Pepys, *Diary*, Bk 4, p. 111 (25 April 1664).

83 Morris, *Observations*, p. 110; H. Horwitz, '"The mess of the middle class" revisited: the case of the "big bourgeoisie" of Augustan London', *Continuity and Change*, 2 (1987), pp. 264, 266, 276.

84 Griffiths *et al.*, 'Population and disease', pp. 196–7; Richard Price, 'Observations on the expectations of lives ...', *Phil. Trans.*, 59 (1769), p. 119.

Chapter 9

Politics made visible: order, residence
and uniformity in Cheapside, 1600–45

Paul Griffiths

'These things are visible'[1]

'IN THE FACE OF THE WORLD'

The central London thoroughfare of Cheapside was placed 'in the face of all
the world'. The monarch, it was said, had 'a perticuler eye' on Cheapside.
It was a ceremonial and commercial centre point – London's 'shopping street'
and 'first and absolutest place'. But this prize promenade belonged to the
nation too; it was 'the starr and jewell of the land'.[2] It was a political space
where verbal and visual statements of meanings of order were emphasized,
and a key point on the map of civic and royal ritual, as well as on the route
followed when offenders were led around the city for public punishment in
busy locations.

Situated 'in the face of the world', people, buildings, and traffic on this
'first' street received much comment. Thousands of passers-by walked along it
each day, pausing to shop, talk, or to look at the sights. Furthermore, Cheapside was imagined as a civil and well mannered space. It saddened John
Chamberlain that Catholics fleeing the collapse of the floor in the French
ambassador's residence in 1623 received rough handling there. 'Even in
Cheapside,' he wrote, 'where they shold be more civil, they were redy to pull
and teare them out of the coaches as they passed to their lodgings or to the
surgeons.'[3]

Above all, however, eyes and minds turned to the south side of Cheapside,
to the 'fair houses and shops' of the Goldsmiths' Row. John Stow gushed with
pride:

> The most beautiful frame and front of houses and shops within the walls of London
> or elsewhere in England [he wrote, is] commonly called Goldsmiths Row between
> the end of Bread Stret and the cross in Cheap. It was builded by Thomas Wood
> (goldsmith and sheriff) in 1491. It contains ten fair dwelling houses and fourteen

shops all in one frame, uniformly builded four storeys high, beautiful towards the
street with goldsmiths arms and likeness of wood-men in memory of his name ...
These he gave to the Goldsmiths with stocks of money to be lent to young men
having those shops. This front was again new painted and gilt over in 1594. The
goldsmiths [Stow concludes] kept their shops and trade here in West Cheap from
ancient times.[4]

The high-ranking and fashionable goldsmiths' trade spread a sense of taste
and wealth. One traveller noted that London's streets 'are very handsome and
clean but that which is named from the goldsmiths who inhabit it, surpasses
all the rest'. Shopfronts were a visual prize, interiors contained riches too: 'all
sorts of gold and silver vessels exposed to sale; as well as ancient and modern
medals, in such quantities as must surprise a man the first time he sees and
considers them'. On his travels in 1599, Platter wrote that only goldsmiths and
money-changers lived in a 'long street called Cheapside ... so that inexpress-
ibly great treasures and vast amounts of money may be seen here'.[5] The
'uniformly builded' houses of goldsmiths boosted Cheapside's high status. As
such, the Row raised both civic and royal honour, providing a lush background
for visual displays of powerful authority.

The late sixteenth century was a high point for the Cheapside Row after its
recent renovation in 1594. Soon, however, this chorus of praise was turned into
a commentary complaining of its shocking decay. In 1622 John Chamberlain
moaned that 'yt is a straunge sight and not knowne in this age till within these
two or three yeares, to see booksellers, stocking men, haberdashers, point-
makers, and other meane trades crept into the Goldsmithes Rowe, that was
wont to be the bewtie and glorie of Cheapeside'.[6] Worse still, Cheapside was a
busy city artery; the rotting Row was very *visible*. The worsening condition of
the Cheapside Row and its near neighbour in Lombard Street where goldsmiths also once traded in a matching line of shops,[7] together with the
growing movement of goldsmiths to places beyond the west walls of the City
where well-heeled clients now settled in large numbers, resulted in campaigns
to reverse both these trends.[8] The policy of forcibly returning the scattered
goldsmiths to the shabby Rows has not passed unnoticed. But previous work
has nearly always treated it simply as an aspect of the political aesthetics of the
'personal rule'. Ashton writes that Charles I, dismayed by the rotting fabric of
a city that appeared likely to burst its seams, planned to fashion 'a more
civilized urban environment [in London] worthy of a great capital city', and
that the 'unpopular' order instructing goldsmiths to return was 'one of the
most striking examples' of this grand imperial design.[9]

Yet, as I will show in this essay, there were several languages calling for the
reform of the Rows and the return there of the 'remote' goldsmiths. The City
and the Goldsmiths' Company also pursued measures to preserve the character of the Rows. Their priorities, I show, came increasingly to clash with

those of the central government, and contributed to the alienation of a substantial number of citizens from the Crown. The events along the Rows were not, therefore, storms in teacups, but were small-scale manifestations of far-reaching troubles that unsettled both the City and the country.

It has also passed largely unremarked that the policy of the forced return began more than a decade before the 'personal rule'. What began in 1619 as a defensive manoeuvre by the Goldsmiths' Company to stop a tide of 'foreign' workers, and to prevent crime, was hi-jacked and remodelled by two kings (by James and especially by Charles I) as a piece of imperial culture. Up to now little has been said about the first fifteen years of the forced return or its complicated roots. The attempt was in fact cut in half by a gap from 1624 to 1634, though there was a short-lived attempt to restart it in 1629. The first campaign lasted from winter 1619 until the close of 1624, and the second stretched over the final half of the 1630s and ran out of steam after 1640. At least twenty-nine 'mean' traders were told to shut up shop along the Rows, and at least seventy-five 'remote' goldsmiths, who had mostly been drawn by the commercial pull of the fashionable West End, were ordered to fill their places (a physical mismatch that did not pass unremarked at the time).[10] They were threatened with legal action and the loss of liberty or their place in the livery, and they put a case against the forced uprooting. Yet, despite some chilling threats, only a few of them actively hunted for a Cheapside shop, and by 1640 the complexion of the Rows remained unaltered.[11]

THIEVES, STRANGERS, AND 'REMOTE' AND 'SECRET PLACES'

The wish to keep the Rows as special spaces in the seventeenth century was not new. In 1555 a draper 'voluntarylly submyted hymself' to the Court of Aldermen 'for the matter in varyaunce betwyn hym and the goldsmythes for settynge upp of a clothe shoppe in the Goldesmythes Row in Cheapesyde'. A compromise was reached and the shop was 'devyded into two parts', so that 'the parte thereof opening into Cheapesyde shall styll be occupied as a goldsmythes shop as yt was wont to be'.[12]

Visual display was a point of intersection between the built environment and politics in the next century too. But unease about thieves, strangers, and 'secret' spots was at the head of the company's concerns. It moaned about street sellers, who were said to tour the city seeking to buy stolen jewels and gold and silver plate. In 1606 the company took steps to combat 'the oppression of straingers', picking Anthony Marlowe to prosecute laws 'against the boldnes of straingers'. But the traffic in goldsmiths' goods did not stop, and protests again flared about these street sellers in 1612. Concern expanded three years later when the company connected its financial worries with the falling worth of the freedom, observing that the fortunes of 'ancient' guilds had plunged in recent years as a result of 'the infinite increase' and 'indirect practizes' of 'foreiners'.[13]

On 3 November 1619, at the close of an otherwise quiet day in court, the Goldsmiths' Company began to plan a policy 'for reducing of the shopps in the gouldsmithes rowe to be inhabited by goldsmiths onely'. The once splendid Rows along Cheapside and Lombard Street were now pockmarked by 'mean' traders who kept shop there and upset the neat visual unity of goldsmiths living side-by-side. Two months later the company petitioned the Crown to seek its backing. In so doing, it situated its initiative in far larger political contexts: seeking support 'to reforme the great inconveniences to the commonwealth by such as keepe goldsmithes shops in the suburbes and other remote places of this cittie not free of this societie'.[14]

The policy of a forced return was set in motion by concern about workers tucked away out of reach in 'secret' corners or 'creeping' through the city (language like descriptions of theft or the passage of the pox through infected bodies).[15] In 1620 the company noted the 'greate inconvenience' of keeping shops in suburbs and other 'remote' spots. Unease about strangers creeping into the trade kept rising. The company blasted the 'increasing nomber' of strangers who grabbed 'a great part of' its workers' 'lyvings' in 1622. Worse still, strangers lived in 'chambers, garretts and other secret places' where it lacked 'access' to search, cutting 'deceiptful jewels' and selling stolen plate. A link was made with the Rows: 'strangers', it was said, were 'partlie the means that the use and exercise of other meane trades are crept into the [Rows]'. So it was decided to petition 'the state to redresse these mischiefes so apparantilie increasing'. In 1624, in the midst of their efforts to force the 'remote' gold-smiths to return, the company promoted a parliamentary Bill to prevent the theft of 'plate, jewells and goldsmiths wares' and for 'reformation of incon-veniences in the Goldsmiths trade'.[16]

The Crown's concern about goldsmiths' goods and the currency at this time switched attention towards the trade's location. A company certificate prepared for the Crown in 1616 listed goldsmiths 'suspected to falsify the sterling of this realm'. The King had a rude confirmation of these dangers two years later when he was sold 'deceiptfull plate'. In the same month as the company first noted the untidy scattering of its workers, it was reported that gold and silver stocks in the Mint were dwindling and being shipped overseas. The exodus of gold and silver across the Channel continued to drain funds and, in 1623, Ministers noted 'a great defect and want of necessary store of plate of all kinds more than formerly has been', and claimed that the honour of the Crown was sinking fast because of a poor display of plate at 'festival times' and state banquets.[17]

The policy of a forced return, therefore, began as a dialogue between the company and the Crown, not as an expression of Stuart aesthetics. Its pace was slow and mostly confined to company petitions to the Crown outlining the bleak state of the Rows and men of 'mean trades' (183 in number) setting up trade as goldsmiths there and in other distant parts.[18] But royal pressure to sweep the Rows free of 'mean' traders mounted in the early 1620s. Privy Councillors sent a cross letter to the City in 1622:

> Yt is a thing that every man's eye meetes with as he passeth up and down [they claimed] that the Gouldsmythes Rowe in Cheapsyde which was ever held a great ornament to the citty shold now grow to be intermixed in a broken fashion with shops of meaner trades ... whereof when you shall but enter into due consideracon, we assure ourselves your owne judgments will tell you that it is noe smale disparagment unto the honour of the citty both in respect of the meannes of the shew and because it may breede an opinion of greater decay then (thankes be to God) there is cause.

They tried to shame the City. What an irony, they said, that a 'blemish and deformitie should be noted and suffered in the heart of the citty' at a time when its suburbs 'are many waies beautified (farr above that they have beene in tymes past)'. The link with civic fame was made plain: 'In things of this nature you ought to account the honour and adorning of the city to be an essentiall parte of the good government thereof.' The City was told to plot a 'meanes to restore' the Cheapside Row to its former 'lustre by causing it to be replenished againe with gouldsmythes shoppes' and stop it being 'defaced' by a motley mixture of 'mean and unsuitable trades' by turning 'shoppes into decent houses of habitacion', so 'that principall streete may be the better beautified and adorned'.[19]

Connections between building, visibility and politics are clear in this 'special command'. A month later, however, the King lectured the City rulers about 'faultes' in the city; 'the principal was that whereas at his first coming the Goldsmiths Rowe in Cheapside was so faire and flourishing, they had now suffered yt to be overrun and blemished with poore pettie trades'. A City committee was set up with the support of the company.[20] This intervention was intensified by the decoration of streets for the celebration of Prince Charles's return with his Spanish princess. It was this royal desire to clean up Cheapside for the imagined procession that marked the first notable entry of the City into the Rows dispute. The mayor and aldermen were warned that 'the care of magnificence and splendor [in the Row]' is 'expected at your hands'.[21] By now the return was a national matter and a point of strain between the Crown and the City. Other parts of the Cheapside landscape also fell under a spotlight, including the cross – an 'ornament of the city' – that had recently been 'new builded in more strong and beautiful manner than the former'. Grumbling about traffic that blocked the street never faded.[22]

In 1623 the Crown asked the mayor and aldermen to run an eye over the 'broken' Rows and not sit still as they formerly had. At the knighting of the mayor in the same year, the King grabbed the chance to slip in mention of 'faultes' in the City, the 'principall' being the shabby Rows and the urgent need to move goldsmiths there 'for the contynuance of the beautie and ornament of the chiefe street of the citie'. And a few days later he rapped the city for its lukewarm response to reforming 'fower things' – the swarm of beggars, the shoddy state of the bridge, the dirty river, and the 'decay of the goldsmithes row' by 'creeping thereinto of other meane and unsuitable trades'.[23]

Pushed by the City, the company collected the names of twelve goldsmiths who were able to move to the Rows. But despite its persuasions to 'conforme', only two agreed to move; the rest claimed 'that they had bene long setled' in other places and that a return to the Rows would be financially crippling. A big stumbling block was high rents in Cheapside. (The company said that its 'increase and povertie' caused its workers to scatter in 'remote and unfitt places'.) In 1624 'divers goldsmiths in the Strand' said that, if they were 'compelled' to move, rents should be fixed at 'ancient' rates as they were at first 'for the supporte and cherishinge of yonge beginners leaste able to sitt at great rents'. A bunch of 'young men' from the same place flatly stated that they were 'no way able' to pay rents 'now demaunded', and turned fears about visibility upside down by pointing out that they were settled in an 'open and eminent place of ancient custome for gouldsmiths in ye high street betwixt the court and city'. The Crown requested that shops along the Rows should be let at 'moderate rents'.[24]

Other company tensions also prompted workers to refuse to co-operate. Quarrels rocked the company after 1620, especially calls by the generality to have a bigger say in elections and 'a yeomanry and government among themselves'.[25] As was mentioned above, the company filed a parliamentary Bill in 1624, but it ran into trouble when it was sent 'to prelates and lordes': '100 persons and upwards' of the yeomanry stormed the committee room 'in a tumultuous manner' shouting 'exceptions' to the Bill. Invited to put their case in a less rowdy way, they sent a written copy two days later that left the committee in no doubt that the return was their chief grievance but that there were divisions in their ranks also:

> for those that dwell out of the liberties of London were unwilling to remove their habitations, some others were willing that all the goldsmiths might dwell within the citie & liberties, [and] some others were of opinion to have their dwelling within the walls of the citie onely, but the generalitie seemed unwilling to dwell in London and the liberties clayming the benefit of the cities charter w[hi]ch geveth libertie to all freemen to exercise theire trades in the citie and liberties.

But they said that if 'yt pleased the lords to confyne them to dwell togeather' in 'speciall streets', they would 'submytt' and consider streets 'as they conceive fittest'.[26] But their discontents lingered. In 1628 the yeomanry turned down the company's bid for a loan for this reason: 'divers things past' had been planned without their 'consent prejudiciall unto them as they conceaved'. No single issue was 'expressed,' except that 'heretofore in Parliament concerning the furnishing of the shops in Cheapside with goldsmiths'.[27]

In autumn 1624 the Rows were still a blot on the landscape and, it seemed to the Crown, a very visible token of indifference to its will. The company and City seemed full of words but little else, though the Privy Council said in 1624 that it had the backing of 'divers goldsmiths of note', who produced an Act from the reign of Edward III 'reduceing the habitation of all goldsmiths to the Goldsmiths Row in Cheapside and the Old Change' to stop trading in 'corners'.[28] The company was warned and promised 'to proceed in the busynes'. Yet little happened, and no 'remote' goldsmiths moved from the West End. The silence in the sources over the next five years marks a pause in the return. Yet the larger contexts in which it was located did not cease to operate – a royal proclamation was issued in 1625 urging 'uniformity' in building; royal rebukes about London's shoddy streets or false stones did not simply stop.[29]

The synchronicity between this pause and the King's death was no coincidence. Nor did this lull occur at a low point: committees had just been set up, and the protagonists seemed poised on the edge of a big push in 1625. The terrible plague that swept through the city in the same year diverted energies elsewhere. So, too, did several tough battles that distracted the attention of the Crown: war, raising funds, the Petition of Right. The next move of the return was in 1631 and the Crown was always in the driving seat thereafter. James I had seen the potential of splendid building and its political advantages; he, after all, planned to refurbish St Paul's and to rebuild London as a city of brick to match the finest days of imperial Rome.[30] But Charles's personal predilection was for building on a grander imperial scale;[31] more muscle was added to this political aesthetics by what has been called the 'Laudian style: order, uniformity' and 'the beauty of holiness'.[32]

At this point we should leave the narrative of the forced return for a short pause to consider the contemporary resonances of such words as 'imperial', 'uniformity' and 'order' in these specific contexts. In so doing, the political meanings contemporaries attached to architectural styles will become apparent. Only then will we be in a position to more fully understand the various political dimensions of the attempted cosmetic engineering in Cheapside. Contemporaries believed that the outward styles of buildings both affected and reflected mentalities; a hotchpotch of building materials, measurements, colours or forms was considered to be a warning sign of wayward emotions or volatile political positions. Scribbling in a sketchbook, Inigo Jones commented that 'inwardly' the 'imaginancy [was] set on fire' in 'publicke places'; as an antidote, he recommended that the 'outward ornaments' of architecture ought to be 'sollid, proporsionable according to the rulles, masculine and unaffected'.

Ronald Freart believed that 'the asymetry of buildings, want of decorum and proportion in houses, reveals the irregularity of our humours and affections'.[33] The tatty jumble of 'mean' traders along the Rows, obvious to the eye as a messy patchwork of shopfronts of contrasting colours and conditions, was a symbol of sickness, of minds that lacked balance and of a politics that similarly appeared topsy-turvy.

In the late sixteenth and seventeenth centuries a run of royal proclamations, starting in Elizabeth's reign but peaking in the next, tried to curb or set high standards for fresh building. 'Uniformity' was a by-word, as it was to be in the matter of the Rows. There was microscopic care for appearance: just as in the Palladian architectural style, precise measurements were set down for the fronts and edges of buildings, and building materials were chosen carefully. Several of the concerns that cropped up in warnings about the Rows also animated the makers of building policy (they were, after all, frequently the same people): policing the poor, sickness and health, 'a strong aesthetic and even ideological dimension'.[34] Building proclamations issued in 1611, 1622 and 1630 said that 'uniformite' would 'grace' the city to its 'honour, beauty and lustre'; that 'uniformity of buildinges will bringe honour to the citty and grace and ornament' to its streets. A draft parliamentary Act 'for the ordering and setting the manner of buildings' in and near the city sank without trace after its first reading in 1621. It too sponsored building 'in such uniforme manner as may reduce' streets 'to decency and conformitye', and connected the 'beautifying of the streets' with 'uniformitye in buylding'.[35]

The return was hatched at a time when environmental regulation, a tidal wave of disorder, and the ornamentation of public spaces and buildings were big concerns in the Guildhall and Whitehall. A royal order of 1615 declared that only with the strict regulation of 'private building' could London become 'the greatest or next the greatest city of the christian world'. The Crown gave its full backing to schemes to 'beautify' its capital city. 'Wee do exceedingly approve and commend all edifices, structures and workes which tend to publique use and ornamente,' its Ministers told the City, listing for approval: 'the paving of Smithfield, the planting of Morefield, the bringing of the new streame unto the west partes ... the pesthouse, Sutton's hospital, Britanes Burse, the reedifying of Algate, Hicks Hall' and 'like workes'. The control of 'private' building, it was said, was a matter of 'honour' rather than 'profit'.[36]

Other public works were planned at this time, including the 'beautifying' of St Mary Spital and the paving of the Strand and Finsbury Fields. These comprised a spirited effort to 'beautify' the city that was matched by high words depicting London as an imperial city that drew envious glances from overseas. Such flattery also had its dark side. It drew much of its energy from its opposite – a bleak picture of a city stretched to bursting point where problems ran out of control. As social and economic difficulties spiralled, so perceptions of civic honour sagged. Such civic pessimism peaked in a plea by the City to the Crown in 1632 that 'the freedom of London which was heretofore of very great esteeme is [now] growne to be [of] little worth'.[37] The rotting Rows also signified this depreciation in civic honour. It is clear from the preamble to civic policy that it was felt that the City was a faint shadow of its former glory.

Building, of course, had always been a political resource; studies of its history couple political and visual order, so that buildings are seen as representations of broader social networks of subordination and power.[38] The dismal complaints of the dilapidation of towns in the first half of the sixteenth century, for example, were partly political – crumbling and poorly kept buildings were seen as both symptoms and symbols of sagging civic prestige. After *c.* 1600, however, architectural politics became more systematized through the intellectual development of the Palladian 'neo-classicism' that stretched from Inigo Jones and Henry Wotton to John Evelyn and Christopher Wren.[39] As in the new building codes, 'uniformity' was a common denominator running through theoretical works. Freart commented that 'The true and essential beauty of architecture' was the 'union and concourse' of 'individual parts' agreeing in 'visible harmony and consent'. 'Uniformity' was, in Wotton's words, an 'affectation' of first-class building. Uniformity was also highly valued in street design; Evelyn was clearly impressed by Amsterdam's 'exactly straite, even, and uniform' streets. 'Nothing can be more pleasing', he wrote.[40]

The Palladian style possessed no single politics but a cluster of understandings that could articulate divergent political positions. Both high-sounding republicanism and the language of imperial monarchy turned to classical architecture to seek expressions of their politics. An opposition between an uncompromising tyranny and more spontaneous individual freedoms was also inferred from building styles: a long sweep of uniform buildings was liable to be viewed as an unrelenting architectural absolutism; a mixed bag of colours, styles and sizes was, by contrast, a mark of liberty. Keith Thomas writes that 'unclassical irregularity was a symbol of English freedom'. In *Gallus Castratus* (1659), a response to John Evelyn's *Character of England*, it was said that 'Diversity of frontings' in buildings 'do declare a freedome of our subjects'. There then followed a direct comparison between English (republican) architectural politics, where people were 'not obliged to build' for 'the will of princes', and French (monarchical) systems, where Parisians were 'so forced to uniformity, that their structures seem to be only one continued magnificent wall loop-hold'.[41]

This architectural politics became more heated during the 'personal rule' at a key point in the push to send the 'remote' goldsmiths back to the Rows. The call for 'uniformity' in London's 'first' street was interpreted by many as another example of royal arbitrariness, in much the same way that large-scale building projects like the additions to St Paul's might be understood as monuments of the 'personal rule' and its deeply controversial religious policy.[42] To reiterate, the tug-of-war between the company and its dispersed workers did not produce a neat meeting of minds between the City and the Crown. This was, after all, a time when spending on civic ritual was rising fast and the Crown addressed the City in a very proprietorial language as 'our royal city', 'imperial seat' or 'chamber'.[43] These images were not incompatible, but sometimes trouble flared – the Crown frequently censured the City, for example, urging a larger commitment to blocking new building or sweeping streets clean of vagrants and filth. We also see a variety of civic responses: support, footdragging or flat refusal. All these positions can be detected in the forced return. The principal protagonists had different concerns and their commitments seesawed, though not at the same time. Ultimately, just as they were soon to be at the first shot of the war, the positions of the Crown and the City on the Rows were poles apart by 1640. Yet another royal intrusion into the City was about to disappear in a puff of smoke.

'ARBITRARY LETTERS' AND 'THUNDERING ORDERS'

Little altered along the Rows in the ten-year lull. In 1631 John Howes noted that now 'and for divers years past' the Cheapside Row 'is much abated of her wonted store of goldsmiths which was the beauty of that famous streete'.[44] Yet a flicker of activity was recorded in 1629 when Ministers passed word that news had reached the King of 'the unseemelynes and deformitie' spoiling Cheapside 'by reason that diverse men of meane trades have shops there amongst goldsmithes'. Legal counsel was asked to hunt for laws to force goldsmiths 'to plant themselves' in the Rows, but the only legal device seemed to be the same Act produced by 'goldsmiths of note' in 1624, reciting anxieties about 'obscure lanes', theft and the 'secret' export of gold and silver.[45] The stage seemed set for a revival of strong interest in the return, but events came to a quick stop. As in the pause of 1624, moaning about filthy streets, trespassing foreigners or increasing theft did not disappear. Royal despair at the 'decay' of St Paul's drew glances to nearby Cheapside. But the City's slow response to calls for money to restore St Paul's was matched by the quiet along the Rows, as this burst of activity fell away after the report of legal counsel was brought to the Privy Council in 1630.

The slow ebb and flow of events in the Rows may partly be explained by the dearth of large-scale royal ritual in the city at this time. Yet the imperial chorus that trumpeted London's global first place among cities and pushed forward the design to 'beautify' to maximize royal honour did not stutter.[46] This rallying call kick-started the return at a key moment in Charles's attempts to refashion the city. In July 1634 the King urged the City to put in place Daniel Nys's plan to 'beautify' the streets 'by raising them to a convenient height and evenness and decency', and by cleaning them day and night with 'pipes of lead'. A City committee was set up to meet Nys. Inigo Jones began work on St Paul's in 1634 and his plans for the new Goldsmiths' Hall were drawn up in the same year. Towards its close the company sent lists of its workers 'of ability to take shops' in the Rows and 'refractory' footdraggers to the Court of Aldermen. These simultaneous bursts of activity were cut from the same cloth.[47] The near coincidence of the restarted return with these major architectural projects along Cheapside's edges is no surprise.

On 12 November 1634 the Goldsmiths' wardens were summoned to the Star Chamber, where they listened to the following order:

> Whereas in the Goldsmithes Rowe in Cheapside and Lombard Streete divers shopps are held and occupied by persons of other trades whereby that uniform shew and seemelynes w[hi]ch was before an ornament to those places and a luster to this citty when all the shopps were used with goldsmithes without the mixture of any other, is now greatly blemished ... alsoe on the other side many goldsmithes not regarding those places which are most proper for them have seated themselves scaterdly in sondrye streets and some of them in obscure places which is not the least occasion of divers abuses and disorders, especially in the passinge away of stollen and embezelled plate.

Privy Councillors 'expressely' ordered the wardens to fill the Rows with goldsmiths trading 'in other parts of the city' or its 'adjacent parts' inside six weeks. Any footdraggers risked losing their place in the livery. Pressure was also placed on new recruits: apprentices were ordered to enter into bonds to set up shop along the Rows at the close of their term.[48]

Sixteen non-goldsmiths working in Cheapside were summoned to the company court on 24 November to hear the council's order; nine 'remote' goldsmiths appeared there soon after. Thirteen foreigners living in Lombard Street Row ('betweene Birchin Lane and The Stocks') were called to the court in the next month, but it was said that 'noe conclusive answer was returned': a draper and a perfumer said that they would put their case to the Crown; a goldsmith asked for a bit of time to mull over his situation. The order was read to thirty-four goldsmiths 'dwelling in remote places' a fortnight later, and all but eight of them 'imediately' agreed to move. The footdraggers offered 'divers reasons' to stay in the West End, claiming that 'it was not in the companyes power' to force them out of their shops. Again, the long-suffering Cheapside goldsmiths who rubbed shoulders with 'mean' men blasted their brethren who worked far away from the Rows – 'the auntient and most proper marketts for our trade' – reeling off the familiar litany of complaint about foreigners, 'secret' commerce and cunning thieves.[49]

The company called these events 'tedious', but the King's patience was running thin and 'remote' workers were ordered to act without 'delay': Westminster workers were singled out. The City also seemed to be doing little and was roasted by a Privy Council lecture: their 'extraordinarie care' to clean up the Rows 'for the greater ornament and lustre of the city' was not matched in the Guildhall, and there was not even a glimmer of 'reformation'.[50] 'Remote' workers still trooped to the company court, so the City and company were not entirely passive – a number of them said that they would try to return to the Rows; two others said 'that they are not free of the city' and did not have to keep shop within its walls; and sixteen more – mostly 'poore men' – pointed to their poverty, but promised to 'endeavor to their powers'. In May 1635, however, twenty-one 'mean' traders reported that 'they could not yett gett tenants' for their shops in the Rows, but were still told that they would be 'shut up' at midsummer if nothing changed.[51]

In the same month goldsmiths in Fleet Street, the Strand 'and other publique places' produced reasons for their staying put: rack-renting by foreigners in the Rows put costs well beyond their reach and how could over 100 families squash into just thirty-four shops? The surplus, they said, should stay 'where they dwell', being 'publique and open streets'. The Crown passed these points to the City with a concession to the housing squeeze – goldsmiths could stay in 'open' places like Fleet Street or the Strand, so long as they did not 'settle' in 'by lanes or alleyes' where 'bad consequences' would inevitably follow.[52] Soon after, the company put on a more severe face as the Crown continued its call for swift results. Seven 'remote' workers (among them warden Allein) were 'suspended' from high office and the livery. Yet there was little movement in or out of the Rows – the West End goldsmiths now treated the May concession as a proof of their case. The company sent the Crown yet another census of the stay-at-home offenders.[53]

Resistance was now more solid and sure: summoned before the company court, 'divers' far-flung workers refused to budge and, the court observed, 'seemed to waive their former submission pretending it to be condiconall'. They again claimed that they would be out of pocket, even though the company was 'fully satisfied' that they 'are able' to move 'if they would endeavor the same'.[54] Royal pressure, however, did not lighten. The company was asked 'to give an accompt' of 'the goldsmithes rows' at the Star Chamber in January 1636, and news of a 'small reformacon' tested patience still further. Privy Councillors ordered the Court of Aldermen to call in footdraggers and it too reported that 'remote' workers were now 'not so inclinable' to move as they had been 'upon the first notice' of the forced return. Hearing that the City had been handed a list of 'refractorie' goldsmiths four months earlier, Privy Councillors protested: 'We find nothing at all thereupon done,' despite many messages. A request to the City to count empty and foreigner-run shops in the Rows turned up fifteen shops in Cheapside and twelve in Lombard Street. We 'hath indeavoured to effect' the return, the City declared, 'but hath wrought little reformacon as yet'.[55]

Yet despite these expressions of commitment to the cause, the Crown remained sure that the City was at best a faltering bit-player. Tempers boiled over in May 1637. Privy Councillors had 'bene eye witnesses very lately' of 'disobedience' in the Rows, where 'mean' traders still settled in a 'great number of howses'. An 'arbitrary letter' and 'thundering order' were soon speeding from the Crown to the City rulers, who were said to be 'very worthy of blame' – aldermen were threatened with prison if their indifference did not lift.[56] Maitland writes that 'City magistrates seem to have paid little respect to this letter'. Other Crown charges of sluggish activity followed in 1638. Give 'such order' to the aldermen and deputies, the mayor was instructed, 'as shall teach them to know that the commaunds of this Board ought not so to be slighted'.[57]

At least one alderman reported that he 'instantly' gave the 'mean' traders in the Rows a dressing down, but they too were locked in a tight predicament – they were 'willinge to let theire houses [but] none came to take them'; one said that cooks had kept shop in his house in Lombard Street for over forty years, and that goldsmiths 'utterly refuse' to take it off his hands, as it was in 'a very darke and narrow place unfit for gouldsmithes'.[58] There seemed to be no give or take. But the doldrums in the Rows continued for a couple more years as the return, for so long a contested issue, faded away. The Scottish war and its funding consumed a great deal of Crown time, and the second part of the return had never benefited from the full commitment of the City. And so, just as it had been at its start, the return became once again a company matter.[59]

The mood in the company court soon changed once the Crown's energies were diverted elsewhere. Beginning in autumn 1638 steps were taken to bridge the gaps that split the fraternity, for the company was also troubled by its stormy internal politics. At much the same time as the shoddy Rows splintered opinion, the Goldsmiths' 'generality' stepped up their struggle for greater participation in policy matters and elections, and a major flashpoint occurred in 1640 when the fall-out from the return had still yet to cool. West End goldsmiths raised their voices in this other matter of trampled rights, putting the case for greater democracy. Six members of a group of fifteen nominated by the generality to put their sentiments to a company committee drawing up a parliamentary Bill in that year were known 'remote' workers.[60]

Relations in the fraternity were further soured by the bitterness of workers who felt that the company's authority to smash faulty plate had been hi-jacked to settle old scores or even for malicious glee. This was no light matter, as money was lost and treasured skills were mocked. Feelings rose high, so much so that a Star Chamber suit in which workmen complained about the company's 'vandalism' dragged on in the 1630s; workers met in alehouses, muttering and drawing up petitions, and Thomas Duffield warned the assayor 'that he would let his guts out above his heels'.[61] The plate of at least twenty-nine 'remote' goldsmiths was smashed. The geographical splintering of the company was matched by the wrangling over plate smashing and discontents about democracy.

The outcast West End workers symbolized yet another division in the company, and so a 'loving order' set up inquiries to test their willingness to return to its fold. The court was disappointed: a group of them 'gave many thanks but said that the leavinge of their shopps they could not doe unless they leave their trade'. Francis Allein of Fleet Street said that he was 'ready to doe the company' service but 'desired to be excused if it were so that he must leave his dwellinge which he could no wayes consent unto without his undoing'. Despite 'many perswasions' to 'willingly embrace the love of the companye', Michael Barkstead stayed outside the livery in 1639. It was claimed (wrongly) in the next year that all 'suspended' liverymen (except Mr Courthop) now attended all 'meetings and reimbraced the companys love'. The company brought the return to a final close in September 1642, when it 'moved that all the bonds taken of apprentices' to force them to set up shop in the Rows 'shalbe cancelled or burned'.[62] But at the close of the return the topography of the trade was still uneven. Goldsmiths still flocked to the West End and other distant spots, and the time when all goldsmiths' lived side-by-side in trade ghettos was by now a very faint memory.

'AGAINST THE RIGHT AND LIBERTY OF THE SUBJECT'

The political nation was sensitized to arbitrary acts in the 1630s. The return, of course, was an act of force that trampled on the rights of the out-of-place workers and it doubtless animated at least their partial politicization. The goldsmiths working outside the walls of the City, who by the second half of the 1630s were locked in a struggle with the Crown, included later radical parliamentarians like Francis Allein, a judge at the King's trial, John Barkstead, the chief army nominee to the committee that drafted *The Agreement of the People*, and Thomas Totney, later Theaureaujohn – the self-styled king of the jews, who put the Bible to the flames and saw the Revolution as a golden opportunity to return stolen common land to its true owners. Allein, Totney and John Barkstead's father all suffered the knock to pride of watching their plate smashed by company order.[63]

Significantly, the company said 'that nothing was done' along the Rows 'but what they were then enforced' to do by the Crown, and a group of 'remote' workers said that they could rejoin the livery only at the call of Ministers, as they had been 'sequestrated' by their policy. The blame was put at the door of an over-mighty court that sought to paint the city in its own colours and remodel the lives of 'remote' goldsmiths. This was the climate of opinion in which the last years of the return were understood by many at its receiving end.

On quarter day 1644 the company noted that 'Parliament hath cast an eye of favour' on Francis Allein, who was still outside the livery. He now sat 'in an eminent place of great creditt and trust within the custom house', and on a committee 'for the raising of moneys for our brethren of Scotland' that was meeting that day in another room in the Hall. It was remembered that Allein 'utterly refused' to rejoin the livery in 1638, but it was moved that the company should once again 'cast an eye of favourable respect' upon this leading parliamentarian. The clerk reported that Allein 'confessed' that it 'was more than hee deserved, yet in respect hee was resolved' that 'hee would live and die a citizen' he 'did embrace the companyes kind offer'. There followed a frank conversation that summed up the remembered political significances of the forced return. Allein 'did protest that his former withholding himselfe from the livery was not in any disrespect to the companye but for that hee conceaved the order to be altogeather illegal and againste the right and liberty of the subject'. Allein was also sure 'that the company did longe since apprehend the like', and the court left him in no doubt of this, answering him with an emphatic 'yes'. Standing once again shoulder-to-shoulder with the company elite, Allein put on his livery gown for the first time in nearly a decade. But bitter memories lingered even as late as November 1646, when a group of former 'remote' goldsmiths still refused the company's offer to take a place in the livery.[64]

It is impossible to measure the politicization of the 'remote' goldsmiths because their words are largely lost. But it is improbable that such a long quarrel as that which made the Rows such a trouble spot would not have been a seeding ground for the sort of grumbling that splintered politics in the years before the Revolution. In an important essay, Norah Carlin argues that a series of artisan grievances in pre-Revolution London – most notably, protests to broaden the scope of electoral politics, to gain a greater degree of control over *their* work, and to resist the incursions of 'foreigners' – in effect radicalized artisans' political opinions and made elements of the Leveller programme – especially the reform of monopolies and guild elections – quite attractive to them.[65] Roughly three-quarters of the distant workers settled in the trouble-spot ward of Farringdon Without, whose alderman refused either to lend money to the Crown in 1639 or to supply the Privy Council with a list of names of ward householders who might contribute to a forced loan in the next year. Moreover, this alderman was the puritan prime warden of the Goldsmiths in the year 1639–40 and future militia committee member, Henry Woolaston.[66] As mentioned, high-profile radicals like Theaureaujohn, John Barkstead and Allein were 'remote' goldsmiths, and there were other future parliamentarians in their ranks.[67] Allein and Barkstead's father were in the small group who filed the 'remote' goldsmiths' petition in 1635.[68] Small wonder, then, that, if only for a few, a line stretches from resistance to the forced move to parliamentary opposition in the next decade. The pressure to shift was not the first cause of diminishing loyalty to the Crown, but this Crown trespass on rights was a bruising formative experience.

Yet positions were not as exact as this neat opposition. Workers also felt stung by the company: their plate was smashed and their say at elections was a mere whisper. Positions were sometimes tangled: at the same time as a 'prime' warden shielded West End workers from a forced loan he was part of a drive to push them back to the Rows that continued after royal pressure had dropped to nothing. No wonder, then, that 'remote' workers returned to the company fold in dribs and drabs, despite its reassuring words that it too felt the tough blows to liberty from the grasping Crown.

And, finally, the perspectives of City governors, who at first surely welcomed the re-edification of their most public street. One thing is certain, however – a sense that their city was teetering on the brink of ruin and that its prestige was under threat influenced their policy formation. So it was that the twists and turns of the forced move took place against a city-wide campaign to clean up crime, irregular work, and the environment: discourses of 'public' and 'private' or 'secret' and 'open' places with their implications for locating, monitoring and curbing threats to order pinpointed problems in the squabble along the Rows as well as in the city more generally. Yet, despite this, the backing of the City for the return dwindled in the 1630s, even though perceptions of civic prestige continued to crumble very much in pace with the speedy growth of the metropolis.

The chief cause of this lukewarm attitude to the reform of the Rows was a regular run of royal interventions in the City – mounting pressure to toe the line in policy matters and a proprietorial tone in royal rhetoric at a time when the Crown was pressing claims to London as its capital city through the fashioning of 'an imperial ideal of metropolitan grandeur'. Relations between the Crown and the City, though usually conducted in a surface rhetoric of reciprocity, were also impaired in a sequence of clashes that included the charter dispute (1619), rising financial demands, waste rights, incorporations, and the Irish Plantation. In this respect, too, Cheapside became a contested street – it was already a parade ground for both civic and royal honour, but in the 1630s it became yet another point of tension in a long process of distancing between the Crown and the City, and a minor mirror of larger political developments. When the City cried that its freedom was of 'little worth' (1632), it was felt that the Crown had done little to stop the plunge in its fortunes, most notably the sudden dip in civic fame.

Ultimately, the planned forced move to the Cheapside and Lombard Street Rows flopped because it was undermined by other sweeping changes in the metropolis, including the seemingly irresistible commercial blaze of the West

End – the City kept spilling over its walls, moving into once green fields towards the west, the stream of foreigners quickened, the regulation of work by the guilds slackened. But it also flopped because of the differences and distances between its principal protagonists. Momentum passed between the company and the Crown. The City was mostly a silent partner in the reform of the Rows, sometimes energized by bursts of royal zeal; resentment grew there, and what was at first a mild itch became through time a contribution to a highly sophisticated political position.

NOTES

I must thank Mark Jenner, Phil Baker, Peter Borsay, Ian Gentles, John Morrill, Maggie Pelling, Bob Tittler and Andy Wood for their very valuable comments.

1 Ronald Freart, *A Parallel of the Antient Architecture with the Modern*, trans. John Evelyn (second edition, 1707), epistle dedicatory, fo. 2r.

2 T. Wright ed., *Queen Elizabeth and her Times* (2 vols, 1838), II, p. 88. The other quotations – from a fourteenth-century description and Michael Drayton – are quoted in Lawrence Manley, *Literature and Culture in Early Modern London* (Cambridge, 1995), pp. 242, 240.

3 Chamberlain, *Letters*, II, p. 521.

4 Strype, *Stow*, III, p. 198. See also *Londinopolis*, p. 318. A classic account of the Cheapside Row is T. F. Reddaway, 'Elizabethan London – Goldsmith's Row in Cheapside 1558–1645', *Guildhall Miscellany*, 2 (1963).

5 Lawrence Manley, *London in the Age of Shakespeare: An Anthology* (1986), pp. 40–1, 38–9.

6 Chamberlain, *Letters*, II, p. 460. It was reported, in 1566, that there were sixty-seven 'goldsmithes nowe in Chepe', and thirty-two in Lombard Street. Three years later, sixty-four goldsmiths were said to be working in the 'Goldsmithes Rowe in Chepe', five others lived 'on the north syde of Chepe', and twenty-four more were in Lombard Street. See GCL K, fo. 462; L, fo. 469.

7 Throughout I will refer to the Rows to mean both the Cheapside and the Lombard Street Goldsmiths' Rows. Nevertheless, it is clear that the principal concern in the policy of the forced return was the Cheapside Row, for reasons that will be made apparent.

8 The movement to the west of the city is described in R. M. Smuts, 'The court and its neighbourhood: royal policy and urban growth in the early Stuart West End', *Journal of British Studies*, 30 (1991); M. J. Power, 'The east and west in early modern London', in E. W. Ives *et al.* eds, *Wealth and Power in Tudor England: Essays Presented to S. T. Bindoff* (1978). The westward drift of barber-surgeons at much the same time is discussed by Margaret Pelling, 'Appearance and reality: barber-surgeons, the body and disease', in Beier and Finlay, *London*, pp. 85–7.

9 Robert Ashton, *The City and the Court 1603–1643* (Cambridge, 1979), p. 168.

10 The occupations of the 'mean' traders in the Rows were as follows: five stationers, four silkmen, three upholsterers, two scriveners, merchants, and haberdashers, and one apothecary, clock maker, confectioner, cook, draper, girdler, hosier, milliner, perfumer, sempster and shear grinder. Fifty-five of the 'remote' goldsmiths lived in the expanding

western parts of the metropolis (73.33 per cent), mostly in the Strand, Fleet Street, Holborn and Westminster. Others gave addresses in Southwark, Fenchurch Street, Aldgate, Tower Street and Foster Lane. An indication of the number of freemen in the company is supplied by the list of 400 contributing and non-contributing goldsmiths to the 1641 loan for the Scottish war reprinted in W. S. Prideaux ed., *Memorials of the Goldsmiths' Company* (2 vols, 1896–97), I, pp. 341–52.

11 See, for example, PRO SP 16/293/3; 16/294/80; GCL S1, fos 217, 238, 239.

12 CLRO Rep. 13ii, fos 256v, 265v.

13 CLRO Rep. 25, fo. 418; GCL O, fos 433, 438; P1, fos 36, 115.

14 GCL Pii, fos 209v, 215.

15 Cf. William Clowes, *A Short and Profitable Treatise Touching the Cure of the Disease Called (Morbus Gallicus) by Unctions* (1579), sig. fo. B5v.

16 GCL Pii, fos 215, 267–267v; HOL Journals, III, fo. 305. The petition to the Royal Solicitor is in PRO SP 14/127/12.

17 GCL P1, fos 130v–133, 133v–134; P2, fos 166v, 168v–169, 170v, 171, 172–172v, 173v, 176; *APC 1617–19*, pp. 318–19; *1621–23*, p. 210; *1623–25*, p. 126.

18 GCL P2, fos 242v, 324v–325.

19 *APC 1621–23*, p. 515.

20 PRO SP 14/146/85; CLRO Rep. 37, fo. 176.

21 *APC 1621–23*, p. 515.

22 CLRO Rep. 39, fo. 219v; *Londinopolis*, p. 115; Howes, *Annales*, p. 1,034.

23 CLRO Rep. 37, fo. 76; PRO SP 14/146/85; GCL P2, fos 340v–341; *APC 1623–25*, p. 20.

24 GCL P2, fos 342v–344; CLRO Remb. 8, fos 24v–25; 6, fo. 49; *APC 1623–25*, pp. 298–9.

25 See my 'Secrecy and authority in late sixteenth- and seventeenth-century London', *HJ*, 40 (1997), esp. pp. 941–5.

26 GCL P2, fo. 361.

27 GCL Q, fo. 76.

28 *APC 1623–25*, p. 234; GCL Q1, fos 6v, 10.

29 See CLRO Jour. 33, fos 96–8; *APC 1623–25*, p. 505; CLRO Remb. 6, fos 172–3; Jour. 34, fo. 297; GCL Q, fos 22, 73v, 183v.

30 The political aesthetics of James's reign are described in J. Newman, 'Inigo Jones and the politics of architecture', in Kevin Sharpe and Peter Lake eds, *Culture and Politics in Early Stuart England* (Basingstoke, 1994), pp. 231–45; John Harris, Stephen Orgel and Roy Strong, *The King's Arcadia: Inigo Jones and the Stuart Court* (1973), pp. 112–25, 142.

31 Smuts writes that '... particularly in Charles's reign the [royal building] commission [headed by Jones] promoted some ambitious projects [the return is listed]', and that ' ... in many ways 1625 was a more decisive cultural watershed than 1603': *Court Culture and the Origins of a Royalist Tradition in Early Stuart England* (Philadelphia PA, 1987), pp. 127, 184. See also Newman, 'Inigo Jones and the politics of architecture', pp. 251–4.

32 Peter Lake, 'The Laudian style: order, uniformity and the pursuit of the beauty of holiness in the 1630s', in Kenneth Fincham ed., *The Early Stuart Church 1603–1642* (Basingstoke, 1993). See also Smuts, *Court Culture*, chap. 8.

33   Inigo Jones, quoted in Timothy Mowl and Brain Earnshaw, *Architecture without Kings: The Rise of Puritan Classicism under Cromwell* (Manchester, 1995), p. 82; Freart, *A Parallel of the Antient Architecture with the Modern*, epistle dedicatory, fo. 4v.

34   The outline of these building programmes in the reigns of Elizabeth, James I and Charles I can be followed in T. G. Barnes, 'The prerogative court and environmental control of London building in the early seventeenth century', *California Law Review*, 58 (1970), and Norman G. Brett James, *The Growth of Stuart London* (1935), chaps 3 and 4. The principal motivations behind these proclamations are discussed in Barnes, 'The prerogative court and environmental control', esp. pp. 1,340–2, 1,346–9; Kevin Sharpe, *The Personal Rule of Charles I* (New Haven CT and London, 1992), pp. 407–12, and Paul Slack, *From Reformation to Improvement: Public Welfare in Early Modern England* (Oxford, 1999), pp. 54–61. The obsession with 'uniformity' was articulated in most of these royal proclamations. The quotation is from Sharpe, *Personal Rule*, p. 411.

35   CLRO Jours 28, fos 243–243v; 32, fo. 109v; 35, fos 214–216v; HOL MP 12 May 1621. Newman, 'Inigo Jones and the politics of architecture', pp. 244, 245, argues that there was 'an aesthetic dimension' to this building policy, 'in that the fronts of houses were ordered to be made "uniform"', and draws attention to 'the political value of an asthetically attractive urban environment'. See also Christopher Friedrichs, *The Early Modern City 1450–1750* (1995), esp. pp. 200–1.

36   CLRO Jour. 29, fos 351–351v.

37   PRO PCR 2/42, fos 305–6.

38   See esp. Robert Tittler, *Architecture and Power: The Town Hall and the English Urban Community c. 1500–1640* (Oxford, 1991); Peter Borsay, *The English Urban Renaissance: Culture and Society in the Provincial Town 1660–1770* (Oxford, 1989), esp. pp. 61–2, 93, 253, 270.

39   See Mowl and Earnshaw, *Architecture without Kings*, pp. 25–99; Harris *et al.*, *King's Arcadia*; Smuts, *Court Culture*, pp. 98–101; J. A. Bennett, *The Mathematical Science of Christopher Wren* (Cambridge, 1982), chaps 9–10; Newman, 'Inigo Jones and the politics of architecture', p. 255.

40   Freart, *A Parallel of the Antient Architecture with the Modern*, p. 3; Henry Wotton, *The Elements of Architecture*, 1624 (Charlottesville VA, 1968), p. 20; *The Diary of John Evelyn*, ed. E. S. de Beer (6 vols, Oxford, 1955), II, p. 46. Evelyn's plan for 'uniform' streets in his model for the redevelopment of London after the Fire is discussed by Mark Jenner, 'The politics of London air: John Evelyn's *Fumifugium* and the Restoration', *HJ*, 38 (1995), pp. 549–50. Its 'uniformly built brick houses' were an elegant feature of the Covent Garden suburb, which was set out in the 1630s and was doubtless a profitable source of custom for the West End goldsmiths: quoting Smuts, *Court Culture*, p. 128.

41   Keith Thomas, 'English Protestantism and classical art', in Lucy Gent ed., *Albion's Classicism: The Visual Arts in Britain 1550–1650* (New Haven CT and London, 1995), pp. 231, 225; Smuts, *Court Culture*, pp. 104–7; Gallus Castratus, *An Answer to a Slanderous Pamphlet Called 'The Character of England'* (1659), quoted extensively as a running footnote in John Evelyn, *A Character of England with Miscellaneous Writings*, ed. William Upcott (third edition, 1825), pp. 148–9.

42   Mowl and Earnshaw, *Architecture without Kings*, p. 9; Newman, 'Inigo Jones and the politics of architecture', pp. 251–5; Smuts, *Court Culture*, p. 275.

43   R. Mackenny, *Traders and Tradesmen* (Beckenham, 1987), pp. 155–65, 172; Michael

Berlin, 'Civic ceremony in early modern London', *Urban History* Yearbook (1986), esp. pp. 24–5; D. M. Bergeron, *Civic Pageantry 1558–1642* (1971), esp. pp. 105, 125, 134, 138; Theodore B. Leinwand, 'London triumphing: the Jacobean Lord Mayor's show', *Clio*, 11 (1982), esp. pp. 138, 146. See also James Knowles, 'The spectacle of the realm: civic consciousness, rhetoric and ritual in early modern London', in J. R. Mulryne and Margaret Shewring eds, *Theatre and Government under the Stuarts* (Cambridge, 1993), esp. pp. 173–4. For the growing emphasis in royal discourses on the 'royal city' see Manley, *Literature and Culture*, esp. chap. 5; Sharpe, *Personal Rule*, pp. 403–4.

44 Howes, *Annales*, p. 1,045.

45 *APC 1629–30*, p. 181; GCL Q, fos 158–158v, 176v, 178v, 181v; PRO SP 16/168/30.

46 See Judith Richards, '"His nowe majestie" and the English monarchy: the kingship of Charles I', *P&P*, 113 (1986); Bergeron, *Civic Pageantry*, p. 105; Smuts, *Court Culture*, pp. 286–7. Paul Slack writes that 'Absolute power was making a bid to shape even the landscape' and that the 'new urban aesthetics also had political implications'. See his *From Reformation to Improvement*, pp. 69, 72, and more generally, pp. 68–74.

47 CLRO Remb. 7, fos 135–6; Rep. 48, fo. 418; Remb. 8, fo. 80; Newman, 'Inigo Jones and the politics of architecture', pp. 247–51. See also Sharpe, *Personal Rule*, pp. 403–4; Brett-James, *Growth of Stuart London*, p. 113.

48 GCL S1, fo. 48; PRO SP 16/277/34; PCR 2/44, fos 214–15; GCL minute book S1, fos 57–8.

49 GCL S1, fos 59–61, 65–6, 67–9, 75, 83–4; PRO SP 16/278/103.

50 GCL S1, fos 93–4, 111–12, PRO PCR 2/44, fo. 343; CLRO Remb. 8, fo. 80.

51 GCL S1, fos 124–6, 173–4.

52 CLRO Remb. 8, fos 86v–87; Rep. 49, fos 210v–211; PRO PCR 2/44, fo. 587; GCL S1, fos 197, 199–200, 200–1, 202–3, 204; PRO SP 16/290/74. See also GCL S1, fos 219–20.

53 GCL S1, fos 214–15; PRO SP 16/293/5; GCL S1, fos 221–3.

54 GCL S1, fos 237–9; CLRO Rep. 49, fo. 216v.

55 GCL S2, fos 345–7; CLRO Remb. 7, fos 178–9; Rep. 50, fo. 137v; GCL S2, fos 359–64; CLRO Rep. 50, fo. 161.

56 CLRO Remb. 7, fos 207, 209; PRO SP 16/357/51; PC 2/47, fo. 446; William Maitland, *The History of London from its Foundation by the Romans to the Present Time* (1739), p. 190.

57 Maitland, *History of London*, p. 191; PRO SP 16/278/65.

58 PRO SP 16/278/86; 16/382/76; 16/386/64.

59 GCL T, fos 85, 107–107v, 109, 109–109v.

60 GCL V, fos 45–45v. Francis Allein was included among these six West End men. A few years later he was also a member of a faction seeking greater democracy in elections to ward office in Farringdon Without. Allein was elected scavenger in 1641, an inquestman in 1643, and a common councillor in 1645. See Keith Lindley, *Popular Politics and Religion in Civil War London* (Aldershot, 1997), p. 185; GL MSS 3016/1, fos 221, 235, 254; 3018/1, fos 126, 135.

61 GCL S1, fos 108–9.

62 GCL T, fos 124, 125v; V, fos 22v, 24v–25, 96; W, fo. 17v. See also GCL T fos 122–123v, 126v, 127v; V, fos 25, 32v. Barkstead and other 'remote' goldsmiths were also pressed to

rejoin the livery by being elected to serve as rentors, an appointment they refused at the risk of a steep fine.

63 See Robert Brenner, *Merchants and Revolution: Commercial Change, Political Conflict, and London's Overseas Traders 1550–1653* (Cambridge, 1993), p. 606; Ian Gentles, *The New Model Army in England, Ireland, and Scotland 1645–1653* (Oxford, 1992), p. 279; Lindley, *Popular Politics and Religion*, esp. p. 321; Christopher Hill, *The World Turned Upside Down: Radical Ideas during the English Revolution* (1972), p. 226; Richard L. Greaves and Robert Zaller eds, *Biographical Dictionary of British Radicals in the Seventeenth Century* (3 vols, Brighton, 1982–84), I, pp. 9–10, 39–40; III, pp. 223–5.

64 GCL W fos 267v–268v, 270. The 1646 events can be followed in GCL X, fos 99–99v, 100–100v, 101v–102, 108–108v, 111v–112.

65 Norah Carlin, 'Liberty and fraternities in the English Revolution: the politics of London artisans' protests 1635–1659', *International Review of Social History*, 39 (1994), esp. pp. 226, 229, 231, 235–43, 251–4.

66 Pearl, *London*, pp. 329–30. Woolaston also served as city sheriff in 1638–39 with Issac Pennington.

67 Including James Prince, who sat on the Westminster Militia Committee, and Richard Morrall, the parliamentary sequestrator. See Lindley, *Popular Politics and Religion*, pp. 220, 331 nn. 130–2.

68 GCL S1, fos 199–200. Barkstead's father was also among the group who delivered the exceptions of the 'remote' workers in 1624. See GCL P2, fo. 361.

Chapter 10

The poor among the rich: paupers and the parish in the West End, 1600–1724

Jeremy Boulton

It may seem strange to write about the poor in London's western suburbs, which, we have been told, 'remained an exclusive preserve of professional men, courtiers, and the landed classes'.[1] To concentrate on St Martin's and its daughter parishes would seem odder still. There were significant numbers of poor living in and around Westminster Abbey and the Houses of Parliament in the parish of St Margaret's. But St Martin's contained the royal palace of Whitehall and associated offices. Large government departments were constructed opposite Whitehall during the seventeenth century.[2] Even in the early eighteenth century, after a disastrous fire in 1698 had prompted a move to St James's, Whitehall could still be described as 'the Royal Palace and Residence of the Kings and Queens of England'.[3] St Martin's also contained a substantial part of the Strand. At the beginning of our period this street included aristocratic palaces. In the 1650s most of it consisted of three or four-storey houses, usually with shops.[4] The far western part of the parish consisted, until the development of Hanover Square in the early eighteenth century, of St James's Park and the royal palace of the same name, much extended and 'beautified' in the later seventeenth century.[5] Early in our period, clusters of housing in St Martin's Lane designed for the social elite readily found tenants amongst Jacobean and Caroline courtiers.[6] The socially exclusive credentials of the district were advanced still further by the development of the Covent Garden piazza during the 1630s,[7] 'for the habitation of gentlemen and men of ability'. It quickly attracted large numbers of appropriate tenants.[8] Further exclusive developments occurred after the Restoration, notably St James's Square, which, with Covent Garden piazza, set the blueprint for architectural planning during England's 'urban renaissance'.[9] Unsurprisingly, work on London's topography has contrasted the superior housing and society in the 'fayre' West End with that found in the east.[10]

This emphasis on the social exclusivity of the West End[11] arguably makes the district a more rewarding place to study the poor. The first reason is that it may well show that the social exclusivity of the district has been exaggerated. Malcolm Smuts has made the important point that even fashionable developments like the Covent Garden piazza were, from the beginning, surrounded by poorer-quality housing.[12] A similar pattern can be discerned in Strype's pithy descriptions of many of the streets and alleys of St Martin's as 'ordinary' or 'not well built'. Off Long Acre, he reported, was Phoenix Alley, 'a pretty open Alley, but ill inhabited, and nastily kept'.[13] Julia Merritt reminds us that 'the needy and dispossessed were to be found here, as in other towns'.[14]

Looking at the poor of the West End, however, should do more than dent the perceived social exclusivity of that district. Bob Shoemaker has portrayed the Restoration West End as, sometimes quite literally, a social battleground. He argues that extreme social tensions in that district were generated by social changes and led to higher rates of prosecution for offences against the peace and for vice.[15] In particular socially exclusive residential enclaves were continually threatened by the erection of poorer housing and its inhabitants. These poorer sort were increasingly seen as socially and morally offensive by their loftier neighbours. Some West End parishes,[16] then, are depicted as facing a growing struggle to retain their social character. The 'West End came *increasingly* [my emphasis] to contain a large number of poor as well as wealthy inhabitants, causing the social character of some inner West End parishes to decline markedly during this period.'[17] According to this account 'as more fashionable streets and squares were erected to the west in St Martin's and St James's parishes, Covent Garden lost its position as London's most socially prestigious parish'.[18] St Martin's, too, suffered during the later seventeenth and early eighteenth centuries: 'a large and *growing* [my emphasis] contingent of the poor threatened the exclusivity of its aristocratic streets and squares ... this social divide [found in the Hearth Taxes] ... persisted and *probably increased* [my emphasis] over the next sixty years'.[19]

There is a conflict here between those who see the West End as subject to the pressures consequent upon the growing poverty or at least declining social status of its inhabitants and those who stress the enduring social mixing in that district.[20] One important agenda for the historian, therefore, must be to assess the reality of social change in the West End. Did poverty increase in the district in our period? Can we measure the course of social change with any precision? More interestingly, perhaps, can we say something about the impact that this unique society had on the relief of the poor, or on the lives of the poor? Do St Martin's poor law records suggest that relief was provided within a 'social battleground'?

Furthermore, to what extent did the administration of poor relief reflect the heady social mix in St Martin's? Steve Hindle has drawn attention to the power relations that determined the granting of poor relief in Holland Fen.[21] In those parishes, surely typical of most parishes in rural England, the 'vestrymen were the better sort of the parish ... The vestry ... dominated parish politics, and nowhere were they more assiduous than in the administration of poor relief'.[22] A further reason, then, why St Martin's may be worth closer attention is that power relations are likely to have been particularly complex. Merritt has uncovered the strong court and Cecil connections of many of the St Martin's vestry in the Elizabethan and Jacobean period.[23] Court and government connections certainly endured thereafter, but we may wonder to what extent the parish's unusual social composition shaped the relief of the poor. Can we reconstruct what Keith Wrightson has called 'the politics of the parish' in London's West End? Tentative answers to such questions suggest ways in which current thinking about social relations may need revision.

Lastly, and more prosaically, this essay attempts to add to our understanding of early modern poor relief by locating paupers as firmly as possible in their immediate historical context. Only recently have historians become sensitive to the multiple ways in which the local economy, power and social structures determined the shape of parochial poor relief measures. To understand the movement of average pensions over time, or the number of paupers relieved, requires more detailed work on local economies and the sociopolitical context.

POPULATION GROWTH IN THE WEST END, 1550–1724

Any assessment of the relief of the poor must begin by reconstructing population growth in St Martin's. The rate of population growth in a pre-industrial economy is a major factor determining the pressure on local resources, housing quality and local government. The space devoted to examining this question, however, should not be taken to imply that demographic factors were the *only* motor of changes in early modern poor relief systems. As we will see, both demographic contraction and expansion might inform the decisions of local policy makers and directly affect the lives (and income) of local paupers. Local responses to population movements, however, were by no means mechanical or straightforward. They depended on a host of other factors, such as the local social structure, the economy and social relations within the taxpaying classes as well as a whole host of perceptions and inbuilt assumptions amongst the parish officers and others who ran the poor relief system.

In the absence of comprehensive listings of the population the best method to estimate demographic growth in a large urban area is to use the number of baptisms recorded in the local parish register. This method is not without sources of inaccuracy, but it does give some idea of changing trends in population growth, as well as a reasonable guess at overall size. What follows represents a major addition to the demographic history of London.[24] It is

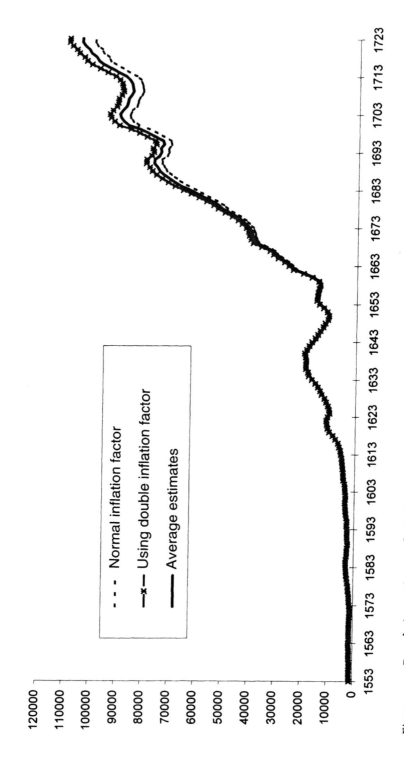

Figure 10.1 Population estimates for St Martin in the Fields and daughter parishes, 1550–1723

based on an aggregative analysis of the baptism register of St Martin in the Fields and its daughter parishes from 1550 to 1724.[25]

Figure 10.1 presents population estimates for St Martin's and all its daughter parishes from 1550 to 1723. The estimates are based on a birth rate of 32·5 per thousand, and apply the correction factors suggested by Wrigley and Schofield.[26] I have used two estimates of the birth shortfall, one based on the latter authors' original estimates, and one where their estimates have been doubled. This procedure takes account of a number of features of London's demography that may well have caused registration of births in the baptism register to deteriorate rapidly in the later seventeenth- and early eighteenth-century capital. Firstly, the rising infant and child mortality rate in the capital and the increasing delay in baptizing children would have caused an increase in the number of children dying before baptism.[27] Secondly, the West End was home to many foreign nationals who often baptized their children elsewhere than their parish churches.[28] There were also many dissenters in London; one estimate suggests a figure as high as one in five.[29]

Taking the average of these estimates, and bearing in mind that they are subject to some uncertainty,[30] the graph reveals the extraordinary population growth of the West End in the seventeenth century. From a population of perhaps 1,400 in the mid-sixteenth century the district had grown to just over 3,000 by 1600. It had tripled to about 10,200 in 1620 and reached around 18,500 by 1640, a sixfold increase since the beginning of the century.[31] Although the fall thereafter must be exaggerated by the failures of parish registration during the Civil War, St Martin's probably suffered a dramatic population collapse during the first Civil War. This began to reverse in the 1650s but dramatic recovery and population take-off occurred only after 1660. With a population of about 19,000 then, its population had doubled to a remarkable 38,800 by 1670. In 1685 the district's population lay around 69,000. By 1700 86,000 people lived in the district and in 1720 its population probably numbered over 100,000.[32] This phenomenal growth was accompanied by division of the original parish. This tended to take the form of prestigious areas being developed and then taken out of the mother parish. St Paul Covent Garden was carved out in 1645, a separation confirmed at the Restoration. St Anne Soho was taken out in 1678 (consecrated in 1686) and St James Piccadilly in 1685. Even then, Strype reported of St Martin's in 1720 that it 'remaineth a very great parish, and too populous for one Church to receive the Inhabitants'.[33] The whole district was easily the fastest growing part of London in the seventeenth century, and may have slightly outstripped the East End by 1700.[34]

Explaining this population expansion is easy enough in general terms. Courtiers increasingly lived near the Stuart palaces, litigants and lawyers flocked to the courts at Westminster. In the seventeenth century the movement of the titled and gentry from the countryside, and also from the old City, gathered pace. With them came those who supplied them, professionals like physicians, luxury tradesmen like goldsmiths and coach builders, and an army of servants, coachmen and messengers. The Great Fire provided another pressing reason to look to the West End. The expansion of the civil service, the development of a permanent standing army and the increasing frequency of parliamentary sessions also lay behind the continued expansion of the West End after 1660.[35]

However, it is clear that the growth of the West End was not inexorable. It seems to have been checked, albeit briefly in the early 1620s. Population was seemingly stagnating during the 1630s and there was a serious population crash at the start of the Civil War. Furthermore, there were two clear checks on growth around 1690 and 1703, after which dates population may have stagnated or even fallen for a five- and ten-year period respectively. It is crucial to establish such developments when studying the fortunes of the poor, since the size of the population determines the number of taxpayers and represents an indirect indicator of the health of the local economy. Moreover, historically, the poorest members of communities are the least able to move quickly in times of difficulty, so that there is likely to be a widening gap between need and local resources in times of local crisis. The flight of richer neighbours during plague epidemics is the best illustration of this phenomenon.[36]

There appear to have been three distinct reasons for population slow-down in the West End, each of which has different implications for the local poor. It is possible that the check on growth in the early 1620s was a direct result of the attempts by the Stuart kings to restrict gentry residence in London. In January 1623 John Coke was informed 'that he could now have his choice of houses in St Martin's Lane at very good rates since the two proclamations have so emptied the City and the suburbs'.[37] It is possible that the population stagnation of the mid-1630s was also linked with another vigorous Stuart campaign against resident gentlemen.[38] The population collapse during the first Civil War seems well attested. Although the depth of the fall is probably exaggerated by unusually defective baptism registration, the loss of the court must have had serious knock-on effects on the West End's economy which were not compensated for by the benefits of a permanent Parliament or the spending on the parliamentary war machine. Porter has the impression 'that Westminster, St Martin's and Covent Garden were distinctly underpopulated during the War'.[39] Unsurprisingly, therefore, in the early 1640s parish pensions in St Martin's were cut across the board, owing to a fall, or perhaps a projected fall, in the yield of the poor rate.[40]

The checks on population growth in the West End at the end of the seventeenth century probably had a different impact on the fortunes of its poor. Both were associated with periods of war against France in 1689–97 and 1702–1714.[41] The 1690s were a time of considerable hardship in the metropolis,[42] but the hardship produced by high food prices and economic depression was mitigated, to some extent, by the impact on the labour market of the large-scale recruitment into the armed forces amongst London's population. This had a contradictory impact on the level of poverty. On the one hand it removed male breadwinners and was clearly, therefore, a direct source of impoverishment. JP's examinations of paupers in St Martin's in the early eighteenth century are full of the effects of impressment and recruitment into the armed forces.[43] On the other hand, warfare mopped up surplus labour, increased employment rates and increased the participation of women in London's labour markets.[44]

THE WORLD OF WORK

If we are to study the West End poor it is important to say something about the economy and society . It would be expected from what has already been said that the West End economy would be dominated by courtiers, government officers and luxury trades. Norden in the late sixteenth century asserted that:

> The Citie of Westminster is known to have no generall trade whereby releef might be administered unto the common sort as by merchandise, clothing or such like ... The first and principal meanes is her Majestie's residence at Whitehall or St James's, whence if her Grace be long absent the poore people forthwith complaine of pennary and want ...[45]

Merritt reported that St Martin's was 'primarily settled by those providing services to Court and local gentry, [and] Crown employees'. She, like Smuts, is sensitive to the fact that the parish 'contained a mix of rich consumers, prosperous tradesmen, struggling manual labourers and paupers ... living in close proximity to one another'.[46]

The purpose of this section is to establish whether this was so for the whole of the seventeenth century. Unfortunately, there is no period when the parish registers record occupations. Table 10.1, therefore, is based on a variety of sources. In general these over-represent the wealthier inhabitants. It is a reasonable guide to the spread of economic interests in the parish, but is a less certain guide to the trades and crafts of humbler inhabitants. Before 1650 the bulk of occupations are of individuals appearing in recognizances at the Middlesex quarter sessions, between 1612 and 1618, and from the 1630s and early 1640s.[47] After 1660, three sources were used. A large number of individuals were given occupational designations when being nominated or chosen as parish officers, ranging from churchwardens to overseers, surveyors of the highways and more humble scavengers.[48] Occupational data were also recorded in three Poll Tax listings of parts of St Martin's parish for 1660, and for a couple of divisions of that parish in rate assessments made by the surveyor of highways in 1711. The 1711 tax clearly omits those too humble to

Table 10.1 Occupations in St Martin in the Fields, 1600–85 (%)

Occupational Classification	Total Sample	Occupations		London all parishes[a]		PCC wills, 1600–85
		Before 1660	1660 and after	1601–40	1641–1700	
Building	7·6	9·4	6·2	6·5	7·2	7·5
Clothing	21·1	22·6	19·8	23·3	22·7	20·3
Decorating/furnishing	5·8	4·9	6·6	2·9	3·6	2·1
Distribution/transport	9·0	8·6	9·4	9·2	7·5	4·6
Labouring	1·4	2·2	0·8	4·0	4·9	0·2
Leather	8·9	10·9	7·2	8·7	8·9	6·4
Merchants	1·1	0·6	1·5	10·9	7·0	2·9
Metalwork	6·8	7·2	6·4	9·1	8·9	5·0
Miscellaneous production	1·9	1·2	2·4	2·3	3·6	1·0
Miscellaneous services	6·2	3·8	8·2	6·2	5·4	7·1
Professions	2·9	2·5	3·3	4·0	2·5	12·0
Local government officials	0·4	0·2	0·6	2·8	1·9	1·2
Royal officials	0·4	0·1	0·6			10·4
Victualling	26·5	25·9	27·0	10·1	15·9	19·3
	100·0	100·1	100·0	100·0	100·0	100.0
No. of cases	2,853	1,281	1,572	3,620	12,259	482

[a] *Source* Beier, 'Engine of manufacture', in Beier and Finlay, *London*, p. 148.

pay it. The 1660 Poll Tax was not, by law, levied on those receiving alms.[49] To represent the richer sort, the occupations recorded by those leaving wills in the Prerogative Court of Canterbury have also been included separately.

The occupational structure reconstructed is largely predictable, although it clearly underestimates humble occupations, notably labouring and domestic service.[50] The parish clearly had a very substantial victualling sector, which expanded in line with a more general expansion in that part of the economy in seventeenth-century London. It seems likely that the West End had a larger victualling sector than comparable extramural suburbs in London.[51] This is to be expected. There was considerable through traffic along the principal streets, notably the Strand and Charing Cross, and some establishments attracted resident gentry. Thus Strype wrote about the King's Head Inn, in Little Suffolk Street, a 'large place for stabling and coaches, nigh unto which, and at the Corner of James Street, is Paulets Ordinary or Eating house, much resorted unto by the Nobility and Gentry'.[52]

The other very substantial sector was the clothing sector. This typically occupied between one-fifth and a quarter of employed adults in Stuart

London, and St Martin's was no exception.[53] What was perhaps more unusual was the relatively limited number of individuals involved in the production or finishing of fabrics, for the clothing sector in St Martin's was dominated by 398 tailors. Many of these would have been selling to consumers living in or around the court. The presence of such fashionable demand explains the presence of thirty-two milliners, seventeen periwig makers, a 'peruke maker', two indian gown sellers and one 'cutter and raser of sattens'. Victualling and tailoring remained the most important Westminster occupations amongst the respectable in the late eighteenth century.[54] Otherwise the absence of merchants in the West End is again confirmed.[55] The sources probably undercount the professional element in the local economy, and only detailed treatment can reveal those whose livelihood might best be categorized as providing luxury goods and services. In our sample we find, for example, a birdcage maker, a globe maker, an instrument maker, two picture drawers and a picture maker, a prospective glass maker, two toyshop keepers and a writing master. One-fifth of those working in the metal trades were goldsmiths, silversmiths or jewellers.[56]

The sources used here dramatically undercount another important occupational group, government officials, whose offices might be subsumed under their honorific titles of gentleman or esquire and courtiers. Charles II's court employed musicians, actors, grooms, liveried footmen, 600 or so horse guards and over 200 grenadiers. There were also forty gentlemen pensioners, and the Yeomen of the Guard, in 1690 '100 in daily waiting, and 70 not in waiting'.[57]

To redress the balance a little Table 10.1 also includes those occupations given in the wills of those dying in St Martin's registered with the Prerogative Court of Canterbury.[58] This highly selective sample again underlines the importance of the clothing and victualling sector but, unlike the other sources, does reveal the substantial wealthy element who found employment at court. This far from dominated the local economy. Only about one in ten of those will-makers gave a government or court employment and although this is certainly an underestimate it does suggest that *direct* employment at court was a minority pursuit. Another under-represented group in Table 10.1 is professionals. Amongst elite will-makers they were, however, more common, representing about 12 per cent of those with given occupations. Most were physicians, surgeons or clerics, some connected explicitly with the court, with a scattering of individuals offering more esoteric skills, notably John Kersey, 'teacher of mathematicks' (d. 1677).

A group omitted from most of the sources were servants. Domestic service was the most commonly experienced occupation for London girls, and many examined female paupers listed a history of serial domestic service.[59] Other sources reveal that servants were numerous. Three poll tax returns, which list those over sixteen in the parish, labelled 673 individuals (some 22 per cent of the adult population of the district) as servants. Female servants were more common than men, a sex ratio of 92 men to every 100 women, a figure entirely comparable with other parts of London in the later seventeenth century and typical of other early modern towns and cities.[60] Servant-keeping was relatively common in this part of the West End. Of the 772 households (more properly housefuls; this definition *includes* lodgers, see below) listed in the poll books used here some 264 (34 per cent) contained servants aged sixteen or over.[61] Such live-in servants were rarely found in large numbers: most employers kept one or two.[62] The average size of the servant group per family was 2·22 and half of all employers kept only one. In the part of St Martin's covered by these three Poll Tax listings (which covered about one in five of its population)[63] only a handful of households kept more than five servants.

The last aspect of the parish's society that ought to be considered in more detail is how far it was dominated by the social elite. Clearly, although there were many high-profile aristocratic mansions and gentry town houses in the parish, most inhabitants were more humble. This is an important topic for any study of pauperism, because those of elevated social rank may have helped local paupers through informal charity and hospitality. The presence of a significant proportion of the nation's social elite in the parish is, of course, a truism in London history. Between one-fifth and one-eighth of ratepayers in the parish before 1640 were gentlemen, and it contained more resident knights and peers on the eve of the Civil War than a 'typical English county'. Smuts also estimated that one-fifth of the population were resident gentlemen or their dependants.[64] Such aristocrats might have a major impact on local affairs. Early in the period the Cecil family dominated the parish and its governing vestry.[65]

The aim here is to achieve a long-term view of the social elite in the parish. It is clearly not enough to count the number of titled residents, since the extraordinary population growth of the parish could well have outpaced any increase in titled inhabitants. I have thus expressed the number of titled residents as a percentage of the number of households in the parish (see Table 10.2). This involves estimating the number of households in the parish, which has been done by dividing the population totals estimated above by a plausible household size. This procedure is intended to give only an *impression* of trends over time. Average households may well have been smaller than that used here, and may not have remained constant. The calculation is also complicated greatly by the difficulty of defining a household. The poll books reveal that about one-third of the population were lodgers in other people's 'houses'.[66] Lodgers are conventionally treated not as belonging to the household in which they were resident but as their own household. Here, however, the houseful is used because it is believed that this was the unit of assessment that was most likely to be identified by those making rates, which after about 1670 were based on the ratable value of houses.

Table 10.2 Proportions of titled households in St Martin's district

Year	Estimated No of 'households'	Total rated households excluding zero rated	Total rated titled 'households' excluding zero rated	% titled ratepayers	% titled households
1601	630	231	13	5.6	2.1
1611	897	356	28	7.9	3.1
1621	1,916	674	44	6.5	2.3
1631	2,635	853	56	6.6	2.1
1641	3,315	1,431	78	5.5	2.4
1651	2,125	1,169	53	4.5	2.5
1661	3,641	2,361	96	4.1	2.6
1671	7,278	3,228	110	3.4	1.5
1681	10,689	4,401	149	3.4	1.4
1691	13,989	6,605	228	3.5	1.6
1701	16,141	7,298	222	3.0	1.4
1711	15,872	7,389	242	3.3	1.5
Total	79,128	35996	1319	3.7	1.7

Source WAC/A1, A2, A37, A38, A56, A57, D16, D23, D7, F328, F338, F348, F358a, F368, F379, F389, F399, F408, F419, F431, F441, H443, H453, H462, H471, H480, H490 (rate books and/or overseers accounts of St Anne Soho, St James Piccadilly; St Martin in the Fields, St Paul Covent Garden).

Table 10.2 presents some preliminary findings regarding the number of titled residents. Not too much importance should be attached to the absolute proportions, given the doubts which surround any estimation of households. It should also be noted that the historians' definition of 'titled' varies. In particular, I have not tried to measure the number of gentlemen. This is because the honorific 'Mr' was used with increasing frequency and with less regard to actual entitlement after the Restoration. Here the titled residents are principally knights (459), ladies (413), lords (190), earls (145) and dukes (47), with a smattering of dames, countesses, duchesses and so on. The exercise is also subject to distortions produced by the varying rate at which titles such as baronetcies were created and sold, and the enthusiasm with which subjects took up knighthoods. Knights, of course, were often successful courtiers who had been mere gentlemen, professionals or merchants until fortune or court favour beckoned. Thus Dr Clergis, a vestryman in St Martin's in 1659, reappears as Sir Thomas Clarges at his first attendance at a vestry meeting after the Restoration.[67] It is certain, too, that the number of titled residents was greater than the rate books suggest. Some titled residents lodged in others' houses and probably escaped rating and others refused to pay.[68]

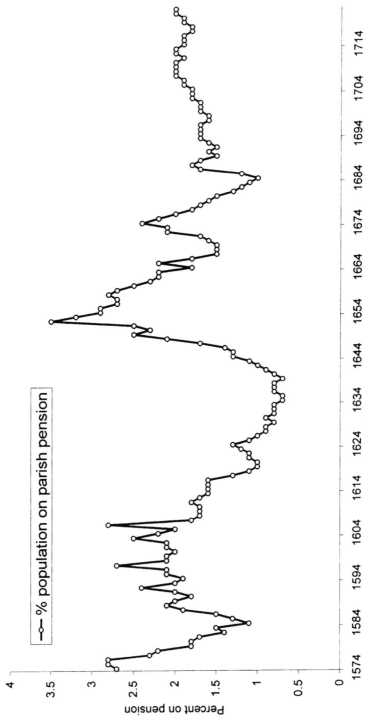

Figure 10.2 Percentage of the population of the West End on parish pensions, 1574–1722

Nevertheless, Table 10.2 does indicate that the proportion of titled residents declined after the 1660s. By the early eighteenth century the proportion of titled ratepayers was about half that before 1641. Titled residents also became less prominent after the Restoration because many sold their often ram-shackle mansions and palaces to property developers. Even titled residents, argues Stone, came to prefer more modest town houses in the new squares and courts.[69] Table 10.2 thus reveals that the West End's most 'aristocratic' phase ended shortly after the Restoration.

THE POOR AMONG THE RICH
SUMMARY MEASURES

Poverty was far from an overwhelming problem in the West End. Table 10.3 demonstrates that only about one in five households in St Martin's and one in seven in St Paul's was considered too poor to pay the tax.[70] Westminster and many districts of suburban London returned twice as many exempt poor.[71]

This section explores whether the number of paupers relieved increased as a proportion of the total population of the West End, and aims to give some idea of the relative number of poor inhabitants compared with other parts of London. Since the emphasis continues to be on the long term, all West End parishes are included, other than St Anne Soho, whose overseers' accounts have not survived.[72] The procedure has been to simply multiply the number on pensions by two, to allow for unlisted dependants, and express this as a percentage of the population estimates made above.[73] This exercise is clearly subject to uncertainties surrounding both the number of dependants and the size of the population. The higher proportions on relief before 1607 are due to the fact that the figures include orphans; thereafter they do not. What is immediately striking is that the proportion of the population on permanent relief did not grow in the long term. Indeed, the numbers entering the books

Table 10.3 Exempt poor in Westminster and the West End, 1664

Parish	Total households	No. of exempt	% exempt
St Clement Dane	858	29	3.4
St Margaret Westminster	3,133	1,486	47.4
St Martin le Grand	264	35	13.3
St Martin in the Fields	3,054	587	19.2
St Mary Savoy	148	61	41.2
St Paul Covent Garden	485	67	13.8
Total households	7,942	2.265	28.5

Source LMA MRTH7, fos 1–60.

Figure 10.3 Location of parish pensioners in St Martin in the Fields, 1716

before the Civil War did not keep pace with population growth, with at best one in a hundred receiving pensions on the eve of the Civil War. Thereafter dependence seems to have reached a peak during the 1650s. After the Restoration the proportion on relief hovered around 2 per cent.

The district was thus relieving a significantly *smaller* proportion of its population with pensions than English provincial cities. York, for example, was relieving between 4 per cent and 7 per cent of its population in the seventeenth century, and 8 per cent by 1716. Other provincial cities like Exeter, Norwich, Salisbury and Bristol relieved similar proportions.[74] Even by early modern European standards, the number relieved is on the low side.[75] What Paul Slack has called the 'growth of social welfare' does not seem to have extended to the pensioner population in these relatively wealthy West End districts. If there was an increase in the incidence of poverty in the West End, as some authorities have suggested, it does not show up in these figures. It is probable, however, that there *was* an increase in the number of paupers relieved by *irregular* cash hand-outs, rather than regular pensions. The number of *permanently* destitute individuals, however, showed little increase.[76]

Why the number of pensioners only kept pace with population growth is a more complex question than may at first appear. Pensions were applied for, and more people applied than were granted them.[77] There was intermittent pressure from the vestry and churchwardens on the overseers to restrict the growth in the number of pensioners. In St Martin's particular efforts (usually coinciding with shortfalls in available income) were made in the 1620s,[78] 1640s and 1650s,[79] and in 1662.[80] Rapid population growth may have caused cash flow problems and helps to explain other flurries of regulatory anxiety in 1671 and 1676–77.[81] Other efforts were made following legislation to the same effect in the late seventeenth and early eighteenth centuries. However, the frequency of the orders, and complaints that they had not been adhered to, suggest how difficult it was to supervise the activities and decisions of the parish overseers, responsible for paying hundreds of pensions and many more casual payments each year. Regulation probably increased at the end of our period, when JPs played a larger role in examining inmates and candidates for poor relief. Such efforts, however, did not necessarily reduce the numbers on parish relief, and could even prove counterproductive.[82]

THE POOR AMONG THE RICH
RESIDENTIAL DISTRIBUTION OF PENSIONERS

It has already been suggested that social exclusivity in the West End has been overstated. It would clearly be interesting to know where parish pensioners lived, since that would tell us something about the degree of social zoning that may have existed. Figure 10.3 maps parish pensioners living in the central

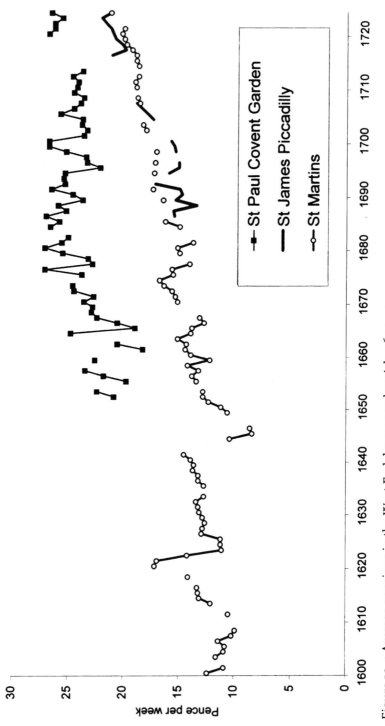

Figure 10.4 Average pensions in the West End, by year and parish, 1600–1724

Table 10.4 Average pensions by cohort (pence per week)

Period	St Martin in the Fields	St Paul Covent Garden	St James Piccadilly (Westminster)	St James Clerkenwell
1601–20	12·1			
1621–40	13·1			
1641–60	12·2	21·7		
1661–80	14·8	23·0		8·0[a]
1681–1700	16·2	25·1	15·3	9·0[a]
1701–20	18·9	24·2	19·1	
1721–24	20·5	26·0	21·4	23·0[a]
No. of pensioners	19,151	2,228	6,534	

Note [a] Clerkenwell years are 1661, 1701, 1723 respectively.

Source Smith, 'Ageing and well-being', pp. 76–7.

districts of St Martin's (excluding the westernmost parts of the parish beyond St James and St Anne Soho) listed in 1716 on a version of the parish map used by Strype's *Stow* in 1720.[83] This exercise is not related to the population at risk in any particular street, and there remain problems with locating all pensioner addresses on the contemporary map.[84] Nevertheless, it indicates that, despite the existence of some alleys, lanes and yards where destitution was particularly common, pensioners could be found in many parts of the parish. Hartshorne Lane[85] and Hungerford Market, next to Northumberland House, contained a significant number. Paupers were also found in significant numbers in Vinegar Yard (about 200–300 yards from Covent Garden piazza), along Bedfordbury, around the church, in the streets and alleys north of Long Acre and in the yards and lanes east of the Hay Market. Pensioners also lived along Long Acre, in St Martin's Lane and around Charing Cross. A few lodged along the Strand and in Newport Street. Although particular streets and courts in this district clearly were only for titled and well-to-do residents, it would be difficult to describe this West End district as socially exclusive, and there is little likelihood that the situation in 1716 was any different from that found fifty years or more earlier.[86]

How generous were pensions paid in this West End district? Did residence amongst the nation's elite produce higher pensions for the parish paupers? Was the West End relatively generous, and did their monetary value change over time? To answer this question the mean pension paid in St Martin's and its daughter parishes are presented summarily in Table 10.4 and annual variations are graphed in Figure 10.4.

Since pensions can be understood only in parochial context the figures are broken down by parish. The following points are worth making. Firstly, the small but more select parish of St Paul Covent Garden (see Table 10.3 for its relative poverty in 1664) was always more generous to its small number of pensioners, although the other parishes' rate of increase was much faster, indicating that pension values were converging over time.[87] Secondly, the supposedly more socially exclusive parish of St James paid similar pensions to its parent parish of St Martin's. Thirdly, the upward drift of pensions was not inexorable. There are sharp annual fluctuations and two periods of especially marked discontinuity. Figure 10.4 reveals that St Martin's pension payments fell in the Civil War and Interregnum period. This consisted of a sharp reduction in the average pension in the mid-1640s and then a slow recovery to the Restoration.[88] There was another sharp drop in average pensions in the early 1620s, specifically in 1622, after a previous increase.[89]

It seems probable that before the Restoration parish pensioners suffered when the parish experienced (temporary) demographic contraction and a consequent fall in available resources. Pensions were reduced across the board during the years 1643–44, presumably because of a fall in real or projected income. Thereafter the vestry made exceptional efforts to regulate access to pensions. It may be more than a coincidence that the average value of pensions had fallen during the check on population growth in the West End during the early 1620s. This was another period when the vestry attempted (with temporary success) to exercise greater control over the granting of pensions by the overseers.[90] As noted above, this is not an argument that relief of the poor was driven in some mechanical way by the rate of population change. We must always avoid demographic determinism.[91] Average pensions, for example, fell shortly after the Restoration and again in the late 1670s at a time when population growth was buoyant.

The size of pension payments must have reflected a range of local variables. The notion, for example, that the size of such doles reflects variations in the local cost of living[92] is clearly far too simplistic. Average weekly pensions in the 1680s ranged from just 9d weekly in Clerkenwell to 15d–16d in St Martin's and St James Westminster and 2s 1d in St Paul's. The latter was surrounded on three sides by St Martin's. Clerkenwell, a northern suburb of London, was about 1·5 km from St Martin's and St Paul's. The value of pensions in London ranged still more widely. In the 1690s the wealthy inner city parish of St Michael Cornhill was apparently spending £11 annually on each of its fortunate pensioners (i.e. about 4s 3d per week). In the poor City parish of St Andrew by the Wardrobe (a ten-minute walk west from St Michael) pensioners were paid, at most, 4s each month. Cost of living, then, was just one, and not necessarily the most important, variable. Others clearly included the amount of available parish income, local social policy, perceptions of need and other available sources of poor relief. Some parishes also may have given more supplemental help to their pensioners. Pearl claimed that a basic parish pension of 10d a week in the mid-seventeenth century could have been inflated to nearly 2s 9d a week by supplemental aid from parish and City companies.[93]

THE RICH AND THE POOR
LOCAL GOVERNMENT AND SOCIAL RELATIONS

Poor relief in the West End challenges the rather 'bipolar' view of power relations in early modern communities. Poor relief, it has been argued, was run 'by the most substantial' parishioners. Relief of the poor became, in the seventeenth century, a system directed by 'the best sort in the parish'.[94] Although this was undoubtedly so for many rural and urban parishes, it was not the case in the West End. In St Martin's the parish was governed by the vestry, but for most of the seventeenth century relief of the poor was conducted by the overseers, with some extra disbursements being made by the churchwardens. The vestry did *not* reflect the upper echelons of the parish. Most vestrymen in St Martin's were substantial tradesmen, wealthy craftsmen, professionals or court or government officials. Few knights and no peers attended regularly.[95]

After the Restoration, and probably before it too, overseers of the poor were mostly local tradesmen and craftsmen.[96] Although some overseers went on to become churchwardens and then vestrymen as part of the local *cursus honorum*, many did not. There was thus probably something of a social and possibly generational gulf between the vestrymen and churchwardens, and the overseers. Overseers took no part in vestry meetings unless they were specifically summoned, a restriction confirmed in 1661, and this must have subverted attempts to place restrictions on their activities.[97]

If there are signs of incipient social division within parish government, perhaps more interesting is that most of the exalted inhabitants took little part. Of course this was partly due to the fact that the select vestry did not expand to match population growth. At the Restoration and just before, average attendance at the St Martin's vestry was just thirteen, in 1682 it was sixteen.[98] This handful of individuals formed the prime local government institution for about 56,000 people. In addition to being swamped by rapid population growth, however, even wealthy vestrymen did not have the social cachet of their wealthiest neighbours. After their separation from St Martin's, the vestrymen of St James's have likewise been described as 'composed very largely of tradesmen. The grandees of St James appear not to have concerned themselves greatly in the government of the area.'[99] For this reason, far from being a relatively 'simple' poor relief system where local power structures corresponded with the realities of the local social structure, and where power and authority flowed downwards from a monolithic parish elite, some parish vestries in the West End may be characterized more accurately as occupying an uncomfortable middle ground, with the true social elite above them, their comfortably-off social counterparts alongside them, and the poor and more humble below them.

For this reason, poor relief involved those running the machine in delicate and sometimes uneasy negotiations with their social superiors (sometimes, indeed, with their patrons).[100] Even enforcing the payment of poor rates might be a contentious issue. For example, in 1617 the vestry had to wait on the Earl of Salisbury, who was detaining church and poor rates 'because no pew is appointed for his Lordships servants'.[101] Although overseers had the legal power to distrain goods in the event of non-payment, the vestry in 1678 thought it better 'that letters be Written to Persons of Quality and other persons of Ability to induce them to pay their Rates to the poore'.[102] Non-payment of rates was a particular problem in the West End because of a belief that the King's servants were exempt from both local taxation and also from taking any part in local government. In 1703, for example, the vestry of St Martin's asked the Attorney General whether a Mr Tuckwell was exempt from serving as overseer 'as being Yeoman of Her Majesties Salt Stores in Ordinary with fee'.[103] Two years earlier they had been constrained to wait on the Officers of the Board of Green Cloth 'to discourse them about such persons who keep houses and Trades in the parish and serve the king, That they may serve Overseers of the poor'.[104] In 1681 vestry complaints that 'persons of quality' had not paid poor rates were sent to the King and his Council.[105]

This is not to deny that the elite played a significant role in local poor relief. Some, not that many, gave free gifts to the churchwardens or overseers, bequeathed legacies channelled through parish officials, or left endowed charities behind them.[106] Even discounting those who evaded payment, the proportionate contribution of titled and exceptionally wealthy residents to the local poor rate was considerable.[107]

More interesting, however, is the extent to which the elite had direct contact with the poorest in the parish. The extent of informal giving is important, since it suggests alternative social arenas where relationships might still be forged outside the structures of parochial poor relief. Unsurprisingly, evidence is fragmentary. We now know that exclusive streets or squares were often close to scenes of desperate poverty in back streets and alleys. We should recall, too, Jütte's reminder that the poor were always more visible than their habitation in side streets and back alleys might suggest.[108] There is plenty of evidence that the begging poor, who seem to have included parish pensioners, could be quite aggressive in their approaches to their more fortunate neighbours. It is also clear that even the wealthiest residents faced insistent demands.[109] The elite, of course, were probably increasingly inaccessible on the street as they travelled in coaches and sedan chairs rather than on foot or by horse.[110] However, even here, direct approaches were made. The poor seem to have congregated at gateways leading through Covent Garden before the Civil War, waiting for the Earl of Salisbury's liveried servants to ride by.[111] Another enduring and highly traditional metropolitan custom was for the begging poor to congregate in the church and churchyard during service time.[112] A vestry order of 1677 indicates something of the range of tactics used:

> Ordered that Badges bee delivered to such of our poore as the Churchwardens & Overseers of the poore shall think fitt Who thereby have liberty to aske and receive broken meate only and not to beg of Coaches or of people going in the streets, and the hours of asking at doores allowed are from one to foure in the afternoone and noe longer, and none are to aske at doores without a badge And if any of the said poore shalbe unruly or uncivil in their asking at doors, then the badg is to bee taken from them.[113]

The extent to which mansions and supposedly exclusive houses were pestered by the begging poor at their doors cast a further blight on the 'socially exclusive' West End. This traditional practice had been a nuisance to London householders in the early seventeenth century, when they were 'continually troubled with relieving of beggars at their doors'.[114] Such activity may have been tacitly encouraged by example in the West End, since the royal court apparently adhered to the medieval rhetoric of hospitality via the office of the royal almoner, who distributed money at the palace gate.[115] Archaic though this practice was, he was indeed distributing money to St Martin's paupers in the early eighteenth century.[116] In the 1640s the steward running Sir Thomas Barrington's imposing house in Queen Street made regular 6d gifts to 'the poor at the door' or the roadside.[117] As Heal has pointed out, London living did not necessarily entail a rejection of the traditional imperative to relieve the poor and needy.[118] In fact, metropolitan life may have made the poor a more familiar and certainly a physically closer presence, even in the socially exclusive West End.

CONCLUSION
SOME IMPLICATIONS AND SPECULATIONS

This essay represents only a first step towards a reassessment of the social and economic history of London's West End. It has focused deliberately on the long term, and has taken the entire district as a whole, rather than breaking it down into its component parts. More work should, and is, being done to illuminate the history of this 'city within a city'.[119] Studying the poor in this area is, however, suggestive. It seems clear that some historians may have overestimated the social exclusivity of the Restoration West End. In fact, the West End was probably most 'aristocratic' before the Civil War. Although the absolute number of parish pensioners increased dramatically after the Restoration, placing strains on the machinery of poor relief, there is little sign that extreme destitution became a more significant problem, at least in proportional terms. The poor were, even in the West End, however, probably more visible, for they pestered the coaches and doorsteps of the rich and titled, as well as more humble parish officials.[120]

Social relations, too, were more complex in the West End. Poor relief may have brought conflict in the early modern West End, but this conflict was as much amongst the rich as between rich and poor. It has been argued elsewhere that out-relief under the old poor law was not a particularly effective means of imposing 'crude' social control on the poorer sort.[121] One may go further here and argue that the process of relieving the poor might itself open up fissures and social divisions within local communities. Collecting and assessing the local taxation that funded poor relief could be contentious and might set the parish governors against their social superiors as well as some of their more humble neighbours. Lastly, this chapter may make one ponder the source-bound myopia that can befall historians. To understand the lives of the poor, we must read parish records. To fully comprehend their experience, however, perhaps in rural and provincial England as much as in the metropolis, we must always remember that there might be other sources of relief and other arenas of social interaction or conflict on the doorsteps or at the gateways of their social superiors.

NOTES

The author would like to thank the editors for their generous assistance.

1 L. Stone, 'The residential development of the West End of London in the seventeenth century', in B. Malament ed., *After the Reformation: Essays in Honour of J. H. Hexter* (Philadelphia PA, 1980), p. 186.

2 For a plan of Whitehall in 1670 see G. H. Gater and W. H. Godfrey eds, *Survey of London*, XVI *Charing Cross (The Parish of St Martin-in-the-Fields, Part I)* (1935), plate 92.

3 Strype, *Stow*, II, p. 76.

4 M. Power, 'The east and west in early modern London', in E. W. Ives, R. J. Knecht and J. J. Scarisbrick eds, *Wealth and Power in Tudor England: Essays Presented to S. T. Bindoff* (1978), p. 172.

5 Strype, *Stow*, II, p. 77.

6 R. M. Smuts, 'The court and its neighbourhood: royal policy and urban growth in the early Stuart West End', *Journal of British Studies*, 30 (1991), p. 143.

7 For the development of the Covent Garden estates see *ibid*.

8 Stone, 'Residential development', p. 198.

9 For the history of individual buildings see the relevant volumes of the *Survey of London*, and also C. L. Kingsford, *The Early History of Piccadilly, Leicester Square, Soho and their*

Neighbourhood (Cambridge, 1925). John Stow was relatively uninterested in the West End: see Kingsford, *Stow*, II, pp. 97–124. Strype, *Stow*, II, is far more informative, pp. 67–80. The standard work remains N. G. Brett-James, *The Growth of Stuart London* (1935), esp. pp. 151–86, 366–98.

10 See Power, 'The east and west'; *id.*, 'John Stow and his London', *Journal of Historical Geography*, 11(1985); *id.*, 'The social topography of Restoration London', in Beier and Finlay, *London*.

11 I follow Brett-James and Power and distinguish between the West End and Westminster proper. Westminster refers to the vill of Westminster, consisting of the parish of St Margaret's. West End parishes were St Martin's and its daughter parishes, St Mary Savoy, St Clement Dane, St Andrew Holborn and St Giles in the Fields: see Power, 'The east and west', p. 181.

12 Smuts, 'Court and its neighbourhood', pp. 145–8.

13 Strype, *Stow*, II, p. 74.

14 J. Merritt, 'Religion, Government, and Society in early modern Westminster *c.* 1525–1625', University of London Ph.D. thesis (1992), chap. 6; quotation from p. 267.

15 R. B. Shoemaker, *Prosecution and Punishment: Petty Crime and the Law in London and Rural Middlesex c. 1660–1725* (Cambridge, 1991), esp. pp. 273–310.

16 Those most subject to social upheaval were St Giles, St Martin's and St Paul Covent Garden. Shoemaker states that the remaining West End parishes – St Margaret's Westminster, St Mary le Strand, St Clement Dane and St Andrew Holborn experienced less social change and 'consequently experienced lower prosecution rates': *ibid*, p. 299.

17 *Ibid.*, p. 292.

18 *Ibid.*, p. 292.

19 *Ibid.*, p. 298. See also, Stone 'Residential development', p. 191.

20 See also Merritt, 'Religion, Government, and Society', p. 305.

21 S. Hindle, 'Power, poor relief and social relations in Holland Fen *c.* 1600–1800', *HJ*, 41 (1998).

22 *Ibid.*, pp. 79–80.

23 Merritt, 'Religion, Government, and Society', esp. pp. 192–205.

24 The best books on London's demography are J. Landers, *Death and the Metropolis: Studies in the Demographic History of London 1670–1830* (Cambridge, 1993), and R. Finlay, *Population and Metropolis: The Demography of London 1580–1650* (Cambridge, 1981). For recent surveys, see R. Finlay and B. Shearer, 'Population growth and suburban expansion', in Beier and Finlay, *London*. They used the printed parish registers of St Margaret's Westminster, St Paul Covent Garden and St Martin's to represent the West End. Since they omitted St Martin's after 1636, they underestimated the rate of growth in the West End: *ibid.*, pp. 58–9. See also V. Harding, 'The population of London 1550–1700', *LJ*, 15 (1990).

25 The baptism registers of St Martin's, St Paul Covent Garden, St James Westminster and St Anne Soho were counted by Jo Bath, kindly funded by the Nuffield Foundation, whose assistance is hereby acknowledged.

26 The birth rate is the mid-point of the two suggested by Finlay, *Population and Metropolis*,

p. 157. For Wrigley and Schofield's inflation factors see E. A. Wrigley and R. S. Schofield, *The Population History of England: A Reconstruction 1541–1871* (Cambridge, 1981), pp. 536–41.

27 Landers, *Death and the Metropolis*, pp. 135–9, 162–8.

28 Strype noticed a large number of French nationals, a French church above Hungerford Market and one in St Anne Soho: *Stow*, II, pp. 68, 74, 76.

29 See J. Boulton, 'Clandestine marriages in London: an examination of a neglected urban variable', *Urban History*, 20 (1993).

30 If London's fertility level followed the same course as that in England, its birth rate would have *fallen* over the seventeenth century, thereby further *inflating* the estimated population sizes presented here.

31 These pre-Civil War population estimates are comparable with those of other authors: cf. Smuts, 'Court and its neighbourhood', p. 118; Merritt, 'Religion, Government, and Society', p. 277.

32 It should be noted that these population estimates are more than *double* those of Shoemaker, *Prosecution and Punishment*, pp. 327–9. This is due, in all probability, to the fact that Shoemaker used partial counts of households, and household size multipliers that were too small. His general finding, that prosecution rates were higher in the West End than in the East End, would still stand, since the same underestimation seems to apply to *all* his population estimates. This disagreement, therefore, does nothing to undermine the central thesis of an excellent book.

33 Strype, *Stow*, II, p. 67.

34 Together the East End, Stepney and Whitechapel, contained about 20,000 people in 1600, and about 90,000 in 1700: M. Power, 'The east London working community in the seventeenth century', in P. J. Corfield and D. Keene eds, *Work in Towns 850–1850* (Leicester, 1990), pp. 103–4.

35 Stone, 'Residential development ', pp. 173–86; Merritt, 'Religion, Government, and Society', p. 188; Smuts, 'Court and its neighbourhood', p. 119. For the value of the Long Parliament to the West End economy see S. Porter, 'The economic and social impact of the Civil War upon London', in S. Porter ed., *London and the Civil War*, (Basingstoke, 1996), pp. 176–7.

36 See P. Slack, *The Impact of Plague in Tudor and Stuart England* (1985), chap. 2.

37 The number of baptisms in the parish supports the notion of a temporary check on unremitting population growth before the 1625 plague. For the proclamations see F. Heal, 'The Crown, the gentry and London: the enforcement of proclamation 1596–1640', in C. Cross, D. M. Loades and J. Scarisbrick eds, *Law and Government under the Tudors* (1988), quoting p. 219. See also F. Heal, *Hospitality in Early Modern England* (Oxford, 1990), pp. 146–51.

38 *Ibid.*, pp. 221–5.

39 Porter, 'Economic and social impact', pp. 190–1. See also Brett-James, *Growth of Stuart London*, pp. 119–20.

40 J. Boulton, 'Going on the parish: the parish pension and its meaning in the London suburbs 1640–1724', in T. Hitchcock, P. King and P. Sharpe eds, *Chronicling Poverty: The Voices and Strategies of the English Poor 1640–1840* (Basingstoke, 1997), p. 25.

41 For the impact of war see, L. D. Schwarz, *London in the Age of Industrialisation: Entrepreneurs, Labour Force and Living Conditions 1700–1850* (Cambridge, 1992); Landers, *Death and the Metropolis*, pp. 78–83, 286–300; D. A. Kent, 'Gone for a soldier', *Local Population Studies* (1990); N. Rogers, 'Carnal knowledge: illegitimacy in eighteenth-century Westminster', *Journal of Social History*, 23 (1989).

42 S. Macfarlane, 'Social policy in the later seventeenth century', in Beier and Finlay, *London*.

43 Thus we have in 1709: 'Mary Cotton ... sayes she is the wife of Daniel Cotton by Trade a Tripeman now in the Queens Service at Sea'; 'Mary Turnor sayes she is the widow of John Turnor who dyed about 10 years ago in the service in Flanders'; WCA F5001, fos 60, 62.

44 J. M. Beattie, *Crime and the Courts in England 1660–1800* (Oxford, 1986), pp. 213–37, notes the trough in indictments for property crime during war years and the 'clear benefits' to London's working population war brought: *ibid.*, p. 230.

45 Brett-James, *Growth of Stuart London*, p. 78.

46 Merritt, 'Religion, Government, and Society', p. 188. See also, Smuts, 'Court and its neighbourhood', pp. 124, 128; Rogers, 'Carnal knowledge', p. 349.

47 The data from the 1630s were kindly lent to me by Professor Malcolm Smuts. The earlier data were taken from W. Le Hardy ed., *Calendar to the Sessions Records 1612–1618* (4 vols, 1935–41). This latter sample includes individuals who were listed as victims of crime, and some criminals.

48 This source lists 551 individuals with allocated trades; sixty-five were before 1629 and the remaining 486 were listed between 1667 and 1684.

49 See T. Arkell, 'An examination of the poll taxes of the later seventeenth century, the Marriage Duty Act and Gregory King', in Schurer and Arkell, *Surveying the People*.

50 I have excluded servants from the Poll Tax occupational data, since none was recorded in sources before 1660.

51 A. L. Beier, 'Engine of manufacture: the trades of London', in Beier and Finlay, *London*, p. 148. Victualling trades occupied between 13·2 per cent and 17·5 per cent of those adult males buried in his extramural parish sample.

52 Strype, *Stow*, II, p. 68.

53 Beier, 'Engine of manufacture', p. 148.

54 E. M. Green, 'The taxonomy of occupations in late eighteenth-century Westminster', in Corfield and Keene, *Work in Towns*, p. 165. See also C. Harvey, E. M. Green and P. J. Corfield, 'Continuity, change, and specialization within metropolitan London: the economy of Westminster 1750–1820', *EcHR*, 52 (1999), p. 483.

55 Beier, 'Engine of manufacture', p. 148.

56 *Ibid.*, p. 155. For the classic statement of the growth of conspicuous consumption in Stuart London see F. J. Fisher, *London and the English Economy 1500–1700* (1990), pp. 105–18.

57 T. Delaune, *Angliae Metropolis: or, The Present State of London: with Memorialls Comprehending a Full and Succinct Account of the Ancient and Modern State Thereof* (second edition, 1690), pp. 106–11.

58 All individuals making a will in the parish of St Martin in the Fields and daughter parishes have been abstracted from the printed indexes to the PCC. Unfortunately the editors of the indexes covering 1631 to 1653 chose not to record 'ordinary' occupations. I have been unable, thus far, to consult a copy of the index covering the years 1661–70.

59 See P. Earle, 'The female labour market in the late seventeenth century in London', *EcHR*, second series, 42, (1989); T. Meldrum, 'London domestic servants from depositional evidence 1660–1750: servant–employer sexuality in the patriarchal household', in Hitchcock *et al.*, *Chronicling Poverty*.

60 For the Poll Taxes see WCA F4534–6. These figures include nine apprentices. Some of the male 'servants' would probably have been apprentices. For an analysis of the 1695 Marriage Duty Act assessment for London see K. Schurer, 'Variations in household structure in the late seventeenth century: toward a regional analysis', in Schurer and Arkell, *Surveying the People*, p. 266. See also L. Schwarz, 'English servants and their employers during the eighteenth and nineteenth centuries', *EcHR*, 52 (1999).

61 More properly one might look at individual families. There were, including those lodging in other households, some 1,404 families in all, of which 302, or 22 per cent, kept servants.

62 Schwarz, 'English servants and their employers', p. 238.

63 The population estimates would suggest about 20,000 individuals living in the parish in the early 1660s, which, allowing for a third of the population under sixteen, would produce a percentage of about 15.

64 Smuts, 'The court and its neighbourhood', pp. 123–4.

65 Merritt, 'Religion, Government, and Society', pp. 194–9.

66 The Marriage Duty Act assessments for London show that the average *houseful* contain 6·1 members, of whom 1·7 were lodgers: Schurer, 'Variations in household structure', p. 268.

67 WCA F2003/228–9. According to the *DNB* Clarges was indeed originally a doctor or apothecary.

68 See p. 214.

69 Stone, 'Residential development', pp. 194–5.

70 For this source and the table see J. Boulton, 'The most visible poor in England? Constructing pauper biographies in early modern Westminster', *Westminster Historical Review*, 1 (1997), pp. 15–16.

71 For comparable information see Power, 'Social topography', p. 205; *id.*, 'The east and west', p. 181.

72 The population totals used in the following calculations have therefore been reduced, by subtracting Soho's estimated population.

73 This is the method used by Paul Slack, *Poverty and Policy in Tudor and Stuart England* (1988), pp. 176–7.

74 *Ibid.* Adding the orphans of St Martin's to the total number of pensioners and their dependants increases the proportions only by about 0·5 per cent.

75 R. Jütte, *Poverty and Deviance in Early Modern Europe* (Cambridge, 1994), p. 54.

76 From the end of the seventeenth century St Martin's spent a greater proportion of its

poor relief funds on the casual or extraordinary poor than on regular payments to parish pensioners and orphans: Boulton, 'Going on the parish', pp. 24–5. By 'permanent' is meant 'on regular relief as a pensioner'. I shall discuss the relatively short duration of parish pensions elsewhere.

77 *Ibid.*, pp. 26–32, esp. p. 46 n. 108. For this point see also S. King, 'Reconstructing lives: the poor, the Poor Law and welfare in Calverley 1650–1820', *Social History*, 22 (1997), p. 321 n. 20.

78 WCA F2001, fos 161–3, setting out new orders regulating the parish poor.

79 Boulton, ' Going on the parish', pp. 27–9.

80 WCA F2003, fos 291–5, 309–11.

81 WCA F2004, fos 70, 73, 79, 85, 179, 190v–198v. See also a campaign against 'all such poore people as are lately come into the parish and have demanded reliefe' in 1680 (fo. 290), an order to have them all listed 'fairly written in three Columes' (fo. 335) in 1682 and restrictions imposed on the granting of casual relief in 1686 (WCA F2005, fos 42–5).

82 In 1708, for example, the churchwardens were asked to wait on the JPs of St Martin's, 'to desire them not to putt any such poor on the Extraordinary or pencon, who have been putt out upon Examincaon & Inquiry, by the Gentlemen of the Vestry and Churchwardens, and a List to be delivered to the Justices of such poor who are so putt Out', WCA F2005, fo. 396.

83 See 1716 listing, WCA F4539.

84 Each pensioner is represented by a black dot. These have been allocated evenly in the appropriate streets and alleys. Throughout it has been assumed that where a street name was given, it referred to that street in the parish of St Martin's. Only pensioners located in the parish have been mapped, although a few lived just across the parish boundary.

85 Many more were to be found there in the 1707 listing, which included more individuals, see WCA F4509.

86 A similar impression is gained from the 1664 Hearth Tax returns.

87 St Martin's pensions increased by 68 per cent between the 1640s and the end of our period, compared with only 20 per cent in St Paul's.

88 See Boulton, 'Going on the parish', p. 25.

89 The overseers' accounts for 1622 show across-the-board reductions in pensions: WCA F349

90 In December 1622 the vestry drew up orders regarding the relief of the parish poor, including clauses preventing the overseers from increasing pensions or spending large sums of money without vestry consent, the appointment of a committee to take a quarterly view of all the 'poore which are weekly releeved' and an order enjoining the local constables to be diligent against inmates and newcomers: WCA F2001, fos 161–3.

91 See B. Todd, 'Demographic determinism and female agency: the remarrying widow reconsidered ... again', *Continuity and Change*, 9 (1994).

92 For a remark finding such a link see Slack, *Poverty and Policy*, p. 176.

93 Cited in Macfarlane, 'Social policy', pp. 255–6. For differences between rural parishes

see L. Botelho, 'Aged and impotent: parish relief of the aged poor in early modern Suffolk', in M. Daunton ed., *Charity, Self-interest and Welfare in the English Past* (1996).

94 Wrightson, 'Politics of the parish', p. 22.

95 For an excellent account of St Martin's vestry in the Jacobean period see Merritt, 'Religion, Government, and Society', pp. 179–99. Legislation in the seventeenth century allowed some social groups, including the peerage, to avoid parish office. See WCA F2006, fo. 20. For an Anglican purge of the vestry, which nonetheless left 'many of those who had attended the meetings of the previous vestry' free to attend subsequently, see P. Seaward, 'Gilbert Sheldon, the London vestries, and the defence of the Church', in T. Harris, P. Seaward and M. Goldie eds, *The Politics of Religion in Restoration England* (Oxford, 1990), pp. 57–8.

96 Analysis of a document supplying information on those nominated or serving as overseers amply demonstrates this: see WCA F2517.

97 WCA F2003, fo. 248. Serving or fining for the office of overseer was, however, made a condition of vestry membership in 1704: WCA F2005, fo. 312.

98 This statement comes from a detailed analysis of the attendance records of every vestrymen attending in the years 1659 and 1662, and 1682: WCA F2003, fos 185–298; F2004, *passim*.

99 F. H. W. Sheppard, *The Parish of St James Westminster*, I, *South of Piccadilly*, Survey of London 29 (1960), p. 7.

100 Merritt, 'Religion, Government, and Society', pp. 194–7.

101 WCA F2001, fos 111–13.

102 WAC F2004, fo. 235v. See also fos 244, 268, 21/7/1679, and esp. 268v citing a Privy Council Order of 18/1/1633 to the effect that the King's servants should undertake parish duties.

103 WCA F2005, fo. 311.

104 *Ibid.*, fo. 261.

105 WCA F2004, fo. 309.

106 St Martin's appears to have been relatively poorly endowed, given the wealth of the inhabitants.

107 Merritt, 'Religion, Government, and Society', p. 284.

108 Jütte, *Poverty and Deviance*, p. 59.

109 Boulton, 'Going on the parish', pp. 32–4. Some beggars who had seen better days deliberately appealed to their erstwhile social counterparts. The failed poet Arthur Brett, who died in his mother's house in the Strand in 1677, 'came up to London, and there fell into poverty, begging from gentlemen in the streets, and especially from Oxford men', *DNB*.

110 Stone, 'Residential development', pp. 179–81. For some striking insights into what he calls the growth of interiorization, and especially the private journeys made possible within London in sedan chairs and coaches, see L. Manley, *Literature and Culture in Early Modern London* (Cambridge, 1995), pp. 505–7.

111 Merritt, 'Religion, Government, and Society', p. 293.

112 Boulton, 'Going on the parish', pp. 32–3. This was an enduring feature of street life in

London: see D. Defoe, *Proposals for imploying the Poor in and about the City of London, without any Charge to the Publick* (1723), p. 3, 'they besiege the Entrance of our Churches, and fill our Ears, in all Places of Resort, with lamentable Complaints of Distress'.

113 WCA F2004, fo. 198v.

114 Heal, *Hospitality*, p. 319.

115 Delaune, *Present State*, p. 113.

116 See the list compiled by the St Martin's officials in 1707, WCA F4001, fo. 18v.

117 A. Searle, 'Sir Thomas Barrington in London 1640–1644', II, 'Life at Queen Street', *Essex Journal*, 2 (1967), p. 69. See also pp. 35–41, for Part I.

118 Heal, *Hospitality*, pp. 180, 319–20.

119 My forthcoming *The Making of the London Poor* will look at many aspects of this. See also my 'Surviving in London's West End', *International Review of Social History*, supplement (forthcoming, 2000).

120 Boulton, 'Going on the parish', p. 33.

121 *Ibid.*, p. 37.

Part IV

Material culture and consumption

Chapter 11

———◆———

'Great quantities of gooseberry pye and baked clod of beef': victualling and eating out in early modern London

Sara Pennell

'There's no place so well furnish'd ... with munitions for the mouth.'[1]

In late twentieth-century London the culture of eating out has been lionized as part of what is making London culturally and globally significant once more; when London cooks, the Western world seems to salivate.[2] As James Howell proudly observed, in the mid-seventeenth-century metropolis, a city of nearly 400,000 inhabitants,[3] there was also little opportunity not to eat. 'Londinopolis' was well provided with 'an abundance of all kinds of provision, as flesh, fish, fowle, fruits, fuel, variety of drinks and wines', a plenitude which much of the kingdom and its nascent colonies were labouring increasingly to furnish.[4]

More recently, and less panegyrically, F. J. Fisher and E. A. Wrigley have cast London's victualling as a crucial component of its early modern economic complexion, in studies that concentrate in great part on the supply of raw foodstuffs and processed staples as central to the 'feeding' of pre-modern London.[5] Yet the foodways of the metropolis – used here to connote the diverse uses and implications of food as a cultural and economic complex, structured around and structuring other aspects of individual and collective existence – are as important to analyse as the quantities and components of provisioning.[6] Neglecting to consider eating as a socio-economic and organizational phenomenon, is to ignore consumption in its profoundly corporeal sense.[7]

Indeed, exploring 'how' and 'why' the vast quantities of food absorbed by Howell's metropolitan 'stomack' for its own consuming purposes were eaten provides an underexplored route into assessing London's status as a (proto-type) modern urban paradigm. Did metropolitan foodways particularize the life styles of early modern London's inhabitants, as opposed to those of other urban and urbanizing centres?[8] The precedence of London as a template for provincial material tastes and practices has been gradually dismantled by certain scholars in past years. However, the complexity of metropolitan tastes, as well as the spatial and symbolic contexts in which consuming was located, remain unfixed within the broader topography of British consumption patterns.[9]

A response to the poles of historiography represented by Fisher's conspicuously consuming Tudor and Stuart city and Dorothy George's bleak Georgian 'uncertainties of life and trade' is certainly necessary. The getting and spending of persons of the modest, artisanal status of Nehemiah Wallington, or of the fledgling legal 'professional' Stephen Monteage, are seldom illuminated, and the omission remains glaring.[10] For the labouring non-elite, towards the lower reaches of the 'middling sorts', there were demographic, spatial and associative considerations which assumed a different magnitude in London, if not being unique to it. Mapping these concerns reiterates the complexity of constructing categories of food consumption for early modern Londoners. How, for example, do we categorize the pie made at the hearth, but taken to the local tavern oven to cook, an action which usually involved payment of the tavern keeper for this service? What follows reflects as much upon spatiality as central in constructing metropolitan experience as upon other environmental or political factors.[11]

The paucity of general studies of victualling derives in part from the difficulties in gathering evidence of food preparation and eating as practical actions, rather than as textual and moral prescriptions.[12] Reliance upon the gustatory preoccupations of 'visible' Londoners like Samuel Pepys, and upon the accounts of foreign travellers, with their culturally predisposed, occasionally idiosyncratic 'gaze', preserves perspectives that render up the extremes of metropolitan eating: Pepys and Henri Misson should not stand as proxies for all early modern metropolitan appetites.[13] This research moves beyond testimonies such as these to sources both public and institutional, visual and artefactual, fictional and promotional. And while these all supply perspectives upon extra-domestic preparation and eating, they also inevitably reflect perhaps the one continuity of London history/histories: its kaleidoscopic yet continually fragmentary variety.[14]

THE LIMITS OF DOMESTIC PROVISIONING

William Fitzstephen's description of twelfth-century London, mined in the sixteenth by John Stow, recorded the presence of a Thameside 'public eating-house', at which 'every day, according to the season, may be found viands of all kinds, roast, fried and boiled, fish large and small, coarser meat for the poor and more delicate for the rich ... This indeed is the public cookery, and very convenient to the city, and a distinguishing mark of civilisation.'[15] Certainly, extra-domestic eating was hardly novel in sixteenth- and seventeenth-century London. But the parameters within which such outlets operated had changed substantively. The ethics of hospitality and urban commonweal which characterized the eating house of Fitzstephen's description were elusive factors in early modern metropolitan provision – a contrast Stow perhaps wanted to emphazise – overshadowed by a demand raised up on necessity.

Suburban development of the City, Westminster and the liberties south of the Thames brought with it demographic pressures upon the spatial and temporal organization of non-elite labour and thus of domestic life.[16] High concentrations of individuals living in lodgings, singly or in fluid, often non-familial groups, and the presence of that prototypical 'consuming' population, domestic servants, often in search of food on their free days or to spend their board wages, made extra-domestic victualling inevitable.[17] Ralph Treswell's usefully annotated surveys reveal that, while kitchen[18] hearths are common in the early seventeenth-century structures, they were not universal. Of the Boroughside, Southwark, housing owned by St Thomas's Hospital, only seven of fourteen dwellings appear to have contained a kitchen at all.[19] Provision of ovens was yet more scattered; where they are noted, they can often be related to industrial or commercial concerns, for example, in the cookshops of Pie Corner, or in brewery complexes.[20]

Lack of ready access to an oven did not preclude domestic food preparation, of course, but other spatial and economic arrangements hindered it. Kitchens could be located almost anywhere in a structure, and St Sepulchre and St Giles inventories reveal kitchens in every conceivable location, from cellar to garret.[21] For those who worked in the food trades, there was the added complication of combining one's kitchen with one's work space, an elision which surely complicated household provisioning.[22]

Perhaps most pressing were the spatial problems experienced in multiple occupancy households. For the labouring Londoner, who more often than not lodged in a larger household, the use of communal spaces – hallways, landings but, above all, the kitchen – could lead to confrontations which made eating out the easier, if not the preferable option.[23] Lodgers might be provided with the means to undertake some cooking of their own, but this could pose too great a temptation: Mary Crab, who leased a room from Sarah Colly, of St Sepulchre, was indicted in December 1731 for stealing a saucepan, a box iron, a plate and some sheets from her landlady, goods with which her room was presumably furnished.[24]

To avoid such losses, demanding payment for board as well as lodging was a common arrangement. Corbet Vezey, indicted at the Old Bailey sessions of January 1732 for the murder of his wife by alleged cruelty and starvation, had lodged with his wife at the Mile End house of one Mrs Finlow. Finlow testified that Vezey and his wife had consumed 'the same as the rest of the Family ...

beef, pork, fish or whatever we had for Dinner ... sometimes hot, and sometimes cold, just as we had it ourselves'.[25] Yet, as cases concerning neglect of apprentices attest, the substance of the 'board' was often less varied and plentiful than that furnished by Mrs Finlow.[26] Even those in a position to choose their lodgings and set a price for their board could be short-changed. In 1698 Robert Molesworth, later first Viscount Molesworth, wrote to his wife in Ireland about the lamentable service his two sons and their tutor were receiving at their London lodgings. 'Really I must hasten their departure to prevent their being starved ... Two dinners and three suppers for ten souls has been made out of a shoulder of veal.'[27]

Although boarding was effectively a domestic relationship, it nevertheless introduced commercial considerations and limited obligations into meal-times. Thus when Mrs Finlow could not, or would not, provide her lodgers with meals, they were dependent on finding sustenance elsewhere. Board wages paid to resident servants were the logical extension of such arrangements, but alternatives did exist, notably tabling.[28] Valentine Persel, a witness of Elizabeth Hewit's alleged theft of jewellery and cash from her master, tailor Andrew Kirk, in July 1734, explained that his presence in the household was because Kirk's wife 'dresses victuals for young men, so we diet with him'.[29] A tabling 'contract' such as this, perhaps set up by his employer, prevented Persel from frittering away a board wage, and losing perhaps more than just money, in local taverns.[30]

Recourse to tabling highlights the mobility of metropolitan labour: where Persel lived and where he worked were not where he dined. The service of Mrs Kirk in providing his meals marks a second constraint upon the domestic sufficiency of many London households: a growing demand for the labour of women, and for their culinary skills in particular. As Earle's study of female witnesses in the city's Church courts between 1695 and 1725 reveals, 16·4 per cent of single female deponents with identified trades were employed in catering, victualling and shopkeeping, whilst the occupation most commonly shared by wives with their husbands was the operation of a victualling outlet.[31]

The nuances of female involvement in metropolitan provisioning – so often poorly captured in the official record – are nicely illustrated in the case against Elizabeth Calloway, who kept a brandy shop and lodging house in Cecil Court, near St Martin's Lane. Accused of committing arson for insurance purposes on her dwelling in 1735, Calloway asserted that she had insured her business because of the fire risk posed by Eleanor Pickhaver's adjacent cookshop. Pickhaver, however, testified that Calloway had recently been a disgruntled customer of hers:

> Five or six weeks before the fire she [Calloway] sent a woman for six pennyworth of boil'd beef, and in a little time the Woman came back with a few scraps of it, and said it was all full of sand, I asked some gentlemen in the house (whose meat had

been cut from the same Buttock) if their meat was Sandy. They said, No, So I bid the woman leave what she brought if she did not like it. She went back, and ... [Calloway] came in a hurry, and said, Hussy, keep my money at your peril, I'll soon cure you of selling meat here.[32]

Why did Calloway patronize her neighbour's shop? It is possible that she simply had too many commitments already to cater for herself. The particularly feminized 'economy of makeshifts' embodied in Calloway's ventures, and its consequences for domestic order, disrupted prevailing normative readings of female labour, enshrined as they were in the moral, economic and spatial responsibilities of the ideal 'good housewife'. Yet paradoxically it also enabled the likes of Pickhaver and Mrs Kirk to exploit traditional female involvement in the culinary aspects of housewifery as a financial resource.[33]

Another Old Bailey case certainly casts into sharp relief the practical and emotional repercussions of extra-domestic female employment. Isaac Smith was indicted in February 1719 for the murder of his wife Elizabeth in a house in Old Bedlam. William Cadwallader, who employed Elizabeth as a washer-woman, deposed that Smith:

> ask'd her [Elizabeth] for some victuals and some strong drink; she told him that she had but a Farthing in her pocket and that would not buy a Pint of strong drink, but that he might go to Mrs Ward's and there have what he wanted; he said he would not go there because she always talk'd to him of what he did not care to hear; and would have had her go

Cadwallader then offered to share with Smith the bread and cheese that he was about to eat, but Smith 'call'd his wife Bitch and Toad and such like Names ... that she should not work for her pride, and he go like a vagabond, etc ... upon which he run at her and with the knife he had in his hand gave her the ... wound'.[34] Smith's inability to cope with his wife's 'pride', her need to earn a livelihood, cost him his life.

This case further highlights the vexed opposition between the notion of ready-made food as a convenience of a nascent topography of metropolitan leisure, where Smith was able to 'have what he wanted', and on credit (given the couple's lack of ready cash), at Mrs Ward's and ready-made food as a begrudged necessity, in a service-driven, spatially-squeezed environment where domestic sufficiency could only be an ideal propagated in cookery and conduct books.[35]

VENUES OF VICTUALLING

Contemporary definitions and data obscure as much as they reveal about the contours of extra-domestic eating. What *are* we looking for? Let us select two extramural parishes, St Sepulchre without Newgate and St Giles in the Fields,

Table 11.1 Involvement in victualling in St Giles in the Fields and St Sepulchre parishes, 1660–1751

No. involved	St Sepulchre	St Giles
Population	7,385[a]	34,800[b]
1660/61[c]	143	n.a.
1663/64[c]	126	n.a.
1720/21[d]	40	136
1751[e]	n.a.	158
Inventories[f]		
1660–80	1	2
1690–1710	7	7
1720–40	8	6

Sources[a](1695) George, **London Life** pp. 408–9. [b](1711) **ibid** [c]CLRO, MS 208A, Lists of recognisances of all vintners, tablekeepers, innholders, cooks, victuallers within the City wards, 1660/61 and 1663/64, information for St Sepulchre in Farringdon Without, pp. 29–35, 278–84. [d]LMA, MR/LV/3/90, 93, recognizances of licensed victuallers taken at general renewal of licences, Finsbury Division (inc. St Sepulchre), March 1720/21; MR/LV/3/92, recognizances of licensed victuallers, Holborn Division (inc. St Giles), February 1720/21. [e]LMA MR/LV/7/3, 12, 13, 14, recognizances of licensed victuallers taken at general renewal of licences, Holborn Division, September and November 1751. [f]Numbers of victuallers (victuallers, inn-, tavern- and alehouse keepers, bakers, cooks) identified in sample of fifty inventories each for three twenty-one-year periods, from both parishes, LGL MSS 9174, 9186, Commissary Court inventories for St Sepulchre and St Giles in the Fields parishes, 1660–1740. For further details of this sample see Pennell, 'Material culture', appendix 1.

with populations of around 7,385 and 34,800 respectively at the close of the seventeenth century. In their rapid demographic expansion, fuelled in part by extensive but temporary in-migration, and with large-scale new construction and infilling promoting increasing socio-economic bifurcation, they characterize many features of early modern metropolitan growth.[36]

In these parishes, licensing and inventory data indicate a sizable proportion of the parochial population between 1660 and 1740 covered by the portmanteau term of victualler (Table 11.1). A more detailed, modern enumeration of another extra-mural parish, St Giles Cripplegate, suggests that the late seventeenth-century population contained numerous specialist food producers, in addition to the conventional victualling categories included in Table 11.1. Between 1654 and 1693, alongside 402 recorded victuallers and thirty-two cooks, there were sixteen confectioners, a wafer maker, a dryer of neats' (young calves') tongues, a gingerbread maker and a noodleman.[37] Such data certainly support Beier's assertion, that by 1700 victualling-related employment, in its increasing diversity, comprised the second largest occupational sector in the metropolis, especially on its expanding extramural 'periphery'.[38] But we should also exercise caution towards such data – notoriously unreliable in capturing irregular, seasonal or peripheral participation in **any** trade – confirming the ubiquity of a metropolitan, food-centred service economy.

This unreliability turns partly upon the definitional problems inherent in contemporary usage of the terms 'victualling' and 'victualler'. 'Victualling' embraces the provision and consumption of both food and drink, but has long served as the legal shorthand for the vending of alcohol. The concerted licensing of victuallers from 1552 was rooted in the need to control the commercial provision of alcoholic drink, and to monitor the establishments in which it was sold.[39] The provision of food in these and other establishments is assumed, and sometimes briefly mentioned, but it is rarely considered crucial to defining this type of victualling, as opposed to the 'victualling' of grain and other raw staples.[40]

Nevertheless, during the early modern period the commercial provision of food began to be more strongly identified as a component of victualling. Two Edwardian proclamations concerning Lenten and fast day abstinence hint at how widespread commercial ready-made food provision was becoming. Although the 1548 decree to enforce conformity to regulations prohibiting the preparation and consumption of meat is silent on extra-domestic food provision, its successor of 1552 explicitly declares that: 'no manner of person or persons keeping, or that shall keep any tavern, inn, hostelry, victualling house, common or usual table for any guests ... [shall] utter any flesh, in any kind of manner their houses or elsewhere'.[41]

The acknowledgement that there were sites where domestic restrictions could be evaded, and which were becoming too numerous to regulate informally, is important. A 1618 complaint by City politicians about the 'multitude of alehouses and victualling houses' within the walls moreover implies that the service of food as well as of drink in commercial establishments was by then a factor used to differentiate such establishments.[42] Nevertheless, a 1663/64 enumeration of 'Vintners, Tablekeepers, Innholders, Cooks [and] Victuallers' within the City wards, taken in 1663/64, containing 1,788 names, remains tantalizing, as it contains only infrequent indications of what an individual's **particular** calling might be.[43] So, while official documentation prioritizes the metropolis's inns, taverns and alehouses as victuallers in the static legal sense of the word, it is to the profusion of businesses which overlapped with these establishments, and where food provision was crucial if not key to the service provided, that we must turn for a sense of how London was catered for.

Perhaps distinguishing between categories such as 'eating house', 'cookshop' and 'ordinary'[44] is irrelevant, in a period when terminology (beyond the legal) could be so fluid, and standards so variable. The forty-six eating houses in and around Westminster visited by Charles Bennet, second Baron Ossulston of Uppark, between 1703 and 1712 while he attended the House of Lords[45] were far removed in quality from the holes in the wall, 'denned in secluded alleys, or back courts, silent and sombre ... devoted to the business of mastication'.[46] A 1785 poem by 'James Smith', celebrating the art of frugal living for the metropolitan novice, acknowledges even more basic facilities in St Giles, where 'the knives are chain'd, and ladder forms the stairs', and in Moorfields, 'where wretched paupers ply / Round clothless tables in an open sky'. Whether these were 'eating houses' or 'ordinaries' is perhaps less important than where they were, and whom they served.[47]

The least fixed victualling presence in the early modern city was that of the itinerant food seller. The folklore of street selling owes much to nineteenth-century antiquarian and reformers' embellishments, but the contribution of street vendors to the decline of the fixed metropolitan market in the preceding two centuries should not be underplayed nor should their role in influencing non-elite appetites and access to ready-made foods. In the wake of the destruction of much of the city and its eastern fringes by the 1666 fire, street hawkers were indispensable, and the first half of the eighteenth century was arguably a 'golden age' for them.[48]

Such trading was hardly remunerative, and to maintain a constant street presence, hawkers were well known for their multiple identities, depending on the hour, or the movement of the seasons.[49] Both staples and speciality foods were hawked. Series of illustrated 'Cries of London', amongst the most popular prints published in the late seventeenth century, depicted sellers of 'Hott bak'd Wardens, hott', 'Dutch bisket' and neats' feet.[50] Strategic selling locales were joined by ingenious sales tricks. In an early modern version of the modern supermarket practice of supplying free recipes with unusual foodstuffs, hawkers sold novel market garden produce – early asparagus, sea kale, soft fruit – ready packaged with instructions for preparation and 'dressing it up'.[51]

The evidence of such variety, albeit supported with sparse quantitative data, suggests a highly adapted metropolitan market for ready-made food retailing, one that could cater for every pocket. But this is slightly misleading for the period before the Restoration. Rigorous attempts were made to control ready-made food provision for economic and ethical ends, both in victualling establishments and by regulation of the open market and its prices.[52] The Cooks' Company (chartered in 1480) battled to shore up its jurisdiction over the distinctive 'art and mystery' of cookery. Never one of the more influential liveries, its active members were drawn from practitioners who ran cook-shops, made pastry goods and confectionery or were cooks in private households. Against a backdrop of declining enrolments into the eighteenth century, frequent territorial battles over the right to prepare and sell food were fought with other free practitioners, such as members of the Bakers' and Vintners' companies.[53] These battles intensified when other interests, notably the Crown, stepped in. Charles I's negotiations with the wealthy Vintners' Company for loans during the 1630s were larded with threats to prohibit company members from preparing and selling cooked food; their eventual compliance was rewarded with a grant to dress victuals without hindrance.[54]

How do we move from such political wrangling, from the slippery terminologies of victualling and from general occupational data, to give substance to important victualling locales such as the Pie Corner cookshops, frequented by Smithfield marketgoers, or to the large taverns of 'Broad St Giles' and the increasing number of eating houses in the tenement cellars and courtyards off Monmouth Street and Drury Lane, (re-)fuelling the public for other neighbourhood entertainments like the theatre?[55] Misson's oft-quoted description of a London cookshop, its limited menu and methods of serving meat, complements inventory listings of equipment owned by decedents described as cooks.[56] Roger Parks, of St Martin's in the Fields, died in 1688 in possession of goods including:

> a jack, weight and chaine, a range in the chimney ... 3 racks, 3 spitts, 2 dripping pans, a pair of tongs and a fork, 2 porridge pots, 3 kettles, 2 saucepans, a brasse ladle, a brasse skimmer ... a brasse mortar, 3 brasse pot lids, a brasse cullender [colander], a gridiron ... 12 pewter dishes, 4 pewter pots [possibly drinking vessels], an old couch, a joynt stool, a chopping block, a little table, a little table, a wooden chair.

These goods, along with some candlesticks and lumber, were valued together at £4 10s, and comprised Parks's only kitchen utensils, and differ only in quantity from the furnishings of many contemporary domestic London kitchens.[57] On a more elegant scale was the business of Thomas Mitchell, also recorded as a cook of St Martin's in the Fields. Mitchell's 1677 inventory records fine brass pots, stewpans and saucepans, and 9 cwt of pewter in his shop (total contents valued at £6 19s), while on the first floor the appraisers noted the contents of two 'Dineing Roomes' which were probably for the use of Mitchell's clientele, furnished with upholstered chairs and tapestry wallhangings.[58]

Cooks' establishments like Mitchell's were no doubt set up along the lines envisaged by Campbell in his guide to London trades.[59] Careful reading of other victuallers' inventories can likewise indicate the culinary possibilities of the taverns, inns, ordinaries and eating houses they ran.[60] But the character and demands of interstitial victualling, associated with non-traditional working practices (embodied most clearly in the prominence of women amongst victualling workers) and non-traditional locales beyond company and Crown jurisdiction, are not recorded in such manuals, nor in probate appraisals. Steeped as we are in a 'fast-food culture', this abundance of food facilities may strike us as a ready and accommodating response to the needs of the metropolitan population. But a demand born of necessity does not necessarily produce a service entirely 'public' in its ends.

CATERING FOR NECESSITY OR CONVENIENCE?

In 1700, after divine service, a (fictional) pedestrian might proceed to a London bookseller's, where he was 'in hopes of getting a Dinner and a Bottle'. But as Thomas Brown, the pedestrian's sardonic guide to London, noted, the hungry visitor was more often than not disappointed with 'a Dish of Coffee and the old talk that trading was dead'. In the 'prodigious and noisy city', food and its procurement were an omnipresent activity, but one not always founded upon a positive construction of convenience: convenience as the hallmark of choice, access and ease.[61]

The ready availability of victuals around the clock certainly suggests itself as one criterion of 'convenience eating'; unsurprisingly, Campbell's estimate of the length of the working day for London tradesmen gives cooks' hours as 'uncertain'.[62] The oyster girls who frequented the entrances to taverns and alehouses could be seen at their 'stations' throughout the day, from noon, when Robert Nichols saw Peter Noakes, accused of murder, run through the door of a Charing Cross tavern, 'where our oyster girl was putting up her oysters', to late in the evening, when Sarah Thompson, an oyster girl at an alehouse in the Hermitage, recalled having seen John Smith walk past her into the building prior to his fatal attack on a customer in 1722.[63] John Perry, a pastrycook, was still hard at work at six on the evening of 27 October 1731, when Elizabeth Bird came to his shop and ordered several pies to be sent to a Ludgate Hill inn.[64] Nocturnal victualling was a common focus of neighbourhood complaint; John Utting of St Martin's in the Fields went before a Jury of Annoyances in March 1614 for permitting unruly consumption at his ordinary during 'all hours in the night'.[65]

Even when there was no set 'ordinary' to be served, or supplies had been exhausted, hosts were willing to feed certain patrons. Lacy Ryan, 'gentleman', came to a Long Acre tavern around half past nine in the evening of 20 June 1718, and 'enquiring what they had for dinner, and being answered that they had nothing left, he desired that something might be got for him'. A tavern servant was sent out to fetch a dish, and returned to witness Ryan's killing of another customer.[66] In another case of murder at a Holborn hostelry, the landlord recalled that, he and his wife having dined, one Saunders 'came in, [and] I asked him if he had dined? He said, No. Upon which I offer'd him a piece of mutton pasty which had been set by in the Bar, and he accepted of it.'[67]

Such availability surely acted as a powerful solvent on fixed mealtimes, as well as sanctioning 'snacking'. It comes as no surprise that this term gained significant currency in the late seventeenth century, attaching to those food-stuffs that increasingly occupied the interstices of structured eating. Snacking was accepted – indeed, expected – in communities where regular mealtimes and a secure domestic location for eating were simply not viable. What the above cases also suggest, however, is that the ever-ready tavern table was really accessible only to a few; 'snacking' was itself structured by money and status. Ryan and Saunders were both described in terms of higher social standing than their hosts, and are treated accordingly. Treatment of clients arguably depended on the latter's ability to convince the host of position as much as upon demonstration of ability to pay.[68]

The ability to ape persons of position, whether in manner or *goût*, to secure access to food or seclusion (as a prelude to theft) was a common deception. Robert Car, alias Ramsey, indicted of stealing a silver spoon from the Cross Keys tavern in Holborn, came there on 21 October 1734 in company and ordered supper. They consumed 'several pints of Wine, fowls and egg-sauce and Jellies', but in court the prisoner admitted that 'having called for more than we were able to pay, we slipp'd out'.[69] Such a ruse could of course run both ways. Ned Ward in *The London Spy* condemned grand Westminster eating houses (probably those frequented by Lord Ossulston): 'for every fop who with a small fortune attempts to counterfeit quality, and is fool enough to bestow twenty shillings' worth of sawce, upon Ten pennyworth of meat, resorts to one of these Ordinaries'.[70]

These establishments could charge highly for their reputations, and be selective about not only their clientele but what they served to whom, as Swift acidly noted in his pillorying of Pontack's, the famed City eating house. His narrator-customer Lindo, the country knight who has not been to the city for forty years, and who wants nothing more than a beefsteak, is unimpressed by 'a Ragoust of fatted snails' offered him instead: 'Adieu Pontack, for I foresee / Thou'lt never take Penny more of me; / If this be counted Eating well, / I never shall in Taste excell.' Even here, patron–client relations were not necessarily constructed upon the precedence of the consumer.[71]

Away from such institutions, and the purse and (real or assumed) persona required to patronize them, experiences of eating out were decidedly more prosaic. The *London Spy's* picaresque description of what was on offer in Smithfield's many cookshops – 'measly Pork and Neck beef stood out in wooden Platters, adorn'd with Carrots, and garnish'd with the leafs of Mary-golds' – may exaggerate for effect. But he exemplified in such depictions locales where quantity, rather than quality, and speed rather than polished service, were paramount.[72]

Convenience for the more humble customer perhaps came in other forms, for in certain establishments they were not limited to eating food prepared and paid for on site. The array of culinary equipment owned by victuallers meant that tavern and alehouse kitchens were frequently used as intermediate locations for food preparation, either by householders short on hearth space or fuel, or by patrons who brought food from other sources to accompany their drinking. Thomas Rawlings, who was killed by the landlord of the Feathers alehouse in Holborn, on 7 October 1725, had 'come into the ... house ... and brought a couple of rabbits, which he order'd to be roasted for supper': these may have been purchased already skinned and gutted from a nearby hawker.[73]

A more insidious, customer-catching interaction between victualling suppliers is implied in other arrangements. The oysters sold at tavern doors usefully stimulated thirst, while hostelries were (literally) good feeding grounds for itinerant food traders, like Susannah Anderson, who frequented West-minster public houses 'with a basket of Pyes to sell'.[74] A 1641 pamphlet deploring the re-emergence of a strictly observed Sabbath had Leatherbeard reminiscing to Rubynose about the profits realised by their late mistress 'by her thin-cut slices of roast beef at prayer time; and how I sold the ale and beer at that time at double prices'. There is clearly nothing novel about the 'free' salty bar snacks provided in modern pubs.[75]

If the necessity underpinning much provisioning ensured that much extra-domestic eating was not primarily sociable, is the link we so easily make between 'eating out' and leisure in the modern period inadmissible for the early modern? The answer has to be a qualified 'no'. Experiences of eating away from home in the course of the working day significantly shaped a growing non-elite consciousness of the locations and composition of oppor-tunities for non-necessary, 'leisure-time' commensality and consumption.[76]

Speciality foods and 'treats' had long been a feature of extraordinary events like Bartholomew Fair.[77] Cookshops, ordinaries and taverns were often venues for sociable eating in connection with rite of passage celebrations, and for ritual occasions such as vestry and county feasts.[78] But these environments were not places for exclusively 'leisured' consumption of food, a phenomenon intimately intertwined with the development of places of resort – spas, promenades, museums of 'curiosities' – distanced from locales of labour. It was this efflorescence, and the role of eating and drinking within such establishments, that contemporary critics decried as the chief cause of the emasculation of the metropolitan labouring population.[79]

Key locations for captive consumers decried in *Low-Life, or, the One Half Knows not how the Other Half Live*, a bleak mid-eighteenth-century view of a Sunday spent amongst the labouring sort, were 'the new breakfasting hutt near Sadlers' Wells, crowded with young fellows and their sweethearts ... drinking tea and coffee', and the 'eel-pie shops' located at the Bromley ferry over the river Lea. Perhaps the most striking example of a novel eating establishment was the bun house. In 'Chelsea, Stepney, Stangate, Marybone [Marylebone]' early on Sunday morning, *Low-Life* observed the bun house bakers 'heating the ovens, cleaning the windows, kneading of dough'.[80] A trade card of *c.* 1718 claimed that Richard Hand of Chelsea was the 'oldest original Chelsey Bunn baker', while David Loudon's clearly rival establishment, 'the Bunn House', advertised around 1730, provided an adjacent museum of curiosities. Ancillary attractions seem unnecessary, however, if the estimate of 50,000 customers on Good Fridays at such establishments at the end of the seventeenth century is at all credible.[81] The popularity of such locales, 'very full of customers, noise, smoke and children', surely explain the less than relaxed expressions of Hogarth's weary 'cit' strollers, departing Sadlers' Wells, in the 'Evening' image from his 1736 'Times of the Day' series.[82]

The moral premise of *Low-Life* is the recovery of Sunday seemliness, and what makes the text such a valuable document for the study of London eating out is its location of sociability around food and drink at the heart of Sabbath-breaking.[83] In this it dovetails usefully with evidence on prosecutions for working on the Sabbath in London's Middlesex parishes; half of those accused of Sabbath labour between 1660 and 1725 were victuallers, bakers and fruiterers.[84] This occupational concentration emphasizes the modest living scraped from many such concerns and the need to be open at all hours, as several prosecutions from the Hackney petty sessions in the 1750s attest. But it also surely reflects demand. For larger establishments the penalties for operating on a Sunday were paltry compared with what could be earned from illicit custom. Ann Kemp, landlady of a substantial tavern on the edge of London Fields, was prosecuted during the 1750s on several occasions for serving drink and baking cakes on the Sabbath, but the 5s she was fined on each occasion did not even merit her attendance before the justices.[85]

Bun houses, breakfasting huts and tea gardens drew the ire of the likes of Daniel Defoe as the locales that lured the spendthrift servant, sponsoring tastes and deportment out of kilter with sobriety and thrift. They were arche-typal venues of visibility, where new shoe buckles might be paraded, their more fashionable successors first spied.[86] But they were also locales which existed in great part *because of* such customers, who sought escape from garrets and lodgings on days off, and whose disposable income, apparent lack of long-term financial objectives and cultivation of dietary habits paralleling, if not equalling, those of their masters and mistresses, surely underpinned expenditure on petty (edible) luxuries.[87] What is also striking is that these establish-ments are far more demotic than the spaces for selective social mingling often described as the cornerstones of 'urban renaissance'. Unlike assembly rooms, bun houses and breakfast huts opened their doors and their menus to all paying customers – the crux of the matter, as commentators observed.

Of course, commercial venues like these did not eradicate *domestic* socia-bility around food. The character of domestic eating nevertheless underwent a realignment with extra-domestic experiences, a shift evidenced in the material culture of inventories (Table 11.2). In this same sample, by the second quarter of the eighteenth century, no fewer than nine households were recorded with dining rooms.[88] Given the spatial pressures already discussed above, the presence of a dining room implies a certain luxury of space, but it arguably

Table 11.2 Presence of goods by ranked frequency, in St Sepulchre and St Giles in the Fields parishes inventories, 1660–1740

1660–80		1690–1710		1720–40	
Object	*Frequency*	*Object*	*Frequency*	*Object*	*Frequency*
Fireirons	38	Spits	42	Saucepans	48
Spits	36	Firegrate	41	Pewter plates	44
Roasting jack	35	Roasting jack	41	Pewter dishes	43
Brass kettles	34	Frying pans	35	Roasting jack	39
Iron pots	33	Saucepans	33	Ceramics[a]	38
Frying pans	28	Pewter dishes	31	Spits	37
Skillets	26	Pewter plates	30	Gridiron	34
Pewter dishes	26	Brass pots	28	Drinking pots	32
Pewter porringers	23	Gridirons	26	Trivets	31
Pewterwares[b]	22	Drinking pots	25	Hot drinks goods[c]	29

Notes Each period sample comprised fifty inventories. [a]'Ceramics' includes all specified and unspecified assemblages of earthen- and stonewares, but not porcelain china. [b]'Pewterwares' denotes parcels of unspecified pewter recorded in inventories, which could contain both table and hearth goods. [c]'Hot drinks goods' denotes equipment for preparing and consuming tea, coffee, chocolate, etc.

Source GL MSS 9174, 9186, Commissary Court inventories for St Sepulchre and St Giles in the Fields parishes, 1660–1740. For further details see Pennell, 'Material culture', pp. 178–80, appendix I.

also suggests a set of priorities which rated commensal displays as highly significant within domestic bounds.

Certainly, the possession of new tablewares does not entail regular (or any) use, nor does the eating of a particular dish in a cookshop inevitably lead to the acquisition of a taste that had to be regularly indulged domestically. But the parameters and the expectations of domestic consumption were reframed. The death of Hannah Brinsden at the hands of her husband Matthias was similarly prompted by little more than Hannah's desire to have some meat for her supper. As Brinsden himself testified:

> my Wife said, What! Must I have no victuals, but bread and cheese for supper as well as for breakfast and Dinner? Why my girl, says I, can't you eat the same as I and the children eat? No says she, I want a bit of meat for I have had none today. Child, says I, be satisfied tonight and we will have some meat tomorrow. No, says she, I won't stay until tomorrow, I'll have some now, and if I can't have it at home, I'll go out and get it.

Such cases highlight the difficulties of sustaining domestic sufficiency in an environment where entitlement and access to food were shaped by more than simply market availability. Brinsden confessed that, in order to escape his wife's scolding, and moments before her stabbing occurred, he had cut off 'a heel of the loaf and a piece of the cheese ... intending to go to the ale-house that I might eat my supper in peace'. The alehouse and its alternatives are here cast as locations which at once compounded the shortcomings of domestic life in the metropolis but also offered themselves as an inevitable substitute.[89]

CONCLUSION
FOOD FOR ALL?

The boasts of London's apologists notwithstanding, not all the city's population was abundantly furnished with victuals, and not all city inhabitants could afford a sixpenny ordinary. Yet there was still another level of food 'retailing' to which the hungry and indigent London inhabitant could turn. What, for want of a more appetising description, might be called the recycling of foodstuffs and meals was a natural by-product of the city's perceived collective stomach. 'Broken victuals' were one of the perquisites claimed by domestic servants, by which their critics characterized the decadence of household oeconomy under servile domination.[90] Daniel Defoe was pointedly direful in his warnings to employers about the practices of servants, who might 'maintain one, two, or more Persons from your Table'. Particularly to be watched were shoe-cleaners, or 'Blackguards':

> if you keep a Table, [you] ... are well-off if [he] has no more than his own Diet from it. I have often observed these Rascals sneaking from Gentleman's doors with Wallets, or hats, full of good Victuals, which they either carry to their Trulls, or sell for a Trifle.[91]

This clandestine passage of left-overs was not an insubstantial trade. It supplied, for example, the chief currency of the Rosemary Lane rag fair: 'The chief customers were Mumpers [rag-dealers] and people as Ragged as themselves, who came to barter scraps for patches; ... it was a very currant swop, to change Food for Rayment.'[92] The *necessity* of food 'perquisites', or simply the temptation of left-overs, for many servants and employees is conveyed in the confession of Mary Herbert. Employed to wash dishes at a St Dunstan's in the West tavern, she was caught stealing pewter and napery from the kitchen, and confessed that 'she being a poor Woman had carried them away with broken Victuals'.[93]

Servants were not the only conduit by which broken victuals left the homes of the well-off. In 1734, also spurred on by hunger, and perhaps remembering the good table at Gerard Bothomley's, William Jellard broke into his former master's house. Jellard claimed he had been in search of victuals, but his defence was countered by the testimony of a current servant, who deposed that 'he [Jellard] knew my Master kept no victuals in the house, but order'd all to be given away'.[94] Bothomley's donation of broken victuals possibly found its way to one of London's prisons, where such foodstuffs were the preserve of impoverished prisoners, unable to afford the crippling fees so often charged by their gaolers for meals and sundries, or not equipped to cater for themselves.[95] Amongst eighteenth-century 'Cries of London' images are at least two portraits of male hawkers collecting 'broken bread and meat for the poor prisoners'.[96] How successful these collections were, and who ultimately benefited from the victuals – prisoners or hawker – is unclear. However, a 1702 report to the Middlesex quarter sessions regarding the ill treatment of debtors imprisoned in the Common Side of Newgate noted that 'there is charity beef sent in and moneys collected and sent for their relief and divided amongst them', but that these benevolences were being embezzled by certain favoured prisoners.[97]

The dietary regimens of the inmates of London's growing number of welfare institutions, with their repercussions on moral as well as physical status, are a subject in their own right.[98] But the city's prisoners, and the difficulties they faced securing provision, offer a compelling image of just how the consumption and commodification of food could not be simply a matter of indulging tastes, stimulating dietary expectations, and sociability. The detritus of London's 'universal stomack' was sought for those most inconvenienced and necessitous of London residents: the indebted, the accused, and the convicted. Their uncertain passage to the inmates of Newgate and London's other prisons embodies the concerns of status, accessibility, (in)convenience and need which underwrote the differing eating experiences encountered in early modern, ever-consuming 'Londinopolis'.

The preoccupation of much metropolitan history with institutional, religious, mercantile and communal concerns is founded upon the difficulty of reconstructing the domestic in metropolitan life. The constructions of commensality and the commercialization of hospitality explored here are not incompatible with viewing eating out and the consumption of ready-made foods as leisure activities, or as components crucial to the forms non-elite leisure practices assumed. Nevertheless, they suggest that leisured eating, or non-essential consumption, was defined extensively through but substantively in distinction from, consumption provoked by necessity, inconvenience or isolation. Locales of leisured eating were clearly escapist venues, where the anonymizing bonds of labouring life in the capital might be temporarily laid aside, and in which an otherwise fragmentary social cohesion might be sought through sociability; they capitalized on conceptions of food, forged for the consumer in the midst of necessity.[99]

'Public cookery', to recall Fitzstephen, might be an indicator of civilization, but it was indubitably also a negative consequence of such 'civilization'. For those who came to the capital seeking a Cockayne of gilded gingerbread, as well as employment, and for those residents whose labouring lives left few opportunities to secure a domestic sufficiency at their own hearths, 'great quantities of gooseberry pye, and baked clod of beef, sold among draymen, slop-shop women, barkers to sale-shops, botching taylors and journeymen translators in the range of cookshops in Broad St Giles' could be enjoyed, ephemerally and ambivalently, as the civilizing fruits of a truly metropolitan existence.[100]

NOTES

1 *Londinopolis*, p. 348.

2 *Newsweek*, 128:19 (November 1996), pp. 44–9.

3 Vanessa Harding, 'The population of London 1550–1700: a review of the published evidence', *LJ*, 15 (1990), pp. 112–15.

4 *Londinopolis*, pp. 347–8.

5 F. J. Fisher, 'The development of the London food market 1540–1640', reprinted in E. M. Carus-Wilson ed., *Essays in Economic History*, I (1954); *id.*, 'The development of London as a centre of conspicuous consumption in the sixteenth and seventeenth centuries', reprinted in Carus-Wilson, *Essays in Economic History*; E. A.Wrigley, 'A simple model of London's importance 1650–1750', reprinted in Philip Abrams and Wrigley eds, *Towns in Societies: Essays in Economic History and Historical Sociology* (Cambridge, 1978). A useful, but still trade-focused critique of Wrigley is offered in J. A. Chartres, 'Food consumption and internal trade', in Beier and Finlay, *London*.

6 For an ambitious attempt to analyse the foodways of another great early modern city see Daniel Roche, *The People of Paris: an Essay in Popular Culture in the Eighteenth Century*, trans. Marie Evans (Leamington Spa, 1987), pp. 242–68.

7 Robert Ashton, 'Popular entertainment and social control in later Elizabethan and early Stuart London', *LJ*, 9 (1983), p. 10.

8 Cf. the relative neglect of this subject in metropolitan studies like M. Dorothy George, *London Life in the Eighteenth Century* (Harmondsworth, 1965); Peter Earle, *The Making of the English Middle Class: Business, Society and Family Life in London 1660–1730* (1991), pp. 271–82. A thesis by Karen Hopkin, 'The victualling trades in London 1666 to 1730, with special reference to cookshops', London School of Economics M.Sc. thesis (1980), supervised and quoted by Earle, has proved impossible to locate. It is hoped this chapter does not rehearse too much of the material presented there.

9 Penelope Corfield, *The Impact of English Towns 1700–1800* (Oxford, 1982), chap. 8; Jonathan Barry, 'Provincial town culture 1640–1780: urbane or civic?', in J. Pittock and A.Wear eds, *Interpretation and Cultural History* (Basingstoke, 1991); Peter Borsay, 'Cultural diffusion and the eighteenth-century provincial town', *LJ*, 19 (1994).

10 Paul Seaver, *Wallington's World: a Puritan Artisan in Seventeenth Century London* (1985); GL MSS 205/1, 205/2, diary of Stephen Monteage, 1733, 1738. Cf. Peter Earle, 'The middling sort in London', in Jonathan Barry and Christopher Brooks eds, *The Middling*

Sort of People: Culture, Society and Politics in England 1550–1800 (Basingstoke, 1994), and Lorna Weatherill, *Consumer Behaviour and Material Culture in Britain 1660–1760* (1988), pp. 47–51.

11 See Gowing in Chapter 7 and John Schofield, *The Building of London from the Conquest to the Great Fire* (1984); F. E. Brown, 'Continuity and change in the urban house: developments in domestic space organisation in seventeenth-century London', *Comparative Studies in History and Society*, 28 (1986). Cf. John Landers's epidemiological approach in *Death in the Metropolis: Studies in the Demographic History of London 1670–1830* (Cambridge, 1993).

12 Sara Pennell, 'The material culture of food in early modern England *c.* 1650–1750', University of Oxford D.Phil. thesis (1997), pp. 1–14, 66–128, 227–55.

13 Jean-Louis Flandrin and Philip Hyman, 'Regional tastes and cuisines: problems, documents and discourses on food in southern France in the sixteenth and seventeenth centuries', *Food and Foodways*, 1 (1986); Ashton, 'Popular entertainment', p. 10. Cf. Annette Hope, *Londoners' Larder: English Cuisine from Chaucer to the Present* (Edinburgh, 1990), pp. 55–72; Sara Paston-Williams, *The Art of Dining: a History of Cooking and Eating* (1993), chap. 3.

14 Valerie Pearl, 'Change and stability in seventeenth-century London', *LJ*, 5 (1979).

15 *Stow*, Wheatley, p. 504, quoting Wheatley's translation of Fitzstephen's *Description of London*; Felicity Heal, *Hospitality in Early Modern England* (Oxford, 1990), pp. 300–1, 306, 351, 387–8; Peter Clark, *The English Alehouse: a Social History 1200–1830* (1983), pp. 133–4.

16 M. J. Power, 'East and west in early modern London', in E. W. Ives, R. J. Knecht and J. J. Scarisbrick eds, *Wealth and Power in Tudor England: Essays presented to S. T. Bindoff* (1978).

17 D. A. Kent, 'Ubiquitous but invisible: female domestic servants in mid-eighteenth-century London', *HWJ*, 28 (1989); Tim Meldrum, 'Domestic Service in London 1660–1750: Gender, Life Cycle, Work and Household Relations', University of London Ph.D. thesis (1996).

18 This term is used as shorthand for the main food preparation space in a dwelling, but it was by no means universally used in the early modern period.

19 Schofield, *Building of London*, pp. 75, 91, 179; John Schofield ed., *The London Surveys of Ralph Treswell*, London Topographical Society, 135 (1987); Brown, 'Urban house'; Alan Thompson, Francis Grew and John Schofield, 'Excavations at Aldgate, 1974', *Post-medieval Archaeology*, 18 (1984); Boulton, *Neighbourhood*, pp. 194–5.

20 Schofield, *Treswell*, p. 20. Hearth Tax returns (1664) for St Giles in the Fields record only seven dwellings with chargeable ovens, while none is recorded in St Sepulchre: LMA MR/TH/1 and 2, Hearth Tax Returns, Holborn and Finsbury divisions, 1664.

21 Schofield, *Treswell*, pp. 19–20.

22 Pennell, 'Material culture', pp. 184, 239, 246.

23 James Peller Malcolm, *Anecdotes of the Manners and Customs of London during the Eighteenth Century ... with a Review of the State of Society in 1807* (2 vols, 1810), II, pp. 414–15.

24 *Proceedings at the Sessions of Peace, and Oyer and Terminer for the City of London and Middlesex ... 8, 9, 10, 11 and 13 December 1731* (1731), p. 6.

25 *Proceedings at the Sessions of Peace, and Oyer and Terminer for the City of London and Middlesex ... 15,17, 18 and 19 January 1732* (1732), p. 47.

26 George, *London Life*, pp. 224–35; Earle, *Middle Class*, pp. 101–2 (esp. n. 36).

27 Manuscripts of M. L. S. Clements, in *HMC Various Collections*, VIII (1913), p. 219.

28 J. J. Hecht, *The Domestic Servant in Eighteenth Century England* (reprinted, 1980), pp. 130–5; Kent, 'Female domestic servants', p. 123.

29 *Proceedings at the Sessions of the Peace and Oyer and Terminer for the City of London and Middlesex ... 24, 25 and 26 April [1734]* (1734), p. 118.

30 For non-metropolitan tabling see Donald Woodward, *Men at Work: Labourers and Building Craftsmen in the Towns of the North of England 1450–1750* (Cambridge, 1995), pp. 147–59.

31 Peter Earle, 'The female labour market in London in the late seventeenth and early eighteenth centuries', *EcHR*, second series, 42 (1989), pp. 338–9; Pamela Sharpe, *Adapting to Capitalism: Working Women in the English Economy 1700–1850* (Basingstoke, 1996), pp. 1, 4, 16–17.

32 *Proceedings at the Sessions of the Peace and Oyer and Terminer for the City of London and Middlesex ... 2, 3, 4, 5 and 7 July 1735* (1735), p. 102.

33 Despite the Cooks' Company prohibition on binding girls as apprentices: GL MS 9994/3, fo. 24v; Pennell, 'Material culture', pp. 210–14, 219.

34 *Proceedings of the King's Commission of Peace and Oyer and Terminer for the City of London and Middlesex ... 25, 26, 27 and 28 February 1718/19* (1719), p. 3. See also Daniel Defoe's defence of the 'poor industrious woman' in *Augusta Triumphans: or, the Way to Make London the most Flourishing City in the Universe* (1728), p. 30.

35 Pennell, 'Material culture', chap. 3. Cf. Earle, *Making of the Middle Class*, pp. 52–6, 273; Peter Borsay, *The Urban Renaissance: Culture and Society in the Provincial Town 1660–1770* (Oxford, 1991), pp. 230–1, 274.

36 Strype, *Stow*, I, pp. 239–46, 282–3, II, pp. 75–85; William Maitland, *History and Survey of London* (2 vols, 1756), II, pp. 965–6, 989, 1180, 1362; John Parton, *Some Account of the Hospital and Parish of St Giles in the Fields, Middlesex* (1822), pp. 107–8, 153, 303–5; George, *London Life*, pp. 41–2, 114, 135, 138; Emrys Jones, 'London in the early seventeenth century: an ecological approach', *LJ*, 6 (1980), pp. 124–5, 131–2. Population figures (St Sepulchre for 1695, and 1711 for St Giles) given in George, *London Life*, pp. 408–9.

37 Thomas R. Forbes, 'Weaver and cordwainer: occupations in the parish of St Giles Cripplegate, London, 1654–93, 1729–43', *Guildhall Studies in London History*, 4 (1979).

38 A. L. Beier, 'Engine of manufacture: the trades of London', in Beier and Finlay, *London*, pp. 147–8.

39 Clark, *Alehouse*, pp. 5–14, 21–34, 39–63.

40 *Ibid.*, pp. 10–11, 132–5, 227–9.

41 Proclamations of 16 January 1548 and of 9 March 1552, in Paul L. Hughes and James F. Larkin eds, *Tudor Royal Proclamations*, I, *The Early Tudors 1485–1553* (New Haven CT, 1964), pp. 413, 511.

42 Clark, *Alehouse*, p. 49.

43 CLRO MS208A, Recognizances of vintners, tablekeepers, innholders, cooks, victuallers, etc., for the City wards, 1660/61 and 1663/64, pp. 197–284.

44 The victualling connotations of this word – a place where a fixed-price set meal could be had – are significantly sixteenth-century in origin.

45 Clyve Jones, 'The London life of a peer in the reign of Queen Anne: a case study from Lord Ossulston's diary', *LJ*, 16 (1992), p. 145.

46 'London eating houses', *Chambers' Edinburgh Journal*, 282 (24 June 1837), pp. 173–4.

47 'James Smith', *The Art of Living in London: a Poem* (1768), p. 17.

48 Maitland, *Survey of London*, I, p. 301; Stephen Macfarlane, 'Social policy and the poor in the later seventeenth century', in Beier and Finlay, *London*, p. 260; Boulton, *Neighbourhood*, p. 76; Sean Shesgreen ed., *The Cries and Hawkers of London: Engravings and Drawings by Marcellus Laroon* (Aldershot, 1990), p. 22; Archer, *Pursuit*, pp. 200–3.

49 Although the goods they sold might be well beyond their own purses: Shesgreen, *Cries*, pp. 37, 116.

50 Shesgreen, *Cries*, pp. xii, 12–15; BODL JJ, Trades and Professions, Box 1, series 1, nos 3, 39, and Box 4, no. 144 ('*Cries of London*', 1711: Peter Tempest edition of Laroon).

51 Dorothy Davis, *A History of Shopping* (1966), p. 204; Malcolm Thick, *The Neat House Gardens: Early Market Gardening around London* (Totnes, 1998), pp. 147–56.

52 A. B. Robertson, 'The open market in the City of London in the eighteenth century', *East London Papers*, 1 (1958); Ian Archer, Caroline Barron and Vanessa Harding eds., *Hugh Alley's Caveat: the Markets of London in 1598*, London Topographical Society, 137 (1988), pp. 5–7, 11–17, 23–5.

53 GL, MSS 3111/1, fos 46v, 105, 243, 259; 9994/4, fo. 71. See also Sylvia Thrupp, *A Short History of the Worshipful Company of Bakers of London* (1933), pp. 67, 117; William F. Kahl, 'The Cooks' Company in the eighteenth century', *Guildhall Miscellany*, 2 (1961).

54 [John Rushworth], *Mr Rushworths Historical Collections Abridg'd and Improv'd ...* (6 vols, 1703–08), II, pp. 340–1.

55 Strype, *Stow*, I, p. 283; Parton, *St Giles*, pp. 237–43; George, *London Life*, pp. 54, 322; *A to Z of Restoration London* (City of London, 1676), with introductory notes by Ralph Hyde (1992).

56 [Henri Misson], *M. Misson's Memoirs and Observations in his Travels over England, with some Account of Scotland and Ireland, Written Originally in French and Translated by Mr Ozell* (1719), pp. 146–7. Earle cites the same observations, suggesting Misson was describing a 'high-class' cookshop, but there is nothing in the original to support this classification: Earle, *Making of the Middle Class*, p. 56.

57 Total inventory value (excluding debts owed and owing), £52 11s 6d: LMA AM/PI (1) 1688/17. Decedents described in their inventories as cooks may not have been members of the Cooks' Company, of course; the absence of company apprenticeship enrolments and freedom records for much of the seventeenth century makes this difficult to corroborate.

58 Total inventory value (minus lease) £167 14s: LMA AM/PI (1) 1677/45.

59 R. Campbell, *The London Tradesman, being a Compendious View of all the Trades, Professions, Arts ... Now Practised in the City of London and Westminster* (1747), pp. 276–8.

60 For example, see GL MSS 9186/4, inventory of William Bates, victualler, St Sepulchre, 1732 (copper fish kettle, salamander); 9186/4, inventory of Dorothy Coleman, widow and victualler, of the Golden Lion, St Sepulchre, 1740 (funnel, salamander, cheese plates, steak tongs).

61 [Thomas Brown], *Amusements Serious and Comical, Calculated for the Meridian of London, by Mr Brown* (1700), p. 127.

62 Campbell, *London Tradesman*, p. 333.

63 *Select Trials at the Sessions House in the Old Bailey* (2 vols, New York and London, 1985) I, p. 130; II, p. 317.

64 *Proceedings ... December 1731*, p. 8.

65 William Le Hardy ed., *Calendar to the Sessions Records, County of Middlesex, new series, I, 1612–1614* (1935), p. 382.

66 *Proceedings at the Sessions of the Peace and Oyer and Terminer for the City of London and Middlesex ... 10, 11 and 12 September 1718* (1718), p. 6.

67 *Select Trials*, II, p. 128.

68 Peter Thompson, '"The friendly glass": drink and gentility in colonial Philadelphia', *Pennsylvania Magazine of History and Biography*, 113 (1989), and personal communication. November 1993.

69 *Proceedings at the Sessions of Peace and Oyer and Terminer for the City of London and Middlesex ... 4, 5, 6 and 7 December 1734* (1734), pp. 15–16.

70 Edward (Ned) Ward, *The London-Spy Compleat: in Eighteen Parts* (2 vols, c. 1700), I, part 9, p. 7.

71 'Pontack's', *Notes and Queries* 8th series, 7 (1895); [Jonathan Swift], *The Metamorphoses of the Town: or a View of the Present Fashions ...* (1731), pp. 11–13. See also Misson, *Memoirs*, p. 34.

72 Ward, *London Spy*, I, part 2, p. 14; part 5, p. 15.

73 *Select Trials*, I, p. 305; BODL JJ, Trades and Professions, Box 1, series 1, no. 27 ('Cries of London', 1711, Tempest edition).

74 *Proceedings ... 23, 24, 25 and 26 April 1718*, p. 6.

75 *The Tapster's Downfall and the Drunkard's Joy*, cited in George Dodd, *The Food of London: a Sketch* (1856), pp. 82–3. See also *A Dissertation upon Drunkenness ...* (1727), pp. 10–11; *Low-life, or, the One Half Knows not how the Other Half Live* (third edition, 1764), p. 32.

76 This point has been made in the context of servants' 'tastes' and their development, but wants emphasis within the broader spectrum of metropolitan victualling.

77 See, for example, Ben Jonson, *Bartholomew Fair*, The Revels Plays, ed. E. A. Horsman (Manchester, 1979), Act II, scene 2, lines 1–10, 32–3.

78 Newton Key, 'The political culture and political rhetoric of county feasts and feast sermons', *Journal of British Studies*, 33 (1994); Jones, 'London life', p. 144; GL MS 205/1, Monteage diary 1733, p. 157.

79 *Low-life*, pp. vi–vii.

80 *Ibid.*, p. 27.

81 Ambrose Heal, *London Tradesmen's Cards of the XVIIIth Century: an Account of their Origin and Use* (1925), pp. 68–9; Dodd, *Food of London*, p. 518.

82 *Low-life*, pp. 46, 72, 76–7; Sean Shesgreen, *Hogarth and the Times-of-the-Day Tradition* (Ithaca NY and London, 1983), pp. 99, 103, 118–19. Stephen Monteage was a weekly visitor to Sadlers' Wells, and an occasional visitor to Hornsey Woods: GL MS 205/2, Monteage diary 1738, p. 67 and *passim*.

83 W. B. Whitaker, *The Eighteenth Century English Sunday: a Study of Sunday Observance* (1940), pp. 121–50.

84 Robert B. Shoemaker, *Prosecution and Punishment: Petty Crime and the Law in London and Rural Middlesex, c. 1660–1725* (Cambridge, 1991), p. 251.

85 Ruth Paley ed., *Justice in Eighteenth Century Hackney: the Justicing Notebook of Henry Norris, and the Hackney Petty Sessions Book*, LRS, 28 (1991), pp. 185, 189–91.

86 [Daniel Defoe] Andrew Moreton, Esq., *Every-body's Business is Nobody's Business, or Private Abuses, Publick Grievances exemplified in the Pride, Insolence and Exorbitant Wages of Women-Servants, Footmen, Etc.* (fourth edition, 1725).

87 Eliza Haywood, *A Present for a Servant Maid*, 1743 (New York and London, 1985), pp. 31–2; Hecht, *Domestic Servant*, p. 223; Kent, 'Female servants', p. 123.

88 Of these only three are identifiably victuallers (out of forty-three inventories which specify room names): Pennell, 'Material culture', p. 239.

89 *Select Trials*, I, p. 243. This argument is developed at length in Alan Jay Epstein, 'The Social Function of the Alehouse in Early Modern London', New York University Ph.D. thesis (1977).

90 For comparable Parisian practices see Roche, *People of Paris*, p. 243.

91 [Defoe] Moreton, *Every-body's Business*, pp. 11–12, 26–7; Mr Zinzano, *The Servants Calling: with Some Advice to the Apprentice ...* (1725), pp. 35–6; Haywood, *Servant Maid*, pp. 29–31.

92 Ward, *London-Spy*, II, part 2, p. 10; *Low-life*, p. 61.

93 *Proceedings ... 23, 24, 25 and 26 April 1718*, pp. 3–4.

94 *Proceedings ... 24, 25 and 26 April 1734*, p. 106. See also *Low-Life*, p. 58 .

95 W. J. Sheehan, 'Finding solace in eighteenth-century Newgate', in J. S. Cockburn ed., *Crime in England 1550–1800* (1977), p. 233; Joanna Innes, 'The King's Bench prison in the later eighteenth century: law, authority and order in a London debtors' prison', in John Brewer and John Styles eds, *An Ungovernable People: the English and their Law in the Seventeenth and Eighteenth Centuries* (New Brunswick NJ, 1980), pp. 269–70, 273, 276.

96 BODL JJ, Trades and Professions, Box 5, nos 7–8.

97 William Le Hardy ed., *Middlesex County Records: Calendar of the Sessions Books 1689–1709* (1905), p. 244; Sheehan, 'Finding solace', p. 234.

98 One touched upon in Macfarlane, 'Studies in poverty', p. 304, and T. V. Hitchcock, 'The English workhouse: a study in institutional poor relief in selected counties 1696–1750', University of Oxford D.Phil. thesis (1985), pp. 166–77.

99 This interpretation is adapted from Anthony Sutcliffe, 'The growth of public intervention in the British urban environment during the nineteenth century: a structural approach', in James H. Johnson and Colin G. Pooley eds, *The Structure of Nineteenth Century Cities* (1982), p. 119. See also Clark, *Alehouse*, pp. 139, 223.

100 *Low-life*, p. 56.

Chapter 12

From conduit community to commercial network? Water in London, 1500–1725

Mark S. R. Jenner

THE MORAL ECONOMY OF THE CONDUIT

One day in either December 1629 or January 1630 Frances Humfreys went down to a Thamesside wharf in Wapping 'to ... drawe water' from the river. She found that it was impossible because a scaffold built by Peter Marsh blocked her way, and so she went back and complained to John Swanton, in whose house she was living. Swanton went down and confronted Marsh, protesting that 'he was annoyed by ... Marsh ... stopping of his water'. Marsh, witnesses agreed, was not conciliatory, lambasting Stanton as 'a sawcy Jacke ... a Copper nose drunckard', and as 'the basest fellowe in the p[ar]ish'.[1]

Historians of early modern London have used such disputes to explore notions of honour and honesty,[2] but the history of water in the early modern capital has attracted less attention.[3] Such relative neglect is surprising. Water, after all, was 'the blood of London', and water pipes its veins,[4] even though no Londoner could rely on a readily available and copious supply. Indeed, as a number of European and American studies have stressed, water was a scarce and valuable resource in all pre-industrial cities.[5] (Remarkably, water is not included in any cost of living index in British economic history.) Admittedly, its cost was not a major cash outlay for most households, although wealthier people and institutions did purchase water from water carriers. Livery company accounts, for instance, record payments to waterbearers among the expenses of their feasts,[6] while when the Apothecaries' Company reedified their Hall in the early 1630s they paid the waterbearers for hundreds of tankards of water to make lime and plaster.[7] For most households the cost of water lay in the hours spent fetching it, a task made even more arduous by the unreliable nature of many of the capital's sources. In 1601, for instance, Jane Harrison told Chancery how Elizabeth, the servant of her neighbour, Jane Pooley, went 'to fetche a payle of water' from the pump in the yard of the Boar's Head inn, Whitechapel, where Mrs Pooley rented lodgings. The pump was broken and 'she could have no water there'. Elizabeth confronted the wife of Oliver Woodlif [head tenant of the inn] and demanded 'how she should do for water, and how it chaunced the poomp was not mended, tellinge her that she well enoughe knewe that her m[ist]ress was to be allowed water there, and not to be driven to seeke yt any where els'. She was told that Woodlif had transferred his lease to Richard Samwell and that she should talk to him.[8]

The problems which she and Frances Humfreys experienced reveal how far access to water was mediated by the micropolitics and material culture of neighbourhood. Disruptions to either meant that Londoners were denied easy access to their supply. When John Coxe, a limeman, built a wharf by the Tower in 1589 he obstructed the brewers and others who came with carts to fetch water there. Early in James I's reign a minor riot in Swan Alley off Thames Street destroyed stairs there, inconveniencing all who 'did use to take water ... theire'.[9] Few histories of London water supply have concerned themselves with such minutiae; their approach has largely been top down, either retelling the lives of men like Sir Hugh Myddelton, founder of the New River Company,[10] or chronicling major technical innovations and the formation of new water companies.[11] In the words of Elaine Stratford, 'the history of water supply ... is written as a history of masculine achievement in the public sphere'.[12] Such studies have also separated the history of water supply from the wider themes of social and cultural history and from the broader political issues of access to the necessities of life.[13]

Clearly the Thames provided the water for a myriad London households like John Stanton's; many of those dwelling farther from the river obtained water from wells or pumps. In 1577 Sir Thomas Ramsey's house in Lombard Street, for instance, had a well yard next to the kitchen; so, too, did the London house of Sir William Garrard in 1571.[14] However, private sources, even ones shared between the inhabitants of a lane or alley, were by no means universal. They were normally closely guarded. In 1626 Sir John Holles wrote to his wife in outraged tones that in his absence the gardener's boy had 'suffered ... [all] who would, to fetche water, that the hows was as common as fleet-street conduyt'.[15]

Holles's comments reveal how sources of water were embedded within clusters of relationships which determined who could use particular sources. These social networks worked at many levels. Property owners might permit thirsty businesses to draw water from their well or Thamesside wharf. Early in Henry VIII's reign, for instance, Southwark brewers reached an agreement with the Bishop of Winchester, who permitted them to 'fetch water with theire Carts' from the wharf on his property there.[16] There were also agreements between households, and between landlords and tenants. The inn yard pump in Whitechapel bound households together in shared reliance upon this facility; people necessarily interacted around this common resource. As we have seen, Elizabeth was accompanied on her fruitless trip by Mrs Harryson, the wife of a local goldsmith. Alice Saunders, wife of a Whitechapel butcher, was also there and witnessed her discomfort.[17]

Such ties might constitute a literal politics of the parish pump. In the early sixteenth century many parishes maintained a well.[18] Over the next hundred years many were converted into pumps.[19] These reduced the danger to children,[20] and the risk of certain kinds of contamination, but, as Mrs Poley's servant discovered to her cost, they required regular maintenance. In the summer of 1590 the aldermen were even commanded to repair the common pumps in their wards 'wheare wells heretofore stoode Or els to cause the same ... to be made agayne'.[21] Some parishes (like St. Margaret Moses in the 1580s) organized collections for their upkeep.[22] Vestries regulated parochial supplies. In 1583, for example, the vestry of St. Martin's Ludgate decreed that only three waterbearers should work from the parish conduit in Old Bailey, that they must be men and should not use the labour of their wives or servants. If they carried water out of the parish they were to lose their position.[23]

Medieval mayors and aldermen similarly sought to construct a civic community by ensuring communal sources of water. Firstly, they guaranteed citizens' legal right of access to the Thames. In the 1270s it was ordered that lanes down to the river must be kept open; in 1417 owners of riverside wharves were forbidden from charging people going down to the river to wash clothes or to fetch water.[24] Secondly, the City governors paid for the piping of water into the City. In 1236 the lord of Tyburn manor granted London the right to pipe water from springs near Paddington to the great conduit built in Cheapside. From the later fourteenth century other conduits were established, and during the 1430s the mayor and aldermen obtained a much improved supply by arranging for water to be piped from the Abbot of Westminster's land.[25] A century later additional sources were piped into eastern parts of the City from Hackney.[26]

Conduits and standards, where all could collect water for their own use gratis, stood in the major thoroughfares of the Tudor City.[27] They were substantial stone structures covered with tiles, enclosing large tanks that were filled by pipes coming from outside the City. Smaller stopcocks or taps from which people received their supply reached out into the street. The conduits' importance was emphasized by architectural embellishment – some were crenellated or even painted with oils.[28] (See Figure 12.1.) By the 1630s the corporation was maintaining twelve conduits, each with a salaried keeper to enforce regulations governing access to the water.[29] The supply was, for instance, supposed to flow only between five and eleven in the morning and one and six in the afternoon (an hour later in winter).[30] Inevitably, disputes erupted among those queuing for water, particularly as the water pressure was low and containers took a while to fill up. As verses appended to the early

Figure 12.1   The little conduit, Cheapside, 1585

seventeenth-century print, 'Tittle-Tattle', put it: 'At the Conduit striving for their Turn, / The Quarrel it grows great, / That up in arms they are at last, / And one another beat.'[31] The City fathers accordingly sought to maintain due order. In July 1553, for instance, a man was bound all day by an iron collar to a post next to the Standard in Cheapside 'for stryffyng at the condytt', while thirty years later the aldermen ordered the erection of a whipping post in Gracechurch Street to punish 'suche lewde p[er]sons as ... shall ... abuse themselves at the Conduite'.[32]

There was as much concern about preventing inappropriate or wasteful use of conduit water as about stopping punch-ups between people waiting there. In July 1345 the mayor and aldermen banned brewers and fishmongers from drawing water from the great conduit in Cheapside to make beer and wash fish because they were depriving the commonalty of their supply.[33] In 1530 the mayor complained that water (especially at Gracechuch conduit) was being 'myspended in Wasshyng of bucks wateryng of horses ... & Wateryng of ffyshe'.[34] The notions of reasonable use for conduit water were perfectly caught in a 1608 letter to the Earl of Suffolk explaining the stopping of his quill (a private pipe attached to the main pipe feeding the conduits). The mayor was

> sorry ... to give your ho[nour] any occasion of mislike, but the water soe scarce unto the cunduittes. And the clamour of the poore is such this tyme of Dearth and scarcity that there could noe other course be taken for their satisfacon, but by

cuttinge of some of the Quiles, w[hi]ch drewe awaie soe much water ... your L[ordshi]p. may be pleased to be advertised that much Complaint hath ben often-tymes made of the exceedinge great wast of water in that house beinge taken not only for the necessary use of dressing Meate, but for the Laundery for the Stable and for such other Offices as might be otherwise served.[35]

The earl and his servants had offended their neighbours through typically aristocratic conspicuous consumption of the supply which the City had granted them from the pipe supplying the conduits. Such conduct was deeply insensitive – like venison or wine, water was part of the currency of civic favour, and quills were granted as a special favour to valued friends of the City.

Such gifts were always politically sensitive because the conduits were symbolic and moral centres of the City. It was no accident that many punishments such as pillorying and whipping were enacted next to them,[36] and that they featured prominently in civic rituals.[37] Bequests to build or repair them were listed prominently in chronicles and other forms of civic commemoration.[38] At regular intervals the mayor and aldermen symbolically reaffirmed their importance by progressing out to inspect the conduit heads, where in the mid-1560s a specially constructed building known as the Banqueting House was built for their celebrations and to mark their control of the area.[39]

There are striking parallels between the rules governing the conduits and those of the City markets. This might seem paradoxical – after all, the public provision of water removed it from the cash nexus. However, both sets of regulations protected small consumers' entitlement to necessities. The hours of both market and conduit were carefully delineated. The regrating of water by industrial consumers like brewers was strictly prohibited; ordinary householders' right to acquire small quantities of water at conduits and their right to buy small quantities of grain in the public markets were thus both guaranteed.[40] Like other measures, waterbearers' tankards were of fixed size and sealed by the City; in 1529 the mayor commanded that none should bring any container to the conduits 'whiche when ... Full ... been [*sic*] more than oon mannes burden'.[41] The reservation of conduit water for cooking and drinking paralleled concern about the proper use of grain. During a dearth of water, wasteful consumers like the Earl of Suffolk were admonished or cut off; during a dearth of bread brewers and starchmakers were forbidden from using grain.[42]

It is clear that sixteenth-century Londoners had a well developed sense of a moral economy of water. Civic supplies were embedded in a framework of expectations about their proper use and allocation deriving from civic ordinance and collective practice,[43] which strongly resembled E. P. Thompson's description of the moral economy of the grain market.[44] In 1561 the aldermen only just averted a planned water riot in which young men and waterbearers were going to tear up the private quill of Lord Paget, which had caused the Fleet Street conduit to dry up. Something similar probably occurred in 1547, when two girdlers were imprisoned for gathering together a crowd and for seditious words about the water at the Standard in Cheapside (where there had been problems with the supply).[45] On occasion the complaints of water-bearers and other inhabitants led the aldermen to cut off quills or to ask aristocrats and other eminent people to desist from excessive consumption.[46] When Charles I leased out the spring at Dame Agnes the Clear, just to the north of the City walls, local people rioted against attempts to enclose it.[47]

Such collective action was possible because the conduit, like the market, was, in Thompson's words, a 'place where the people, because they were numerous, felt for a moment that they were strong'.[48] Water sources were centres of neighbourhood life and were thus the forum of gossip, ribald commentary and collective sanctions. The minor Elizabethan writer Richard Robinson complained that in his years of poverty 'the Prentices and Children with ... malicyus myndes and mowthes' derided him 'in the Shoppes, in the Streetes, and at the Conduictes'; in 1620 George Williams told Sir William Maurice how, after Mr James Price had railed against some local inhabitants, 'All the women in the street hard by holborne cunditte ... abused him vilie: they called him ... foolish welsh Justice'.[49] Words were not the only sanctions meted out in such places. Petty criminals and others who offended local sensibilities might be harshly pumped as an extra-judicial punishment.[50]

As Robinson and Williams noted, the conduit was particularly the resort of women and the young. This reflected the unequal distribution of labour. Carrying water was one of the most arduous forms of women's work.[51] It also often fell to the youngest apprentice, and older apprentices resisted the task. Texts celebrating male apprentice culture constructed a mythology of life around the conduits, presenting it as a kind of initiation into the homosocial world of guild labour. When, for instance, Simon Eyre was the youngest apprentice in his master's house,

> [he] was often sent to the Conduit for water, where in short time he fell acquainted with many other prentices comming thither for the same intent. Now their custome was ... that every Sunday morning divers of these prentices did use to go to a place neer the conduit, to break their fast with pudding Pies, and often they would take *Simon* along with them: but upon a time it so fell out, that he should draw mony to pay the shot with the rest, that he had none: whereupon hee merrily said unto them: My faithfull friends, and Conduit companions, treasurers of the Water-tankerd, and maine pillars of the pudding-house; I may now compare my purse ... to a bad nut, which being opened, hath never a kernell.[52]

He therefore begged to be excused from paying his round, promising instead to buy all the apprentices a breakfast if he ever became lord mayor. His companions, surprisingly perhaps, agreed. Sure enough, Simon Eyre became wealthy, was elected mayor of London, and established a Shrove Tuesday breakfast for all the City apprentices.

TRANSFORMATIONS

As early modern London's population grew, it placed increasing demands upon the limited natural resources in its vicinity. It has, for instance, been argued that Elizabethan London was facing a fuel crisis because readily available supplies of wood had been exhausted.[53] While Londoners were never expiring with thirst, there was a growing shortage of potable water, especially in the northern areas of the city, where the expanding population polluted many springs and wells.[54] In 1642 the aldermen even claimed that London had grown so much that its people 'can hardly bee gov[er]ned, fedd, or provided w[i]th water'.[55]

The City overcame the worst of this nascent water shortage by increasing the supplies available to its inhabitants. In 1543 an Act of Parliament gave the City the right to improve its conduits by bringing water from Hampstead and to exploit all large springs within a five-mile radius.[56] Much of the response simply extended the late medieval civic culture of water. New pumps were sunk, often going deeper than before. In 1576 workmen had to dig nearly 20 ft down to find water for the new pump in St. Andrew Undershaft.[57] New conduits were established through a mixture of civic initiative and private endowments. In the late 1560s, for instance, the aldermen established a conduit at Dowgate supplied with water from the Thames,[58] while between 1577 and 1580 the godly clothworker William Lambe spent some £1,500 rebuilding the conduit at Holborn and piping additional water from its head springs.[59]

To increase their water resources more drastically, the City fathers sought out the best water-raising technology available. Their own workmen were highly experienced in maintaining the conduits and the conduit heads,[60] but as the sixteenth century progressed the mayor and aldermen turned more frequently to foreign projectors and engineers.[61] In 1542 the City plumber and carpenter were sent to Hampton Court to inspect Henry VIII's new engine 'for the redye drawyng of Water', and the following year the chamberlain was instructed to take down all that the King's plumber knew of the City's conduit pipes.[62] In the early 1590s the aldermen paid the Italian engineer Frederico Genebelli for increasing the City's supply from Paddington and consulted him about maximizing supplies to Dowgate.[63] From 1574 they had protracted dealings with Peter Morris, a Dutchman or a German, who was granted a royal patent for 'engines for raising water'.[64] It was agreed that Morris would raise water from the Thames not far from the north end of London Bridge to a tank 30 ft in the air and pipe a supply from it to cisterns in Leadenhall and next to St. Magnus's church.[65] As he was finishing Morris approached the City with a grander scheme.[66] After the exchange of legal and financial guarantees, in 1582 the City granted him a 500 year lease of the right to erect an engine on London Bridge. This waterwheel used the current under the arches to raise water, which was then piped through the City.[67]

Morris had many successors. In May 1593 the City leased Bevis Bulmer, a projector with extensive experience in mining,[68] a plot of land by the Thames at Broken Wharf on which he established a horse-driven pump to raise water and supply parts of the City.[69] The engine was finished the following year and the enterprise continued for over a century as the Broken Wharf Water Company. Most importantly, between 1609 and 1613 the goldsmith Sir Hugh Myddleton and his partners, drawing on the expertise of a range of surveyors and engineers, several of whom had themselves proposed schemes to increase London's water supply, dug a canal, soon known as the New River, from springs at Amwell and Chadwell in Hertfordshire to a reception pond at Islington. From there the company used gravity to convey water through the northern and western areas of the City in elm pipes laid under the streets.[70]

When the City wrote to the Lord Chancellor in 1582 urging him to support Morris's scheme, their letter described how he was bringing water to Old Fish Street and Leadenhall, and would 'by the waie ... serve the private houses of a great number of ... Citizens'.[71] In fact, the sale of *private* supplies was a *raison d'être* of the London Bridge, Broken Wharf and New River companies from their inception. As early as 1594 Bulmer leased a supply to William Awbrey, Master of the Requests.[72] The New River had only 350 tenants at Christmas 1614, but had exceeded 1,000 customers by Michaelmas 1618. Nine years later the company was supplying 1,514 tenants.[73] The figure had grown to 2,154, perhaps a tenth of the houses within the City's jurisdiction, in 1638.[74] The number taking piped water continued to grow through the seventeenth century. The Broken Wharf engine was supplying 600 houses in the 1650s.[75] In the central ward of Bassishaw roughly 9 per cent of properties were connected to the New River in 1618.[76] Sixty per cent of houses there had piped water in 1677, as did slightly over a third of households in the poor district of Whitefriars.[77]

Between the late sixteenth century and the early eighteenth the civic moral economy of water was largely eclipsed as these and smaller waterworks established to supply the western and eastern suburbs transformed the social organization of London water. In *c.* 1550 most Londoners acquired water in a classically Lockean fashion, by going and collecting it. As the *Second Treatise of Government* put it, 'Though the Water running in the Fountain be every ones, yet who can doubt, but that in the Pitcher is his only who drew it out?'[78] Only monasteries like the Charterhouse and Greyfriars, and a few privileged individuals (generally those who purchased former monastic property) had supplies of piped water.[79] People who purchased water did so from the water-bearers: they paid people to carry water from the conduits, a public resource. By the late seventeenth century many Londoners had entered into contracts with capitalist water companies which provided them with a private supply of water to their households: they thus purchased water as a commodity from a private company which owned it.

Such companies' supplies were much cheaper per gallon than a water-bearer's load, but only wealthier London households could afford it. The lowest rent for a year's supply from the New River in 1629 (paid by almost half the company's tenants) was £1,[80] 4 per cent of a building craftsman's annual income, assuming he was in work for fifty weeks.[81] The companies insisted on quarterly cash payment and an entry fine of a year's rent. Both would have been beyond the liquidity of many middling, let alone labouring, households. Living in a society in which running water is regarded as a basic amenity, we tend to regard the decision to acquire piped water as a natural one. Piped supplies certainly had many advantages. In 1621 the Goldsmiths decided it would be 'lesse charge & farre more benefitt ... to take in the Thames Water' for £1 a year. In previous years 'the often repairing ... of the pomp in the back yard' of the Hall used by the company tenants in Gutter Lane had been 'verie chargeable' and they had had 'no use of it for a long season'.[82] In fact the adoption of piped water was neither smooth nor instantaneous.

Firstly, many Londoners probably had doubts about the financial viability of the new enterprises and may have been unwilling to pay the entry fine until they were convinced of their long-term viability. Their scepticism was well founded. Large waterworks required enormous initial investment and produced returns only after years. None of these schemes would have survived without substantial financial assistance from the City and/or the Crown. Much of Morris's engine was paid for by a bequest from the common serjeant of the City, but the aldermen lent him a further £1,000 in 1586.[83] They lent Bulmer a total of £3,000; it is unclear how soon they recovered the money.[84] In 1588 Morris sought to sell his waterworks, but the City declined to buy, probably because they were not yet profitable.[85] Between 1610 and 1612 Myddelton faced complete failure as his costs soared and the progress of the canal was halted by the resistance of landowners through whose property the New River was to pass. He only brought his 'fyve yers hard laboure' to its conclusion with a large loan from the City and by persuading James I to take a half share in the scheme.[86] Their investment was slow to mature. At the end of 1614 Myddelton had spent over £18,500 and received under £1,000; the New River did not begin making profits till after his death in 1631.[87]

Secondly, there was resistance to how the City's support for Myddelton allowed 'that w[hi]ch was intended for a publick good [to] ... be converted to a privat gayne'.[88] Such concern about the commercial exploitation of water was intensified by the fountain and conduit images pervading early modern England: the fountains of charity, of divine grace and of justice.[89] All were premised upon the representation of waters, often urban waters, as universally available without the intervention of the market. Protestant sermons styled preachers 'God's conduits'. Preaching before the mayor in 1661, William Bell was even more explicit:

> You must let *judgement run down like water, and righteousness as a mighty stream; free*
> as *water* from a *spring*, ... And free as your *Conduit-water*, that fills the *earthen pitcher*,
> as well as the *silver goblet*. And free as your *Thames water* that flowes to all that will
> *fetch* it, and not as your *New-River-water*, that is imparted to none but those that will
> *pay for it*[90]

Despite (or because of) such scruples, the Crown and the City leaned on the citizenry to take New River supplies (and thus safeguard their investment). In December 1616 the Privy Council wrote to the mayor and aldermen, noting James VI and I's gracious support for Myddelton and the benefits which the City was likely to receive from his supplies of 'sweete and holesome water', and commanding them to 'provide ... that the ... water may be taken into all such houses within that citty and liberties, as ... out of necessity or conveniencie may make use of the same'.[91]

The aldermen did indeed press citizens to make 'use of the same'. In July 1618, for instance, the ward of Bassishaw drew up lists of 'Such as have the water' and 'Such as are thought fit to take in the s[ai]d water'. The latter had to explain their reluctance to rent a supply. John Bancks's answer survives. '[H]is famely' was small; he had 'a pump yelding store of water [and] a lardg Cesterne to receive Rayne water Contynually'. His house was 'very unfitt' to have the water, as the stone pavements of his house would have to be taken up to lay the pipes; he maintained a 'poore aged man in bringing Cundit water 4 tanckers a penny'.[92]

Bancks's final point is particularly significant. It shows how far in early modern London the provision of water was embedded within social relationships and intermingled with the more affluent households' obligations to poorer neighbours. The carriage of water often functioned as a make-work project and a form of charitable support for indigent neighbours. William Lambe bequeathed money for 120 pails with which poor women might earn a living.[93] Some waterbearers, like Joan Starkye's in 1589, were household servants. Even when they did not reside in the house, their work regularly brought them into the household. In May 1640, for instance, George Sprat, a waterbearer of St. Giles Cripplegate, had 'occasion to go into the house of' an apothecary near Aldermanbury conduit, where he heard apprentices discussing a planned anti-Catholic riot.[94] The wills of the sixteenth-century London elite often contained bequests to their waterbearers. In 1576 the goldsmith Thomas Hartop not only left gowns to four waterbearers but directed that they should carry his coffin.[95]

Taking in New River water was thus not simply to get extra plumbing it transformed the relations by which an urban household was sustained. For wealthier Londoners, the 'natural' tenants of the company, it involved laying off servants or turning away poorer neighbours and severing bonds of charity and mutual obligation. At a time when poverty was an urgent problem many

Londoners were surely reluctant to abandon such public manifestations of neighbourly charity. This reluctance was redoubled by the symbolic importance of the waterbearer. Tankard bearing was rather more than 'an honest shift of living, though somewhat toilsome', as William Lambe's biographer sanctimoniously described it. In Robert Wilson's 1590 allegorical drama *The Three Lords and the Three Ladies of London*, '[P]ainful Penury' was 'faine to carry three Tankerds for a penie'.[96] The aldermen made considerable efforts to protect the employment of the waterbearers, the 'Almes-folkes' of the Conduit Head, as Thomas Middleton styled them.[97] So when the City informed the Lord Chancellor of their agreement with Peter Morris they emphasized that the waterbearers would 'neverthelesse ... have as much worke' as they could perform. In the early years of the New River, Myddelton was obliged to set up standpipes from which the waterbearers could draw water and continue their trade.[98]

Civic support was part of the complex negotiation of the waterbearers' position within the City. As drawers of water their work embodied Old Testamental signs of accursed bondage and was seen as particularly degrading. In 1600 one poet represented 'Poore-tankard-slaves' as among the lowest of 'base artificers';[99] members of the Weavers' Company complained in the 1620s that new looms and foreigners were destroying the livelihood of poor weavers so that they were forced to 'become Labourers Porters, Waterbearers'.[100] Yet, like the porters, the London tankard bearers were also an organized fraternity, and from the 1490s they even had a hall.[101] It was sold off in the 1560s, when the fraternity was engulfed by internal disputes between freemen and non-freemen.[102] Declaring that most freemen waterbearers were 'of the greatest disorder, simplest of discrecon and most troublesome', the aldermen intervened, insisting that their rulers be 'the wysest and discretest men' of the fellowship and placing all under the supervision of the chamberlain.[103] The size as well as the symbolic importance of the fraternity doubtless stirred the aldermen to action. In 1621 the fraternity claimed that they and their families numbered 4,000. During the 1630s and 1640s between twenty-five and thirty men entered the fraternity every year – equalling the carpenters or bakers – but the figure fell thereafter and was a derisory trickle after the Fire.[104]

This was part of the wider decline of City conduit culture. Unlike *ancien régime* Paris or Rome,[105] Restoration and Augustan London was not a fountain city. Visiting England in the 1660s the French physician and natural philosopher, Samuel de Sorbière, was struck by the meanness and obscurity of London conduits. They were, he noted, almost devoid of architectural embellishment; you could walk by them without realising their purpose.[106] Although the City went to considerable expense rebuilding them after the Fire,[107] their supply seems to have become less reliable and less important over the later seventeenth century. The wide diffusion of piped water amongst the better sort probably sapped the aldermen's will to maintain free public supplies, and their annual inspection of the conduit heads degenerated into boozy beanfeasts.[108]

However, they did spend large sums maintaining the system, and did face formidable practical difficulties. Several times 'sheepstealers and other Thieves' got into the Banqueting House and 'made it their Shelter & place of entertainm[en]t; by the early 1670s 'greate quantities' of the conduit waters were being stolen 'by reason of ye multitude of buildings' erected over the pipes as London expanded westward.[109] A decade later, after 'the totall failer' of several conduits, the City solicitor and the City plumber were despatched to Lord Chief Justice Pemberton to get a warrant permitting them to enter houses and search for the conduit water, as the aldermen suspected it was 'unjustly taken away and used by great numbers of persons'.[110] Repeated complaints over the subsequent decades indicate that such inspections were not successful.[111]

Although London waterbearers were not as disruptive as those of eighteenth-century Paris,[112] they did not give up passively. They lobbied against the New River and petitioned Parliament about the 'great defect of water ... in the ... conduits' in 1621.[113] On Midsummer Day 1654 the waterbearers of St. Leonard's Eastcheap conducted a mock funeral to mourn the absence of water.[114] The 'Poor Water-Tankerd Bearers' were still agitating about the conduits thirty years later. In 1682 *The Moderate Intelligencer* reported how they had petitioned the aldermen about how, through the neglect of the people who were supposed to maintain them, 'they had wanted water in four of the Conduits for several weeks'. A month later it was reported that 'the Poor men and Women, that used to get their Bread' by carrying water from the conduits were 'almost Starved', and they petitioned for two months before they 'received any satisfactory answer' from the aldermen.[115] In September 1698 the tankard bearers of St. Giles Cripplegate petitioned similarly that 'Water may be Conveyed to the ... Conduit as formerly'.[116]

By this stage the City, effectively bankrupt with the Orphans' debt, had privatized its water resources and its statutory right to all springs within a five-mile radius.[117] In January 1693 the City leased ponds and springs in Hampstead, Hornsey and St. Pancras to a consortium including William Patterson, founder of the Bank of England.[118] The following June all the springs at Dalston, Marylebone and Paddington were leased to the projector, Thomas Houghton. For just over £2,500 in cash and an annual rent of £700 he gained the right to use all water there to supply private customers as long as he supplied the City conduits and prisons.[119] Both schemes became embroiled in prolonged litigation and there was bitter recrimination between Houghton and the City until he surrendered his lease in 1703. Ultimately, the Hampstead Waterworks Company found a measure of commercial success providing piped water to the western suburbs and the Conduit Waters Company amalgamated with the London Bridge waterworks,[120] but supplies to the City's public conduits were never satisfactory.

In 1700 Newgate prison gave up on its traditional supply of conduit water and rented one from the New River. Eight years later many Cheapside residents had lost patience with the conduit altogether, complaining that it was a hazard to traffic and that 'Especially since the water ... hath bin stopt' the ground around it had become a laystall for foul-smelling filth. It was, they concluded, 'neither ornamentall nor usefull'.[121] Several City conduits were thus demolished as an obstruction to traffic in 1730 and by the 1780s the only official water tankard used in the City was carried by Cob in productions of Ben Jonson's *Every Man in his Humour*.[122] The introduction of piped supplies may even have made life harder for people like Edward Goslin, whose residence was 'destitute of Water but what was fetched ... by Pails'.[123]

NEW NETWORKS

It is important to strike a balance between romanticizing sixteenth-century conduit culture and writing panegyrics to the new capitalist water companies. The latter's achievements were considerable. Compared with the inhabitants of many European cities even the poorest Londoner was well provided with water. James Howell wrote that Sir Hugh Myddelton deserved a statue in his honour and noted that the inhabitants of Amsterdam had 'neither well nor fountain or any spring of fresh water ... but their fresh water is brought unto them by boats'.[124] The companies vastly increased the volume of water available within the capital. In *The Honest Lawyer* (1616) one character contrasts two men's urinatory capacity by observing that one 'dribbles like the pissing Conduit: but his joviall sonne with a streame like Ware water-spout'.[125] The cost of their supply remained steady and thus fell in real terms over the course of the seventeenth century, while by the 1650s some City landlords were laying on piped water to low-rent property and even almshouses.[126]

Nevertheless, seventeenth-century water companies could offer only limited supplies. When in 1692 Elizabeth Pourter leased a New River Company supply, she was granted '*Water running ... through one small ... Pipe of Lead*' and '*one small Cock of Brass*', which was to be turned on '*three days in every week ... according to the usage ... of the Company*'. Companies could not always fulfil this promise. Leases disclaimed liability for any interruption in supply caused by '*Reparations, ... mischance, ... Fire*' or icy weather. John Evelyn noted how the water pipes had frozen during January 1684; clearly the recommended use of heaps of horse manure to warm them was not sufficient when the Thames had frozen.[127] Although early advocates of the New River claimed that its supply would reach 25 ft in any house, ultimately water pressure was low and most houses received water to a cistern in the basement. When George I insisted that the recently founded Chelsea Water Company should pipe water to the upper floors of Kensington Palace he was gaining an exceedingly rare comfort.[128]

One should not, therefore, exaggerate the speed of the transition to piped water and the dessication of the moral economy of the conduits. The change was most marked in the City, and the City was not typical of the seventeenth- and eighteenth-century metropolis. Its medieval hydraulic infrastructure, administrative resources and financial resources were far greater than those of most suburban parishes. Far more of its inhabitants could afford piped water than in the poorer eastern suburbs, where the Shadwell Water Company was supplying some 1,370 houses in 1722.[129] Nevertheless, notions of entitlement and fair price articulated by late medieval civic custom and Tudor statute remained of legal consequence till the early nineteenth century, and the City still contained forty public pumps and wells in 1866.[130]

Elsewhere in London pumps, wells and water carriers remained vital. Residents with a piped supply might need it for various domestic tasks; in less favoured areas pumps remained centres of neighbourhood life and neigh-bourly brawls. In 1703, for instance, Elizabeth Thomas of St. James in the Fields came 'with a Tubb' into Warwick Court, off Derry Street, 'to fetch some water from thence'. Martha Harris came out of an adjacent house and knocked the tub on to the ground. Elizabeth Thomas apparently exploded, 'You nasty spitefull Whore, if you had not been nasty spitefull Whore you would not have kicked my tubb down into ye dirty water'.[131] Outside the City water carriers continued to ply their trade; in the 1820s William Hone described a plebeian moral economy of water resistant to water companies' blandishments:

> the prejudices of old-fashioned people [were] in favour of water brought to the door, and their sympathy with ... the water-bearer.... 'I'll stick to the carrier as long as he has a pail-full and I've a penny, and when we haven't we must all go to the workhouse together'. This was the ... reasoning of many honest people ... who preferred taxing themselves to the daily payment of a penny and ... twopence to the water-carrier, in preference to having 'Company's water' at eighteen shillings per annum.[132]

Although this moral economy of water was clearly grounded on notions of commonality, it was also, as we have seen, structured by inequalities based on sex and age. More than any other innovation of the sixteenth or seventeenth century, therefore (except perhaps the spread of ovens), piped water could transform patterns of domestic labour and extra-domestic sociability. The advent of piped water to a kitchen saved women or servants many back-breaking trips to well, pump or conduit. Yet new technology did not simply 'liberate' women: in Ruth Schwarz Cowan's words, 'the introduction of modern water systems had multiple effects'.[133] Increased availability of water often laid more work on women's shoulders because they were in consequence expected to meet new standards of domestic cleanliness. As we have seen, raising any water above ground level required extensive domestic labour.

One should also note that the lower orders played an active role in the reconstruction of conduit culture. As the tankard bearers drifted away other groups colonized these spaces. As the wardmote inquest of Farringdon Within complained early in the eighteenth century, 'the Conduit at the Upper end of Cheapside ... [was] a Common and Publick Nusance, ... being a Nest for Chimney Sweepers, a Lodge for Dirt and Nastyness and in no ways an Ornament ... to this ... City'.[34] Although the conduits would have been a convenient and prominent place from which to tout for business, the sweeps' appropriation of this location was a potent symbolic reversal. Phythian-Adams has shown how over the eighteenth century London chimneysweeps and climbing boys burlesqued and then displaced the milkmaids' rituals on May Day, manipulating the opposition between soot – filthy urban waste – and milk – white, clean, rural produce.[35] There was a similar ironic reversal whereby the sooty sweeps placed themselves next to cleansing waters.

The congregation of such groups round the conduits should remind us, then, that the history of London's water supply was not a simple transition from *Gemeinschaft* to *Gesellschaft*. The piped water supplies of the London Bridge, Broken Wharf and New River companies individuated and privatized households, reducing their involvement in the hurly-burly of the public water sources, but they were also the first network technologies, binding thousands of households into a common system.[36] Inscribed within the rent books of the water companies were new collectivities, defined not by parish or ward boundary but by their shared connection to a main.

This created a greater sense of technological dependence,[37] well illustrated by lurid fantasies after the Fire. Gilbert Burnet was told that 'at Islington ... there is a great room full of pipes that convey it through all the streets of London'. Just before the Fire a Roman Catholic, who had insinuated himself on to the company board, entered this vital room and turned off all the cocks supplying the City. He then absconded with the keys, leaving the citizens at the mercy of the conflagration.[38] This story captures perfectly how Londoners saw themselves as bound together by the new technology. Similar fears surfaced at other moments of social crisis. During the Gordon riots, for instance, guards were mounted on the New River and London Bridge waterworks because of rumours of planned attacks by papistical (!) foreign arsonists. In 1803 the lord mayor warned the governors of the New River 'that the Persons employed to supply the Metropolis with Water ... are mostly Irish and ... have been heard to Declare that in Case of Invasion or Insurrection they should ... assist the Enemies of this Country by preventing the Supply of Water in Cases of Fire'. They responded by sending detailed information about their employees to the Secretary for War.[39]

Such technological networks were also thus clearly social networks. Customers of a water company were not just linked by a main – they shared a turncock, the man who turned the water on and off, and a collector who came round to collect the rent and sign their receipt each quarter.[140] These were the crucial human brokers of network technology and, like waterbearers, were the intermediaries between the source of water and the consumer. London water companies, therefore, continually monitored the sobriety, probity and politeness of their 'servants', for they could win or lose customers.[141] In 1684 one of Sir John Reresby's London servants reported how 'very troublesome' the collectors of the Thames water had been. The 'offecers of the ye new river water' had been more amenable and so they adopted its supply.[142] Furthermore, piped water supplies did not simply individuate households, they produced collective action whereby inhabitants of a district joined together to approach a water company to request a supply. In April 1671, for instance, a dozen householders in Cross Street, Islington, wrote to the New River informing it that they 'should be glad to become your Tennants for the New River Watter to be laid down the ... Street', and that it would be worth the company's investment, 'as there is many new Houses fitting up for Tennants'.[143]

Addressed to the governors of the company, not to the vestry or alderman, such petitions were part of a redrawing of the boundaries of government in late seventeenth-century London. From the 1690s street lighting and the night watch were less and less the responsibility of individual citizens and were increasingly taken over by salaried and commercial operators. Moreover, as Paul Slack has noted, in the late seventeenth and early eighteenth centuries there was a proliferation of bodies providing social relief which were more or less independent of the traditional structures of parish and town government. Many of these borrowed the organizational and financial forms of joint stock companies and shared the latter's seamy reputation.[144] The history of London's water over the seventeenth century paralleled this broader shift in the boundaries of government. Water moved from being a resource regulated by local governors – aldermen, vestrymen – and by neighbourhood pressures (the culture of the conduit) to being a resource which was substantially allocated by groups of shareholders and by the governors of companies. The City's willingness in the 1690s to lease the springs which supplied the conduits marked a new acceptance of the role of commerce in the running of the civic state.

NOTES

My thanks to seminars in Aberdeen, London and Oxford where I presented papers on this theme, to Mike Berlin, Laura Gowing, Sara Mendelson, Margaret Pelling and James Robertson for references, to Derek Keene for letting me read his unpublished paper, to the Wellcome Trust for funding the research and to Paul Griffiths for comments on a draft. Above all, my thanks to Patricia Greene for reading versions with her perceptive eye and for so much else as well.

1 LMA DL/C 233, fos 141v–142, 154. This dispute is discussed in Gowing, *Domestic*, p. 117.

2 Gowing, *Domestic*; T. Meldrum, 'A women's court in London: defamation at the Bishop of London's consistory court 1700–1745', *LJ*, 19 (1994).

3 See, however, Gowing, *Domestic*, p. 117. Medieval water supply has been discussed more extensively: J. Schofield, *Medieval London Houses* (New Haven CT and London, 1994), pp. 117–18; D. Keene, 'Issues of water in London before 1300', forthcoming.

4 S. Rolle, *Burning of London* (1666), quoted in J. G. Harris, 'This is not a pipe: water supply, incontinent sources and the leaky body politic', in R. Burt and J. M. Archer eds., *Enclosure Acts* (Ithaca NY, 1994), p. 205; *Londinopolis*, p. 397.

5 D. Roche, 'Le temps de l'eau rare du moyen-âge à l'époque moderne', *Annales ESC*, 39 (1984), pp. 383–99; J-P. Goubert, *The Conquest of Water* (Oxford, 1989), I; S. Hoy, *Chasing Dirt* (Oxford, 1995), chaps 1–3.

6 For example, GL MS 2883/3, fos 18–19, 317; G. Parsloe ed., *Wardens' Accounts of the Worshipful Company of Founders of … London 1497–1681* (1964), pp. 9, 160, 286.

7 GL MS 8230 (unfoliated), 24 February, 4, 21 May.

8 PRO C24/290/3, fo. 7. No deponent gives Elizabeth's surname. This case is discussed in C. J. Sisson, *The Boar's Head Theatre* (1972), p. 53.

9 BL MS Lansdowne 60/16; PRO STAC8/61/11.

10 S. Smiles, *Lives of the Engineers* (5 vols, 1861), I, chaps 3–4; J. W. Gough, *Sir Hugh Myddelton* (Oxford, 1964); G. C. Berry, 'Sir Hugh Myddelton and the New River', *Transactions of the Honourable Society of Cymmrodorion* (1956).

11 For example, W. Matthews, *Hydraulia; An Historical and Descriptive Account of the Waterworks of London* (1835); W. R. Scott, *The Constitution and Finance of English, Scottish and Irish Joint Stock Companies to 1720* (3 vols, Cambridge, 1910–12), III, pp. 3–36; H. W. Dickinson, *The Water Supply of Greater London* (1954); A. Hardy, 'Water and the search for public health in London', *Medical History*, 28 (1984). B. Rudden, *The New River: A Legal History* (Oxford, 1985) is an exception, but is less interested in the social history of London water.

12 E. Stratford, 'Gender and environment: some preliminary questions about women and water in the South Australian context', *Gender, Place and Culture*, 2 (1995), p. 212.

13 Cf. C. Hamlin, *Public Health and Social Justice in the Age of Chadwick* (Cambridge, 1998).

14 F. W. Fairholt, 'On an inventory of the household goods of Sir Thomas Ramsey, Lord Mayor of London, 1577', *Archaeologia*, 40 (1866), p. 332; Hertfordshire Record Office, MS 27423, m. 13.

15 P. R. Seddon ed., *Letters of John Holles 1587–1637*, II, Thoroton Society Record Series 35 (1983), p. 324.

16 LMA P92/SAV/602, copy lease, 26 November 1513.

17 PRO C24/290/3, fo. 8. Cf the situation of Katherine Oxinden described by Margaret Pelling above.

18 For example, Machyn, *Diary*, p. 211; Kingsford, *Stow*, I, pp. 164, 292.

19 CLRO Reps 18, fo. 225v; 23, fo. 82v; Kingsford, *Stow*, I, pp. 138, 160, 164, 174–5, 219, 290, 292; II, p. 79.

20 In 1563–65 the wardmote inquest of St. Dunstan's in the West presented an ill maintained well as very dangerous to all 'passyng by the same in the nyght tyme': GL MS 3018/1, fos 12–14.

21 CLRO Rep. 22, fo. 182v. Wells too require regular maintenance, e.g. W. F. Cobb, *The Church of St. Ethelburga the Virgin ... The Churchwardens and their Accounts* (1905), p. 22.

22 GL MS 3476/1, fos 114–142v.

23 GL MS 1311/1, fo. 72. The vestry continued to appoint and regulate the three parish waterbearers until at least the middle of the seventeenth century, *Ibid.*, fos 77v, 104v; GL MS 1311/2, Part II, fo. 7.

24 Keene, 'Issues of water', p. 5; H. T. Riley ed., *Memorials of London and London Life in the XIIIth, XIVth, and XVth Centuries* (1868), pp. 648–9.

25 D. Keene and V. Harding, *Historical Gazetteer of London before the Great Fire*, I: *Cheapside*, pp. 522–6; C. M. Barron, 'The Government of London and its Relations with the Crown 1400–1450', University of London Ph.D. thesis (1970), pp. 266–77.

26 Stow, *Survey*, I, p. 128; CLRO Rep. 11, fos 13v, 230, 314v.

27 For the location of the conduits, M. J. Power, 'John Stow and his London', *Journal of Historical Geography*, 11 (1985), fig. 5.

28 B. R. Masters ed., *Chamber Accounts of the Sixteenth Century*, LRS 20 (1984), 176g; CLRO Rep. 41, fos 316–316v; Keene and Harding, *Cheapside*, pp. 525–6. For contemporary representations of them, L. Manley, *Literature and Culture in Early Modern London* (Cambridge, 1995), fig. 11a–d.

29 CLRO City Cash 1/1, fo. 45.

30 CLRO Rep. 10, fo. 191; Jour. 49, fo. 141v; Misc. MS 143.1. Cf. GL MS 1311/1, fo. 91v.

31 Reproduced in D. Lindley, *The Trials of Frances Howard* (1993), plate 9.

32 Machyn, *Diary*, p. 34; CLRO Rep. 20, fo. 425v.

33 Riley, *Memorials*, p. 225 (see also p. 617).

34 CLRO Jour. 13, fos 188v, 206v.

35 CLRO Remb. II, fo. 321.

36 For example, CLRO Reps 14, fo. 133; 22, fo. 324v; *Londinopolis*, pp. 77–8.

37 Manley, *Literature and Culture*, pp. 223–7, 231–2.

38 For example, J. Stow, *A Summarie of Englyshe Chronicles* (1565), fos 144, 145v.

39 *Chamber Accounts*, 314, 316.

40 *The Lawes of the Markette* (1562); E. P. Thompson, 'The moral economy of the crowd', reprinted in *Customs in Common* (paperback edition, 1993), pp. 193–7.

41 Keene and Harding, *Cheapside*, p. 526; CLRO Jour. 13, fos 188v, 206v.

42 CLRO Jour. 24, fos 7, 133v, 135v; BL Lansdowne MS 152/7; M. Pelling, *The Common Lot* (1998), p. 44.

43 For the ways popular sanctions derived from civic punishments, M. Ingram, 'Judicial folklore in England illustrated by rough music', in C. Brooks and M. Lobban eds, *Communities and Courts in Britain 1150–1900* (1997).

44 Thompson, 'Moral economy'. In adopting this formulation I am not suggesting that

there is only one moral economy or that the commercial distribution of water is not frequently invested with moral value: see M. Jenner, 'Political economy, the parish and the public in the politics of London water *c.* 1790–*c.* 1830', in S. Sturdy ed., *Medicine and the Public Sphere*, forthcoming.

45 CLRO Reps 14, fos 519–520v, 523v; 11, fos 324, 325–325v.

46 CLRO Reps 21, fo. 466v; 24, fo. 396.

47 PRO SP16/439/7.

48 Thompson, 'Moral economy', pp. 256–7.

49 G. M. Vogt, 'Richard Robinson's *Eupolemia* (1603)', *Studies in Philology*, 21 (1924), pp. 647–8; A. Roberts, 'Letter to Sir William Maurice from William ap William', *The Antiquary*, 2 (1880), p. 251.

50 PRO STAC8/49/6; Gowing, *Domestic*, p. 100; *Dawk's Newsletter*, No. 288 (21 April 1698) and 299 (17 May 1698).

51 C. Davidson, *A Woman's Work is never Done: A History of Housework in the British Isles 1650–1950* (1982), chap. 1.

52 *The Novels of Thomas Deloney*, ed. M. E. Lawlis (Bloomington IN, 1961), p. 140.

53 W. H. Te Brake, 'Air pollution and fuel crises in pre-industrial London', *Technology and Culture*, 16 (1975). Rappaport, *Worlds*, pp. 144–5, suggests London's transition to coal was smoother than Te Brake's Malthusian account.

54 Stow, *Survey*, I, pp. 15–16; *Lords' Journal*, II, fos 1092–3.

55 CLRO Jour. 40, fo. 33.

56 35 Henry VIII c. 10; CLRO Rep. 11, fo. 62; R. R. Sharpe, *London and the Kingdom* (3 vols, 1894), II, p. 18.

57 Stow, *Survey*, I, p. 160, CLRO Rep. 19, fo. 86.

58 CLRO Rep. 16, fos 249v–250, 268v; *Chamber Accounts*, 315; Kingsford, *Stow*, I, pp. 230, 232.

59 A. Fleming, *A Memoriall of the Famous Monuments ... of ... William Lambe ... 1580* (1875), pp. 23–4; CLRO Reps 19, fos 178, 219v; 20, fo. 161v.

60 In 1580 the Earl of Sussex urged the City to prefer their own plumber, John Martyn's, proposal for raising water to that of 'any straunger': CLRO Remb. I, fo. 45.

61 The City employed Flemish water-raising expertise in the 1490s: C. Welch, *History of Tower Bridge* (1894), p. 86.

62 CLRO Rep. 10, fos 285, 327. On Hampton Court's water supply, S. Thurley, *The Royal Palaces of Tudor England* (New Haven CT and London, 1993), pp. 164–7.

63 CLRO Reps 22, fos 232v, 257, 270, 320v, 345v, 376v; 23, fo. 440. Genebelli was granted a patent for some kind of machine and also found employment from the Crown and Privy Councillors; *Draft Calendar of Patent Rolls ... 1585–1587*, List and Index Society 242 (1991), I, p. 14; M. J. Rodriguez-Salgado and the staff of the National Maritime Museum, *Armada 1588–1988* (1988), pp. 120, 255.

64 CLRO Rep. 18, fo. 307; *Calendar of the Patent Rolls, Elizabeth I*, VIII, 1575–1578 (1982), no. 3672.

65 CLRO Rep. 18, fos 375, 377.

66 CLRO Rep. 20, fos 75v, 83, 95, 97, 102v. It is not clear whether the first engine was ever completed – certainly its construction was greatly delayed while Morris was employed on fen drainage: CLRO Rep. 19, fos 3v, 188, 210v; Remb., I, fo. 28.

67 CLRO Rep. 20, fo. 201; Jour. 21, fo. 245v. For the moves up to the signing of this lease, Rep. 20, fos 120v, 168v, 170v. For a copy of the lease, Thames Conservancy Papers 181/4/30.

68 R. Jenkins, 'Bevis Bulmer', *Notes and Queries*, eleventh series, 4 (1911); J. Shaw, *Water Power in Scotland 1550–1870* (Edinburgh, 1984), pp. 62, 71 n, 77–8.

69 CLRO Jour. 23, fos 189v, 196; Reps 22, fo. 435v; 23, fos 56, 58, 62, 186, 245, 310, 313v.

70 Gough, *Myddelton*, chap. 3; Berry, 'Myddelton'.

71 CLRO Remb. I, fo. 449.

72 PRO REQ2/170/67.

73 Berry, 'Myddelton', pp. 42–3; PRO LR2/43.

74 PRO E178/6032 m. 10. This figure is a 'guestimate'. To approximate the number of houses in the City I took the ward totals returned for the 1638 tithe survey of the City and supplemented them with estimates made in 1632. This produced a total of 19,083 houses within the liberties: R. Finlay, *Population and Metropolis* (Cambridge, 1981), p. 173; GL MS 17080/1, unfoliated. The resultant 11·3 per cent is too high because a significant number of New River customers lived outside the liberties.

75 Sheffield University Library Hartlib MS 26/51/1.

76 GL MS 3505, fo. 13, lists eighteen people taking the New River. T. C. Dale, *The Inhabitants of London in 1638* (1931), pp. 141–3, lists 198 households in Bassishaw in 1638.

77 M. S. R. Jenner, 'Early Modern English Conceptions of "Cleanliness" and "Dirt" as reflected in the Environmental Regulation of London, *c.* 1530–*c.* 1700', Oxford University D.Phil. thesis (1991), chap. 6.

78 J. Locke, *Two Treatises of Government*, ed. P. Laslett (Cambridge, 1988), p. 289.

79 C. J. Bond, 'Water management in the urban monastery', in R. Gilchrist and H. Mytum eds, *Advances in Monastic Archaeology*, British Archaeological Research, British Series 227 (1993).

80 Six hundred and twenty-six out of 1,314 who paid the full six months' rent in 1629.

81 J. Boulton, 'Wage labour in seventeenth-century London', *EcHR*, 49 (1996), p. 288.

82 GCL Pii, fo. 517.

83 CLRO Remb. I, fo. 449; W. K. Jordan, *The Charities of London 1480–1600* (1960), p. 204; CLRO Rep. 21, fo. 353. At least part of this loan was still outstanding in the 1590s: Rep. 22, fo. 293.

84 CLRO Jour. 23, fos 270v, 286; Rep. 25, fos 92, 124v.

85 CLRO Reps 21, fo. 576; 22, fos 22v–23.

86 Berkshire Record Office D/EN O24/4; Gough, *Myddelton*, pp. 39–48; Rudden, *New River*, pp. 13–17 and 268–73.

87 Berry, 'Myddelton', pp. 41–2.

88 Duke of Northumberland MSS vol. 8, fo. 171 (BL Microfilm 282). This is quoted by kind permission of the Duke of Northumberland.

89 Harris, 'This is not a Pipe', pp. 217–18.

90 W. Bell, *City Security Stated: in a Sermon Preached at St Pauls August 11th 1661. Before the ... Lord Mayor* (1661), p. 22.

91 *APC 1616–17*, pp. 99–100.

92 GL MS 3505, fo. 13.

93 Jordan, *Charities of London*, p. 99.

94 PRO C24/211 Allen *v.* Versalyme, evidence of Joan Starkey; SP16/267/89.

95 N. Adamson, 'Urban Families: The Social Context of the London Elite', University of Toronto Ph.D. thesis (1983), p. 91; PRO PROB11/64/45. Cf. the bequest of alderman James Cambell, W. H. and H. C. Overall eds, *Analytical Index to the ... Remembrancia ... of the City of London 1579–1664*, p. 553 n.

96 Fleming, *Memoriall of ... William Lambe*, p. 24; H. S. D. Mithal, *An Edition of Robert Wilson's 'Three Ladies of London' and 'Three Lords and Three Ladies of London* (New York, 1988), p. 59.

97 T. Middleton, *Honorable Entertainments, Compos'd for the Service of this Noble Citie* (1621), sig. [B7].

98 CLRO Remb. I, fo. 449; Gough, *Myddelton*, p. 48.

99 C.G., *The Minte of Deformities* (1600), sigs. Civ–ii.

100 GL MS 4647, fo. 81v.

101 H. C. Coote, 'The ordinances of some secular guilds of London, 1354 to 1496', *Transactions of the London and Middlesex Archaeological Society*, 4 (1871), pp. 55–8. On aldermanic sponsorship of the porters, W. M. Stern, *The Porters of London* (1960), Part I.

102 Coote, 'Ordinances', p. 58. In 1591 the waterbearers had a house in Whitecross Street where they met. LMA DL/C/214/45 Bridges c. Stockdale, fos. 46, 51, 52

103 CLRO Letter Book V, fo. 255.

104 *To the Honorable Assembly of the Commons ... The Humble Petition of ... the poore Water Tankerd-bearers* (s.sh., n.d., [1621]); *Chamber Accounts*, 11p, 157c; CLRO City Cash 1/1–19

105 D. Garrioch, *Neighbourhood and Community in Paris 1740–1790* (Cambridge, 1986), pp. 27, 33–4 , 121.

106 S. de Sorbière, *Relation d'un Voyage en Angleterre* (1664, facsimile edition, with introduction by L. Roux, Saint-Etienne, 1980), p. 29.

107 CLRO ex GL MS 359 details the expenditure of over £4,500 on the conduits in the 1660s.

108 C. Carlton, *The Court of Orphans* (Leicester, 1974), p. 96.

109 CLRO City Lands Committee Papers 1677, no. 174; CLRO Jour. 47, fo. 138v.

110 CLRO Reps 87, fos. 143v, 163v, 221, 253; 88, fo. 8.

111 For example, CLRO Court of Aldermen Papers 1710. See also Rep. 112, fo. 432.

112 A. Farge, 'L'espace parisien au XVIIIe siècle d'après les ordonnances de police', *Ethnologie Française*, 12 (1982), p. 124.

113 PRO LR2/27B 11 September 1611; *To ... the Commons ... The ... Petition of ... the ... Water Tankerd-bearers.*

114 P. S. Seaver, *Wallington's World: A Puritan Artisan in Seventeenth-Century London* (1985), p. 53.

115 *The Moderate Intelligencer*, 27 (11–14 September, 1682); *The Loyal London Mercury*, 16 (11–14 October 1682), and see 24 (8–11 November 1682).

116 CLRO Rep. 102, fo. 382. The waterbearers of Cheapside petitioned that spring: *ibid.*, fo. 205.

117 This process can be followed in CLRO Committee for Improvements, Minutes, I (1692–94). On the Orphans' Debt see Carlton, *Court of Orphans*, chap. 6.

118 CLRO City Lands Deed 39.8; C. E. Lee, '"Plentyfull Sprynges at Hampstede Hethe": the story of Hampstead Water Company', *Camden History Review*, 3 (1975), pp. 2–3.

119 CLRO City Lands Deed 44.15; PRO C8/455/25. Houghton fronted a consortium including his more famous brother, John. The often fantastical scale of his projecting vision can seen in *The Alteration of the Coyn, with Feasible Method to do it ... To which is annexed, A Projection ... for establishing a Firm and General Peace in Europe* (1695).

120 PRO C6/322/41, C24/1257/33; Scott, *Joint Stock Companies*, III, pp. 3–7, 12–15.

121 CLRO Alchin Box O/LXXV(6); Jour. 54, fo. 651.

122 W. Maitland, *History of London* (1739), p. 450; 'Memoirs of William Lamb', *Gentleman's Magazine*, 53 (1783), p. 136.

123 CLRO Court of Aldermen Papers, November–December 1719, 'The Case of Edward Goslin'.

124 *Londinopolis*, p. 11; J. Howell, *Epistolae Hoelianae*, ed. A. Repplier (2 vols, Boston MA and New York, 1907), p. 21.

125 S.S., *The Honest Lawyer* (1616), sig. F. 'Ware water' is New River water.

126 For example, GL MS 4524/2, fo. 277.

127 GL MS 191; *The Diary of John Evelyn* ed. E. S. de Beer (6 vols, Oxford, 1955), IV, p. 363; J. Houghton, *Collection for the Advancement of Trade and Husbandry* (facsimile edition, Farnborough, 1969), 27 September 1695.

128 BODL MS Tanner 98, fo. 47; D. Cruickshank and N. Burton, *Life in the Georgian City* (1990), p. 88; LMA Acc. 2558/CH/1/1, fo. 137.

129 LMA Acc. 2558/MW/C/15/98. This is approximately 9.35 per cent of the 14,644 houses estimated to be in this area in 1708. The area's population had grown rapidly by the 1720s and further research is needed to determine the extent of the company's service. M. D. George, *London Life in the Eighteenth Century* (second edition, 1966), pp. 409–12.

130 D. Hay, 'The state and the market in 1800: Lord Kenyon and Mr Waddington', *P&P*, 162 (1999); S. E. Brown, 'A just and profitable commerce: moral economy and the middle classes in eighteenth-century London', *Journal of British Studies*, 32 (1993); H. Malchow, 'Free water: the public drinking fountain movement and Victorian London', *LJ*, 4 (1978), p. 183.

131 LMA DL/C/248, fo. 8 (Harris c. Thomas).

132 R. Allen, 'Shepherd's Well: Hampstead's early fresh-water source', *Camden History Review*, 15 (1988), pp. 7–9. W. Hone, *The Table Book* (1827), pp. 733–4, quoted in Gough, *Myddelton*, p. 66.

133 *More Work for Mother* (1989), p. 88.

134 CLRO Court of Aldermen Reports and Papers: Petitions n.d., 'F'.

135 C. Phythian-Adams, 'Milk and soot: the changing vocabulary of a popular ritual in Stuart and Hanoverian London', in D. Fraser and A. Sutcliffe eds, *The Pursuit of Urban History* (1983), esp. pp. 100–3.

136 Historians of nineteenth- and twentieth-century technology use the term to describe technological systems – gas, electricity, telephones – which reach into the domestic sphere, connecting households, neighbourhoods and even towns to an integrated system, e.g. T. P. Hughes, *Neworks of Power* (Baltimore MD, 1983); J. Tarr and G. Depuy eds, *Technology and the Rise of the Networked City in Europe and America* (Philadelphia PA, 1988).

137 Machyn's note that in November 1560 there 'was no water in [any] condyth ... but in Lothbere', reveals another form of technological dependence, Machyn, *Diary*, pp. 245–6.

138 *Bishop Burnet's History of his own Time* (6 vols, Oxford, 1823), I, pp. 401–2.

139 G. Rudé, 'The Gordon riots: a study of the rioters and their victims', in *id., Paris and London in the Eighteenth Century* (1970), p. 278; LMA Acc. 2558/MW/C/15/361/1 and 2.

140 For such receipts, LMA Acc. 2558/MW/C/15/45.

141 For example, LMA Acc. 2558/NR/1/1 fos 1, 3v; Acc. 2558/CH/1/1 fos 193, 200, 208–11.

142 Leeds Archives Department, Reresby MSS 27/3.

143 LMA Acc. 2558/NR13/207/3.

144 E. S. de Beer, 'The early history of London street lighting', *History*, 25 (1941); P. Slack, *From Reformation to Improvement* (Oxford, 1998), chaps 5–6.

Index

Note: 'n.' after a page reference indicates a note on that page.

Index

numbers 209–11, 217–18
policing 59, 181
residential patterns 211–13
poor relief 5, 15, 48, 197–225 *passim*
entitlement 59–60
levels 213–15
non-payment 216
Popish Plot 9
population 2, 49, 53, 58, 61, 69, 155, 157, 199–203, 206, 211, 215, 216, 219n.24, 220n.34, 220n.37, 230, 233, 256, 271n.29
Porter, Roy 3, 6, 108
Portlock, Richard 75
Pourter, Elizabeth 262
poverty 7, 49, 95, 96, 101, 124, 158, 181, 187, 197–225 *passim*, 255
Pratt, Geraldine 131
Price, Mary 95
print culture 3, 9, 123
privacy 134, 136, 148–9n.19, 166
private sphere 12, 132, 133–7, 191
Privy Council 39, 182, 185–9 *passim*
probate inventories 135, 233–4, 236, 247n.57, 249n.88
prostitution 7, 11, 12, 73, 76, 86, 87, 88, 90, 91, 92, 93–101, 139, 142, 144, 145–6
providentialism 41, 72, 163
provost marshals 71, 76
Prynne, William 36
public sphere 9, 50, 132, 133–7, 140, 147, 191, 251
Pulman, John 78
punishments 176
cage 60
carting 60, 133, 140–1, 143
ducking 60
executions 10, 33, 34–6, 123, 163
pillory 36, 41, 254
prison 98, 243, 261
public penance 50–1
pumping 255
stocks 60
whipping 60, 96, 141, 253–4
Purbeck, Lady 165
Pym, Philip 99

Ramsey, Sir Thomas 251
rakes 96, 101
rape 96
Rappaport, Steve 5, 49–50, 60
receiving stolen goods 67, 79, 100
recorder, City 31, 69, 77
Redmore, Christian 146–7
Reformation 30, 36–8
charity, impact on 60
church fabric 47–8

historiography 50
iconoclasm 47
propagation 36–7
resistance to 50
ritual and 47–66 *passim*, 140
Reformation of Manners
societies 11, 72–3, 76, 86
remembrancer, City 28–9
rents 181, 187
reputation 36, 77, 100, 108, 132, 134, 137, 144–5, 238
Reresby, Sir John 265
residential patterns 15, 197–8, 206–9
intermingling 29, 198, 211–13
Restoration 3, 5, 9, 14, 90, 163, 198, 201, 207, 209, 211, 214, 215, 235
Rewse, Bodenham 67, 74, 75, 76, 80
riot 5, 251, 255, 259
Robinson, Richard 255
Rogationtide 57–9, 65n.66
Rose, Gillian 131
Ross, William 99
Royal Injunctions (1559) 57
rumour 29, 264
see also libels; news
Russell, Sidney 144

Sabbath-breaking 240
Sacks, David Harris 31
Saker, Mrs 79
Saker, Robert 68, 74, 75, 79, 80
Salisbury 211
Salisbury, Earl of 217
Salter, James 120
Saunders, Alice 252
scavengers 55, 195n.60, 203
scolding 141, 242
Scory, John 35
seasons 140, 235
and residential patterns 160–5
sedan chairs 217, 224n.110
seditious words 255
Sell, Ann 115
separate spheres, theory of 108, 133–7
sermons 33, 34–5, 37–8, 39, 40, 74, 123, 258–9
servants 28, 54, 88, 90–1, 96, 97, 99, 112, 134, 139, 142, 165, 168, 240, 242, 248n.76, 250, 259, 263, 265
living quarters 13, 135, 136, 166, 206
numbers 3, 205–6
wages 94
Shadwell Waterworks Company 263
Shaftsbury, Anthony Ashley Cooper, Earl of 77
Sharpe, Joan 141
Sheffield, Edward 90
Sheriffs 28, 36, 67, 76, 78
Ship Money 28

282